DATE DUE

			PRINTED IN U.S.A.

CLIFFS NOTES

HARDBOUND LITERARY LIBRARIES

SHAKESPEARE LIBRARY

Volume 3

<u>*The Histories; The Sonnets*</u>

7 Titles

ISBN 0-931013-02-X

Library distributors, hardbound editions:
Moonbeam Publications
18530 Mack Avenue
Grosse Pointe, MI 48236
(313) 884-5255

MOONBEAM PUBLICATIONS
Robert R. Tyler, President
Elizabeth Jones, Index Editor

FOREWORD

Moonbeam Publications has organized **CLIFFS NOTES**, the best-selling popular (trade) literary reference series, into a fully indexed hardbound series designed to offer a more permanent format for the series.

Hardbound volumes are available in a **BASIC LIBRARY**, a 24 volume series. The current softbound series (over 200 booklets) has been divided into five major literary libraries to help researchers, librarians, teachers, students and all readers use this series more effectively. The five major literary groupings are further subdivided into 17 literary periods or genres to enhance the use of this series as a more precise literary reference book.

Hardbound volumes are also available in an **AUTHORS LIBRARY**, a 13 volume series classified by author, covering 11 authors and over 70 Cliffs Notes titles. This series helps readers who prefer to study the works of a particular author, rather than an entire literary period.

**CLIFFS NOTES HARDBOUND
LITERARY LIBRARIES**
1990 by
Moonbeam Publications
18530 Mack Avenue
Grosse Pointe, MI   48236
(313) 884-5255

Basic Library - 24 Volume
ISBN 0-931013-24-0

Authors Library - 13 Volume
ISBN 0-931013-65-8

Bound in U.S.A.

SHAKESPEARE LIBRARY

Volume 3

The Histories; The Sonnets

CONTENTS

KING HENRY IV
PART 1

NOTES

including
- *Introduction*
- *Characters*
- *Synopsis*
- *Summaries and Commentaries*
- *Medium: Verse and Prose*
- *Sixteenth-Century Political Theory*
- *Review Questions*
- *Selected Bibliography*

by
James K. Lowers, Ph.D.
Department of English
University of Hawaii

NEW EDITION

INCORPORATED

LINCOLN, NEBRASKA 68501

Editor

Gary Carey, M.A.
University of Colorado

Consulting Editor

James L. Roberts, Ph.D.
Department of English
University of Nebraska

Cliffs Notes, Inc.   Lincoln, Nebraska

CONTENTS

This volume of Notes is based on the text in *The Complete Plays and Poems of William Shakespeare*, edited by W. A. Nielson and C. J. Hill (Boston: Houghton Mifflin, 1942).

King Henry IV, Part I Notes

INTRODUCTION

In the Stationers' Register, the official record of licensed booksellers and publishers in London, appeared the following entry for February 25, 1598:

> *The historye of Henry iiiith with his battaile of Shrews-*
> *burye against Henry Hottspurre of the Northe with the*
> *conceipted mirth of Sir John Ffalstoff.*

Later in the same year the First Quarto edition of the play was published, the title having been modified to read *the battell at Shrewsburie, betweene the King and Lord Henry Percie, sur-named Henrie Hotspur of the North. With the humorous conceits of Sir Iohn Falstlaffe.* Prior to the play's inclusion in the First Folio, 1623, five other quarto editions of the play were published. Among the ten chronicle-history plays written by Shake-speare, only *Richard III* provides comparable evidence of sustained popularity, both plays excelling in this respect all of the fifteen other Shakespearean dramas which were published in quarto editions during this period. *1 Henry IV* was and remains a favorite stage piece.

The reasons for its great popularity are not hard to find. The subtitle of the Stationers' entry and to the main title of the quarto points to the first and most important one: the *conceited mirth*, the *conceits*, that is, the jests, of one Sir John Falstaff. Not only is it that in this chronicle-history play for the first time comic scenes alternate with the serious ones, but in the portrayal of Sir John Falstaff, Shakespeare created the greatest comic character certainly in English literature and quite possibly in world liter-ature. And among all characters in drama this same Falstaff emerges as one of the most complex.

The reference to "Hotspur of the North" in both subtitles points to a second reason. Henry Percy, or Hotspur, emerges as the most prominent of the rebel leaders, an attractive if head-strong young man, one not devoid of heroic and tragic stature. The role of Hotspur in the main plot brings up the subject of structure. The typical chronicle-history play, of which Shakespeare's *Henry VI* plays are representative, tends to be epic in structure; that is, it tends to lack focus and to present action characterized by a series of climaxes prior to the resolution. The subtitles of *1 Henry IV* give some indication of what the dramatist has accomplished: this is a play about rebellion; the royal forces are pitted against rebels among whom Hotspur is pre-eminent. But in the play, although King Henry is the titular hero and does lead his forces against enemies of the Crown, it is his son and heir, Prince Hal (as he is called familiarly), who directly opposes Hotspur. In all likelihood influenced by his contemporary, Samuel Daniel, whose narrative history in verse, *The Civil Wars between the Two Houses of Lancaster and York,* Books I-IV, was published in 1595, Shakespeare made Hotspur the young con-temporary of Prince Hal, although the rebel leader was actually somewhat older than Henry IV. The structural advantage of all this should be apparent. There is an admirable centralizing of the conflict as the action rises to its climax and falls to its resolution at Shrewsbury. Furthermore, Shakespeare compressed the historical action, which extended from June, 1402, to July, 1403, into a few months.

1 Henry IV ranks high among all of the thirty-seven plays in the Shakespeare canon for superior portrayal of characters, leading and subordinate. Brief notice has been made already to the prime example, Sir John Falstaff, who unquestionably disreput-able, is endowed with such a superior wit in his comic revolt against law and order that some critics would elevate him to the status of hero. In important ways both Prince Hal and Hotspur are leading characters who are no less well realized, and much can be said for the characterizations of lesser figures, including Worcester, Glendower, and even Poins. In addition to these virtues, one should also consider the maturity of style, both in verse and in prose, a style notable for its wide range, vivid imagery, and strong verbs. Excepting only romantic love (found, for example, in that later chronicle-history play, Henry V), Henry IV gives us God's plenty.

For the main plot Shakespeare depended chiefly upon Holinshed's *The Chronicles of England, Scotland, and Ireland,* Vol. III, 1587, avoiding any change in sequence of historical events with the exception of that in which the king and Prince Hal achieve reconciliation (III.ii), which actually took place nearly ten years after the Battle of Shrewsbury. The way in which the dramatist selected and changed specific details to suit his purpose may be illustrated by the following quotation from Holinshed:

> The king, in deed, was raised, & did that daie manie a noble feat of armes for, as it is written, he slue that daie with his owne hands six and thirtie persons of his enimies. The other [Prince Hal] on his part, incouraged by his dooings, fought valiantlie, and slue the lord Persie, called sir Henrie Hotspurre.

In Shakespeare's play, it is Prince Hal, especially, who is accorded the laurels of the peerless warrior, refusing to retire from battle despite his wounds, rescuing his royal father from the renowned Douglas, and defeating Hotspur in single combat. King Henry, the titular hero, is not given comparable prominence in this culminating episode, although his kingly virtues are not ignored.

When this play was first produced, Falstaff was identified not by that name but as Sir John Oldcastle. Evidence of this original identification remains, for Prince Hal calls the fat knight "my old lad of the castle" in the first comic scene (I.ii.46). Moreover, in 2 *Henry IV*, the 1599 quarto uses *Old.* for *Fal.* as one of the speech prefixes (I.ii.137) and the epilogue to 2 *Henry IV* includes the statement that "Oldcastle died martyr, and this is not the man." The historical Sir John Oldcastle was a well-known aristocrat during the reign of Henry V, and a leader of the Lollards, that faction whose religious views were considered heretical, for which reason he ultimately was burned at the stake. Descendants of Oldcastle, the Lords Cobham, flourished in Protestant sixteenth-century England and understandably were offended by the use of their ancestor's name.

The historical Oldcastle received some notice in Holinshed's *Chronicles*, but that is not the source used by Shakespeare in this instance. He found the name in the anonymous *Famous Victories of Henry V*, a comedy-history play which was produced as early as 1588, but not published until a decade later. This excessively inept drama deserves brief attention as a second source used by Shakespeare, especially for the comic scenes in his play.

In *Famous Victories* Sir John Oldcastle, familiarly called "Jockey," plays a subordinate role. A comparison of him with Shakespeare's Falstaff is one of the surest ways of attaining a sound appreciation of our dramatist's creativity. But the playwright's debt, however slight, must be acknowledged here. This is also true of Hal's relationship with the habitués of the Boar's-Head Tavern and especially the robbery at Gadshill. Indeed, the confusing name Gadshill for one of the participants in the robbery derives from the earlier play, and in it Prince Hal is no more than an irresponsible, dissipated prodigal.

The name *Falstaff* may well derive from the Sir John Falstoffe, a historical figure, who makes a brief appearance in Shakespeare's *1 Henry VI* and who, according to many chronicles, was one-time owner of the Boar's-Head Tavern.

Historically, *1 Henry IV* continues the action set forth in Shakespeare's *The Tragedy of Richard II* (1595), and the dramatist necessarily includes in it many references to events dramatized in the earlier play. These include the events leading up to the usurpation of the throne by Bolingbroke (who thus became Henry IV), aided by the powerful baronial family of the Percies; the ominous prophecy of the fallen Richard, for whose death Bolingbroke was responsible; the new king's determination to do penance for his heinous crimes by fighting the enemies of Christendom in the Holy Land, once political matters in England are settled.

The Earl of Northumberland, as leader of the Percy faction, is quite prominent in *Richard II*, and his son Henry Percy, better known as Hotspur, is also among the *dramatis personae*. Hotspur describes himself as "tender, raw, and young" (II.iii.42); he fights courageously in behalf of Bolingbroke and is present at the deposition of the anointed monarch, Richard II. Young Prince Hal does not make an appearance in this earlier play, but in it he is set in opposition to the valiant Hotspur. Late in the action, the triumphant Bolingbroke asks, "Can no man tell me of my unthrifty son?" (V.iii.1). And he makes reference to Hal's "unrestrained loose companions," to the "dissolute crew" with whom the prince, "wanton" (carefree) and "effeminate" (refusing to accept manly responsibility), fraternizes. Thus the public characters of Hotspur and Hal are already well established. But, in *Richard II*, when Hotspur reports Hal's impudent reply to the news of his father's triumph, Bolingbroke replies,

> As dissolute as desperate; yet through both
> I see some sparks of better hope, which elder years
> May happily bring forth. (V.iii.20-22)

In this way Shakespeare prepares the way for the full-length portrait of the prince who will emerge as the Ideal Prince, the leader who was to become the prototype of the Hero-King, the model of all English sovereigns, as he was depicted by all the chroniclers and as he appears in Shakespeare's own chronicle-history play.

CHARACTERS

King Henry IV

The eldest son of John of Gaunt, Duke of Lancaster, and grandson of Edward III, Henry had returned from banishment on July 4, 1399, to claim the rights of inheritance denied him by

Richard II. As these events were dramatized in Shakespeare's *Tragedy of Richard II*, he led a revolt against the Crown, forced Richard to abdicate, and became the first of the Lancastrian rulers of England; subsequently he had the hapless Richard put to death. In Shakespeare's *Richard II* and on occasion in *1 Henry IV*, he is referred to as Bolingbroke, from the place of his birth. History reports him as a brave, active, and temperate man who had been welcomed to the throne by all classes, pledging "to abandon the evil ways of Richard II" and to govern "by common counsel and consent." He is further described as being a good soldier, a careful administrator, and a wise statesman. Nevertheless, his position was insecure and trying because of the manner in which he attained kingship. Bitter experience was to make him somewhat suspicious and calculating.

Henry, Prince of Wales

Prince Hal, as he is usually called in this play, the high-spirited eldest son of Henry IV, had indeed been a carefree, boisterous youth, and the "wild prince" stories were circulated beginning in his own lifetime. History records also that he distinguished himself in the Welsh wars and gained valuable experience in government. Holinshed, Shakespeare's chief source, says: "Indeed he was youthfullie given, growen to audaucitie. . . . But yet. . . his behavior was not offensive or at least tending to the damage of anie bodie." That he did become alienated from his royal father is historical fact. Again in the words of Holinshed, "The king after expelled him out of his privie councell, banisht him the court, and made the duke of Clarence (his yoonger brother) president of the counsell in his steed." Reconciliation followed, but much later than in Shakespeare's play. In the *Henry IV* plays, the dramatist depicts the apparent waywardness of the prince and the profound concern of the king, both happily resolved by Hal's chivalry and heroism at Shrewsbury.

Henry Percy, surnamed Hotspur

Son of the Earl of Northumberland and nephew of the Earl of Worcester, Hotspur emerges as the impetuous leader of the northern rebels. Again it was Holinshed who provided the basic elements of his character; but it remained for Shakespeare to so develop that character, consistent with his purpose of providing a strong contrast primarily to Prince Hal and secondarily to King Henry, that the Hotspur of this play is almost an original creation. He is identified only as "Percy" in *Richard II;* in the present chronicle-history play, he is a major figure whose name suggests that he is indeed, in the words of Holinshed, "a capteine of high courage" spurring on the horse that carries him into battle.

Henry Percy, Earl of Northumberland

This is Hotspur's father, the titular head of the House of Percy, most powerful baronial family of the North Parts. He appears as he did in *Richard II* — cold and politic, in marked contrast to his son, a man who is, from the royalist point of view, certainly "a haughty, insulting" enemy of the Crown.

Thomas Percy, Earl of Worcester

Brother of the Earl of Northumberland and uncle of Hotspur, it is he who has especially influenced his impressionable young nephew. According to Holinshed, his "studie was ever . . . to procure malice, and set things in a broile." So he appears in this play.

Owen Glendower

First referred to as "the irregular and wild Glendower" (I.i.40), he was a Welsh nobleman, descended from Llewellyn, last of the Welsh kings. It was he who defeated and took captive Edmund Mortimer, Earl of March, who married one of Glendower's daughters. Incensed because Henry IV had not provided him redress against a grasping neighbor in a quarrel over landed property, Glendower led a great following of his countrymen against English rule. Traditionally certain supernatural powers were attributed to him.

Edmund Mortimer, Earl of March

Mortimer is presented in this play as the son-in-law of Glendower, the brother-in-law of Hotspur, and claimant to the throne of England. For the record, it was his nephew, a younger Edmund, who married Glendower's daughter and who, as son and proclaimed heir of Roger Mortimer, Earl of March, was claimant to the throne of England. By taking liberties with history here, Shakespeare magnified the dangers faced by Henry IV.

Prince John of Lancaster

Younger brother of Prince Hal, he appears in the very first scene and on the battlefield at Shrewsbury, where he is distinguished for his courage. To some extent he functions as a foil to his older brother, the Prince of Wales.

Archibald, Earl of Douglas

This "ever-valiant and approved Scot," as he is called by the Earl of Westmoreland (I.i.54) was a leader of the forces defeated by Hotspur at Holmedon. He then became an ally of the Percies in their revolt against Henry IV.

Sir John Falstaff

Knight of the realm, enormously fat and white-bearded, he is the companion of the carefree Prince Hal. Falstaff is concerned largely with pleasures of the flesh and cheerfully rejects conventional ideas and behavior especially suitable to his rank and age. He emerges as the most paradoxical character in all fiction, dramatic or non-dramatic. His irrepressible humor and superior wit, by means of which he retrieves himself from embarrassing or difficult situations, make it practically impossible for one to pass moral judgment on his character.

The Earl of Westmoreland

One of the noblemen who lead the king's army.

Sir Walter Blunt

Another nobleman loyal to King Henry and a commander of the royal forces at Shrewsbury. He functions especially as an emissary for the king.

Sir Richard Vernon

His role is exactly that of Sir Walter Blunt, but he serves the rebellious Percies, not the king.

Richard Scroop

The Archbishop of York and the ally of the Percies in the rebellion.

Sir Michael

A follower of the Archbishop of York.

Poins

Prince Hal's companion at Boar's-Head Tavern in East-cheap, it is he who devises the plot to gull Falstaff at Gadshill. His special relationship with Prince Hal suggests that he, in contrast to Peto and Bardolph, comes from a genteel family.

Gadshill, Peto, Bardolph

These three are the riotous and rascally associates of Falstaff. The first (whose name is identical with that of the scene of the robbery) serves as advance man among the rogues, the one who ascertains all the necessary facts relating to the planned robbery; the last named functions as a kind of parasitical serving man to Sir John Falstaff.

Lady Percy

Hotspur's sprightly, affectionate wife, she is the sister of Mortimer.

Lady Mortimer

Daughter of Glendower and wife of Mortimer, who dotes upon her. She speaks no English and her husband speaks no Welsh.

Mistress Quickly

This is the kindly, if rather stupid and disreputable, hostess of the Boar's-Head Tavern in Eastcheap.

SYNOPSIS

The main plot of *1 Henry IV* has as its subject the rebellion of the Percies, the northern baronial family who had helped Henry depose Richard II and attain the crown. They are joined by the Scottish Earl of Douglas, Edmund Mortimer, Earl of March, claimant to the throne, and Owen Glendower, a Welsh noble.

Henry is presented first as a ruler who has been beset with troubles from the start: civil strife in England, attacks by Scottish forces moving across the northern border, and the defeat and capture of the still loyal Mortimer by Glendower. He thus is unable to fulfill his earlier vow to lead a crusade to the Holy Land. But there is one piece of good news: English forces led by young Hotspur have defeated the Scots at Holmedon and have captured the renowned Earl of Douglas. Yet this especially gives the harassed king reason to lament the dereliction of his son and heir, Prince Henry, who sedulously has avoided the court and public responsibility and spends his time in the company of the elderly, high-spirited Sir John Falstaff, as well as the lowly habitués of the Boar's-Head Tavern in Eastcheap.

The comic subplot deals most amusingly with this same Falstaff and his boon companions, including Prince Hal, as he is appropriately called in this setting. In the initial episode, Hal joins with Poins, Bardolph, and Peto in a plan to gull Falstaff, contriving to have him participate in a robbery at Gadshill, be robbed in turn, and finally exposed as a coward and liar. Alone, Prince Hal soliloquizes, letting the audience know that, although he now chooses to enjoy himself in riotous company, he has no illusions about the character of his associates and will redeem himself publicly at the proper time.

The main plot takes precedence at this point. Once more at the court, King Henry confronts the Percies — Northumberland, Worcester, and Hotspur. He sternly rebukes them and especially demands to be told why the ranking Scottish prisoners taken by Hotspur have not been turned over to the Crown. The Percies, deeply resenting the fact that the man they helped to the throne now intends to enforce absolute obedience, begin to plot their revolt. They will make peace with Glendower and gain his support and that of Mortimer. Then, aided by Welsh and Scottish forces, the latter led by Douglas, they will war against the usurper, King Henry IV.

It is time to advance the comic subplot. Arrangements are completed for the robbery at Gadshill during the night. When the victims, a group of travelers, approach, Poins and the prince use an excuse to separate themselves from Falstaff and the others. Falstaff, forced to proceed on foot, is the leader of the robbers, who then are set upon by the disguised prince and Poins and robbed in turn. Falstaff exhibits almost miraculous alacrity in beating a retreat.

Again the action shifts to the main plot, wherein Hotspur is presented reading a letter from an English noble whose aid he has solicited. He can hardly contain himself as he reads the excuses offered and he denounces the writer as a coward. Then, in an exchange with his attractive young wife, Kate, he reveals himself as a man practically obsessed with matters relating solely to the planned revolt against the Crown.

In Eastcheap at the Boar's-Head Tavern, Falstaff is exposed as the dupe who has been tricked by the prince and Poins. But, not unexpectedly, in view of his already demonstrated wit, he not only survives the ordeal of being derided as a coward and liar but emerges comically triumphant. Prior to all this, Hal had made satiric reference to the prowess of Hotspur; now an emissary from the king informs Hal that he must appear at court promptly. This turn of events provides the prince the opportunity to participate with Falstaff in a "play extempore," each successively enacting the role of King Henry rebuking the wayward son and heir.

At the residence of the Archdeacon in North Wales, Hotspur, Worcester, Mortimer, and Glendower hold a parley, one not without some dissension. They plan the campaign against the royal forces and the later division of England into three parts. The absence of the Earl of Northumberland is significant in light of later events.

In the meantime, the confrontation between the king and Prince Hal takes place, the former sternly rebuking his son and comparing him unfavorably to the valiant Hotspur. But when Hal soberly vows to redeem his tarnished reputation at Hotspur's expense, the king not only forgives him but places him in command of royal forces. At that very moment the two learn that the rebels will be assembled at Shrewsbury.

Once more the action shifts to the Boar's-Head Tavern, where Falstaff is flourishing in the company of Bardolph and Mistress Quickly. The prince and Peto arrive, and we learn that Hal has reimbursed the travelers who had been robbed at Gadshill and has arranged for Falstaff's commissioning as a leader of the king's forces.

Hotspur, Worcester, and Douglas learn that the Earl of Northumberland and his retainers will not join them. Apparently illness has incapacitated him. Not for long is Hotspur dejected by this bad news; sure of victory, he sees this as providing a greater opportunity to impress the multitude, whose support the rebels must gain and retain. Vernon arrives with the news that the royal army has set forth for Shrewsbury and that second in command to the king himself is the Prince of Wales. Hotspur, at first depressed by Vernon's glowing description of Hal, quickly recovers himself and declares that he will oppose the prince in single combat. Yet a third report is received: Glendower will require fourteen days to raise a force of Welshmen. But nothing can dampen the ardor nor restrain the impetuosity of Hotspur.

Now we meet Falstaff as a military commander. Unscrupulously he has managed to enlist a group of pitiful, physically unfit "soldiers" whom he will lead to Shrewsbury. Both Prince Hal and Westmoreland remark on their unfitness but do nothing to stop Falstaff.

Sir Walter Blunt, emissary from King Henry, arrives in the rebel camp and addresses the rebel leaders, voicing the orthodox condemnation of their disloyalty and conveying to them the king's willingness to listen to their grievances. Hotspur restates the rebel's arguments, and the royal offer is rejected.

In Yorkshire, the Archbishop of York and one Sir Michael, both in sympathy with the rebellious Percies, discuss the impending battle at Shrewsbury. Learning that Mortimer and his battle forces will not be able to join the rebels, the archbishop expresses his deep concern for the success of the enterprise. He directs Sir Michael to leave at once to enlist support, for he knows that King Henry, aware of his disaffection, will move against him "if Lord Percy thrive not."

The action now moves to the king's camp at Shrewsbury. There, Worcester and Vernon meet with Henry IV, are given a chance once more to voice their grievances, are lectured on the subject of loyalty, and are offered generous terms if they will disband their forces. Prince Hal speaks words of praise for Hotspur, modestly concedes that he himself has been derelict, and offers to fight his rival in single combat. The two rebel leaders depart, ostensibly to report to Hotspur what has been said by the king and prince. Present during all this was Sir John Falstaff, who, left to himself, soliloquizes on the impractical aspects of heroism and honor.

Worcester does not tell his nephew about the king's offer, convinced that under any circumstances the older leaders of the revolt will be the objects of Henry's wrath. But Vernon reports honestly and clearly to Hotspur how Prince Hal conducted himself. When a messenger announces the approach of the royal forces, Hotspur sounds the call to battle.

In the course of that battle, Douglas slays Blunt, mistaking him for the king, and he exchanges words of warlike determination with Hotspur. A contrast is provided by Falstaff, who suddenly appears after the two have left. We learn that he has committed his tattered troops to battle, wherein they, with the exception of one or two, have been slaughtered. When the prince appears, deadly serious, Falstaff employs his verbal wit once more — and is sternly rebuked.

Prince Hal rescues his father from the sword of Douglas and meets and slays his great rival, Hotspur. After the prince's departure for another part of the battlefield, Falstaff reappears. Then, when Hal returns with his brother, Prince John of Lancaster, Falstaff claims to have slain the young rebel leader. Neither of the princes bothers to refute him at any length. Worcester and Vernon are captured and later put to death. But Douglas, also a captive, is set free by the generous Prince Hal. The rebel forces have been badly defeated. King Henry then dispatches John of Lancaster to the North, where he will oppose Northumberland and the Archbishop Scroop; he himself will leave with Prince Hal to fight the forces led by Glendower and Mortimer.

SUMMARIES AND COMMENTARIES

ACT I — SCENE 1

Summary

An exhausted King Henry describes the horrors of civil strife which his realm has endured during the twelve months that he has ruled England. At last he will be free to lead a united force of English soldiers to fight the enemies of Christendom in Jerusalem. But the Earl of Westmoreland brings news which forces the king to postpone this crusade. In Wales Mortimer's forces have been badly defeated by Glendower and Mortimer himself has been taken captive. Furthermore, English troops led by young Henry Percy, "the gallant Hotspur," are engaged in a battle at Holmedon against the Scots commanded by Douglas. The king has already learned the outcome of this battle, thanks to the services of Sir Walter Blunt. Young Percy has won a great victory and taken many prisoners. This is indeed, as Westmoreland states, "a conquest for a prince to boast of" (77). The king sadly replies that he wishes his own derelict son were more like the valiant Hotspur. He is concerned also because that admirable son of the Earl of Northumberland refuses to turn his prisoners over to the Crown, especially because many of them are ranking nobles. Westmoreland informs him that Hotspur's arrogance is the result of his uncle's influence: "This is his uncle's teaching; this is Worcester,/ Malevolent to you in all aspects. . . ." The king announces that he will hold council at Windsor and instructs Westmoreland to order the Percies to be present.

Commentary

The titular hero, King Henry IV, whom we meet and hear in this opening scene making what amounts to a formal address, had made the vow to fight the infidel in the Holy Land shortly after his usurpation of the throne from Richard II and the death of his predecessor for which Henry himself was responsible (*Richard II*, V.vi.30-52). Primarily, therefore, it is Henry, the sinner, the man guilty of the heinous sins of usurpation and regicide, who appears here — one who hopes to atone for his sins by going to the Holy Land. From a doctrinal point of view, never to be ignored in Shakespeare's chronicle-history plays, Henry is already enduring divine punishment, although, under God's authority, he rules England and merits the obedience of all subjects. This was the orthodox Tudor, sixteenth-century view which informs this play.

Understandably, then, King Henry appears "shaken [and] wan with care" (1), as he tells us in his speech, dwelling with vivid detail on the "furious close of civil butchery" (13). The rising of the Welsh led by Glendower points to the fact that Henry will not yet be given the opportunity to do penance for his sins. And with these internal troubles, there remains the threat from Scotland, still an independent kingdom. The seriousness of this threat is apparent: Sir Walter Blunt has ridden hard to bring the news of Hotspur's victory.

As he did in the last act of *Richard II*, Shakespeare now introduces the contrast between "young Harry," the king's eldest son and heir, and the dedicated, courageous Hotspur. The former's brow is stained with "riot and dishonour" (85); the latter is "the theme of Honour's tongue,/ Amongst a grove the very straightest plant" (81-82). Little wonder that the distraught Henry would like to exchange sons with the Earl of Northumberland, especially since Hotspur has been winning glory not in civil strife but in fighting a foreign enemy.

In view of the second reference to the postponement of the king's "holy purpose," that of leading a crusade to Jerusalem, it follows that the reported failure of the Prince of Wales is part of Henry's punishment for his sins. So Shakespeare's generation would conclude.

The titular hero has been introduced in this first scene, and we have gained an insight into one aspect of his character; the connection between this chronicle-history play and the preceding one has been indicated tacitly; and the dominant theme of rebellion has been established. Although neither Hotspur nor the Prince of Wales has made an appearance, the two have been set in opposition, and as a result the secondary but important theme of honor has been set forth.

ACT I – SCENE 2

Summary

The action now shifts to the Prince's apartment in London, and the participants are Prince Hal himself, Sir John Falstaff, and Poins. Prince Hal, far from engaging enemies of the Crown in armed combat, is amusing himself in witty verbal exchange with Falstaff. The subject of this discourse ranges from drinking to purse-snatching. The two vie with each other in trading amusing insults. Falstaff shows little deference for the prince, twitting him about his lack of grace and his devil-may-care attitude and behavior. Hal, whose initial speech provides a full-length portrait of the knight as a glutton and lecher who is too "fat-witted" to be concerned about the time of day, proves to be a rather worthy opponent in this combat of wits. But Falstaff matches him in rebuttal; indeed, some critics argue that the fat knight excels him.

Since the subject of robbery has been introduced prior to the arrival of Poins, the way has been prepared for details about the Gadshill enterprise in which Hal and Falstaff are asked to participate. Hal amuses himself at Falstaff's expense. First he refuses to go along with the others even "for recreation sake"; then, after listening to Falstaff's denunciation of him, he changes his mind; and finally he refuses once more to be one of the thieves at Gadshill. After Falstaff has departed, the prince learns from Poins that the robbery will provide a wonderful opportunity to gull Falstaff. Let Sir John, Bardolph, and Peto rob the travelers; then Hal and Poins, disguised, will rob the robbers. The great sport will be to expose Falstaff as a coward and liar. Prince Hal cannot resist such a good chance to trick his old companion; he will take part in the robbery at Gadshill.

All the dialogue so far has been in prose. Left alone, the prince now soliloquizes in blank verse. He makes it clear that he is fully aware of the character of his chosen companions, likening them to "contagious [poisonous] clouds." He states that he chooses for a time to remain in their riotous company for recreation's sake but will, at the right moment, surprise and gratify the world by standing forth in his true character.

Commentary

Appropriately, prose is the medium used in this first scene of the broadly comic subplot wherein matters of state have no immediate place. But one should note that, colloquial though it is predominantly, it is the prose of upper-class, sophisticated speakers. Occasional vulgarisms in the man-to-man exchange between Falstaff and Hal should not mislead the reader. Sir John here, and throughout the play, is a speaker of superior prose, prose marked by a vivacity, brilliance, and finish evidenced from the very beginning in his first two speeches with their balance, antitheses, and allusive elements. Hal, and even Poins, uses the same general style, which provides a significant contrast to that used, for example, by the lowly carriers in Act II, Scene i.

But most important in this scene are the characters of Falstaff and Prince Hal. What is learned about Falstaff as he exchanges spontaneous, good-natured insults with the prince? He is, to be sure, a knight of the realm, apparently a not unfitting associate of the prince, whom he meets now, not in a disreputable tavern but in the prince's London apartment. If, for the moment, we take literally what Hal says about him in his first speech (2-13), Falstaff emerges as one devoid of any sense of responsibility. Time, a symbol of the ordered life as used here, could not possibly concern one whose hours are spent largely in drinking sack (a strong sherry-type wine, especially popular in the days before gin and whiskey), overeating, and wasting half the day in sleep induced by gluttony. Add to all this Falstaff's alleged interest in bawds and houses of prostitution. Quite an indictment, and one which Falstaff does not refute: "Indeed, you come near me now, Hal," he replies (14). Yet he is anything but embarrassed. Is his way of life unknightly, ignoring as he does *noblesse oblige*, the obligations of rank? Well, let Hal remember that Falstaff "takes purses by moonlight" and thus does not follow "Phoebus, he, 'that wand'ring knight so fair'" (16-17). Here, demonstrating for the first of many times his upper-class learning, he provides a brilliant rhetorical commentary on gross reality and, as always, is fully aware of what he is doing. Moreover, only a superior wit could accomplish all this in such an adroit way, effectively answering what may well be a serious indictment of his character. Cheerfully, he adds to his offenses: he is one who engages in robbery by night and thus goes "by the moon," not by Phoebus the sun. The figurative language here admits to interesting interpretation relevant in a play, the main theme of which is rebellion.

Traditionally the sun is a common symbol of royalty; in this instance, it represents the king, who stands for law and order. Rhetorically and poetically, the moon may represent more than one thing; here it is unmistakably a symbol of instability, not only because it does not remain the same size to one's eyes as time passes, but because (as Hal points out) it governs the tides of the sea, which ebb and flow. One of the leaders of the Northern rebels of 1569, a later Earl of Northumberland, was denounced by loyalists as "the wavering moon." As a knight who follows the moon, then, Falstaff is a rebel (though a comic one) against law and order. And this conclusion finds support in his witty, elegant circumlocutions and epithets: when Hal becomes king—and Falstaff is always aware of Hal's status as heir apparent—let robbers be honored; let them be called "squires of the night's body, not "thieves of the day's beauty" (27-28). The opposition of day and night is that of order and disorder. "Diana's foresters, gentlemen of the shade, minions [favorites, darlings] of the moon," which is described as "noble [and] chaste," are other refined terms used by Falstaff to describe criminal activity.

When Hal's reply makes this very point, Sir John is quick to change the subject, or to try to do so. But the reference to the gallows and hanging, the usual punishment for robbery in Shakespeare's England, has been introduced by the young prince, who will not, for the moment, let his lively companion ignore it, thus the reference to the "buff jerkin" worn by sheriff's officers and to "durance," meaning not only "long lasting" but "imprisonment" (48-49). The culmination of Falstaff's rejection of law and order comes in his comic plea to the prince, urging him to have nothing to do with "old father antic [buffoon] the law" and to honor thieves, who are admirable men of "resolution" (65-70).

Hal obviously enjoys this repartee with Falstaff, who indeed is, as he will say later, not only witty in himself but the cause of wit in others. The young prince lays a verbal trap for the knight: as king he will not hang malefactors; Falstaff shall. Immediately Falstaff pictures himself as a learned judge—and then is told that, far from being elevated to the bench, he will function as the common hangman. Wit rescues him from this ignominious position, as he makes a play upon the word *suits* (petitions or solicitations made at court; suits of clothing). This is grim humor, appropriately like a jest on the gallows itself, for in Elizabethan times the hangman received the clothes of his victims and therefore was referred to ironically as the best-dressed man in England.

Wit or no wit, the subject of hanging is not a pleasant one, and Falstaff changes the subject and mood. He is "as melancholy as a gib cat or a lugg'd bear." And Hal matches him simile for simile. Falstaff's reply, "Thou hast the most unsavoury similes and art indeed the most comparative, rascalliest, sweet young Prince" (89-91), underscores at once his favored position as a kind of privileged jester and, surely, a genuine affection for the prince.

This by no means exhausts the facets of his complex character. Earlier (54-60), it was made clear that Falstaff willingly let the prince foot all the bills at the tavern. Now, having been matched by Hal in the combat of wits, he adopts another role. For the moment he becomes the penitent old sinner, acknowledging that he is "little better than one of the wicked." The style he adopts is that of the pulpit, biblical in its simple parallelisms and repetitions (95-98). How serious, how repentant he really is becomes clear at once. In mock sorrow, he, this white-bearded old man, attributes his moral downfall to young Prince Hal, whose use of biblical paraphrase in reply reveals his continued awareness of Falstaff's comic tricks.

But once more Sir John's ludicrous statement has made him vulnerable. When Hal suddenly asks, "Where shall we take a purse tomorrow, Jack?" (111), Falstaff responds with enthusiasm: "'Zounds, where thou wilt, lad; I'll make one." And yet once more his wit saves him when Hal dryly comments on this sudden shift from "praying to purse-taking": thieving is Falstaff's profession; is it not proverbial that the wise man should follow his own vocation?

When Poins arrives with the details relating to the proposed robbery, we learn more about Sir John. He declares that, if Hal does not join in the enterprise, Hal lacks honesty, manhood, and good fellowship; and that, in retaliation, Falstaff himself will be a traitor when the prince rules England. Ostensibly finding such virtue in thieves, Falstaff sustains the force of his earlier reference to robbers as "squires," "gentlemen," and "Diana's foresters." If one chooses to analyze this amusing reversal of values closely, it becomes apparent that Falstaff and all who willfully engage in robbery as a vocation are rebels against the Crown. Thus, much of the action in this comic subplot stands as a parody of the serious, public action in the main plot; moreover, the theme of rebellion is common to both. "Comic relief" will not suffice to describe the action in the subplot; there is much more.

Finally, as regards Falstaff, there is the question of cowardice, one much debated by commentators early and late in view of the knight's behavior later in the play. From Poins' remark made to Hal alone in order to persuade him to join in tricking Falstaff, one may conclude properly that cowards are not all of one piece. Peto and Bardolph are "true-bred cowards"; but Falstaff is a coward on principle, a practical realist, as it were, who will fight no longer than he sees reason (207-8). Nor will he prove to be an ordinary liar; he will tell the most "incomprehensible lies" about his experience at Gadshill.

How does Prince Hal appear in this scene? In popular tradition he is connected with various escapades including robbery; thus the early introduction of the theme of robbery would be immediately understood by Shakespeare's audiences. But the dramatist handles this subject carefully as far as the prince is concerned. It is Hal who is rather insistent in reminding Falstaff that thieves end up on the gallows. When asked to participate in the Gadshill robbery, the prince asks: "Who, I rob? I a thief? Not by my faith" (154). And we are to understand that he goes along only for the sake of duping Falstaff.

So amusing is Sir John that there is danger of underestimating Hal's wit. Falstaff indeed is the cause of wit in others, but time and again it is a remark made by the prince which provides Falstaff with the opportunity to scintillate. Surely one of the reasons that these two enjoy each other's company so much is that they share in the exhibition of verbal wit. For example, when Falstaff expresses his willingness to be hangman rather than judge because it "jumps with [his] humour as well as waiting in the court" (77-78), Hal gets the point immediately. "For obtaining of suits?" he asks. His last words addressed to the fat knight in this scene are brilliant: "Farewell, thou latter spring! Farewell. All-hallown summer!"

Prince Hal's final soliloquy has disturbed many readers. Some find it "priggish and hypocritical," and one may well conclude that it leaves the reader with an unflattering impression of Hal. Perhaps it is best here to remember that Shakespeare is dealing with a beloved, honored historical character whose youthful escapades and subsequent reformation had become part of treasured tradition. In a sense, the speaker is not Hal, Falstaff's "sweet wag," but Henry, Prince of Wales, who one day will lead English troops to victory over the traditional enemy, France. Here he functions as a kind of chorus. But once he gets beyond the indictment of his unprincipled associates as "contagious clouds" and "foul and ugly mists," his charm and breadth come through:

> If all the year were playing holidays,
> To sport would be as tedious as to work.
>
> (227-28)

These lines rescue him from the charge of calculation or hypocrisy.

Summary

A determined King Henry strongly reproves the Earls of Northumberland and Worcester, and Hotspur, who have obeyed his summons to appear before him. His threat to use force if necessary to curb their opposition leads Worcester to remind him that they, the Percies, were largely responsible for his rise to the throne. The king promptly orders Worcester to leave. Now it is Northumberland who addresses Henry IV, voicing words of conciliation. Hotspur, he states, has been maligned, for his son never intended to ignore a royal command. Hotspur himself explains what happened. Battle weary, he found it impossible to respond affirmatively to the request made by the king's messenger, a pretentious, unmanly coxcomb. Although the loyal Sir Walter Blunt puts in a good word for Hotspur, the king does not accept this excuse. He is convinced that young Percy intended to use the Scottish prisoners in bargaining with him for the ransom of Mortimer, Earl of March, Hotspur's brother-in-law, whom he denounces as one who foolishly betrayed the forces he led and now has married the daughter of his captor, "that great magician, damn'd Glendower." Hotspur vehemently defends Mortimer, but the king refuses to believe that he is not a traitor. Ordering Hotspur to talk no more of the Earl of March, he adds: "Send us your prisoners, or you'll hear of it." The king and members of his retinue leave.

Hotspur is beside himself. Even though he risks his life he will not obey King Henry. Just as Northumberland urges his son to control himself, Worcester returns to hear another outburst from his nephew. When Hotspur says that the king turned pale at the very mention of Mortimer's name, Worcester replies, "I cannot blame him." And this leads to a review of past events: Richard II's designation of the Earl of March as his heir to the throne, the role of the Percies in Bolingbroke's successful revolt, the ignominious position in which this proud and ungrateful Henry IV has placed the members of the House of Percy.

Worcester interrupts to announce that he has a plan, one "deep and dangerous," which he will reveal to his kinsmen. Hotspur is exhilarated by the very mention of a dangerous exploit to be carried out in the name of honor. Henceforth, he declares, he will dedicate himself solely to opposing "this Bolingbroke" and the Prince of Wales. Only after Northumberland has succeeded in calming his son can Worcester proceed. Hotspur is to pacify Henry IV for the time being by turning the prisoners over to the Crown, but he will make peace with Douglas and soon will ally himself with Glendower and Mortimer. Augmented by the Scottish and Welsh forces, the Percies will then confront the usurper Henry IV.

Commentary

The action in the main plot has risen to the point where the conflict is brought into the open. Following the audience with the king, the Percies are on the verge of rebellion. The danger to the Crown is very great indeed as Hotspur's speech beginning "Send Danger from the east unto the west" (195-97) makes clear. Henry faces not only the opposition of the most powerful baronial family in the North, but also, if the rebels' plan succeeds, the forces of Mortimer (legal heir to the throne according to the will made by Richard II) and the fearsome Glendower.

In this scene King Henry is represented not as the sinner, weary and wan with care, but as the forceful, competent ruler determined to maintain order within his kingdom as he faces baronial opposition. Yet he has been politic. The opening lines of his first speech tell us that he has sought to placate troublesome subjects, who nevertheless must respect him as one "mighty and to be fear'd" (6) if they prove recalcitrant. In the language of sixteenth-century political philosophy, Henry is a man gifted with the "specialty of rule." Nor does this conclusion rule out the fact that, in the words of Hotspur, he is a "subtle king,"—one capable of calculation, as a successful head of state has to be, at least in an era of power politics.

But this does not mean that Henry's crimes are to be forgotten. To Hotspur are assigned speeches which recall the sins of usurpation and regicide. For these the king and the Percies alike "wear the detested blot/ Of murderous subornation" and must suffer "a world of curses" (163-64). In counsel with his father and uncle, young Percy frequently disdains to refer to Henry as king; rather he is "cank'red [malignant] Bolingbroke," a thorn or canker in comparison to the lawfully anointed Richard II, "that sweet lovely rose." In the plant kingdom the rose is the appropriate symbol of royalty, just as the lion is in the animal kingdom.

All this may confuse the modern reader. Who actually is in the right, King Henry or the Percies, if either? The only way to answer this question is by recourse to Tudor political policy which, as has been stated earlier, informs this play. Henry remains a sinner; usurpation and regicide cannot be justified. But now a just God permits him to rule England. God may permit the rebel to rage as part of the punishment of a sinful ruler; but the rebel himself is guilty of mortal sin for his revolt against the Crown. A perceptive student may recall Richmond's leading a revolt against Richard III and emerging triumphant as Henry VII, first of the Tudor monarchs. Loyalists of the sixteenth century had an answer: Richmond (grandfather of Elizabeth I, ruler of England during the larger part of Shakespeare's lifetime) was the divinely appointed savior of the country and thus not a rebel. Perhaps it is well to remember that what most Englishmen cherished was stability—law and order within the kingdom. Richard II, in his latter years, was guilty of gross misrule; his successor, Henry IV, proved to be a strong, capable ruler.

Hotspur's basic character is firmly established in this scene. His high spirits and undoubted courage, his forthright answer to King Henry make him appear admirable. Unlike his uncle, the crafty Worcester, architect of the planned revolt, he is completely aboveboard. His sincerity is not to be questioned when he inveighs against "half-fac'd fellowships" (208) and the alleged ingratitude of the king. He is dedicated to winning new laurels in the only way he knows how; craft and selfish motive have no place in his character.

But Hotspur lives up to his name in more ways than one. Patience and contemplation are foreign to his nature; only in violent action is he at home. Time and again either his father or his uncle must rebuke him. Will he obey the king's order to relinquish the prisoners? "An if the devil come and roar for them,/ I will not send them," he exclaims (125-26). Northumberland's rebuke is hardly exaggerated: "What, drunk with choler?" No less revealing are Hotspur's words when Worcester first broaches his "deep and dangerous" plot: "O, the blood more stirs/ To rouse a lion than to start a hare!" (197-98). This Hotspur of the North is dedicated to winning honor after honor and now relishes the prospect of facing his major opponent, the king himself. Again it is his father's remark which provides telling comment on his son's limitations as a leader:

> Imagination of some great exploit
> Drives him beyond the bounds of patience.
>
> (199-200)

In martial affairs this young man is indeed the soul of courage; but he lacks discretion, he is too impetuous. Subsequent lines with reference to plucking "bright Honour from the pale-fac'd moon" emphasize once more Hotspur's special concern with honor as he conceives it (and about which, perhaps, he talks too much). In the words of his uncle:

> He apprehends a world of figures here,
> But not the form of what he should attend.
>
> (209-10)

To be noted also is that Hotspur is again pitted against "that same sword-and-buckler Prince of Wales," as he contemptuously calls Hal. By the end of this scene in which we learn that the Percies will be allied not only with Mortimer and Glendower but possibly with the disgruntled Archbishop of York, second ranking churchman in England, Hotspur can hardly contain himself: "O, let the hours be short/ Till fields and blows and groans applaud our sport!" (301-2). His choice of the word *sport* referring to bloody conflict is as revealing as anything else as regards his character. Hal, we recall, has been manifesting a far different attitude toward what constitutes sport; and he is about to engage in an enterprise which is against law and order within the kingdom ruled by Henry IV.

ACT II – SCENE 1

Summary

Two carriers complain about the accommodations of the inn at Rochester as they prepare to drive their pack horses to the market in London. Gadshill, the professional thief to whom Poins had made reference, enters and asks to borrow their lantern, but the wary carriers refuse to lend it and leave. At Gadshill's call the chamberlain, an informer, appears. He confirms what he told Gadshill earlier: a franklin (middle-class landowner) with three hundred marks in gold will be among the travelers soon to depart from the inn. Unlike the chamberlain, Gadshill has no fear of the hangman because he is joined in the robbery by Sir John and, to paraphase his own words, persons of higher rank.

Commentary

The inn-yard setting is a little masterpiece of vivid writing. It is picturesque in the literal sense, evoking a memorable picture – the darkness of a winter's morning with Charles' Wain (the constellation of the Great Bear) visible over the chimney, and the flea-infested inn itself. The note of homely realism is enhanced by the reference to the death of Robin Ostler, his passing lamented by the lowly carriers, whose colloquial discourse provides an interesting contrast to that between Prince Hal and Falstaff. And all this has its place in a play, the theme of which is rebellion. The carriers are representative of a goodly proportion of the English people, going about their work in their unglamorous way. The quarrel between king and lords affects all Englishmen, including these carriers concerned about the comfort of their poor horses and getting their produce to market.

Gadshill, appropriately named after a stretch of road notorious for robberies, and the unscrupulous chamberlain provide the contrast to the hard-working, honest subjects of the Crown. Gadshill's speech is larded with the argot of the Elizabethan underworld; consider, for example, the references to "foot landrakers" (footpads), and "long-staff sixpenny strikers" (thieves who will bash a person on the head for a pittance). But more important is his reference to the exalted company who are to join him in the robbery; they are ones who

> pray continually to their saint, the commonwealth;
> or rather, not pray to her, but prey on her, for they ride
> up and down on her and make her their boots.
>
> (88-91)

His sardonic words unmistakably are applicable to the Percies with their plot against the commonwealth, represented by the king, just as they are to Falstaff and Prince Hal. One may well recall the words spoken by Henry IV at the beginning of this play. Speaking of the grave civil disturbances which have occurred in the commonwealth during the first year of his reign, he said:

> No more shall trenching war channel her fields,
> Nor bruise her flowerets with the armed hoofs
> Of hostile paces.
>
> (I. i. 7-9)

Again the thematic connection between main plot and subplot is made clear.

ACT II – SCENE 2

Summary

Prince Hal and Poins appear together on the highway near Gadshill. Poins has succeeded in depriving Falstaff of his horse, and the fat knight himself arrives calling for Poins, who has withdrawn into the darkness. Hal offers to find Poins, and Falstaff is left alone to complain about Poins' perfidy. When the prince returns, Sir John is no less voluble in his denunication of any one who would so "colt" (fool) him. When Hal refuses to serve as Falstaff's groom—that is, get his horse for him—the knight unrestrainedly and wittily excoriates him.

Gadshill, Bardolph, and Peto enter. The victims of these robbers are now coming down the hill; all must put on their masks and be ready for them. Prince Hal instructs all but Poins to confront the travelers in the narrow lane, while he and Poins wait farther down the hill, ready to waylay their victims if they escape the first encounter. Falstaff has a moment of trepidation but agrees to stand fast. Hal and Poins leave to put on the disguises which will serve their purpose later.

Rendered helpless, perhaps chiefly by the verbal explosions of Falstaff, the travelers are quickly robbed and bound. The thieves are about to share the loot when the disguised Hal and Poins set upon them. Bardolph and Peto take to their heels at once; Falstaff remains only to strike a blow or two and then runs off, leaving the loot. The thought of the corpulent Falstaff footing it all the way to London delights Hal and Poins.

Commentary

One may wonder how it happens that the travelers, including the well-heeled franklin, are not mounted and proceed afoot. Obviously, Shakespeare, actor and shareholder in his company, was the practical man of the theater; stage entries on horseback were impractical. Not only does he deprive the travelers of horses but capitalizes on this necessity by having Hal and Poins deprive Falstaff of his horse.

In this scene farcical action, the broadest type of comedy, is dominant: Falstaff is the victim of Prince Hal, aided by Poins, and is paying the price for his enormous girth and brave words, but Shakespeare does not permit him to become the object of derisive laughter. Again his lines are superb of their kind. Here especially he is the master of witty paradox. He will be "accurs'd to rob in that thief's company" (10); hourly during the past twenty-two years he has vowed never to endure Poins' company again. Yet he cannot bring himself to forego "the rogue's company." He calls down a plague upon all thieves who cannot be true men. Paradox is carried even further. This corpulent old man, for whom twenty-four feet up hilly ground is the equivalent of seventy miles for any one of his companions, is the personification of vitality when he confronts the travelers. His best line is "What, ye knaves! young men must live" (95-96); here is the Falstaff who, despite his advanced years and white beard, is the very spirit of carefree youth.

From one point of view, Hal and Poins function as the wits who so manipulate events that folly is exposed—specifically, the folly of Sir John. But a serious crime *has* been committed, and it is not easy to dismiss all this as no more than an escapade in which the prince amuses himself prior to his promised reformation. For the time being, however, judgment must await the outcome of the gulling of Falstaff.

Some readers may be disturbed by Hal's refusal to show any pity for Falstaff who "sweats to death,/ And lards the earth as he walks along" (115-16). But that would be sheer sentimentality; there is no occasion to conclude that Sir John is in great discomfort. He is enduring comic punishment, as it were, for his sin of gluttony.

ACT II—SCENE 3

Summary

At Warkworth Castle, Hotspur reads a letter from a noble whom he has asked to join in the rebellion. The noble advances one excuse after another for declining the invitation. Young Percy is indignant and scornful of the writer, who ignores the fact that the Percies have powerful allies, some of whose forces already have set forth for the place of assembly. Hotspur suspects that this timorous lord may betray the plot to the king. Vehemently he expresses his defiance.

Lady Percy enters. She is deeply worried about her young husband, whose preoccupation with some serious business has made him neglect her and most normal activities. Hotspur will tell her nothing, and she suspects that he faces great danger. He does assure her, however, that she will join him at an unidentified destination.

Commentary

An occasional earlier commentator has argued that this scene may be justified largely on the grounds that we must be given a recess from Falstaff. This is a wholly unwarranted conclusion. First, the scene reveals the progress of the rebellion planned by the Percies in the first act; second, it adds appreciably to what is now becoming a full-length portrait of Hotspur, the "theme of Honour's tongue," as Henry IV called him at the beginning of the play.

Young Percy's choleric asides, filled with contemptuous epithets ("lack-brain" . . . "frosty-spirited rogue" . . . "dish of skim milk") are sufficiently revealing. In writing to the unidentified noble, Hotspur has eliminated any possibility of surprise; inevitably the king will be informed. Enraged to the point where he could "divide [himself] and go to buffets" (34), he nevertheless will brook no delay; he will set forth that very night, still convinced that the revolt is an "honourable" action. The figure of speech he uses to reassure himself is admirable: "out of this nettle, danger, we pluck this flower, safety" (9-10). Especially characteristic is his rough, yet good-natured, sparring with his wife. Declaring that this world is not one for playing with mammets (dolls) or tilting lips, he adds:

> We must have bloody noses and crack'd crowns,
> And pass them current too. God's me, my horse!
>
> (96-97)

It is hard to imagine anything that could be more revealing and graphic than Lady Percy's speech describing her husband's obsession with thoughts of armed conflict—a set speech, replete with rhetorical questions and balanced lines: "Of sallies . . . Of palisadoes . . . Of basilisks . . . Of prisoners' ransoms" (40-67).

But another side of Hotspur's character comes through strongly, one that is most attractive—a bluff manliness and wit of sorts. No one can doubt that he deeply loves his Kate, just as she dotes on him. His last words to her echo the well-known passage from the Book of Ruth and leave no room for doubt concerning the relationship between this attractive young couple: "Whither I go, thither shall you go too. . . ." There is irony in the fact that he will not tell her what the "heavy business" exactly is, since he indiscreetly wrote all about it to a fellow nobleman.

ACT II—SCENE 4

Summary

At the Boar's-Head Tavern, Prince Hal and Poins are entertaining themselves. Hal tells his companion that he has won much honor by being accepted as "sworn brother" to the lowly tavern servants. He engages Francis, one of them, in a bewildering game with Poins' help. First the prince, then Poins, calls for poor Francis, who, striving to please both, runs up and down stairs in a ridiculous manner, answering each call with "Anon [at once], sir." Hal makes the newly-arrived Falstaff and the rest of the thieves wait at the door while he comments on the significance of Francis' behavior, curiously shifting to a comparison of himself with "the Hotspur of the North."

Falstaff and his companions enter, the fat knight complaining bitterly about the prevalence of cowardice and calling for sack. He then tells how courageously he fought at Gadshill against enemies who, first said to number one hundred, are successively reduced to six or seven; and, as he testifies, two particular ones in buckram suits become successively four, seven, nine, and finally eleven. Hal and Falstaff exchange derogatory epithets. At last the prince gives the true account of what happened and challenges Falstaff to explain away the fact that he has proved himself to be a coward and liar. Falstaff, in his special way, does exactly that. Valiant though he is, never would he be one to kill the heir-apparent whom he recognized immediately by instinct. His spirits are uplifted, for he now knows that

Hal has the money taken from the travelers. Let all be merry, he exclaims and suggests a "play extempore" — a bit of amateur play acting — as a source of amusement.

A messenger from the king is announced. At Hal's request Falstaff leaves to "send him packing." During Sir John's absence Bardolph and Peto tell how the old knight coached them to back up his preposterous story. When Falstaff returns with news of the revolt of the Percies, the prince seems almost totally unconcerned. The names of renowned Hotspur ("that same mad fellow of the North," as Falstaff calls him), Mortimer, Douglas, "that devil Glendower" leave him unperturbed; unlike Sir John, he cannot be a coward.

But Hal must appear before his royal father, and this provides the subject for the play extempore, a kind of rehearsal, in which the prince and Falstaff play alternate roles.

The arrival of the sheriff and "all the watch" at the tavern door interrupts this merriment. At Hal's request, Falstaff hides behind the arras and the others go upstairs, leaving the prince with Peto to face the law. The carrier who accompanies the sheriff into the tavern identifies one of the thieves as a gross fat man — "as fat as butter." Hal assures them that the man is not present and that he will answer personally for any charges made.

After the sheriff and the carrier have left, Falstaff is discovered fast asleep and snoring behind the arras. "Search his pockets," says Hal to Peto, who finds only a tavern bill for a bit of food and vast quantities of sack. On inspiration Hal decides to pester Falstaff by giving him a command of foot troops which he will have to lead against the rebels. Hal himself will report to his father in the morning and will see that the stolen money is returned.

Commentary

This scene of broad comedy is at once one of the most hilarious in all literature and also one of the most significant in this play. No reader will want to miss any part of the fun; but no careful reader should be so carried away by Falstaff's superb performance as to miss the ideas relating to the theme and to the characterizations.

First to be explained is the import of Hal's remarks about his relationship with the tavern tapsters and apprentices, to whom he refers as "loggerheads" (blockheads) and "a leash (a pack, as of leashed animals) of drawers." To many, this episode hardly reflects favorably upon the character of Prince Hal, particularly the trick played upon the lowly Francis. Perhaps Hal's exploits with the drawers may be considered "miserable attempts at mirth" introduced "to show the quality of the prince's wit when unsustained by Falstaff's," the whole comprising "a very strange incoherent rhapsody" best explained by the prince's volatile nature and by the fact that he has "spent several hours drinking with the drawers." This is the view taken by an early commentator (*New Variorum*). More recent Shakespearean critics have taken a far different view and have found coherence and relevance in this episode.

In our century of the common man and with the prevailing tendency to create Shakespeare in our own image, it is easy to go astray here. For one thing, contemporary sources tell us that the gallants in Renaissance England took a sort of pride in being on quite familiar terms with drawers and that only favored guests were invited to the cellar to sample the wine in the hogsheads. Democratic sentiments must not mislead us. The prince of Shakespeare's *Henry IV* is at the highest rung of the ladder in a hierarchical society; in contrast, the drawers, worthy subjects of the Crown, are at the lowest rung. Yet Hal has won their admiration and affection, and they compare him favorably to Falstaff, that "proud Jack." In so conducting himself he has "sounded the very base string of humility." This could well be the best way to prepare for the day when he will rule all the people of England, all levels of society. In a word, in the first part of this comic scene, we are given an insight into the education of the prince, one who will lead an English army to France and be able to move freely among his soldiers on the eve of the decisive battle of Harfleur, listening to and understanding their conversation. From this point of view, Prince Hal has won a certain kind of victory. In *2 Henry IV*, the Earl of Warwick, seeking to console the dying King Henry IV, who again has great reason to worry about his son's behavior, has this to say:

> My gracious lord, you look beyond him quite.
> The Prince but studies his companions
> Like a strange tongue, wherein, to gain the language,
> 'Tis needful that the most modest word
> Be looked upon and learned.
>
> (IV.iv.67-71)

As Hal explains to Poins, the trick played on Francis is a "precedent" (36), or example, one in which he has proved himself to be a man of "all humours." That is to say, he is willing to indulge himself in all the varieties of life, including the present kind of merriment. His devastating burlesque of Hotspur (114-25) logically follows. Young Percy, according to Hal, is like Francis in his concentration on one narrow field of human activity, for Hotspur is obsessed by thoughts of carnage in battle — with "crack'd crowns and bloody noses." Indeed, there is much special pleading here; Hal has been and still is a truant from noble exercises. He has yet to prove himself and to make good the promise he made at the end of Act I, Scene ii. Virtue must manifest itself in positive action.

To compare Hal's wit with that of Falstaff in this scene, or elsewhere in the play for that matter, is wholly irrelevant. Whatever Falstaff's limitations may be, no one can deny him pre-eminence in the realm of wit.

Falstaff is in rare form as he enters, denouncing Hal and Poins as cowards and identifying himself as one endowed with true "manhood," as one of the few "good" men left in a bad world. He manifests again his constant awareness of Hal's status as heir-apparent and his own status as privileged jester by declaring his intent to beat Hal out of his kingdom with a wooden dagger and drive Hal's subjects before him like a flock of geese —

including, to be sure, the lowly ones whom Hal has just been winning over.

When Sir John brazenly denies that he has had a single drink, although we have seen him quaff a cup of sack almost as soon as he entered the tavern, the way is prepared for his gargantuan lies concerning the number of assailants at Gadshill. His immediate reply to Hal, who points out that Falstaff's lips are still wet with wine (170), provides a key to the old knight's tall stories: "All's one for that" (What difference does it make?). Surely it is futile to waste one's time debating whether or not Falstaff expects Hal and Poins to believe him. He remains the great wit at his calling; exaggeration, as is apparent here, can be wonderfully amusing.

And so when, with assumed solemnity, he justifies his conduct at Gadshill, having been exposed as a liar and coward. As Hal knows, he is "as valiant as Hercules; but beware instinct: the lion will not touch the true prince." In identifying himself with the great exemplar of strength and courage in classical mythology, and with the lion (a symbol here, not of royalty, but of courage and ferocity in the animal kingdom), Falstaff illustrates another aspect of his complex character. Here he is the braggart warrior, a well-known type character in classical comedy, long since naturalized in Renaissance European drama, including English. But let us give Falstaff credit; he is aware of the full import of his words.

The nobleman at the door, an emissary from the king, is dismissed by Falstaff as "Old Gravity"; the elderly, white-bearded knight in whose life seriousness has no place is glad to "send him packing" (328). The epithet Falstaff uses here is at one with "old father antic," which he used earlier to describe the law. The implication is the same: he has no use for responsibility, for law, for order. They interfere with life conceived as a perpetual holiday.

There follows an exchange between Hal and Bardolph and then between the prince and Falstaff; these have some special interest in the realm of the comedy of physical appearances (340-60) and also have some thematic relevance. Bardolph's flaming nose invites Hal's witty comment; it provides a constant glow which should have served Bardolph as well as his sword during the Gadshill robbery, and yet Bardolph ran away. Perhaps, in contrast to Falstaff's undisturbed good humor, there is rancor in Bardolph's reply: "My lord, do you see these meteors? Do you behold these exhalations?" (351-52). But Shakespeare is making a typical play on words here. On one level, meteors and exhalations stand for drunkenness and poverty; on a second level, not to be ignored in a play about rebellion, they stand for violation of law and order.

In the comedy of physical appearances, Falstaff's enormous girth, which invites Hal's merciless comments (357-61), provides much fun. "Bare-bone" Falstaff, Hal suggests, has been blown up by bombast, implying that the old man is devoid of real substance. There is, perhaps, pathos to be found in Sir John's reply: if he has not been able to see his own knees since he was a youth of Hal's age, once, long ago, he was becomingly slender. And, to be sure, he has his own explanation for his corpulence—"a plague of sighing and grief" has blown him up "like a bladder." We are not allowed to sentimentalize; Falstaff's wit drives away sentimentality.

The subsequent dialogue relating to the fearful opponents of Henry IV is especially revealing of Hal's character. Despite all that Falstaff says to undermine the courage of the young prince, Hal remains nonchalant and (thanks probably to the presence of Falstaff) quite witty. What should come through, especially since Hotspur dominated the previous scene and his character has had an important part in the present one, is that Prince Hal finds no occasion to become voluble and boastful about what he intends to do. News of impending conflict does not drive him beyond the bounds of patience. Deeds, not words, are called for, certainly not advertisement of one's self.

The "play extempore," culminating in Falstaff's brilliant defense of himself and his way of life, is a comic masterpiece. Sir

John's genius is fully revealed here as he throws his considerable self into the role of an irate father and king reproving an errant son and heir. He is especially appreciated by the hostess of this disreputable tavern, whom he calls, in lines of heroic verse, his "sweet . . . tristeful queen." Earlier, attention has been called to Falstaff's rather wide range of knowledge, to the fact that his discourse reflects an education appropriate to a knight of the realm. This aspect of his character is again shown, as when he speaks of "King Cambyses' vein," a reference to the ranting style used by Thomas Preston in the widely popular tragedy *Cambyses*, written some twenty-eight years before *1 Henry IV*. More emphatically, it is shown by Falstaff's matchless burlesque of euphuism, the highly contrived style used in the even more widely popular and influential prose romance *Euphues* (1579), by John Lyly. That style, which for a time was widely imitated, is marked by interminable parallelisms and antitheses, rhetorical questions, maxims, and curious allusions and similes which derive from the *Natural History* of Pliny, classical mythology, and the bestiaries of the Middle Ages. All these stylistic devices Falstaff makes use of in his speech, which includes insulting and even scandalous comments on the royal family. He concludes with words of highest praise for "a virtuous man" with whom the prince keeps company. Ah, yes — now he remembers the name. It is Falstaff. Let Hal "him keep with," the rest banish.

When Hal asks that they exchange roles, Falstaff asks, "Depose me?" And he challenges the prince to match him in gravity and majesty. At this point some will be reminded of Hal's solemn promise to break "through the foul and ugly mists/ Of vapours that did seem to strangle him" (I.ii.225-26). If he is to do so, this king of jesters must be deposed.

Actually, Prince Hal, in the role of his father, makes no attempt to rival Falstaff; he makes use of this change to berate the fat knight as (among other things) "that grey iniquity, . . . that villainous abominable misleader of youth, Falstaff, that old white-bearded Satan" (449-509). Then Falstaff, suddenly serious and dutiful in tone as he plays the role of the young heir to the throne, makes his memorable reply, one that is so eloquent, so appealing that generations of theatergoers and readers have taken Falstaff to their hearts—and uncritically have kept him there, whatever his actions have been or will be. Here indeed is verbal brilliance if any is to be found anywhere in literature, dramatic or nondramatic.

There is fine irony in his first statement: he sees no more harm in Falstaff than he sees in himself. He follows this with an appeal for charity. Falstaff is old, he is white-haired; but let no one say he is a whoremaster! It is the strait-laced Puritan who is tacitly denounced in the reference to sack and sugar, fondness for which Falstaff does not deny. Here one of several biblical references used by the knight in the course of the two *Henry IV* plays serves his purpose. Are Pharaoh's lean kine to be loved? And then the incremental refrain on "Jack Falstaff" serves as the peroration. Banish all the other hangers-on at the Boar's-Head Tavern, but banish not Falstaff—the sweet, the kind, the true, the valiant, if old, Jack Falstaff from the prince's company. "Banish plump Jack, and banish all the world."

The commentator who dares to say a word against Sir John at this point of the action risks the charge of lacking a sense of humor (perhaps the most damning charge that can be made against an individual), with the resultant misunderstanding of Falstaff's worth. And yet he has been established as a glutton, one who is devoted largely to the pleasures of the flesh. As Shakespeare has occasion to say elsewhere, wine, used wisely, is a good companion (*Othello*, II.iii.313). In this play, the evidence is complete: Falstaff uses wine in great excess. Nor are all the references to his grey hairs and white beard necessarily intended to invoke pity. Shakespeare's generation belived that age should bring wisdom and a sense of decorum. Carefree escapades may be amusing, even excusable in youth; but in an older person, one who is a ranking member in a hierarchical society, they cannot be laughed away, despite the fact that the rebel latent in many people applauds Falstaff's defiance of the establishment and the sheer brilliance of his defense.

It is with all this in mind that one must evaluate Hal's one-line response after Falstaff has said, "Banish plump Jack, and banish all the world." Says the prince: "I do, I will." Thus, playing the role of king in this play extempore, the heir-apparent embraces law and order; not for long can life be no more than a holiday for him; he has a sacred obligation to fulfill, one that affects the lives of all Englishmen.

Little explication needs to be added. Understandably Falstaff hopes that Hal will not permit the sheriff to enter his tavern sanctuary. His reply to Hal, who once more accuses him of being "a natural coward," is worth brief comment. "I deny your major," he says (544). Falstaff thus spontaneously uses the vocabulary of formal logic, again displaying the range of his knowledge. Moreover, he is not a *natural* coward, as are Bardolph and Peto; he is a coward on principle, that is, when self-interest and self-preservation are involved. He falls asleep behind the arras, confident that the prince will take care of troublesome people like the sheriff.

There is no need to belabor the point relating to the "intolerable deal of sack" consumed by Falstaff — and still not paid for. By the end of this comic scene, preparations are being made for another enterprise involving Hal and his tavern companions, one that will offer a marked contrast to the Gadshill affair. And we learn that Hal, who had told Falstaff that he would not be a thief (I.ii.154) yet had gone along with the rest, will return the money with interest to the travelers.

ACT III – SCENE 1

Summary

In Bangor, Wales, Hotspur and Worcester confer with Glendower, their host, and Mortimer. Young Percy and the Welsh leader, after exchanging compliments, engage in a personal dispute and are interrupted by Mortimer. A map is produced, whereupon the rebel leaders proceed to divide England into three parts—the north going to the Percies, the west to Glendower, and the south to Mortimer. It is Mortimer who explains the immediate action to be taken. He will set forth with Hotspur and Worcester to meet Northumberland and the Scottish forces at Shrewsbury; Glendower, who will need time to muster his forces, will join them later.

Hotspur expresses his dissatisfaction with the division, insisting that the course of the River Trent be changed so as to enlarge his share. Glendower protests, but the two reach an accord.

Mortimer's wife is desolate because her husband must leave her. The couple try to communicate, although neither speaks the other's language. She then sings a Welsh song to the accompaniment of music invoked by Glendower's magic. Hotspur promptly urges his wife to join him in an amorous interlude, and they exchange witty remarks devoid of sentimentality. In short order, however, Hotspur puts an end to this interlude. He will sign the articles of partition and depart for Shrewsbury within two hours.

Commentary

This is the "division" scene; in terms of political doctrine it is especially important. Conceivably some members of Shakespeare's audiences, like many today, had their doubts about the titular hero of this play, Henry IV, recalling not only the illegal manner in which he came to the throne, but also finding him too much the politician, too calculating. For them, Falstaff's comic rationalizations of his own actions to some extent parody those of the king. But few, if any, Englishmen would have tolerated even the thought of division of their country. Their sympathies inevitably would have been on the side of the Crown. Therefore, however valid any complaint by the Percies may have been, their present action, in which they are joined by Mortimer and

Glendower, cannot be justified. In opposing them, the king and his son will emerge as saviors of England.

Fortunately, the heavily doctrinal elements here and elsewhere in the play are rendered sufficiently palatable, thanks largely to superior character portrayal. Not only does Hotspur continue to attract, especially because one sees him in contrast to Prince Hal, but others, including Glendower and Mortimer, interest reader and audience alike. Glendower, it may be noted, is anything but the wild, barbaric figure of the prose histories. And, of course, the scene includes a delightful romantic interlude with music.

Appropriately, it is the character of Hotspur which receives greatest attention in this scene, and his very first speech is revealing. One may question the ultimate worth of a leader who, even momentarily, cannot recall whether he has forgotten or mislaid the important map. This would suggest that he is hardly the one for planning an action, however capable he may be in other areas. Most serious is young Percy's absolute inability to restrain himself, or to tolerate what he considers to be conceit and superstition in Glendower, his host and ally and a man of genuine military greatness. Well along in this scene, Worcester lectures his headstrong nephew, and his words are weighty with import:

> In faith, my lord, you are too wilful-blame;
> And since your coming hither have done enough
> To put him [Glendower] quite beside his patience.
> You must needs learn, lord, to amend this fault.
> Though sometimes it show greatness, courage, blood,—
> And that's the dearest grace it renders you,—
> Yet oftentimes it doth present harsh rage,
> Defect of manners, want of government,
> Pride, haughtiness, opinion and disdain;
> The least of which haunting a nobleman
> Loseth men's hearts and leaves behind a stain
> Upon the beauty of all parts besides,
> Beguiling them of commendation.

(177-89)

"Loseth men's hearts": one recalls that, in the previous scene, Prince Hal had been winning men's hearts!

This is not to say that Hotspur loses one's sympathy in this scene. Quite the contrary. There is graciousness and good heartedness in his reply to his uncle: "Well, I am school'd. Good manners be your speed!" The reader enjoys his satiric thrusts, well illustrated by his reply to Glendower, who claims the ability to "call spirits from the vasty deep":

> Why, so can I, or so can any man;
> But will they come when you do call for them?
>
> (54-55)

Young Percy is no less amusing, but just as tactless and intolerant, when he comments on "lovely English ditties" and Welsh airs and what he calls "mincing poetry." These cultivated subjects have no place in the life of the Hotspur of the North. Although at one point Lady Percy says that her husband is "governed by humours" (237), it is really the single humour insisted upon by Prince Hal in the previous scene which rules him. Compared to either Mortimer or Glendower, whose cultural as well as military accomplishments receive attention, Hotspur is a personable barbarian. It may be added that, although Glendower probably would have had serious difficulty in calling up devils from the vasty deep, Shakespeare does give some evidence of his supernatural powers; for it is Glendower who magically provides the music for the Welsh love song. But, admittedly, the dramatist introduces this rather casually; perhaps, like Hotspur, we are not much impressed.

Something more can be said to the credit of Hotspur. As in Act II, Scene iii, his relation with the lovely Lady Kate, who affectionately calls him a "giddy goose" (232), is delightful. Hotspur's bluffness, his boyish attractiveness comes through strongly. Moreover, gallantry and fair-mindedness remain prominent in his character. When Glendower agrees that the Trent must be "turn'd," Hotspur replies:

I do not care. I'll give thrice so much land
To any well-deserving friend.

(137-38)

ACT III – SCENE 2

Summary

At the palace in London, Prince Hal appears before his father, who dismisses members of his court so that he can speak alone to his son. He passionately censures the heir-apparent for "inordinate and low desires" and for indulging in "such barren pleasures" in the company of such "rude" individuals (12-14), ignoring his status and obligations as a prince. The king seems to believe that Hal's dereliction may be evidence of God's punishment for "some displeasing service" he (the king) has done. Hal does not claim to be blameless, but he states that busybodies and scandalmongers have exaggerated accounts of his behavior.

The king voices his deep concern at considerable length. Hal has absented himself from councils of state, letting his younger brother take his place. If the king himself had chosen, as Hal has done, to cheapen himself in "vulgar company," he never would have won the allegiance of Englishmen. He especially sees in his son the same fatal weaknesses which led to Richard II's downfall. At that time, the king himself was like young Percy, who, no older than Prince Hal, commands "ancient lords and reverend bishops" into battle and has won "never-dying honour" by capturing the renowned Douglas. To Henry IV it seems that Hal is his greatest enemy, not the Northern rebels and Mortimer.

Chagrined by this strong reproof, Prince Hal urges his father not to believe those who have led the king to misjudge him. He solemnly promises to "redeem all this on Percy's head" (132); that is, he will prove his loyalty and worth by performing glorious deeds in opposition to the valiant Hotspur.

Overjoyed, the king declares that Hal will be placed in command of royal forces. The king himself, joined by Westmoreland

and Prince John, will lead another army which will join Hal's in the North.

Sir Walter Blunt arrives with the news that Douglas and the English rebels even now have assembled their troops at Shrewsbury.

Commentary

In this scene the climax and turning point are reached. Because of Hal's vow and his appointment as supreme commander of one large force, the way is prepared also for the shift in the comic subplot. The thematic relationship between main plot and subplot is sufficiently clear, for the reader has come directly from the scene in which this meeting between prince and king has been parodied.

To some, King Henry may appear especially calculating in parts of this scene. Why, for example, should he say to his son:

> I know not whether God will have it so,
> For some displeasing service I have done,
> That, in his secret doom, out of my blood
> He'll breed revengement and a scourge for me.
>
> (4-7)

Perhaps, it is argued, he is not sure that Hal's apparent failure is a sign of God's displeasure; but he is well aware of the "displeasing service" he himself had done — usurpation and regicide. Moreover, his second and much longer speech (29-91) is practical instruction on how to influence people — the right people — what with his remarks on dressing himself "in such humility that [he] did pluck allegiance from men's hearts" (51-52). The point of view represented here is surely not to be ignored, but it may do Henry IV less than justice.

In the first place, it is primarily Henry IV, upholder of law and order, not Henry the sinner, who appears here and in the rest of the play — quite logically, since increasing attention has been paid and will be paid to the rebels. He is the man who, unlike his unfortunate predecessor, is gifted with the arts of kingship. If indeed, according to sixteenth-century political philosophy, the ruler was God's lieutenant on earth, responsible ultimately only to God, he nevertheless must "pluck allegiance from men's hearts," which means that he must win their respect and hold it if his reign is to be successful; after all, God helps them that help themselves. The many contemporary discussions of kingship made all this abundantly clear. The king and father has heard only scandalous reports about his son's behavior. His concern about the succession to the throne is deep and proper; it was a dominant concern of Shakespeare's generation in an England ruled by the Virgin Queen.

Most emphatically now, Prince Hal is pitted against Hotspur. Earlier young Percy had been praised by the king as the "theme of honour's tongue" (I.i.81); now he is "Mars in swathling clothes" (112), a youth no older than Hal who leads high-ranking subjects (a reference to Northumberland, Mortimer, and the Archbishop of York, who are all mentioned in lines 118-19), and who defeated the great Douglas.

At the end of Act I, Scene ii, Hal promised to redeem his tarnished reputation, but he spoke in soliloquy, voicing his secret thoughts, as it were. Now he makes his pledge directly to his king and father. This is not the casual, debonair Prince Hal of the Boar's-Head Tavern speaking. His father's words have penetrated deeply. The very simplicity of his first line underscores his sincerity and determination: "Do not think so; you shall not find it so. . . . (129). He takes his oath "in the name of God" (153). Most readers share the king's elation: "A hundred thousand rebels die in this" (160).

ACT III – SCENE 3

Summary

Falstaff deplores his alleged physical decline resulting from lack of activity since the Gadshill "action." Bardolph's frank comment on the knight's corpulence leads him to a rhetorical exercise, the subject of which is Bardolph's flaming nose. When Mistress Quickly enters, Sir John accuses her of having picked his pockets and he refuses to pay his bill for wine, food, and even items of clothing. The hostess has occasion to mention the prince, whereupon Falstaff calls him a "Jack" (knave) and declares that he would cudgel him if he were present.

The prince enters, marching with Peto. Falstaff joins them, playing on his truncheon (a short staff) as if it were a fife. Falstaff then renews his altercation with the hostess, but when Hal tells him that *he* directed the search of Sir John's pockets, the old knight magnanimously forgives her.

Falstaff is much relieved to learn that all matters relating to the robbery have been settled. Yet the news of Hal's reconciliation with the king hardly elates him, particularly when he is told that he is to command foot soldiers. A serious Prince Hal then gives orders to Bardolph, Peto, and Falstaff, all relating to their services in opposing the rebels.

Commentary

Falstaff's reference to "this last action," a term commonly used for military activity, serves to remind the reader of the connection between the comic subplot and the main plot in this chronicle-history play. One hardly needs the testimony of Bardolph to know that Falstaff has not "dwindled," not "fallen away," either physically or mentally. He is his redoubtable self. His answer to his own questions which begin this scene, complete with witty similes ("like an old lady's loose gown . . . like an old apple-john") tells us as much. Like an old apple, he keeps his flavor; unlike it, he is not shrivelled. We have seen him before in a mood of apparent repentance like the one which follows and are not at all surprised to hear him attribute his fallen state to "company, villainous company", no more than we are surprised to witness the sudden revival of his spirits, thanks to his recourse to hedonist philosophy. When Bardolph remarks that he cannot live long, Sir John replies: "Why, there is it. Come sing me a bawdy song; make me merry" (15-16).

But it is his brilliant comments on Bardolph's physical appearance (27-59) which dominate the first part of this scene. This is an unsurpassed example of the comedy of physical appearance and of words — more specifically the "comedy of noses" (See Rostand's *Cyrano de Bergerac*, wherein the titular hero expounds wittily on the subject of his own nose). To put it another way, this is a comic aria, a bravura piece, all action stopping to give the performer his special opportunity to demonstrate his virtuosity. His evoking of the image of hell's fire (and making another accurate biblical reference) is especially effective; at this point he sounds like a zealous preacher putting the fear of the Lord into the hearts of his listeners.

One additional point may be added. Falstaff has provided the wine for Bardolph for some thirty-two years, we are told (51-55). The time element, probably exaggerated to add to the fun, is not applicable, but the Falstaff of this play has depended upon Hal for the same courtesy. Thus the parasitical aspect of his character again receives notice. As a matter of fact, the interlude involving Mistress Quickly develops this. One learns that the old knight has been victimizing the kindly hostess, who has provided him with drink, food, and clothing.

In this kind of skirmish, or action, be it with the lowly tavern mistress or with the prince himself, Falstaff shows a kind of military genius. His method is to attack; that, quite often, is the best defense. Not irrelevant in this connection is the amusing military pantomine when Hal and Peto march in.

Falstaff is no less accomplished in his responses to the prince. When the hostess reports that Sir John had claimed Hal to be in his debt to the extent of one thousand pounds (a fortune in Shakespeare's day), Falstaff has an unanswerable reply: his love for Hal is worth millions. Nor does he hold the prince in awe, for that emotion is properly to be reserved for the king. He caps all this, tacitly admitting that his pockets had contained only "tavern-reckonings, memorandums of bawdy houses, and one poor penny-worth of sugar-candy" (178-80). He reminds Hal that Adam, progenitor of the human race, fell from a state of innocence, proving that all flesh is weak—and does not he, Falstaff, have more flesh than any other man? Clearly, it will not do to see Falstaff as symbolic of Prince Hal's irresponsible youth any more than it will to reduce him to a single comic type character. He is uniquely himself.

But that is not to say that his wit absolves him from all faults. His status as privileged jester makes it possible for him to urge Hal to "rob . . . the exchequer" at once, now that the prince is on good terms with the king; to suggest that Hal steal a horse for him so that he will not have to lead his soldiers afoot; and to praise rebels on the grounds that they offend only "the virtues" (205 ff.). But the course of life cannot be determined by the atmosphere of an Eastcheap tavern—not if one is to follow it honorably. Unlike Prince Hal, Falstaff is unwilling to give up life as a long series of holidays, even though the fate of the nation is at stake. Quite in character, then, he has his own way of applauding the prince's stirring call to arms ("The land is burning; Percy stands on high"):

> Rare words! brave world! Hostess, my breakfast, come!
> O, I could wish this tavern were my drum!
>
> (229-30)

His sensitive appetite must be satisfied under all circumstances. And it is suggested that he would like to transfer the tavern to the battlefield. Perhaps, in a metaphorical sense, he will do exactly that.

ACT IV—SCENE 1

Summary

The scene now shifts to the rebel camp near Shrewsbury, where Hotspur, Worcester, and Douglas appear. Young Percy and the Scottish warrior exchange compliments. A messenger arrives with news from the Earl of Northumberland. It seems that Hotspur's father is ill and cannot lead his followers to Shrewsbury. Shocked to hear this, Hotspur quickly recovers himself and finds reasons to remain confident: it would be bad strategy to risk his strength in a single encounter; moreover, a victory by the reduced rebel army will redound all the more to their credit, helping to convince the populace at large that the revolt will be successful. Douglas readily endorses these opinions.

Sir Richard Vernon brings news concerning the royal forces. The Earl of Westmoreland and Prince John lead seven thousand soldiers toward Shrewsbury, and the king himself has set forth with another army. Hotspur remains undaunted; he welcomes the opportunity of opposing the royal power. But what, he asks, of Prince Hal? Where is he? Vernon then describes the young heir-apparent "all furnish'd, all in arms," also headed toward the field of battle. Hotspur interrupts Vernon; he cannot bear to hear such words of praise about his royal contemporary. Nevertheless, he now can hardly restrain himself, so anxious is he for the conflict to begin.

There is more news. Vernon reports that Glendower needs more time to muster his power. Worcester and even the fearless Douglas concede that this is the worst news of all. Not Hotspur. When Vernon tells him that the royal forces number 30,000, he exclaims: "Forty let it be!" Douglas joins him in challenging death itself.

Commentary

Although the Battle of Shrewsbury is yet to be fought, the action in the main plot, having reached its climax in Act III, Scene ii, is now falling, structurally speaking. The fortunes of the Percies have been in the ascendent prior to this scene. Now the three items of intelligence mark the turn toward adversity: neither Northumberland nor Glendower will appear with their troops to join those led by Hotspur; the Prince of Wales, having done no more than voice his good intentions, is now acting positively.

The Hotspur in this scene is something more than the limited individual who deserved to be the object of Prince Hal's satire in Act II, Scene iv. He emerges as more than the vain, rather boastful (if courageous) warrior. Although the initial exchange between him and the Earl of Douglas may suggest that the Scotsman is young Percy's alter ego, it is Douglas, not Hotspur, who is the exemplar of unreflecting dauntlessness. Perhaps this difference is implicit in the fact that Douglas is hailed for his courage, Hotspur for his honor. But it is explicit in Hotspur's reaction to the adverse reports — the first brought by the messenger, the second and third by Sir Richard Vernon.

When he learns that his father will not arrive because of "inward" illness (an intentionally ambiguous term), young Percy recognizes the extent to which the odds have shifted and momentarily he loses heart: "This sickness doth infect/ The very life-blood of our enterprise" (28-29); it is "a perilous gash, a very limb lopp'd off" (43). But as a leader he knows that he cannot appear daunted. Promptly he recovers himself and advances reasons for complete confidence in the success of the enterprise. And, of course, Douglas can be depended upon to second him. This is equally true of their reaction to the news about Glendower's inability to muster troops in time, although he had assured the Percies that he would not need even fourteen days. Perhaps there is significance in the Scotsman's reply when Hotspur declares that all goes well: "As heart can think," he says (84). Emotion, not intellect, is his guide.

Vernon's description of the Prince of Wales and Hotspur's reaction call for special comment. From the start, these two have been set in opposition to each other. Young Percy is endorsing little more than the public reputation of the prince (who appropriately is never called "Hal" in these serious scenes of the main plot), one which had been held by King Henry prior to the reconciliation, when he, Percy, refers to him as the "nimble-footed madcap . . . that daff'd [thrust] the world aside and bid it pass" (95-97). Up to end of Act III, the prince in this play has completely ignored public responsibility, so far as positive action is concerned.

Vernon's portrait is that of the Ideal Prince, one that might have been depicted in a rich medieval tapestry. The prince and his followers, wearing the ostrich feather, heraldic emblem of the Prince of Wales, are endowed with spirit and ardor. The prince himself is compared to the Roman god Mercury, a tribute to his prowess: certainly vaulting into the saddle with ease when armor-clad is an impressive accomplishment! Superior horsemanship, it may be added, was an essential accomplishment of the ideal Renaissance man.

Now it is Hotspur alone, not he *and* his comrades, who is momentarily crushed by this report of a battle-ready Prince of Wales: "Worse than the sun in March,/ This praise doth nourish agues," he exclaims (111-12). When he recovers himself, his words comprise a challenge for individual trial by arms:

> Harry to Harry shall, hot horse to horse,
> Meet and ne'er part till one drop down a corse.
>
> (122-23)

In a word, the conflict in the main plot is now assuming the characteristics of a medieval tournament, with an admirable centralizing of the action.

ACT IV – SCENE 2

Summary

Falstaff and Bardolph appear on a public road near Coventry, followed by a newly enlisted company of soldiers. Sir John orders Bardolph to replenish his supply of sack and to tell Peto to meet him at the town's end. He dislikes the idea of marching his men through the town in their rags and tatters. Abjectly impoverished, not one of them could pay him, as so many others had, for release from military service. In Falstaff's own words, "No eye hath seen such scarecrows" (41).

Prince Hal and Westmoreland meet him on the road and comment on the poor creatures whom Falstaff leads. The knight remains undisturbed and is philosophical in the face of this criticism. And, for that matter, the prince seems amused rather than indignant. All are to make haste, says Hal, for Percy is already in the field.

Commentary

Sir John Falstaff, knight of the realm and an officially appointed commander of troops, is off to the wars. A new Falstaff, then? Not at all. This latest "action" provides another occasion for plunder, another chance to show what he thinks of "old father antic the law." Well he knows that the soldier must have his provisions; therefore his first concern has to do with a bottle of sack. In his brilliant soliloquy (12-52), he practically boasts of the disreputable means he has employed to fill the ranks of his company. Nor has he spent a farthing to outfit the beggarly creatures. He had been careful to demand in the king's name those men who would, by one means or another, be able to pay for their release. Then, thanks to the cooperation of minor local officials, he filled the ranks with jail birds—which does not mean that any had been guilty of any serious offense, since roving beggars were subject to arrest in sixteenth-century England. And so these ragged specimens of humanity "march wide betwixt the legs as if they had gyves [fetters] on" (43-44). Led by the corpulent, well-fed Falstaff these bare-boned, lowly subjects are a grotesquely incongruous sight, all the more so if one recalls the splendor of the prince and his fellow warriors in their plumes and glittering gold coats, as described by Sir Richard Vernon in the preceding scene. These "pitiful rascals," as the prince calls them, will win no glory, no honor in the wars. In Falstaff's callous words, they are just "food for powder" (72).

If Falstaff remains a speaker of brilliant prose in this scene, his humor now is grim. Here he is not victimizing a tavern hostess or engaging in robbery devoid of physical violence; he is dealing with the lives of his fellow men, but again he is concerned only with personal gain. He remains "as vigilant as a cat to steal cream" (65). Falstaff must be allowed to follow his course with logical consistency. Significantly, the Prince of Wales does not reprove him; he is permitted to proceed on the march to Shrewsbury.

ACT IV – SCENE 3

Summary

Worcester and Vernon try to convince Hotspur that the rebel forces should not attack at once. Douglas sides with young Percy. The sound of a trumpet announces a parley, and Sir Walter Blunt enters "with gracious offers from the king." This gives Hotspur the occasion to review the story of how Henry was helped by the Percies when he returned from exile and how he then usurped the throne. Now, says the young rebel commander, Henry has proved ungrateful to his benefactors and has ignored the proper claims of Mortimer. When Blunt asks if this is Percy's final answer, he is told that it is not. In the morning Hotspur will send Worcester to hear the king's terms and to present their own.

Commentary

The Hotspur of this scene is admirable; he is anything but the foolhardy, impetuous youth. As supreme commander of the rebel forces, he reasons well. Already facing a numerically superior power, he knows that the odds against him will increase unless he commits his troops immediately. In his recital of grievances he invites understanding and sympathy. He expresses a willingness to negotiate if the terms are honorable. The scene thus ends on at least a faint note of hope.

ACT IV – SCENE 4

Summary

The Archbishop of York instructs Sir Michael to deliver in all haste certain written instructions and information to his allies and relatives who have a substantial number of followers. The archbishop has learned that Hotspur faces the king's power without the support of Northumberland, Glendower, and Mortimer. Convinced that young Percy will be defeated, he knows that the king will then move against him for his part in the conspiracy.

Commentary

The consensus is that this scene is to be justified solely on the grounds that it looks forward to the main action in *2 Henry IV*, wherein royal forces indeed move against the archbishop and Lord Mowbray, his most powerful and dependable ally. Yet there is some reason for its inclusion here strictly with reference to *1 Henry IV*. It provides Shakespeare with the opportunity to summarize major events, to foreshadow the rebels' defeat, and to emphasize the seriousness and magnitude of the entire action.

The Sir Michael of this scene does not find a place in history. He may well be a priest, since priests often were given the courtesy title of "Sir."

ACT V – SCENE 1

Summary

The Earl of Worcester and Sir Richard Vernon arrive as emissaries at the king's camp near Shrewsbury. Present are the king himself, the Prince of Wales, John of Lancaster, the Earl of Westmoreland, Sir Walter Blunt, and Falstaff. As Hotspur did earlier in his reply to the king's emissary (IV.iii), Worcester voices at some length the grievances of the Percies, chief of which is Henry's alleged perfidy when, returning from exile, he assured them that he sought no more than the restoration of confiscated Lancastrian estates. The king does not deign to answer this charge; instead he dismisses it as no more than a pretext for rebellion against the Crown. He refuses to permit the Prince of Wales to settle the dispute in single combat with Hotspur. Instead, he offers the rebels free pardon if they will lay down their arms. After Worcester and Vernon leave, the prince states that both Hotspur and Douglas, supremely confident and proven warriors, will reject the offer. The king agrees and orders all officers to their posts.

Falstaff shows little desire to risk his life in any kind of conflict. He asks Hal to keep an eye on him and to help him if necessary. Alone he soliloquizes on the subject of honor and finds no profit in being a dead hero.

Commentary

The opening lines help establish the mood of this scene, the action of which takes place not long before the battle starts. There is rather obvious irony in the speeches of both Worcester and the king. The former makes much of Henry's violation of an oath to the effect that he sought only redress of grievances and not the throne of England, implying that the Percies had no intention of becoming traitors to Richard II. But the reader will recall Hotspur's words spoken early in the play. Northumberland and Worcester "wear the detested blot/ Of murderous subornation . . . Being the agents or base second means,/ The cords, the ladder, or the hangman rather" who made possible the crowning of Henry (I.iii.162 ff.). His solicitude for the fallen Richard, coming so tardily, does not conceal the basic selfish motives of the House of Percy.

It is no less evident that Henry, not content with retrieving the confiscated Lancastrian estates, was strongly motivated by self-interest, specifically, with ambitions toward the throne. But the overwhelming fact now is that he is England's king and has not been guilty of gross misrule as was his predecessor. He is in the process of suppressing "pell mell havoc and confusion"; he seeks to restore law and order in England. If one keeps in mind the view that, in the larger sense, the State is the greater protagonist in the chronicle-history plays, there is a logic here.

Some commentators see calculation in the king's refusal to let his son meet Hotspur in single combat, arguing that Henry is too adroit to take a risk of this sort when he has numerical superiority. Certainly such a conjecture is admissible, but there is also the fact that the demands of recorded history weigh upon the playwright: a Battle of Shrewsbury *must* be fought.

Prince Hal's demeanor is admirable. His offer to meet the renowned Hotspur in single combat is motivated not by a desire to win personal glory but the wish to save lives. His gracious, magnanimous praise of young Percy (85-93) is in the best chivalric tradition, and there is not a hint of false modesty in the deprecatory remarks he makes about himself. Calmly he accepts the fact that death is a constant of armed conflict; he knows that he, like all mortals, "owest God a death" and he will not seek to postpone payment.

Not so Falstaff. Yet his soliloquy on honor, as he conceives it, is a thought-provoking piece in which he develops his theme with such telling particulars that one's immediate reaction may be to endorse his view wholeheartedly. As much as any of his speeches, this one illustrates his wit and verbal skill. Nor can one logically deny the major premise upon which his argument is based. For at the personal level, the utter pathos, even futility, of all armed conflict is exposed. But note that it is the strictly personal, the individual, which concerns Falstaff. Thus, this gifted comic presents at best a half-truth, and perhaps not even that if one recalls this same knight's bland unconcern about the lives of the poor wretches whom he recruited to fight for king and country.

There have been many references to honor in this play: Hotspur's concept of honor to be won and held largely in warfare; Hal's concept, not explicitly defined, but implicit in his burlesque of Hotspur (II.iv), and in the restrained way in which he vowed to make young Percy his "factor" (III.ii). Now Falstaff, who in the comic scenes found occasions to speak of his valor, has given us his concept of honor, one based on self-interest to the exclusion of all else.

ACT V – SCENE 2

Summary

Back in the rebel camp, Worcester insists that Hotspur must not be told that the king has offered all of the insurgents free pardon. He argues that, although his young nephew's trespass will be forgiven, Henry IV will never place his trust in the elder leaders of the rebellion. Vernon reluctantly agrees to remain silent. Accordingly, Worcester tells Hotspur that the king is merciless. Like Douglas, the youth is ready to fight.

When Worcester then tells Hotspur that the prince has challenged him to single combat, the young rebel fervently expresses his wish that such a meeting could take place. He remains skeptical regarding the worth of the prince, even though Vernon describes the latter's chivalric behavior and becoming modesty.

Learning that even now the "King comes on apace," Hotspur exhorts his companions to fight nobly, and then he embraces them as the trumpets sound the start of the conflict.

Commentary

Worcester's decision to keep from Hotspur the "liberal and kind offer of the King" (2) is wholly dishonorable, a monstrous act of treachery against his own flesh and blood, against the unselfish, if misguided, youth who has risen to the position of supreme commander of the insurgents. It is not by mere chance that this episode immediately follows Falstaff's soliloquy on honor. In comparsion to Sir John, the Earl of Worcester is high in the baronial ranks of England; his is an act of betrayal on the grand scale. If the reader has been tempted to accept Falstaff's view of honor as realistic and eminently practical, he may find occasion now to reassess that view. Even in terms of self-interest, Worcester's act of infamy will prove to be impractical.

Vernon's agreeing to go along with Worcester is disappointing, for he has earned the reader's respect and sympathy by his chivalrous conduct. Indeed he does so in this scene by making the generous report of Hal's demeanor (52-69). He too will pay a great price for his compliance.

The character of the Prince of Wales continues to be elevated, thanks to the testimony of Sir Richard Vernon—the testimony of a hostile witness, as it were. The prince's claim made to his royal father, namely, that he had been maligned

(III.iii.130-31) is supported here. Vernon states that the prince has been the victim of envy, or malice, and will be England's "sweet hope" — that is, the Ideal Prince — if his true character is revealed to all.

But the elevation of the prince is not achieved by the denigration of Hotspur's character. If young Percy finds it hard to accept Vernon's flattering description of the prince, he makes use of no term of contempt for his royal rival. In appropriate lines, Percy's courage and honor, as he conceives it, make him an attractive and a worthy opponent. Aware as the reader is that the Percy forces are outnumbered, Hotspur's brief but stirring battle oration (93-101) and his embrace of his fated companions elicit admiration and sympathy.

ACT V — SCENE 3

Summary

On the battlefield Sir Walter Blunt, wearing armor the same as that of the king, meets Douglas, who has slain the Lord of Stafford, similarly arrayed for the obvious purpose of misleading the foe. Now the Scotsman is convinced that it is Henry IV himself whom he faces, and he demands that Blunt surrender. Sir Walter does not reveal his true identity. The two fight and Blunt is slain.

Hotspur enters, speaking words of high praise to the jubilant Douglas, who believes that now "All's done, all's won" (17). Young Percy recognizes Blunt and disillusions his fellow warrior. Both leave to renew the fight elsewhere.

There is the sound of sudden attack. Then Falstaff appears alone. He finds things quite different from what they had been in London; it is not so easy to get off "shot-free" on the battlefield; he may have to pay the bill, which is a rather steep one. Looking down at the body of Sir Walter Blunt, he finds new reason to believe that seeking honor has its grave limitations. From his soliloquy, it is learned that he led his ragged "troops" into the heart of battle and that all but two or three have been slaughtered.

Now it is the prince who arrives. His mood of complete seriousness and dedication to duty is established at once, as he sternly rebukes Falstaff for idleness and asks for the use of his sword. Falstaff boasts about his alleged valor and even claims to have taken care of Hotspur. When Hal assures him that the young rebel survives to slay Falstaff, the fat knight refuses to relinquish his sword, but offers to give Hal his pistol. It is a bottle of sack, not a weapon, which he draws from the case. Hal seizes it, strongly reproves Falstaff, and throws the bottle at him.

Alone once more, Falstaff declares that he will slay Percy if that fearsome enemy survives. But he makes it clear that he is not about to go out of his way to find such "grinning honour" as that possessed by the dead Sir Walter Blunt. Clearly, Hotspur will survive to old age as far as Falstaff is concerned.

Commentary

The report of Douglas' slaying of the Lord of Stafford, his actual slaying of Sir Walter Blunt, and Hotspur's report that the insurgents "stand full fairly for the day" have the important effect of at least equalizing matters relating to the two opposing forces, despite the fact that the royalists outnumber the rebels. In other words, suspense is sustained; it is still touch and go.

Nothing could be much more incongruous, more grotesque, than the appearance of the corpulent, white-bearded, unheroic Falstaff on the battlefield. His brash claims to valor, which are at one with those made in the Boar's-Head Tavern after the Gadshill affair, his irrepressible verbal wit ("Ay, Hal; 'tis hot,'tis hot./ There's that will sack a city.") provide a counterbalance to the heroics in this scene, which, by themselves, might well be given such emphasis as to be a bit ludicrous — excessively melodramatic in dramatic fiction.

Falstaff *has*, in a metaphorical sense, brought the tavern to the battlefield. The bottle of sack, in place of the pistol in the case, is emblematic. The braggart warrior, one of the facets of his complex character, finds expression here when he assures the prince that "Turk Gregory" never matched his deeds in arms. The allusion, in all probability, is to Pope Gregory VII, noted for ferocity, here given the title of "Turk" since the Turks were held to be exemplars of cruelty.

Now in the midst of battle, the prince has no occasion to indulge in the slightest witticism in his exchange with Falstaff. Sternly he rebukes Sir John: "What, is it a time to jest and dally now?" (57). Certainly the knight's sense of timing is lamentably bad.

ACT V – SCENE 4

Summary

The king bids the Prince of Wales and his brother, John of Lancaster, to rest. Despite his wounds, the prince will not do so: ". . . God forbid a shallow scratch should drive/ The Prince of Wales from such a field as this,/ Where . . . rebels' arms triumph in massacres" (11-14). He has high praise for his younger brother, whose courage inspires them all. The two depart.

Douglas enters, faces Henry IV, and exclaims: "Another king!" He identifies himself and demands to know the true identity of his foe. The king expresses his regret that, until now, the Scottish warrior has met only "his shadows" — nobles whom he mistook for the king. While his son seeks out Percy, Henry will take on Douglas.

The king is in danger of defeat when Prince Hal enters. The latter identifies himself as the heir-apparent, engages Douglas in single combat, and forces his adversary to flee for his life. King Henry is particularly touched by this evidence of his son's courage.

After the king leaves, Hotspur enters, addresses the prince by name and identifies himself. Now at last Harry *does* meet Harry face to face in combat. Falstaff appears to cheer Prince Hal, who will, as he says, "find no boy's play here" (76). At this point in the action, Douglas re-enters and engages Falstaff, who soon falls down as if he were dead. Just as Douglas leaves, Hotspur himself is wounded and falls.

In moving words, young Percy begins to recite his own epitaph but dies before he can finish. It is the prince who, in generous terms, completes it.

The prince sees the fallen Sir John Falstaff. Believing his old companion to be dead (if one takes his words literally), he now provides an epitaph for "Poor Jack," referring to him as "so fat a deer" and declaring that he will see him "embowell'd" (103-10). Hal departs.

Falstaff promptly revives and rises up. As in earlier, far less serious, episodes, he indulges in witty rationalization for his unheroic behavior—specifically, in this case, counterfeiting death. Next, he expresses his fear of "this gunpowder Percy," who is apparently dead. Perhaps, he says, young Percy is "counterfeiting" as Falstaff himself did. He decides to "make him sure"—and then to claim that it was he who killed the valiant rebel leader. No living person is nearby to see him; so he stabs the corpse of the fallen Hotspur. He lifts the body onto his back just as Prince Hal and John of Lancaster re-enter.

Prince John is puzzled: did not Hal tell him that the old knight had been killed? Hal replies that indeed he saw Falstaff "dead,/ Breathless and bleeding on the ground" (137). Sir John, he concludes, is not what he seems.

Indeed he is not, replies Falstaff. As conqueror of the great Percy, he looks to be made either an earl or a duke. He is deeply shocked to hear the prince claim to have slain Hotspur. Prince Hal is not perturbed; he is not concerned with refuting Sir John. As he says to his brother, if a lie will serve Falstaff, he will not interfere.

A trumpet sounds retreat. All know that the rebels have been defeated. The two princes leave to find out how their comrades have fared. Falstaff will follow—for his reward, as he makes clear.

Commentary

Although another scene follows, this one provides the essential resolution of the action. From the start, the character of Prince Hal is enhanced. He refuses to leave the battlefield, despite his wounds; he demonstrates at once his humility and his magnanimity in praising the deeds performed by his younger brother. Even more impressive is the fact that he saves the life of Henry IV, exponent and symbol of law and order in the realm. That the father should be deeply touched comes as something of a surprise. He had distrusted his son, believing that Hal wanted him to die. Now the reader knows how malicious indeed were the slanders against the spirited young prince who had chosen to play the truant for a while.

Although the battle necessarily is presented in a series of separate episodes, the encounter between Prince Hal and Hotspur is the climactic one, for it conveys the impression that the prince's triumph ended the conflict. It will be recalled that Douglas, believing that he had slain the king, was convinced that his action meant total victory for the rebels. Young Percy was the leader of the insurgents.

Hotspur, whose high courage and gallantry have received increasing emphasis, invites one's whole-hearted sympathy as he falls before the prince's sword; his indeed was "a great heart." Surely no one would care to gloat over the fact that this same Hotspur had spoken contemptuously of Hal, refusing to believe that the prince was capable of serious action. For one thing, it was not life *per se* but his matchless reputation as a great warrior which concerned him most. Nor does this suggest undue vanity. He had been no braggart warrior; his titles had been won honestly. Like other dying great men elsewhere in Shakespeare, but perhaps unexpected in this heretofore unreflecting young soldier, Hotspur philosophizes in almost a medieval fashion, seeing himself as "time's fool." Those near death were thought to have the gift of prophecy; Hotspur, had he time, could prophesy. What could he foresee? Unquestionably the triumph of Henry V over the numerically superior French — the emergence of Prince Hal as hero-king of England. Just as Hotspur's courage, sense of honor, and gallantry were stressed increasingly in the later scenes, so Prince Hal's pre-eminence is emphasized. Young Percy has been established fully as the most worthy of all opponents; his conqueror emerges as a completely heroic figure, one almost larger than life itself. Appropriately, there is no suggestion of personal triumph in Hal's words. Magnaminity determines their tone, for he dwells upon young Percy's knightly virtues, his breadth of spirit, the high respect merited by one of such "great heart."

If valid military honor is the subject of this episode, the Falstaffian one which follows provides a grimly comic exercise on bogus military honor. When Hal sees Falstaff lying on the battlefield, he has a valediction for him, one no less appropriate than the one for Hotspur. The prince's statement that he could have "spar'd a better man" (104) probably is purposely ambiguous. For holidays, those occasional times when care may be put aside, there is no better man than Falstaff in the sense of being more entertaining. But life, certainly for the heir to the throne, cannot remain a perpetual holiday. It follows that the prince is not so much in love with "vanity" as to be crushed by the end of all that Falstaff represents.

There is another possibility here. "I know you all," the prince soliloquized at the end of Act I, Scene i; and his remarks to and concerning Falstaff throughout the play have left no doubt that he does fully understand his amusing companion. With this in mind, it may be argued that he is fully aware now that Falstaff is up to his old tricks again. Perhaps his play on the words *heavy* ("O, I should have a heavy miss of thee") and *deer* ("so fat a deer") and the reference to "embowelling," may well be taken as an indication that Hal knows Falstaff hears every word spoken. But admittedly all this is conjecture.

The Gadshill episode established the fact that Falstaff was a coward on principle, not a born coward like Peto or Bardolph. So he is here, as his famous line, "The better part of valour is discretion; in the which better part I have saved my life"

(120-22), makes clear. To be sure, there is an important element of truth in what he says, just as there was in his comments on honor. But there is also a cynical perversion of an abiding truth. Young Percy, prior to the Battle of Shrewsbury, well could have employed discretion without sacrifice of valor, for he was far above self-centered consideration. Discretion to Falstaff means self-preservation and no more.

There was sufficient falling off in the character of Falstaff, with reference to his recruits; there is more now. Sir John Falstaff, knight of the realm, stabs the fallen Hotspur in the thigh, an act which involves complete renunciation of the chivalric code. It is an act of monstrous desecration, absolutely inexcusable.

One may presume that he no more expects to be believed when he claims to have slain Hotspur than he had expected Hal and Poins to believe his story of what happened at Gadshill, for one cannot deprive the witty, knowledgeable Falstaff of ordinary common sense. Hal had tricked him there; now he tricks Hal. And, if on principle he is cowardly where physical action is involved, in the realm of rhetoric he is dauntless. "There is Percy," he exclaims, throwing the body to the earth (142) — a salvo defying refutation. With the same confidence, he expects great reward. At the end of this scene, he says: "I'll follow, as they say, for reward. He that rewards me, God reward him" (166-67). That too has been a great part of his life's philosophy; throughout the play he has followed for reward.

But Falstaff will not permit us to dismiss him scornfully, for his superior wit never deserts him and, in a sense, he has considerable capacity for self-criticism. The thought strikes him that, should he be elevated to a dukedom, actually he will "grow less," for such high rank has its obligations: the king of jesters would have to abdicate.

One other point relating to Falstaff's conduct needs to be settled. Those who refuse to find any fault in this man, who is to them the true hero of this play, make much of his statement that he led his men into the heart of battle. This, it is argued, is irrefutable proof of his personal valor. But is it? Did he actually place himself at the head of his company when he committed it to battle? And did he then, thanks to great martial prowess, survive without a scratch despite his enormous girth? In the next episode he counterfeits death as a means of escaping once more "shot free." Perhaps that was not the first time in which he employed the ruse. Certainly Elizabethans would not interpret the word "led" as proof of Falstaff's courage—not in view of the frequent charges made against leaders who committed their troops to battle but avoided danger themselves. These charges may well provide a revealing insight into Falstaff's actions—and may be at one with his having "misused the king's press damnably" in recruiting his soldiers.

Prince Hal deserves the last word. His superiority and his magnanimity are well illustrated by his refusal to argue with Falstaff or to show the slightest concern about being deprived of the credit for the defeat of a great adversary. He is quite willing to humor this knight of the "latter spring." Nevertheless, it is worth noting that, since Shakespeare indubitably had the sequel to this play in mind, Falstaff cannot be rejected at the end of *1 Henry IV*.

ACT V – SCENE 5

Summary

The insurrection having been repressed, King Henry orders the execution of Worcester and Vernon. The fate of the other rebels will be decided later. Prince Hal intercedes on behalf of the Earl of Douglas, and his life is spared. Prince John of Lancaster is given the honor of setting the Scotsman free. The king then announces that he will divide his forces. One army, led by Prince John and the Earl of Westmoreland, will move against the forces assembled by Northumberland and Archbishop Scroop in northern England. Accompanied by Prince Hal, Henry himself will march to Wales to fight Glendower and Mortimer.

Commentary

"Thus ever did rebellion find rebuke." This opening line, spoken by the titular hero, summarizes the major theme of the play. Another line spoken by the king at the end of this scene points to the theme of *2 Henry IV:* "Rebellion in this land shall lose its sway" (41).

Henry's strong words indicting the Earl of Worcester serve a two-fold purpose. First and most important, these leave the impression at the end of the play that Henry IV is a strong, yet fair-minded ruler, one who gave the rebels every chance to embrace law and order before he moved against them. Second, if a villain is to be found in the main plot, he must be Worcester, who was largely responsible for schooling young Percy and who, as Henry reminds him, had not borne "true intelligence" from the king to the other rebel leaders at Shrewsbury.

Hal now is the Ideal Prince. Properly, it is he who saves the life of the "noble Scot, Lord Douglas" and who delegates to John of Lancaster the "high honour" of freeing Douglas without ransom. Since Vernon has been depicted as no less noble and admirable, one may question why the prince's generosity did not extend to him. It is to be remembered, however, that Douglas, a valiant foe, is not an Englishman, not a rebel against a king to whom he had sworn allegiance.

MEDIUM: VERSE AND PROSE

Quite properly verse is overwhelmingly the medium used in the main plot, the wholly serious action; no less appropriately prose is used almost entirely in the broadly comic subplot. Of the nineteen scenes, ten are devoted entirely to the serious action, six largely to the comic, and three (wherein Falstaff appears on the battlefield) to a mixture of the serious and the comic. The principle of decorum invariably determines the choice of medium. When Hal speaks as the heir-apparent, he does so in iambic pentameter lines, usually blank verse. Not only is this true when he soliloquizes at the end of the first comic scene (I.ii.218-40), but elsewhere. At the end of Act II, Scene ii, just after he and Poins have confronted Falstaff, Bardolph, and Peto and relieved them of the booty and put them to flight, Hal speaks to Poins in blank verse:

> Got with much ease. Now merrilly to horse.
> The thieves are all scatter'd and possess'd with fear
> So strongly that they dare not meet each other;
> Each takes his fellow for an officer.
> Away, good Ned. Falstaff sweats to death,
> And lards the lean earth as he walks along.
> Were't not for laughing, I should pity him.
>
> (111-17)

One may have his misgivings regarding the morality here, since it is not until later that the prince returns the booty with interest. But it would seem that Shakespeare intends us to understand that the heir-apparent is already giving evidence of his true character, looking forward to the day when he will provide more convincing evidence of his dedication to law and order. Even more appropriate is the prince's shift to verse at the end of Act III, Scene iii, when he is about to leave for the wars. To Falstaff he says:

> There [in Temple Hall] shalt thou know thy charge,
>   and there receive
> Money and order for their furniture.
> The land is burning; Percy stands on high;
> And either we or they must lower lie.
>
> (225-28)

As one reads these measured lines, he knows that, in this play, Hal has said goodbye to the carefree life at Boar's-Head Tavern.

Blank verse belongs especially to the main plot, where the very fate of the realm is the issue. Often it is quite formal, notably an idealization of ordinary discourse. Decorum calls for such verse when King Henry is addressing recalcitrant nobles (Act I,

Scene ii) and when he is addressing his truant son (Act III, Scene ii); it is also used when Sir Walter Blunt, emissary from the king, conveys his important message to the rebel leaders (Act IV, Scene iii). But to compare the blank verse in this play with that, say, of the *Henry VI* plays and *Richard III*, all of which date several years earlier, is to realize how great has been the poet-dramatist's advance, how impressive the mastery of the medium. Not only are some twenty-three percent of the blank verse lines in *1 Henry IV* "run-on" lines (that is, running the sense and grammatical structure past the end of a given line and thus avoiding what has been called "iambic monotony"), but over fourteen percent contain speeches ending within the line. Consider, for example, the following quotation:

> *Wor.* Good cousin, give me audience for a while.
> *Hot.* I cry you mercy.
> *Wor.*   Those same noble Scots
>   That are your prisoners,—
> *Hot.*   I'll keep them all!
>   By God, he shall not have a Scot of them;
>   No, if a Scot would save his soul, he shall not!
>   I'll keep them, by this hand.
> *Wor.*   You start away
>   And lend no ear unto my purposes.
>   Those prisoners you shall keep.
> *Hot.*   Nay, I will; that's flat.
>   (I.iii.211-18)

No one with any sensitivity to rhythm can miss the iambic beat in these lines, which conveys as well as prose possibly could the sense of reality, vivid and dramatic.

Rhymed iambic pentameter couplets occur thirty-two times, usually at the end of speeches and of scenes, for which they provide a particular kind of emphasis, as in these lines:

> *Hot.* Uncle, adieu! O, let the hours be short
>   Till fields and blows and groans applaud our sport!
>   (I.iii.301-2)

> King. Our hands are full of business; let's away.
> Advantage feeds him fat, while men delay.
>
> (III.ii.179-80)

> Hot. Harry to Harry shall, hot horse to horse,
> Meet and ne'er part till one drop down a corse.
>
> (IV.i.122-23)

By the time he came to write the *Henry IV* plays, Shakespeare habitually used prose for comic scenes, even for high comedy, not solely for broad or "low" comedy. When the comic element is to the fore, Prince Hal and all the others speak prose. Falstaff has already been identified as a speaker of great prose. His discourse has wide range and always reflects his sophistication and wit. His careful use of repetitions, rhetorical questions, apt allusions, balance, and antitheses is remarkable. His burlesque of euphuism, used when he plays the role of Hal's father, provides sufficient evidence that he recognizes the affected, the contrived, and the artificial for what it is. The following quotations will serve, perhaps, to illustrate his skill:

> Marry, then, sweet wag, when thou art king, let not us that are squires of the night's body be called thieves of the day's beauty. Let us be Diana's foresters, gentlemen of the shade, minions of the moon; and let men say we be men of good government, being govern'd, as the sea is, by our noble and chaste mistress the moon, under whose countenance we steal.
>
> (I.ii.26-33)

> But, Hal, I prithee, trouble me no more with vanity. I would to God thou and I knew where a commodity of good names were to be bought. An old lord of the council rated me the other day in the street about you, sir, but I mark'd him not; and yet he talk'd very wisely, but I regarded him not; and yet he talk'd wisely, and in the street too.
>
> (I.ii.83-98)

If first honors belong to Falstaff, it must be acknowledged that Prince Hal exhibits great skill in prose discourse, matching

Sir John similitude for similitude on occasion, as in the following lines:

> *Fal.*   'Sblood, I am
> as melancholy as a gib cat or a lugg'd bear.
> *Prince.* Or an old lion, or a lover's lute.
> *Fal.* Yea, or the drone of a Lincolnshire bagpipe.
> *Prince.* What sayest thou to a hare, or the melancholy of
> Moor-ditch?
>
>   (I.ii.82-88)

The prose of both prince and knight provides an interesting contrast to that of the lowly carriers at the beginning of Act II, Scene i—and, for that matter, to the prose used by Gadshill a bit later in the same scene.

The range in kinds of prose may be further illustrated. Hotspur employs a style appropriate to subject, mood, and character in two different scenes: first, when he reads and provides commentary on the letter from the timorous lord whose support he has sought (II.iii.1 ff.); second, in the dialogue with his Lady Kate, the amusing if tactless satire of Mortimer and his Welsh-speaking wife (III.i.241 ff.).

SIXTEENTH-CENTURY POLITICAL THEORY

Since the *Henry IV* plays are basically political ones, it is necessary to understand the political doctrine behind them if one is to do justice to Shakespeare's intentions. Elizabeth I, the fifth Tudor to rule England, had come to a throne which was in many ways insecure because of rival claims. Henry VIII, her father, had found it especially necessary to inculcate the doctrine of absolute obedience to the Crown after the break with Rome in 1536. During his reign he had experienced the Pilgrimage of Grace, a rebellion in northern England, and, later, the Exeter Conspiracy, an alleged attempt to depose Henry and place a Yorkist on the throne of England. After Henry VIII's death,

England endured the Western Rebellion of 1549; during Elizabeth's reign there occurred the Rebellion of 1569, as well as plots against the queen's life, notably the Babington Plot, which led to the trial, conviction, and execution of Mary, Queen of Scots. Throughout the century and beyond, England had reason to fear an invasion and the rising of native Catholics. The danger was by no means restricted to the year 1588, when Philip II of Spain sent his Armada to subdue England.

In view of such challenges to Tudor supremacy, there was a need for a political philosophy which would prevent challenges to royal authority and devastating civil war. The basic arguments were developed during the reign of Henry VIII and augmented as new crises arose during the reigns of Edward VI and Elizabeth I. It found expression in officially approved pamphlets and tracts, and also in drama and non-dramatic poetry. Especially it was emphasized in official sermons, the first group of which was introduced in the year 1549. These included strongly worded instruction on the subject of obedience. They were augmented in 1570, following the Rebellion of 1569 and the papal decree of excommunication of Queen Elizabeth I. Every Englishman was required to hear the sermons on obedience three times during the year. The gist of the doctrine was this: the ruler was God's lieutenant on earth; no subject, however exalted, had the right actively to oppose him. To do so was a sin against religion punishable by suffering here and now and by eternal damnation after death. Even if the ruler were a tyrant, the subject had no right to oppose him; for the head of state ruled with God's sufferance. In support of this doctrine, appeals were made primarily to biblical authority. Texts such as Romans 13 and Proverbs 8, as well as ones in Matthew, were cited repeatedly. John of Gaunt, Duke of Lancaster, summed up the doctrine accurately and concisely in his response to his sister-in-law, the Duchess of Gloucester, who reminded him that the reigning king, Richard II, had been responsible for the death of her husband and Gaunt's brother:

> God's is the quarrel, for God's substitute,
> His deputy anointed in His sight,

Hath caus'd his death; the which if wrongfully,
Let Heaven revenge; for I may never lift
An angry arm against His minister.
                              (*Richard II*, I.ii.37-41)

That Henry IV should so suffer is to be explained by the fact
that he, son of John of Gaunt, did "lift an angry arm against
[God's] minister." He endures rebellion; he sees the apparent
waywardness of Prince Hal as part of his punishment; he is not
permitted to lead a crusade against the foes of Christianity and
do penance for his grievous sins. But, according to Tudor
political theory, he wore the crown by God's authority; no subject had the right to oppose him. All this should make understandable the Percies' position and make unacceptable the view
that Henry IV is a hypocrite.

REVIEW QUESTIONS

1. In what sense are there *two* kings of England in this play?

2. In terms of debits and credits, what are the chief facets of
   Falstaff's character?

3. In your opinion what is the chief contribution made respectively by:

     a. Bardolph

     b. Francis

     c. Vernon

4. What are the virtues and the limitations of Hotspur?

5. Hotspur refers to Henry IV as "this vile politician Bolingbroke." What justification does he have for this term?

6. How does the character of Hotspur compare with:

    a. Prince Hal

    b. Douglas

    c. Worcester

7. What do you find especially revealing in these lines as regards theme, plot, or character?

    a. *Falstaff:* O, I could wish this tavern were my drum!
                                 (III.iii.230)

    b. *Prince Hal:* If all the year were playing holidays,
       To sport would be as tedious as to work;
       But when they seldom come, they wish'd for come,
       And nothing pleaseth but rare accidents.
                               (I.ii.227-30)

    c. *King.* A hundred thousand rebels die in this.
       Thou shalt have charge and sovereign trust therein.
                              (III.ii.160-61)

8. To whom is reference made and what is the explanation of:

    a. "Mars in swathling clothes" (III.ii)

    b. "thou latter spring!" (I.ii)

    c. "Harry to Harry shall, horse to horse, meet" (IV.i)

    d. "time's fool" (V.iv)

9. What possible relationship is there between:
    a. The planning of the Gadshill robbery and the scenes in which the Percies discuss the revolt against Henry IV?

b. The gulling of Falstaff in Act II and Falstaff's claim to have slain Hotspur in Act V?

10. What excuse is there for the presence of Archbishop Scroop in this play?

SELECTED BIBLIOGRAPHY

Texts

HEMINGWAY, SAMUEL B. (ed.). *Henry the Fourth, Part I.* A New Variorum Edition. Philadelphia: J. B. Lippincott, 1936. Includes text, textual notes, sources, general criticism, stage history, and bibliography.

HUMPHREY, A. R. (ed.). *The First Part of Henry IV.* The Arden Shakespeare. London: Methuen, 1960.

NIELSON, W. A., and C. J. HILL (eds.). *The Complete Plays and Poems of William Shakespeare.* Houghton Mifflin, 1942. The Notes are based on this complete edition of Shakespeare's works.

Bibliographies

BERMAN, RONALD. *A Readers' Guide to Shakespeare's Plays. A Discursive Bibliography.* Chicago: Scott, Foresman, 1965.

Criticism

CAMPBELL, LILY B. *Shakespeare's 'Histories': Mirrors of Elizabethan Policy.* San Marino, California: 1947. Completely sound study of the *Henry IV* plays as exemplars of rebellion.

CHAMBERS, E. K. *William Shakespeare: A Study of Facts and Problems.* 2 vols. Oxford, 1930. Basic to textual study of the play.

DANBY, JOHN. *Shakespeare's Doctrine of Nature*. London: Faber and Faber, 1949. Includes provocative discussion of what the author considers to be the increasingly secular outlook in the chronicle-history plays.

EMPSON, WILLIAM. *Some Versions of Pastoral*. Norfolk, Conn: New Directions, 1950. Includes short but stimulating study of the *Henry IV* plays in which the critic identifies three worlds, each with its own hero: the rebel camp, the tavern, and the court.

PALMER, JOHN. *Political and Comic Characters of Shakespeare*. London: Macmillan, 1962. Good discussion of Falstaff and politics.

TILLYARD, E. M. W. *Shakespeare's History Plays*. London: Chatto and Windus, 1944. Excellent discussion of Prince Hal in particular, relating his character to certain Renaissance values.

TRAVERSI, D. A. *Shakespeare from Richard II to Henry V*. Stanford University Press, 1957. Scene by scene analysis, with particular attention paid to the themes of policy, honor, and retribution.

WILSON, J. D. *The Fortunes of Falstaff*. New York: Macmillan, 1944. Searches for Falstaffian origins in pre-Shakespearean drama; includes a good analysis of Falstaff's character and actions in the *Henry IV* plays.

———. Shakespeare's *Histories at Stratford*. New York: Theatre Art Books, 1952. Warns against over-moralizing in *Henry IV*.

KING HENRY IV, PART 2

NOTES

including
- *Introduction*
- *Scene-by-Scene Synopses*
- *Commentaries*
- *Suggested Questions*
- *Character Sketches*
- *Critical Notes*
- *Selected Bibliography*

by
James K. Lowers, Ph.D.
Department of English
University of Hawaii

Cliffs Notes

INCORPORATED

LINCOLN, NEBRASKA 68501

Editor

Gary Carey, M.A.
University of Colorado

Consulting Editor

James L. Roberts, Ph.D
Department of English
University of Nebraska

ISBN 0-8220-0026-1
© Copyright 1963
by
C. K. Hillegass
All Rights Reserved
Printed in U.S.A.

1990 Printing

Cliffs Notes, Inc.   Lincoln, Nebraska

CONTENTS

INTRODUCTION

It is apparent that Shakespeare planned both parts of *Henry IV* at the same time. In Holinshed's *Chronicles of England, Scotland, and Ireland* (1587 ed.), the chief source for his English chronicle history plays, he found the story of three rebellions against the English King. He chose to reduce these to two phases of a single rebellion. For the action relating to Prince Hal and the Lord Chief Justice, Shakespeare depended upon Sir Thomas Elyot's account in *The Book Called the Governour* (1531) and an old play entitled *The Famous Victories of Henry V. Henry IV, Part I,* was published in 1598, and that is the date accepted for the composition of the second part. An indication of its popularity is the fact that a quarto edition of the play was printed two years later after successful performances.

The first play ended with the royal victory over the rebels at Shrewsbury. "Thus ever did rebellion find rebuke" were the words of the King. But in the north parts of England civil war threatened, and King Henry ordered John of Lancaster and the Earl of Westmoreland to lead forces "against Northumberland and the prelate Scroop"—that is, against Hotspur's father and the disgruntled Archbishop of York. It is at this point that the second part of the play begins.

Shakespeare's source did not provide him with such a figure as the gallant, impetuous Hotspur, who, as adversary of Prince Hal, made possible effective dramatic contrast and an exciting climax and resolution to the action. John of Lancaster, not Prince Hal, leads the King's forces against the rebels in this play. He defeats them by means of a ruse, not through valor. Prince Hal flourishes especially in the comic subplot throughout most of the play. Yet since the young Prince is to succeed his father and to become the Hero King of England, his role in the comic scenes is diminished appreciably toward the end, for Shakespeare carefully prepared the way to the rejection of Falstaff.

If there is no great foe like Hotspur in the main plot, it nevertheless has its own facets of interest. Chief among these is the attention given to the King's relation with Prince Hal. In scenes replete with irony, the conscious-stricken father is never able to push from his mind the knowledge that he was a usurper, and he misunderstands entirely the motives and actions of his son and heir. Audiences agree that the King's suffering has been movingly realized.

Falstaff, one of the most complex characters in literature, remains a superb comic creation. If anything, he is even less repressed. Poins, Bardolph of the flaming nose, and Peto reappear — the first as Prince Hal's companion at the Boar's-Head Tavern, the other two as cronies of Falstaff. Joining them is a new comic figure, the swaggering Pistol, whose explosive discourse fails to conceal his cowardice. Not only does Mistress Quickly, hostess of the Boar's-Head, find a place in the play, but her role is wonderfully developed. Thanks especially to her genius for misusing words, she makes a notable contribution to the broad comedy of the subplot. With her is another new character, the unrestrained Doll Tearsheet, whose startling vocabulary rivals that of Pistol, if in a different way.

But this is not all. In Act III, Shakespeare introduces two other original comic characters. These are two country justices-of-the-peace, the vain Shallow and Silent, his naive kinsman and admirer. The scenes in which these two appear hold their own with any others in the *Henry IV* plays for sheer hilarity.

If some are less satisfied with *Henry IV, Part II,* it is primarily because of the fate of Falstaff. In a memorable speech in the earlier play (II.iv.521) he had addressed these words to Prince Hal:

No, my good lord. Banish Peto, banish Bardolph, banish Poins. But for sweet Jack Falstaff, kind Jack Falstaff, valiant Jack Falstaff, and therefore more valiant, being old Jack Falstaff, banish not him thy Harry's company, banish not him thy Harry's company. Banish plump Jack, and banish all the world.

Yet he is banished. "I know thee not, old man," says the newly crowned Henry V. And these words seem heartless when spoken to that very embodiment of mirth, the man who was not only witty in himself but the cause that wit is in other men. The judicious reader, however, will recall that, basically, this is a play about rebellion — about disorder — in the State. Without failing to be vastly amused by Falstaff, he nevertheless will recognize that plump Jack *is* a rebel against order. That so many should lament the fate of Falstaff is one of the finest tributes to Shakespeare's ability to create a character who seems actually to live. Legend has it that Queen Elizabeth I herself was so amused by Sir John that she urged Shakespeare to write another play in which the knight would trod the boards once more.

INDUCTION

The induction, a device rarely used by Shakespeare, is a forty-line prologue which serves to link the two parts of *Henry IV*. It is spoken by Rumour, an allegorical figure who appears before Warkworth Castle in Northumberland "painted full of tongues," as described in part by Virgil *(Aeneid,* IV. 174). Rumour's function is to confuse all and sundry as to what actually was the outcome of the Battle of Shrewsbury. At first Rumour tells the truth: King Henry's forces had crushed the rebels. Then Rumour spread false reports: Hotspur killed Harry Monmouth (Prince Hal); the Earl of Douglas subdued King Henry; the rebels won an overwhelming victory.

ACT I – SCENE I

SYNOPSIS

This scene first reveals how well Rumour has done its work. The setting is Warkworth Castle, seat of the House of Percy, the head of which is the Earl of Northumberland, who had remained "crafty sick" at home, rather than joining his son and brother at Shrewsbury. Lord Bardolph arrives and jubilantly tells Northumberland that the rebel forces commanded by the Earl's son have triumphed. According to him King Henry was wounded and is near death; Henry Percy had slain Prince Hal and taken prisoner John of Lancaster; the Earl of Douglas had killed Sir Walter Blunt. Northumberland is assured that this information came from "a gentleman well bred and of good name," who had just come from the site of the battle. At this moment Travers arrives with a far different story which he had learned from another who claimed to have been an eye-witness. His report is that the rebels suffered a crushing defeat and that Northumberland's son had been killed. Although Lord Bardolph is willing to wager his barony on the truth of his report the Earl does not know which to believe. All doubts are settled when Morton arrives direct from Shrewsbury and gives his first-hand account. The King had indeed triumphed. Hotspur had been slain; the Earls of Worcester and Douglas are captives. Moreover, Morton states that even now John of Lancaster and the Earl of Westmoreland lead troops against Northumberland and his faction.

For a moment the Earl gives way to stormy passion. But Travers and Lord Bardolph urge caution and restraint. Morton in particular advises him to remember how many lives are at stake and how necessary it is to wait until a large force is mobilized. A telling point is his reminding Northumberland of the great risk Hotspur had taken with his father's approval. But there is no question of flight. Lord Bardolph concedes that, in the first venture, the risk was great, but points out that the possibility of gain was no less great. In ringing words he voices the sentiments of all: "Come, we will all put forth, body and goods." Morton is quick to concur, for now he has good news. The Archbishop of York has raised a force to oppose King Henry. Northumberland states that he was aware of the powerful Archbishop's activities, and he directs his followers to waste no time in seeking the best counsel in order to insure safety and revenge.

CHARACTERS IN SCENE 1

THE EARL OF NORTHUMBERLAND—Henry Percy the elder, father of Hotspur. As leader of the House of Percy, the most powerful baronial family in northern England, he had led the triumvirate which included his brother and his son in support of Henry Bolingbroke and was largely responsible for placing Henry on the throne. Later, he and his faction accused the King of failing to keep his promises to them and rose in revolt. Pleading illness, he had absented himself from the battlefield at Shrewsbury and had survived to threaten the King with rebellion once more.

LORD BARDOLPH—Thomas Bardolph, a noble mentioned by Holinshed, who is a leading member of the Percy faction.

TRAVERS AND MORTON—Two loyal retainers of the Earl of Northumberland who, like so many in the north parts of England, "knew no Prince but a Percy."

CHARACTERS NOT PRESENT BUT MENTIONED

KING HARRY—King Henry IV (also referred to as Bolingbroke, a place name), son of John of Gaunt and grandson of Edward III. In deposing and succeeding Richard II he founded the Lancastrian dynasty of English rulers.

PRINCE HARRY—Prince Hal (also referred to as Harry Monmouth), son and heir to Henry IV, who, after apparent disregard of his princely obligations, had emerged the hero of the Battle of Shrewsbury.

DOUGLAS—Archibald, fourth Earl of Douglas and first Duke of Touraine. A famous Scottish warrior, he was first an enemy and then an ally of Hotspur. Captured by the royal forces at Shrewsbury he lived to become a supporter of Henry V in the French wars.

WESTMORELAND—Ralph Neville, Earl of Westmoreland

and brother-in-law to the King. He had opposed Richard II and had assisted at the coronation of Henry IV.

SIR JOHN—None other than Falstaff, who dominates the comic scenes in both parts of *Henry IV*. Interestingly enough, he is here identified as one of the most important leaders of the royalist forces.

WORCESTER—Thomas Percy, the wily Earl of Worcester, brother of Northumberland, who fought with his nephew, Hotspur, at Shrewsbury.

ARCHBISHOP OF YORK—Richard Scroop (Richard Le Scrope), who had attained his high office at the request of Richard II. Although he supported Henry IV for a time, early in that King's reign he issued an indictment of the government and raised a body of supporters.

SIR WALTER BLUNT—A stalwart Lancastrian and friend of John of Gaunt, Henry IV's father. He was a minor but useful character in *Henry IV, Part I*, serving principally as the King's emissary.

PURPOSE OF THE SCENE

1. To establish the basic theme of the main plot.

2. To clarify the relationship between the first and second parts of *Henry IV*.

3. To introduce the leader of the rebellious Percy faction and to identify important adherents to their cause.

4. To provide the inciting incident which, in a technical sense, starts the action rising toward its climax.

5. To impress upon the audience the momentousness of the issues involved—the new dangers which now face Henry IV and all England.

SUGGESTED QUESTIONS

1. In lines 20-23, exactly what does Lord Bardolph mean by reference to "Caesar's fortunes"?

2. How may one paraphrase lines 60-61?
   Yea, this man's brow, like a title leaf,
   Foretells the nature of a tragic volume.

3. What is meant by the reference to the Archbishop of York as a man "with double surety"?

ACT I – SCENE 2

The opening dialogue between Falstaff and his newly acquired page deals successively with the latter's report on three matters and with Falstaff's reaction to each report. The first is the doctor's diagnosis of the knight's physical condition, which is hardly flattering. Falstaff, remarking that many take pride in gibing him, cites the latest prank played on him by Prince Hal—sending him the page whose dimunitiveness offers such a comic contrast to the fat knight. But Falstaff, never at loss for words, expresses his views at length, concluding that the Prince is now almost out of grace with him. Next, the page says that the tailor from whom Falstaff had ordered twenty yards of satin has refused to honor the knight's credit, particularly when Bardolph was his security. Finally, the page reports that Bardolph has gone to buy Falstaff a horse. And this bit of intelligence gives Sir John another chance to display his wit.

At this point the little page announces the arrival of the Lord Chief Justice of England, identifying him as the man who had sent the Prince to prison for attempting to circumvent justice on behalf of Bardolph after the Gadshill robbery (see *Henry IV, Part I,* Act II). Falstaff pretends that his new appointment as a commander of troops moving against the northern rebels makes it impossible for him to concern himself with other matters. But the Chief Justice will not be put off. As he reproves the knight for ignoring his summons to appear before him, Falstaff attempts to avoid the issue by expressing concern for the Justice's health and then, at greater length, for the King's—even going so far as to offer a diagnosis. In so many words, Falstaff is denounced as a wastrel, as one who has misled the young Prince, and as one who defies convention and the principle of decorum befitting an elderly man. All this serves only to inspire audacious, witty replies. Falstaff concedes that Prince Hal should not have boxed the ears of the Lord Chief Justice, adds that he had "checked him for it," and concludes that the Prince remains unconcerned, as obviously does Falstaff himself. Then he confirms the report that he has been asked to serve his King once more by joining the royal forces against the Archbishop of York and the Earl of Northumberland. And when the Chief Justice gives his blessings on the enterprise, Sir John brazenly asks him for the loan of a thousand pounds.

Alone with the page, Falstaff voices a complaint on his near-empty purse. In order to raise money, he sends the page with letters to John of Lancaster, to Prince Hal, and to "old Mistress Ursula," whom he weakly had promised to marry. As he concludes, "A good wit will make use of anything."

CHARACTERS IN SCENE 2

FALSTAFF—Sir John, the most famous comic character of Shakespearean drama who has won a place in the company of Prince Hal because of his matchless wit and incessant gaiety, his unfailing ability to incite laughter. Indeed, so gifted is he that generations of audiences have taken him to their hearts, often refusing to believe that he has any basic shortcomings and that his derelictions are all part of a game he plays for the sake of merriment. It may be argued that, in a sense, Falstaff embodies the rebel against seriousness and authority which is latent in many of the most respectable people. Grossly fat, white bearded, he appears as the very spirit of irresponsible youth. His final line in this scene very well sums up his philosophy of life.

LORD CHIEF JUSTICE OF THE KING'S BENCH— England's premier legal official, an elderly, sober, dedicated man intent on seeing to it that order and justice in civil life are maintained within the realm. In this scene he functions as a foil to Falstaff and helps to provide the link between the first and second parts of *Henry IV*.

THE PAGE—The witty little servant, a present to Falstaff from Prince Hal.

CHARACTERS NOT PRESENT BUT MENTIONED

BARDOLPH—Falstaff's serving man and one of the habitues of the Boar's-Head Tavern. Memorable for his bright red nose, he was the source of good comedy of physical appearance in the earlier play.

JOHN OF LANCASTER—Prince John, Duke of Lancaster, third son of Henry IV and general of the royal forces sent against the northern insurgents.

ARCHBISHOP OF YORK—Richard Scroop, powerful leader of the malcontents in Yorkshire.

EARL OF NORTHUMBERLAND—Henry Percy the elder, leader of the Percy faction opposed to Henry IV.

PRINCE HAL—Henry, heir apparent to the throne of England who, after the Battle of Shrewsbury, had joined his royal father in the Welsh wars.

PURPOSE OF THE SCENE

1. To start the subplot and introduce the theme of order therein.
2. To present a full-length portrait of Falstaff.
3. To make clear the fact that, despite the King's injunction, Falstaff and Prince Hal will soon appear together again.
4. To keep to the fore the major theme of rebellion and thus to link main plot and subplot, which is not to be considered as mere "comic relief."

SUGGESTED QUESTIONS

1. What facets of Falstaff's character are clearly revealed in this scene?
2. What does the servant exactly mean when he says, "I pray you, sir, then set your knighthood and your soldiership aside and give me leave to tell you you lie in your throat..." (lines 95-97)?
3. In addition to trying to evade the Chief Justice's reprimands, what is a probably explanation of Falstaff's concern for the King's health?

A C T   I – S C E N E   3

SYNOPSIS

Present at the Palace of Richard Scroop, Archbishop of York, are the Archbishop himself, Lord Hastings, Mowbray (Earl Marshal of the North Parts), and Lord Bardolph. This is a council of war to determine the course of events. The Archbishop has explained the reason for the move against the King and indicated what forces are at his disposal. Mowbray, at one with Scroop as regards grievances, questions that the insurgents are strong enough to oppose the King. Lord Hastings reports that already 25,000 men have been mustered and that reenforcements from Northumberland are expected. Judiciously, Lord Bardolph points out that the basic question is whether or not the rebels can survive without reenforcements. His own position is that it would be foolhardy for the rebels to commit themselves until they are sure of Northumberland's help. The Archbishop agrees: they must not make the fatal mistake which Hotspur made at Shrewsbury. It is Lord Bardolph who sums up the argument, emphasizing the fact that they seek "almost to pluck a kingdom down/ And set up another." Caution, he concludes, must be the watchword.

But Lord Hastings argues that the present force is large enough, and he has good reasons to support his case. King Henry faces danger from the French and from the Welsh led by Glendower, as well as from the northern insurgents: "So is the unfirm King/ In three divided." Moreover, Hastings reports that the Royal treasury is depleted.

This argument seems irrefutable. It is agreed that Henry IV cannot possibly commit all his forces against the Scroop-Percy faction and leave the realm defenseless against the Welsh and the French. Once more the audience learns that the Duke (John of Lancaster) and the Earl of Westmoreland lead the royalists northward, and the King and Harry of Monmouth (Prince Hal) will move against the Welsh. Who will oppose the French, if they should attack England, is not known.

The Archbishop then urges that the insurgents publish their list of grievances in which the King's government will be indicted for misrule. Both Mowbray and Hastings, fired with enthusiasm, call for prompt action: "We are time's subjects, and time bids be gone."

CHARACTERS IN SCENE 3

ARCHBISHOP OF SCROOP—Richard Scroop, to whom important reference was made in Scene 1. Here he emerges as a powerful opponent of Henry IV. He has been able to muster a force of 25,000 men. If one recalls that Henry V led a force of only 15,000 against the French, and that Henry VIII's forces opposing the rebels of 1536 numbered less than 9,000 men, he can appreciate the seriousness of the threat against the Crown. The Archbishop wisely invites and listens to contrary points of view before making up his own mind on what action should be taken.

MOWBRAY—Thomas, second Duke of Norfolk. He was the elder son of Thomas Mowbray, first Duke of Norfolk, who had been banished by Richard II because of his quarrel with Henry Bolingbroke, the man who now rules England. Perhaps because, for a time, he had been excluded from his father's honors, he joined the Archbishop and the Percies in the treasonable action of the year 1405. Anything but foolhardy, he is a determined, strong adversary.

LORD BARDOLPH—His adherence to the Percy cause having been well established in Scene 1, he now represents the

Earl of Northumberland and shares the latter's sense of caution.

LORD HASTINGS — Sir Edward, eighth Lord Hastings, scion of an important baronial family which had included Earls of Pembroke. The fifth Lord Hastings had married Philippa, daughter of Edmund Mortimer, Earl of March, to whom Richard II had willed the Crown of England.

PURPOSE OF THE SCENE

1. To advance the main plot by presenting the council of rebel leaders, who, after an estimate of all factors, voice their determination to take to the field.

2. To introduce personally the powerful Archbishop of York, co-leader of the northern insurgents.

3. To make even clearer the grave dangers confronting King Henry IV: the odds are weighted heavily against him in view of the threats from Wales and France.

SUGGESTED QUESTIONS

1. Exactly how did Hotspur "line himself with hope," in the words of Lord Bardolph (line 27)?

2. What does Lord Bardolph mean by the term *winking* in his reference to Hotspur (line 33)?

3. How may one paraphrase and explain lines 87-88?
The commonwealth is sick of their own choice,
Their overgreedy love hath surfeited.

ACT II — SCENE 1

SYNOPSIS

On a London street Mistress Quickly, Hostess of the Boar's-Head Tavern, asks Fang, the Sheriff's sergeant, whether or not he has served notice of the legal action she has brought against Falstaff. He assures her that he has done so. Snare, the Sergeant's man, appears on call and is ordered to arrest the knight. When Snare voices concern for his life, the Hostess urges caution. In lines packed with *double-entendre* hardly complimentary to her own character and to Falstaff's, she recalls how she had been victimized. Vocally, at least, Fang is all courage and determination; he "cares not his (Falstaff's) thrust."

The Hostess fills in the details in lines marked by the repeated misuse of words. Falstaff, she insists, owes her one hundred marks (about seventy-eight pounds). He may be expected to appear in one of three public places. And at this moment Falstaff indeed appears, along with Bardolph and the page.

Falstaff demands to know what all the fuss is about: "Whose mare's dead?" Fang promptly declares him to be under arrest. Lively action ensues. Falstaff calls upon Bardolph to cut off Fang's head and to throw the Hostess in the gutter. First crying out "Murder! Murder!" Mistress Quickly then adds her voice to that of Fang in an appeal to passers-by for help—although it would seem that she is doing very well without assistance. The page adds to the din, scurrilously denouncing her, just as the Chief Justice and his men arrive on the scene.

The Chief Justice upbraids Sir John for street brawling, particularly at a time when he should be hurrying to join the royalists in Yorkshire. He is then told that Falstaff has imposed grievously upon Mistress Quickly, using worthless promises as the coin of the realm. Asked if he is not ashamed of himself for imposing upon a poor widow, Falstaff calmly asks the Hostess for a bill of particulars. A new charge against him is included in her reply: as she had dressed the head wound he had received from Prince Hal for insulting the King, he had promised to marry her, had even kissed her—and had borrowed thirty shillings.

Falstaff assures the Chief Justice that the poor woman is demented, in proof whereof he states that she had declared her oldest son to be the very image of the Chief Justice. How to account for her sad state? Once prosperous, now indigent, she had lost her wits. Magnanimously, he does not bring charges against her. But as for Fang and Snare, that is a different matter.

The Chief Justice refuses to be misled by what he calls Falstaff's "impudent sauciness," pointing out that long since he has been familiar with the knight's behavior. He orders that Falstaff make restitution and mend his ways.

Sir John, unmistakably irritated by this "sneap" (insult), as he calls it, moves to the attack. He is not impudent; he is honorably bold. Nor will he curtsey to the Chief Justice or deign to be a suitor. Instead, he claims immunity on the grounds that he is engaged in the urgent business of the King.

As the Chief Justice firmly tells Falstaff to pay his debt, Gower, a messenger, enters with news for England's leading legal official: the King and Harry, Prince of Wales, are near London.

Falstaff and the Hostess hold the center of the stage while the two converse.

Now Falstaff uses all his wit and gives the audience a demonstration of his skill in victimizing the Hostess and, incidentally, substantiates her charges against him. He succeeds in getting her to agree to sell treasured furnishings of the tavern in order to raise money for him. "Will you pay me altogether," she asks, not without pathos. "As I live," replies Falstaff, and in an aside he instructs Bardolph to go with her and see that she does not change her mind. Before she leaves, however, she agrees to have Doll Tearsheet join the knight at the Boar's-Head, where he will continue to indulge himself and stretch his credit.

Falstaff and the Chief Justice now remain alone on stage. In their final exchange, it is revealed that the King has sent 1500 foot troops and 500 horses to augment the force led by the Duke of Lancaster. Falstaff is unable to learn whether or not the King plans to return to London at once.

Patently ignoring the Chief Justice, Sir John twice asks Gower, the messenger, to dine with him. The Chief Justice reproves him for loitering in London streets at a time of national peril and for a display of bad manners. Voicing his pride in his ability at verbal dueling, Falstaff says in effect that the Chief Justice had been his teacher as far as manners were concerned. "Thou art a great fool," replies the latter as the scene ends.

CHARACTERS IN SCENE 1

THE HOSTESS—Mistress Quickly, the credulous, kindly hostess of the Boar's-Head Tavern, who has been victimized by Falstaff in more ways than that relating to pounds, shillings, and pence. A devout lover of long words, she has her difficulty in getting them right and thus provides first-rate comedy of words. She strives to hang on to some reputation for respectability, insisting that Falstaff had promised to marry her and using such phrases as "saving your manhoods" (line 29), which were usually voiced after inadvertently making an improper remark.

MASTER FANG—The Sheriff's sergeant, charged with the duty of delivering notices of action in civil cases and insuring the appearance of the accused in court. The obtuse Fang repeatedly strives to impress others with his efficiency and courage.

SNARE—The Sergeant's assistant, whose timidity provides a comic contrast to the apparent valor of his superior. Like Fang, and for that matter most of Shakespeare's characters at this social level, he is a realistic, well-delineated individual, despite his minor role.

FALSTAFF—Remaining his unique self, the knight once more demonstrates his utterly carefree attitude, his mental resiliency, his wit—and his impudence when confronted by the Chief Justice. At one point, however, Falstaff's animosity toward the latter nearly causes him to lose his usual self-confidence.

THE LORD CHIEF JUSTICE—Again he serves as severe critic of and foil to Sir John Falstaff, and as the voice of order and respectability. His character is developed somewhat in this scene, for he finds the opportunity to vie with Falstaff in punning and comes off quite well.

BARDOLPH—Falstaff's serving man.

THE PAGE—Falstaff's servant. Judging by the action in this scene and particularly by the page's two-line speech, there is no question of his loyalty to his master.

CHARACTERS NOT PRESENT BUT MENTIONED

HARRY, PRINCE OF WALES—Prince Hal, upon whose tolerance and good favor Falstaff depends.

MY LORD OF LANCASTER—John, Duke of Lancaster, brother to Prince Hal and leader of royalist troops.

THE ARCHBISHOP—Richard Scroop of York, leader of the Yorkshire rebels.

NORTHUMBERLAND—Henry Percy the elder, Earl of Northumberland and leader of northern rebels in his bailiwick.

PURPOSE OF THE SCENE

1. To give further insight into the character of Falstaff, whose disregard of law and order is emphasized by his cavalier attitude toward the Lord Chief Justice.

2. To introduce the Hostess of the Boar's-Head Tavern in person.

3. To prepare the way for the re-appearance of Prince Hal.

4. To add expository details relating to the action against the insurgents and in this way to keep to the fore the theme of rebellion.

1. Why is Falstaff especially interested in learning whether or not the King plans to return soon to London?

2. What do you find revealing in the fact that Falstaff twice invites Gower to dine with him?

3. Are there any details to support Falstaff's contention that Mistress Quickly was indeed quite prosperous at one time?

ACT II — SCENE 2

SYNOPSIS

Prince Hal and Poins appear on a London street and engage in an exchange characterized by light, brilliant wit. In the amusing backchat between the two, it is made clear that Hal, very much aware of what he is doing and what the public reaction will be, chooses again to seek out the company of regulars at the Boar's-Head Tavern.

Ironically, the Prince remarks that he should not be sad because the King, his father, is sick. And cynically Poins replies that Hal's grief can not be very deep. Still good humoredly, Hal protests that his reactions to such circumstances are not to be confused with those of Falstaff or of Poins. He adds that his heart bleeds inwardly, despite the fact that, in such "vile company," he makes no outward show of grief. Poins flatly states that tears would be a sign of hypocrisy in one who associates with Falstaff. The Prince reminds him that he is no less guilty of association with Poins, and the latter makes a defense of his character just as Bardolph and the page enter.

The Prince greets Falstaff's serving man as "noble Bardolph" and remarks that the page has been transformed into an ape. Again Bardolph's "malmesey nose" becomes the source of comedy. The page declares that, seen through the red lattice windows of the tavern, Bardolph's face was indiscernible. A scurrilous interchange follows, and the Prince, amused by the page's wit, gives him a crown, to which sum Poins adds sixpence.

When the Prince inquires about Falstaff, Bardolph hands over a letter addressed to Hal. Both the Prince and Poins have a choice selection of epithets for and comments on Sir John as they peruse it. Beginning in an excessively formal manner, Falstaff has written a warning to Hal. Poins, he insists, boasts that his sister Nell is betrothed to the Prince. He then urges Hal to report "at idle times," and adds a self-laudatory close to the letter. The incensed Poins vows that he will soak the letter in sack and force Falstaff to eat it.

"Well, thus we play the fools with the time, and the spirits of the wise sit in the clouds and mock us," the Prince concludes.

Hal learns that Falstaff is at the Boar's-Head Tavern in company with the old group as well as Mistress Quickly and Doll Tearsheet. About the latter's unsavory character neither Hal nor Poins is in any doubt. The two agree to "steal upon them," and Bardolph is warned not to give advance notice that the Prince is now in London.

Alone, the Prince and Poins discuss how they can arrange to eavesdrop on Sir John without being discovered. The ingenious Poins has the answer: they will disguise themselves as lowly drawers in the tavern.

CHARACTERS IN SCENE 2

PRINCE HENRY—Hal, the heir-apparent, who again chooses to tolerate the unrestrained behavior of Falstaff and his cronies. Despite his keen wit and apparently devil-may-care manner, he is not without deep concern for his royal father nor unperturbed about affairs in the realm. Consistent with his character as drawn in *Henry IV, Part I,* he appears as a man of "all humors that have showed themselves humors since the old days of Goodman Adam." (See II. iv. 104 in the earlier play).

POINS—Hal's companion at the Boar's-Head, who delights no less than does the Prince in trapping Falstaff. It will be remembered that it was he who proposed to trick the fat knight in connection with the Gadshill robbery. In view of the accusation made in Falstaff's letter, Poins now has special reason for baiting Sir John.

BARDOLPH—Falstaff's serving man.

THE PAGE—Falstaff's little servant, now decked out in new livery.

CHARACTERS NOT PRESENT BUT MENTIONED

HAL'S FATHER—King Henry IV, who is now gravely ill at this time of national emergency.

MISTRESS QUICKLY—Hostess of the Boar's-Head Tavern.

DOLL TEARSHEET—Prostitute at the Boar's-Head Tavern.

PURPOSE OF SCENE 2

1. To re-introduce Prince Hal and Poins, filling in the outlines of character, particularly that of the former.

2. To start the action involving comic conflict between Hal and Falstaff.

3. To provide expository details regarding the King's health.

SUGGESTED QUESTIONS

1. Why does Poins believe that Hal cannot be deeply worried about the King's health?

2. What possibly could be the motivation for Falstaff's libel of Poins?

3. What does Prince Hal mean when he says to Poins, "Never a man's thought in the world keeps the roadway better than thine" (lines 62-63)?

ACT II – SCENE 3

Before Warkworth Castle the Earl of Northumberland, Lady Northumberland and Lady Percy seriously discuss the Earl's plans. The two ladies vehemently urge Northumberland to avoid participation in the rising against Henry IV, but he replies that his honor is at stake since he has given his word to join the insurgents. Lady Percy reminds him that honor had not prevented him from failing to appear at Shrewsbury when Hotspur sorely needed his father's help. Describing her late husband as the "miracle of men," she bitterly argues that with half the number now led by the Archbishop and the Lord Marshal (Mowbray), he would have defeated the royalists and have survived.

Lady Northumberland urges her husband to hurry to Scotland and to remain there until he learned how the insurgents fared in battle. At first unable to make up his mind, the Earl then agrees to follow her counsel.

CHARACTERS IN SCENE 3

NORTHUMBERLAND—Henry Percy the elder, Earl of Northumberland. His decision to leave for Scotland after having given his word to lead his forces in support of those raised by the

Archbishop of York points to the conclusion that the same concern for his own safety explains his failure to appear at Shrewsbury, where Hotspur, his son, faced the royal forces.

LADY NORTHUMBERLAND—Wife of the Earl and mother of the slain Hotspur, understandably concerned for the safety of her husband.

LADY PERCY—Katherine (Kate), sister of Edmund Mortimer, Earl of March, and widow of Hotspur. Her deep love for her dead husband, well established in the earlier play, is underscored in this scene.

CHARACTERS NOT PRESENT BUT MENTIONED

THE ARCHBISHOP—Richard Scroop, Archbishop of York, active critic of Henry IV.

THE MARSHAL—Thomas, second Duke of Norfolk and Earl Marshal of England, now allied with the rebellious Archbishop.

HOTSPUR—Henry Percy, son of the Earl of Northumberland, slain by Prince Hal at Shrewsbury.

MONMOUTH—Prince Hal (Henry of Monmouth).

PURPOSE OF THE SCENE

1. To advance the main plot, making clear the fact that the numerically inferior troops led by John of Lancaster at least will not have to deal with forces mustered by Northumberland.

2. To provide another link between the first and second parts of *Henry IV* by reference to Hotspur and to events dramatized in the earlier play.

SUGGESTED QUESTIONS

1. What is meant by Northumberland's phrase "visage of the times" (line 3)?

2. How may one paraphrase "nothing but the sound of Hotspur's name/ Did seem defensible"?

3. Aside from his promises, why is the Earl at first convinced that he must join forces with the Archbishop?

ACT II – SCENE 4

SYNOPSIS

From the conversation of two lowly drawers at the Boar's-Head Tavern, the audience learns of another way in which Prince Hal had baited Falstaff by giving him five apples with wrinkled skins and identifying the knight as the sixth. They further learn that, at Doll Tearsheet's request, musicians have been sent for, and that the Prince and Poins will soon appear and borrow the drawer's jerkins and aprons.

The Hostess and Doll Tearsheet enter, the former complimenting Doll on her improved health – that is, on having recovered from the excessive drinking of wine. Next, Falstaff makes his appearance singing a ballad. He is solicitous about Doll's health, and the two engage in their respective types of badinage, often a bit scandalous. The Hostess is an appreciative audience, and her comments admit to interpretation at two levels, one inadvertently uncomplimentary to both parties. At the end of this verbal exchange, Doll remarks that she will remain friends with Falstaff since he is going to the wars.

The First Drawer announces the arrival of Pistol, who wants a word with Falstaff. At the mention of Pistol's name, Doll vociferously denounces him as a "swaggering rascal" and a "foul-mouthed rogue." The Hostess, once more striving to keep up the appearance of respectability, vows that no swaggerers are welcome in her establishment. Falstaff then identifies Pistol as his "ancient" (a standard-bearer for a leader of troops) and states that he is a "tame-cheater" (confidence man) who is as gentle as a puppy. After the Hostess engages in another exercise in the misuse of words, Pistol is called for. He enters with Bardolph and the page.

Falstaff invites Pistol to drink a toast first to the Hostess and then to Doll. But the latter will have none of it. She and the ancient have a virulent interchange, Doll excoriating Pistol and Pistol making blood-curdling threats to avenge himself. It remains a question who is the more devastating – the billingsgate which pours from the lips of Doll or the ranting of Pistol.

The disguised Prince Hal and Poins now follow the musicians into the room. Completely unaware of their presence, Falstaff talks freely and most indiscreetly to Doll Tearsheet, who is seated on his lap. He blandly informs her that the Prince is a shallow fellow fit only to be a pantryman, and that Poins ("that baboon") is tolerated only because he is young and wild like the Prince. Hal and Poins exchange witty and appropriate remarks on the slander and on Falstaff's behavior with Doll Tearsheet.

At last Falstaff notices the two drawers and makes unflattering remarks on their resemblance to the Prince and to Poins. Hal's denunciation of the fat knight gives the show away, and the Hostess welcomes Hal, as does Falstaff in his own brash style. But Doll, who had lauded Falstaff as a valorous man, now denounces him as a coward for permitting Hal to insult him.

Poins warns the Prince that Falstaff will surely extricate himself from his predicament if there is any delay in attack. Flatly stating that he had overheard every word, Hal ironically adds that plump Jack, no doubt, will revive the specious argument he had used after running away at Gadshill and claim that he was aware of Hal's presence all along. But the knight, well aware that such a story will not serve him now, calmly admits that he did not recognize the Prince. He has a new, original defense: so far from abusing the Prince he had sought to defend him from the wicked. If he, Falstaff, had voiced praise, they would have fallen in love with the heir-apparent. Hal seizes upon the word "wicked." Who are these "wicked" Falstaff speaks of? Surely not this "virtuous woman," Doll Tearsheet; surely not the Hostess! Did the knight then mean Bardolph, "whose zeal burns in his nose"? Or the page, perhaps?

Falstaff's wit does not desert him. He argues that all named are, in one way or another, wicked—even the little page, despite the "good angel about him." The Hostess, once more sensitive about her reputation, protests; and the two engage in an amusing colloquy.

Peto enters with important news. The King is at Westminster, and messengers have arrived from the North. Moreover, no less than a dozen captains have been asking for Falstaff. Prince Hal reproves himself for wasting time, calls for his sword and cloak, and bids Sir John goodnight. Poins, Peto, and Bardolph leave with him.

Bardolph returns immediately with the news that the captains are waiting at the door for Falstaff, who must leave at once for Court. Sir John says his farewells to the Hostess and Doll Tearsheet, urging them to note "how men of merit are sought after." Both women are distraught as he leaves. But a moment later they hear Bardolph call from another room: "Bid Mistress Tearsheet come to my master." "Oh, run, Doll, run," blubbers the Hostess.

CHARACTERS IN SCENE 4

FALSTAFF—For the first time in *Henry IV, Part I*, the audience views Sir John at his calling in the Boar's-Head Tavern, where he reigns supreme. He is revealed as one devoted to the pleasures of the flesh and as a gargantuan liar—but also as one who is indeed not only witty in himself but the cause of wit in other men. It is to be noted that, however much he has taken advantage of the Hostess and used Doll Tearsheet, both are devoted to him.

PISTOL—For the first time the audience meets one of Shakespeare's "humors" characters, a man who is comically unbalanced in a particular way. Pistol's humor is that he poses as a man who is a ferocious warrior, laconic but startling in speech. Shakespeare uses him partly to burlesque characters in plays notable for bombast which had wide popular appeal. Close students of Elizabethan drama recognize many verbal echoes in Pistol's lines. For example, when he speaks of the "pampered jades of Asia," he borrows a phrase from Christopher Marlowe's *Tamberlaine, Part II*. There are several more inferior plays presented by a rival company. Actually this "fustian rascal" is a poltroon, an arrant coward. Thus Shakespeare makes the most of comic incongruity.

MISTRESS QUICKLY—The kindly, if weak, owner of the Boar's Head Tavern—still the mistress not only of the tavern but of malapropisms.

DOLL TEARSHEET—A prostitute who is "as common as the way between St. Albans and London," to borrow Poins' words (II.ii.184-185), she is a spirited character who is never at loss for words, usually invectives. If her charms are usually for hire, she nevertheless reserves a special place for Falstaff in her affections.

PRINCE HAL—At the comic level, the Prince who had vindicated his honor at Shrewsbury, once again crosses swords with Falstaff. Perhaps some will call the encounter a draw. But one should observe how Hal urbanely controls himself and, once more endorsing the precept that life should have its lighter moments, joins with Poins in gulling Sir John.

POINS—The ingenious baiter of Falstaff and therefore welcome as Hal's associate in the comic subplot.

PETO—One of Falstaff's companions.

BARDOLPH—Falstaff's serving man.

THE PAGE—Falstaff's serving boy.

PURPOSE OF THE SCENE

1. To present the initial encounter between Falstaff and Prince Hal, one which balances the Gadshill episode in *Henry IV, Part I*.

2. To advance the action of the comic subplot and at the same time not to lose sight of the theme of rebellion.

3. To develop the characters of the newly created Doll Tear-sheet and Pistol.

4. To add to the characterization of Prince Hal and Mistress Quickly.

SUGGESTED QUESTIONS

1. Doll Tearsheet praises Falstaff as "valorous as Hector of Troy, worth five Agammemnons, and ten times better than the Nine Worthies" (lines 236-238). How may one explain these allusions?

2. What does Doll Tearsheet mean when she denounces Pistol as a "fustian rascal"?

3. How well does Falstaff come off in this scene as compared to the one following the Gadshill robbery in *Henry IV, Part I*?

ACT III – SCENE 1

SYNOPSIS

It is past midnight. Henry IV, now at the Palace in West-minster, instructs a page to call in the Earls of Warwick and Sur-rey to consider the import of the news received from the north. Ailing and exhausted, the King invokes sleep and laments the fact that its soothing balm, freely enjoyed by the lowliest of subjects, is denied him: "Uneasy lies the head that wears a crown."

The two earls enter and, in reply to the King's question, state that they have studied the letters and are aware of the "rank dis-ease" which now infects the realm. Warwick reassures the worried Henry, arguing that good advice and little medicine will effect a cure—that is, Northumberland (whose decision to fly to Scotland they know nothing about) will be subdued. Henry exclaims that, if one could see into the future and become aware of the perils which await, not even the happiest youth would choose to live. These thoughts lead him to recall earlier events relating to Richard II, Northumberland, and himself, most of which were dramatized in Shakespeare's earlier chronicle history, *Richard II*. He speaks of how Northumberland, once loyal to Richard, had joined forces with Henry himself against the reigning monarch. Especially Henry recalls Richard's ominous prophecy that the day would come when Northumberland would turn traitor again. Warwick discounts the possibility of there being anything supernatural in Richard's prophecy. The King replies that, since such events seem to be unavoidable, they must be accepted. But he remains deeply troubled, for he has heard that the northern rebels now have a force of 50,000 men. Again Warwick reassures him. The report is rumour which always exaggerates. He expresses confidence that the royal army now in the field will defeat the insurgents. And he has one piece of good news: Glendower is dead. Warwick then urges the King to rest. Henry accepts this counsel and declares that, once order is restored, he and his lieutenants will leave for the Holy Land.

CHARACTERS IN SCENE 1

HENRY IV—The ailing King of England, exhausted by loss of sleep and beset by worries. As was true in the earlier play, Shakespeare presents him as a ruler who, determined and capable though he is, suffers the "unquiet mind" of one who is guilty of usurpation and regicide. It is necessary for one to recognize the two-fold point of view here. Henry *is* a sinner, and that he should endure rebellion is part of his punishment; yet he wears the crown on God's sufferance. Those who rebel against him are in turn grievous sinners who have invited God's vengeance.

WARWICK—Richard de Beauchamp, Earl of Warwick, a man famous as a brave and chivalrous warrior who had fought against the King's enemies in the Welsh wars and at Shrewsbury. In this scene he is erroneously referred to as Neville.

SURREY—Thomas FitzAlan, Earl of Arundel and Earl of Surrey. Since his father had been beheaded for treason during the reign of Richard II, his adherence to the Lancastrian cause is readily understood.

CHARACTERS NOT PRESENT BUT MENTIONED

THE EARL OF NORTHUMBERLAND—"This Percy," chief of the baronial family now opposed to the man they had helped to put on the throne.

THE BISHOP—The Archbishop of York, active leader of the rebel force now assembled in Yorkshire.

GLENDOWER—Leader of Welsh forces opposing the King.

PURPOSE OF THE SCENE

1. To introduce the King personally and to show how he suffers from the problems of conscience and kingship.
2. To review some of the events dramatized in *Henry IV, Part I*.
3. To emphasize the elements of conflict in the main plot, notably those relating to the grave dangers which threaten Henry's government.

SUGGESTED QUESTIONS

1. What evidence is there of an adverse turn in the fortunes of the northern insurgents?
2. Why does the King hope to go to the Holy Land?
3. What is meant by "partial sleep" (line 26)?

ACT III – SCENE 2

SYNOPSIS

Before his home in Gloucestershire, Shallow greets Silent, his fellow justice and kinsman. He inquires about the health of Silent's wife and daughter, and about the progress of son William, a student at Oxford. William, he says, must go on to the Inns of Court, the law schools in London. Shallow himself had attended Clement's Inn, and he is confident that his reputation as a wild young fellow still survives there. Among the roisterers whom he recalls is Sir John Falstaff, whom he identifies as one-time page to Thomas Mowbray, Duke of Norfolk. It is this same knight who will arrive soon to obtain recruits, so Shallow informs Silent. And he rambles on, commenting on Falstaff's prowess in brawling when both were young. He continues to talk now of the inevitability of death, now of the price of livestock.

Bardolph and another of Falstaff's men enter. When Shallow identifies himself, Corporal Bardolph (such is his new military title) conveys his master's greeting. The delighted justice lauds Falstaff as an expert with the backsword and inquires about the knight's health and that of "his lady his wife." Bardolph replies that a soldier is better accommodated than with a wife. Shallow is enchanted by the expression "better accommodated." Respectfully, the Corporal points out that it is not a phrase but a word—a soldier-like word.

And he defines it in terms of itself. Accommodated, it seems, means accommodated.

Falstaff enters and is effusively welcomed. When Shallow introduces him to Justice Silent, the knight remarks that a man with such a name is well fitted to administer the law. Then to business. Shallow assures Sir John that he has a dozen fit men among whom good recruits may be found. Four are successively called to be questioned, and the name of each gives Falstaff wonderful opportunity to display his wit.

The first is Ralph Mouldy, described as "a good-limbed fellow, young and strong and of good family." Falstaff remarks that Mouldy should indeed be put to use. Shallow, anxious to prove that he is not obtuse, explains the joke—"things mouldy lack use." Despite Mouldy's protests that his wife will object, he is chosen as the first recruit.

Next is Simon Shadow, who helpfully identifies himself as his mother's son, giving Falstaff the chance to make the inevitable conclusion that Shadow is the natural son of some unknown male. Sir John approves of the name, however, for he needs man "shadows" to complete his roster. So Simon becomes the second recruit.

Thomas Wart, the third to be considered, does not pass muster; he is far too ragged—a "very ragged wart," indeed.

Francis Feeble next steps forth and is identified as a woman's tailor. Falstaff ironically observes that he will be "as valiant as the wrathful dove or most magnanimous mouse." He is accepted as the third recruit.

Then comes Peter Bullcalf, protesting that he is a "diseased" man. But his explanation that he had caught cold while ringing bells on Coronation Day does not help him. Falstaff curtly states that Peter will "go to the wars in a gown"—that is, whether he is sick or not.

Shallow interrupts to invite Sir John to dine with him, but Falstaff politely refuses, adding that he is most happy to see his old friend. With this cue, the harmlessly vain justice recalls more wild episodes in which the two had been involved during their student days. At last Silent manages to say something. He remarks that fifty-five years have passed since his kinsman was at Clement's Inn. Humoring Justice Shallow, Falstaff exclaims, "We have heard the chimes ring at midnight," and he leaves the stage in company of the two.

Immediately both Peter Bullcalf and Ralph Mouldy offer money to Bardolph to secure their release from duty. Peter argues that he is not concerned about himself; it is just that he does not want to go to the wars. In fact, he would rather be hanged. Ralph has a better reason. His wife is old and needs his help. Surprisingly, the "most forcible Feeble" proves to be the soul of courage. "A man can die but once," he declares, and adds that "no man's too good to serve his prince."

When Falstaff and the justices return, the knight is pleased to learn that Bardolph has had three pounds from Peter Bullcalf and Ralph Mouldy. He acts promptly. Although Shallow includes the names of these two in his list of those selected, Falstaff releases them. The perplexed justice cannot understand why, but Sir John makes every thing clear: spirit, not appearance, is the test. Ragged Wart (rejected earlier), thin-faced Shadow, and Francis Feeble — they are the men for him. Ralph must be a man of spirit, since he obviously has nothing else. As for Shadow, the enemy will find him a very poor target. And Feeble, fleet of foot, will prove first-rate for retreating.

Satisfied with this explanation, Shallow once more reminisces about the good old days. Then Falstaff expresses his thanks to both justices and orders Bardolph to give coats to the new recruits. Shallow urges the knight to return and renew their old friendship, and Falstaff commands his corporal to march the men away.

In soliloquy, Falstaff makes it clear that he will indeed return to capitalize on the credulity of Shallow, whom he describes as an inveterate teller of tall tales about the past. He had remembered the justice as one who was "like a man made of cheese paring." And yet, says Falstaff to himself (and to the audience), this same Shallow is now a squire who speaks familiarly of John of Gaunt. He will prove an easy victim; Falstaff will "snap him up."

CHARACTERS IN SCENE 2

FALSTAFF—The audience now witnesses Sir John as he carries out, in his own way, initial duties as a royalist leader. It will be recalled that in *Henry IV, Part I,* he had performed the same task; but the actual recruitment was not dramatized. As he led his ragged army to Coventry, he said to Bardolph (IV.ii.12-15):

> If I be not ashamed of my soldiers, I am a soused gurnet. I have misused the King's press damnably. I have got, in exchange of a hundred and fifty soldiers, three hundred and odd pounds.

Now Shakespeare lets the audience see exactly how the artful Falstaff capitalizes on his commission to raise troops. After all, had Sir John not said that "a good wit will make use of anything?" Yet however much one may deplore Falstaff's action, he cannot avoid being vastly entertained by the wit and ingenuity. And so with the suave manner in which the knight manages his old school fellow, the gullible Justice Shallow.

JUSTICE SHALLOW—Robert Shallow, a country squire—that is, a well-born member of a prosperous county family, whose title (esquire) places him just below the rank of knight. He flourishes as justice-of-the-peace in Gloucestershire, the small county just south of Shakespeare's Warwickshire. Advanced in years, as is Falstaff himself, he lacks Sir John's incisive mind and spirit of perpetual youth. He has reached the stage where he lives much in the past, and it is his loquaciousness and uncertain re-creations of the past which result in good comedy.

JUSTICE SILENT—Shallow's admiring kinsman and fellow justice-of-the peace, whose inarticulateness provides comic contrast to the volubility of Shallow.

BARDOLPH—Falstaff's serving man, now a corporal, whose value to his master is well established in this scene.

RALPH MOULDY—The first recruit examined by Falstaff. He is identified as a member of a good, substantial family and can afford to buy his way out of service in the army.

SIMON SHADOW—The second recruit who is so thin that he is no more than a shadow of a man, and one of no family whatsoever.

THOMAS WART—The pathetically thread-bare third man to be examined by Falstaff.

FRANCIS FEEBLE—The fourth recruit, a woman's tailor, and therefore hardly a manly type. He nevertheless speaks more courageously than any of the others.

PETER BULLCALF—The bovine last recruit to be called up. His timidity provides an amusing contrast to the valor of Francis Feeble.

PURPOSE OF THE SCENE

1. To present Falstaff in his capacity as one of the King's officers exercising his commission to raise troops.

2. To introduce and develop two new, original comic characters, Shallow and Silent.

3. To prepare for one of Falstaff's later escapades which will be carried out at the expense of Justice Shallow.

4. To satirize actual malpractice relating to the recruiting of soldiers in Elizabethan England.

SUGGESTED QUESTIONS

1. What is revealing in the fact that Sir John Falstaff had been a page in the household of the Duke of Norfolk?

2. What is the point of Falstaff's remark on Silent's name: ". . . it well befits you should be of the peace"?

3. Aside from his youth and good physical condition, why should Falstaff be especially pleased to have Ralph Mouldy presented as a recruit?

4. What does Falstaff mean when he says ". . . we have a number of shadows to fill up the muster book" (lines 145-146)?

A C T   I V – S C E N E   1

SYNOPSIS

At Gaultree Forest in Yorkshire, the rebel leaders await the return of scouts who have been sent out to ascertain the size of the royal forces led by Prince John of Lancaster. The Archbishop of York tells his lieutenants, Mowbray and Hastings chief among them, that he has received more news from Northumberland. The Earl has written that, since he has been unable to raise a large force as befits his rank, he has retired to Scotland to wait until times are more favorable. He has only good wishes to offer the rebel leaders.

A messenger then reports that the royalists, in good formation and 30,000 strong, are no more than a mile to the West. Mowbray, noting that the insurgent's own estimate of size has thus been confirmed, is anxious to meet the enemy at once.

The Earl of Westmoreland enters. He brings greetings from his "general the Prince, Lord John and Duke of Lancaster," and a message for the Archbishop. But first he has words of reproach for the latter: why has the "Reverend Father," a man of position, learning, age, turned rebel? The Archbishop concisely states his case. Using the metaphor of "disease," he indicts the rule of Henry IV and argues that the same affliction had fatally infected the deposed and now dead Richard II. He further argues that, so far from being an enemy of peace, he is one that seeks redress of grievous wrongs. He complains that, although articles of grievance had been offered to the King, false counsellors had seen to it that no audience had been granted.

When, asks Westmoreland, had the appeal been denied? Who had stood in the Archbishop's way? In a word, he argues that there is no valid reason for such a gross misuse of high ecclesiastical office. The Archbishop then charges that Henry IV had been responsible for the death of his brother. But the Prince's emissary insists that Scroop has no need for personal redress. Mowbray breaks in to say that *all* need redress of grievances. Westmoreland goes as far as to concede that, in view of the general lawlessness, some injustices may have been inevitable. But he denies that the King is to be held responsible. He goes on to point out that the title and the estates of Mowbray's father (Duke of Norfolk) had been restored. The mention of his father's name leads Mowbray to recall the quarrel between the late Duke and Bolingbroke, now Henry IV, which had led to the banishment of both parties. He insists that, had Richard II permitted them to settle their differences in the lists of Coventry, Richard would not have lost his crown and life. But Westmoreland will have none of this. According to him, if the late Duke of Norfolk had defeated Henry in single combat, he would not have lived to leave Coventry, so great was public opinion aligned against him and in favor of Henry. All this, he adds, is mere digression. He has come to learn exactly what are the complaints of the rebels and to inform them that Prince John not only will give them audience, but, if the demands are just, great prompt redress.

Mowbray voices the first of his suspicions, arguing that this offer may be a trick. Westmoreland insists that it is an honest one, the motive for which is mercy, not fear. The royal army, confident and strong, he states, is better led than is that of the rebel leaders. In reply to a question by Lord Hastings, he assures them that, as the King's general, Prince John has full authority to act in this serious matter.

Having listened to arguments on both sides, the Archbishop requests Westmoreland to take the articles of grievance to the Prince. He promises that, if each is satisfactorily settled, the insurgents will disband. Westmoreland agrees to do so, and says that the decision will be made while both armies await within eyesight.

Again Mowbray objects. He is sure that the King will not forget their action against him and will find an excuse to punish them. But the Archbishop shares Hastings' optimism. He believes that Henry is tired of "petty" grievances and has learned that the death of one traitor leads to the birth of two others. Moreover, he argues, Henry is well aware that those who oppose him are closely allied to his friends; he dares not offend the latter. Hastings adds that, having had to commit forces elsewhere in the kingdom, Henry is now a "fangless lion." Further to conciliate the wary Mowbray, the Archbishop assures him that, if the peace does not endure, the rebel power will be all the greater.

So when Westmoreland returns with the information that John of Lancaster will meet the insurgent leaders at a place equidistant between the two armed camps, the Archbishop and his lieutenants leave promptly. "My lord, we come," are the Archbishop's final words.

CHARACTERS IN SCENE 1

THE ARCHBISHOP OF YORK — Richard Scroop, now full established as the leading spirit among the insurgents. It is he who had drawn up the articles of grievances; it is he who, after listening to opposing points of view, makes the command decision. His address to Westmoreland, as well as his success in raising a large army, emphasizes his status as a formidable opponent.

MOWBRAY — Thomas, second Duke of Norfolk and Earl Marshal of England, who, as in Act I, Scene 3, remains the cautious, skeptical leader among the rebels. But if he is dubious as regards human motives and performance, he remains confident that the rebels can defeat the royal forces.

HASTINGS — Edward, Lord Hastings, whose optimism regarding the possibility of a bloodless settlement of issues approaches wishful thinking. He serves as a foil to Mowbray in the debate at Gaultree Forest.

WESTMORELAND — Richard Neville, Earl of Westmoreland, second in command to Prince John. Here he functions as the Prince's emissary, just as Sir Walter Blunt had done for the King prior to the Battle of Shrewsbury. Like Sir Walter, he is the voice of political orthodoxy, summing up the royalist arguments against the rebel leaders.

CHARACTERS NOT PRESENT BUT MENTIONED

HENRY BOLINGBROKE AND THE EARL OF HEREFORD — The name and title of Henry IV prior to his coronation.

PRINCE JOHN — John of Lancaster, third son of Henry IV and leader of the royal army. He is referred to also as "our Princely General" and as "Lord John and Duke of Lancaster."

THE KING (referred to by Mowbray in his address to Westmoreland) — Richard II.

34

PURPOSE OF THE SCENE

1. To advance the action in the mainplot, bringing the major issues to a head and pointing to the possibility of an amicable settlement.

2. To clarify the respective arguments of the insurgents and of the royalists.

3. To provide a review of antecedent action, going back to the quarrel between the first Duke of Norfolk and Henry Bolingbroke, the man who now rules England.

SUGGESTED QUESTIONS

1. Why is the Archbishop convinced that Prince John will honor the conditions of peace demanded by the rebels?

2. Why is Mowbray convinced that the rebels will not be safe under any conditions?

3. What is meant by "well-appointed" in the Archbishop's reference to the newly arrived Westmoreland (line 25)?

A C T   I V – S C E N E   2

SYNOPSIS

Prince John of Lancaster courteously greets Mowbray, the Archbishop, and Hastings as the three arrive for the parley arranged by Westmoreland. As his emissary had done in the previous scene, the Prince deplores the fact that chief among the enemies of the Crown is the Archbishop of York, who appears not in the vestments of his religious calling nor in the act of explaining God's Word to his flock, but in armor and in the act of "turning the word to sword and life to death." The Archbishop concedes that he now appears in an unnatural form, but insists that he is not the King's enemy. He repeats his earlier argument: the articles of grievance which he had sent to the Court never received consideration; if those "most just and right desires" are honored, the insurgents will prove their loyalty to the King. Mowbray interposes the statement that, if the wrongs are not righted, the rebels stand ready to fight to the last man. Hastings adds that they have reinforcements to back up their demands and warns that, if the parley fails, members of their families will take up the quarrel. Prince John expresses doubt that Hastings possesses the wisdom and power to see into the future, and then, at Westmoreland's suggestion, gives his decision regarding the articles of grievance. He states that he is well pleased with them and insists that his father is not to blame for any injustice: the royal intentions have been misunderstood and some officials misused his authority. The Prince vows that "these griefs shall be with speed redressed." If the rebel leaders accept his assurance, he continues, "let the armies be disbanded at once and peace and friendship restored."

The Archbishop is quick to take John of Lancaster at his word, and Hastings promptly orders a captain to report the news to the rebel troops: "Let them have pay, and part." The leaders of the opposing factions now exchange courtesies. When shouts from the jubilant rebel forces are heard, Mowbray states that the sound would have been pleasing if it had signaled a victory.

The Prince orders Westmoreland to see to it that the royal troops are disbanded and then asks that the rebels pass in review before their dismissal. Hastings leaves to make the arrangements for carrying out the request. Westmoreland reappears and reports that, since the men had been ordered by the Prince to stand fast, they will not leave until they receive direct orders from him. "They know their orders," says the Prince significantly.

When Hastings returns with the news that the men had lost no time in leaving for their homes and places of amusement, Westmoreland immediately declares that Hastings, Mowbray, and the Archbishop are under arrest for treason. Orders are also given for the apprehension of any stragglers among the dispersed rebel forces. Protests regarding justice and honor and good faith are of no avail. The Prince bluntly tells them that he had pledged no more than a redress of grievances — a pledge which he will keep. As for the three leaders, he concludes, let them expect to receive the punishment which awaits all traitors. "God, not we, hath safely fought today," he adds as he orders the traitors to be brought to the "block of death."

CHARACTERS IN SCENE 2

PRINCE JOHN OF LANCASTER — Third son of Henry IV and general of the royal forces. He appears here as a Machiavellian figure, one who will use any means to achieve his purpose. As was stated in the introduction above, his apparent perfidy seems inexcusable to modern audiences. To them he emerges as a hypocrite. Certainly it would be more pleasing to see him manifest the chivalry and courage which marked his older brother's conduct at

Shrewsbury. It may be argued that Shakespeare was restricted by his source or sources, that he could not take gross liberty with history known to all literate members of his audience. Or it may be argued that, had John of Lancaster won a victory in honorable combat, he may well have emerged as the hero of the play. Finally, the historical approach must not be ignored in passing judgment on Prince John. According to orthodox Tudor political theory, which informs the chronicle history plays by Shakespeare and which was to a large extent based upon the Scriptures, the King was indeed God's deputy on earth—God's "substitute," as the Prince calls him (line 28). No subject for any reason had the right actively to oppose him. Just such promises as those made by the Prince were made to the rebels against Henry VIII in 1536. When the insurgent leaders accepted the King's promises for a redress of grievances and dismissed their followers, Henry VIII's officers arrested them as traitors, and they went to their deaths. At that time the question of perfidy was not even raised. Shakespeare's audiences, we may assume, were not offended by Prince John's action.

THE EARL OF WESTMORELAND—Ralph Neville, second-in-command of the royal troops and dependable instruments of Prince John's strategy.

THE ARCHBISHOP OF YORK—Richard Scroop, the courageous spirit of the northern insurgents, but a leader who is proved to be tragically gullible.

HASTINGS—Edward, Lord Hastings, who is the complete optimist, believing that the rebels will win a bloodless victory.

MOWBRAY—Thomas, second Duke of Norfolk, the realist among the rebel leaders, whose misgivings early and late regarding the intent of the royalists mark him as a man of keen insight.

CHARACTER NOT PRESENT BUT MENTIONED

THE KING—Henry IV, who, according to Prince John, is not to be held responsible for any injustices against his subjects.

PURPOSE OF THE SCENE

1. To provide the resolution to the main action as regards the dominant theme of rebellion.

2. To fill in the outlines of Prince John's character, actually in contrast to that of the heir apparent, Prince Hal. Prince John is depicted as a cold politician, a man who lacks the breadth and charm

of his older brother.

3. From a doctrinal point of view, to show that "Thus ever did rebellion find rebuke."

SUGGESTED QUESTIONS

1. How do you explain the metaphor used by the Archbishop when he refers to "this Hydra son of war" (line 38)?

2. What does Mowbray mean when, in reply to Westmoreland's toast, he makes the following comment (lines 79-80)?

You wish me health in very happy season,
For I am, on sudden, something ill.

A C T   I V – S C E N E   3

SYNOPSIS

Noise of armed conflict is heard as Falstaff and a stranger enter. In response to questioning, the latter identifies himself as Colevile of the Dale, a knight. Falstaff charges him with being a traitor who belongs in a dungeon. Asked if this is not Sir John Falstaff who addresses him, the fat knight goes no further than to say that he is as good a man; and he demands that Colevile surrender rather than suffer "fear and trembling." Colevile, convinced that this is Sir John, agrees to submit. His captor then reflects on the fact that his enormous girth always reveals his identity.

Prince John of Lancaster, the Earl of Westmoreland, and one Blunt arrive. The Prince orders the Earl to assemble the troops since the fighting is over, and then asks Falstaff where he had been, pointedly making reference to the knight's "tardy tricks"—his gift for turning up only when the danger is over. Falstaff is injured innocence personified. Heretofore, he states, he had not known that rebuke and check were the rewards for valor. He insists that he had exhausted many post horses in his dash to the battlefield. Now he is here, "in . . . pure and immaculate valor," the captor of a dangerous enemy. Comparing himself to Caesar, Falstaff concludes that he came, he saw, he conquered. But the Prince is sure that Colevile's courtesy, not Sir John's bravery, explains the capture. Falstaff remains Falstaff. As he turns Colevile over to the Prince, he demands that his valor be celebrated in a broadside ballad illustrated with a picture of Colevile kissing Falstaff's foot. Then he will be sure to get true credit, outshining all others. There follows a brief colloquy between the Prince and Colevile, who conducts himself with courage and dignity. Falstaff interrupts on three occasions, anxious to make good his latest fabrication.

Westmoreland returns to report that the Prince's orders have been carried out and the royal forces are now re-assembling. The Prince then orders his men to take Colevile and all other captives to York for immediate execution. Joined by his chief lieutenants, he himself will leave for Court, where his father lies ill. Falstaff asks permission to return by way of Gloucestershire and urges the Prince to report him favorably at Court. Bidding him farewell, John of Lancaster says that he will speak better of Falstaff than the knight deserves.

Alone, Falstaff soliloquizes. He is aware that Prince John has little use for him. And little wonder. This "sober-blooded boy" drinks no wine; all such abstainers are notorious weaklings—and usually fools and cowards. Falstaff then expounds the virtues he finds in sherris sack. According to him, it enters the brain, making a man lively, inventive, witty; it warms the blood, giving him courage; it illumines the face, which then serves as a beacon warning the whole man to arm himself. And this moves the heart to direct the performance of valorous deeds. Thus it is, Falstaff continues, that Prince Henry is valiant. Like Prince John, he had interited cold blood from his father, but good wine had transformed him. If Falstaff had one thousand sons, each would be taught the virtues of sack.

Bardolph enters and tells his master that all the soldiers have been discharged and dispersed. In effect, the knight says, "Good riddance." As for him, he will waste no time in seeking out Master Robert Shallow, whom he has already softened up for his purpose.

CHARACTERS IN SCENE 3

SIR JOHN FALSTAFF—Once more on the battlefield, Falstaff is presented in this scene which balances the one in *Henry IV, Part I,* wherein he claimed to have slain Hotspur. So well individualized is the knight that it would be misleading to reduce him to a type character. Nevertheless, one aspect of his complex character is that of the Braggart Warrior, a favorite in comedy dating back to Roman comedy and taken over into popular drama of Western Europe during the Renaissance. Some among Falstaff's admirers will argue that he does not expect to be believed, so patently false are his claims; and from that point of view is not a liar at all. At least one thing is indisputable, however: Falstaff again proves that "a good wit will make use of anything." His soliloquy on the virtues of sack is a justly famous bravura piece, completely in character.

SIR JOHN COLEVILE OF THE DALE—A representative of the upper class in northern England, many members of which answered the Archbishop of York's call to arms. His obvious good breeding and courage invite the sympathy of the audience.

PRINCE JOHN OF LANCASTER—However one may judge the Prince as a result of the ruse which led to the collapse of the revolt, it must be recognized that he is a firm, competent leader who moves relentlessly against enemies of the Crown. Aware of Falstaff's tricks, he does not hesitate to reprove the knight, but does not deign to engage in argument or raillery with him.

WESTMORELAND—Ralph Neville, Earl of Westmoreland, who continues to function as the Prince's dependable right-hand man.

BARDOLPH—Falstaff's serving man.

CHARACTER NOT PRESENT BUT MENTIONED

MASTER ROBERT SHALLOW, ESQUIRE—The justice-of-the-peace in Gloucestershire who assisted Falstaff in the recruitment of troops.

PURPOSE OF THE SCENE

1. To present Falstaff at his calling now in the rebellious north, showing how he executed his commission as one of the King's officers and thus to enlarge the comic characterization of the knight.

2. To provide Falstaff with the opportunity to explain once more his philosophy of life and, in the process thereof, to illuminate not only his own character but the characters of Prince Hal and Prince John as well.

3. To forge the link between main plot and comic subplot of the play.

SUGGESTED QUESTIONS

1. In what ways does Sir John Colevile of the Dale serve as a foil to Falstaff?

2. What does Falstaff exactly mean when he says, "Colevile shall still be your name..."?

3. Why does Prince John go so far as to say that he will report Falstaff better than the knight deserves?

ACT IV — SCENE 4

SYNOPSIS

King Henry IV lies ill in a room known as the Jerusalem Chamber. Two of his sons, Princes Thomas of Clarence and Humphrey of Gloucester enter with the Earl of Warwick and others. Addressing the group the King states that, if civil dissension has been surpassed and his health improves, he will lead the flower of England on a new crusade to the Holy Land. The ships and troops are ready for such an enterprise. He then asks Humphrey where Prince Henry is. The younger Prince can only reply that his elder brother may be hunting in Windsor Forest. Learning that Thomas of Clarence is present, the King then asks why he is not with his oldest brother, who always had favored Clarence. He urges him to cherish the affection so that he can help his brother when the latter assumes regal authority.

All this leads King Henry to comment on the heir-apparent's character: if Prince Hal is humored, he is gracious and kind of heart; if aroused he can be like flint. Therefore he must be carefully studied. The younger brother must reprove him when he is unduly mirthful, but must do so tactfully. In this way Clarence will prove to be a strong support to Prince Hal.

When the King learns that Hal is actually dining in the company of Poins and other lowly associates, he grieves for his son and heir, using the metaphor of "weeds" to describe those whom the Prince now seeks out. What will happen to England, he asks, if Hal's "headstrong riot has no curb?" Warwick speaks up and argues that the King misjudges his son. According to him, the Prince is schooling himself to understand even the lowliest subject. He predicts that Hal will "turn past evils to advantage." Sententiously the King expresses doubts about the probability of sudden reformation.

Westmoreland enters and is welcomed as the bearer of happy tidings. Harcourt immediately follows and reports that Northumberland and Lord Bardolph are captives of the Sheriff of Yorkshire. But such good news does not improve the health of the now physically weak King. All try to comfort him. Warwick is sure that he will soon recover. But Thomas of Clarence is more realistic. He points out that incessant care and labor have brought his father close to death. When Humphrey voices his concern about possible trouble among the King's subjects incident to the succession,

Thomas of Clarence is reminded that the river Thames had over-flowed its banks three times, just as it had done when Edward III lay at death's door. At last the King revives and asks to be removed to another chamber.

CHARACTERS IN SCENE 4

KING HENRY IV — After having heard several earlier references to the King's health, the audience now sees the ruler desperately ill in the Jerusalem Chamber. His concern about Prince Hal emphasizes one of the important conflicts in the play.

HUMPHREY OF GLOUCESTER — Youngest son of Henry IV, who survived to become regent of England for a time after the death of Henry V.

THOMAS OF CLARENCE — Second son of Henry IV, who became the trusted lieutenant of Henry V in the French Wars.

WARWICK — Richard de Beauchamp, Earl of Warwick, famous as a brave and chivalrous warrior who distinguished himself in the Welch wars and at Shrewsbury.

WESTMORELAND — Ralph Neville, Earl of Westmoreland, chief lieutenant to Prince John of Lancaster.

HARCOURT — An officer in the royal army.

CHARACTER NOT PRESENT BUT MENTIONED

PRINCE HENRY — The heir-apparent whose absence from his father's bedside makes understandable doubts about his real character. The King's words to Thomas of Clarence help to make clear the breadth and complexity of his character.

PURPOSE OF THE SCENE

1. To advance the important theme of the King's relations with his eldest son.

2. To add details concerning the character and reputation of Prince Hal and thus to prepare for the resolution of the play.

3. To provide additional exposition regarding the present state of the realm and the King's aspirations.

SUGGESTED QUESTIONS

1. What are the debits and credits in Hal's character as described by the King?

2. What does the King mean when he announces the intention of drawing "no swords but what are sanctified" (line 4)?

3. In what sense are "the old folk, time's doting chronicles" (line 126)?

A C T   I V – S C E N E   5

SYNOPSIS

Attending the ailing King is the same group who were present in the previous scene. Henry, oppressed by the respectful silence, asks for "some noise" and specifically for some music to minister to his weary spirit. As Warwick gives the order for music to be played in the next room, the King directs that his crown be placed on a pillow next to him.

Prince Henry enters and learns that his father is gravely ill and now disposed to sleep. All leave except the heir-apparent, who says he will keep watch at his father's bedside. Observing the crown, he philosophizes about it as a symbol of care and anxiety. On his father's lip he notices a feather which, he assumes, would not remain stationary if the King were breathing. He therefore concludes that his father has died. In soliloquy, the Prince states that he owes his father heart-felt grief and will pay the debt, and that his father owes him the imperial crown. Young Henry then lifts the crown and places it on his head, reflecting that just as he lawfully inherits it from his father, so he will pass it on to his heir and thus maintain unbroken the line of succession. He leaves the chamber through a door not leading into the one where the others await.

Suddenly awaking, the King calls for Warwick, Gloucester, and Clarence, who immediately enter. He learns that his eldest son has been in the chamber. Correctly assuming that Hal had taken the crown, he orders Warwick to find the heir-apparent and "chide him hither." To the King, his son's action is as great a cause of suffering as is the illness which has brought him close to death. He points the moral in words addressed to Gloucester and Clarence: gold leads sons to turn against fathers who have exercised every care in their training and welfare. Warwick returns to report that Prince Henry is in the next room washing tears of grief from his face. When the Prince enters, all others are asked to leave.

Prince Henry's first words are that he had not expected to see his father alive—words which the King interprets to mean that his son had hoped to find him dead. In a touching speech he reproves the Prince for being so impatient to wear the crown. Thus, says the King, the Prince has proved that he had no love for his father, and adds that unruly behavior all along had pointed to such a conclusion. He urges young Henry to dig his father's grave and order the ringing of "merry bells" announcing the crowning of a new ruler. As for himself, the King sadly concludes, let him be buried and forgotten. In despair Henry IV then predicts what he is sure will ensue: vanity and misrule will flourish; wise counsellors will be dismissed; "apes of idleness" and ruffians will flock to the court; the new ruler will give license to disorder and vice.

At last the Prince speaks. Had he not been choked by grief, he says, he would not have remained silent so long. Kneeling before the King, he declares that the crown belongs solely to his father, and he expresses the fervent hope that his father may live long to wear it. He assures the King that he respects Henry IV's honor and renown and remains his obedient subject. Prince Henry goes on to explain that he honestly believed that his father had died and that the very thought had chilled him to the heart. He insists that, if his words are false, he himself should not survive to realize his father's hope for reformation. Young Henry further explains that he had taken the crown, symbol of royal power and awful responsibility, and had upbraided it: the crown had fed upon the body of his father, and since it had "eaten the bearer up," other gold than that of the crown was to be more prized. At that moment, the Prince continues, he had placed the crown on his head—not with any thought of pride or pleasure, but as a kind of challenge to its tyrannical power. He concludes by saying that, if selfishness had motivated his action, he deserved to become like the poorest slave who kneels before the crown in awe and terror.

Obviously affected by Prince Henry's words, the King replies that God had led his son so to comfort him. He bids his son listen to his last words. Sorrowfully, the elder Henry admits that he had come to the throne "by . . . bypaths and crooked ways, as God knows," and had experienced a troublesome reign. But young Henry, he is sure, will fare better; for his son will wear a crown by right of succession. Old animosities will have died. Nevertheless, the King fears that his son will not be firm enough. He points out that, in order to forestall dissension among restive subjects, he had planned to lead a crusade to the Holy Land. The King then implores God to forgive him for deposing an anointed ruler (Richard II) and to grant that his son have a tranquil reign.

Prince Henry vows that, since his father won the crown, wore it, and gave it to him, he will defend it against all the world.

Prince John of Lancaster enters and greets his father. The King praises him for bringing "happiness and peace," but says that Prince John sees him fatally ill. Prince Henry promptly calls for Warwick, who enters with the others. When the King asks the name of the chamber where he "first did swoon," he learns that it is called Jerusalem. He recalls that, years earlier, it had been prophesied that he would die in Jerusalem, but he had assumed that the name referred to the Holy Land. Henry IV finally directs that he be carried to the chamber: "In that Jerusalem shall Harry die."

CHARACTERS IN SCENE 5

HENRY IV—Here the titular hero of the play emerges as a fully realized human being who wins the sympathy of all who behold and listen to him. He is above all the loving father, mourning because, now having reached the end of life, all the care he had bestowed upon his son and heir seems to have been wasted. Second, he is the conscience-stricken and penitent sinner, tormented by the knowledge that he had deposed an anointed ruler. He is sure that the civil dissension which characterized his reign and Prince Henry's waywardness are part of the punishment meted out by a just God. But his grief transcends the personal; he is deeply concerned for the safety and well-being of England.

PRINCE HENRY—The heir-apparent, misunderstood by his royal father as in the earlier play, finally vindicates himself in his father's eyes. If there are any doubts about the sincerity of his avowals, one should recall earlier evidence in this play pointing unmistakenly to young Henry's genuine affection and respect for his father. In this scene, Shakespeare takes special care to prepare the way for the Prince's rejection of Falstaff.

HUMPHREY OF GLOUCESTER—Youngest son of Henry IV.

THOMAS OF CLARENCE—Second son of Henry IV.

JOHN OF LANCASTER—Third son of Henry IV.

WARWICK—Richard de Beauchamp, Earl of Warwick and trusted counsellor of Henry IV.

SUGGESTED QUESTIONS

1. Aside from the reason given by Henry IV himself, why may he have been so anxious to lead a crusade to the Holy Land?
2. What examples of irony do you find in this important scene?
3. To whom and to what does the King refer in lines 205-207?

And all my friends, which thous must make
　　thy friends,
Have but their stings and teeth newly ta'en out,
By whose fell working I was first advanced. . . .

A C T　V — S C E N E　1

SYNOPSIS

At his home in Gloucestershire, Master Robert Shallow insists that Sir John Falstaff remain his guest for the night and hospitably refuses to accept an excuse. He calls for Davy, one of his servants, and in his bumbling manner proceeds to give him instructions. Here the immediate source of the comic effect is incongruity and anticlimax. Orders and reports relating to preparations for dinner are mixed with those relating successively to planting wheat, a bill received from a blacksmith, the repairing of a chain for a well bucket, and fining the cook for losing sack at a local fair. Finally Davy is told that Falstaff ("the man of war") will stay all night. As the justice says, it is a good thing to have a friend at Court. Davy is instructed to treat Sir John's men well, for they are "arrant knaves" and may "back-bite." The term "back-bite" gives Davy the chance to pun on the fact that all of Falstaff's men wear soiled linen infected with vermin.

Although dismissed, Davy remains to intercede on the behalf of one William Visor, who is to appear in a law suit before the Justice. He agrees that Visor is an arrant knave (one of Shallow's favorite expressions), but argues that, in view of his eight years of service he — Davy — should be allowed to gain special consideration for a knave who is an honest friend. Shallow says that Visor will not suffer and again dismisses Davy.

After greeting Bardolph and the page, the Justice invites Falstaff to follow him. Sir John gives orders to his servants and remains alone on the stage long enough to express his thoughts on the comic appearance of Shallow and to make some unflattering comments on the character of the Justice and of those who serve him. Shallow, it is clear, is as thin as his kinsman, Silent. If Sir

John were cut into staffs he would make no less than four dozen, each the size of Shallow. And if Falstaff had a case to be tried before the foolish Justice he would go to work on the servants. He concludes with the moral reflection that all men should be careful of the company they keep if they are to avoid boorish behavior. Finally, plump Jack says that he will have enough fun at Shallow's expense to entertain Prince Hal continuously for a year. He then answers the Justice's call and leaves the stage.

CHARACTERS IN SCENE 1

ROBERT SHALLOW—The country Justice who once more provides excellent comedy of physical appearance and words. If some are inclined to feel that Falstaff is taking advantage of a well-meaning friend, it is well to note that Shallow's insistence that Sir John remain his guest is not motivated wholly by unselfishness, and that the Justice's conduct on the bench is not exactly faultless.

SIR JOHN FALSTAFF—The fat knight, in constrast to Shallow, now appears as the urbane courtier and soldier. Content for a time to observe and listen, he is a keen judge of and commentator on what he sees and hears. His comic portrait of the emaciated Shallow, his shrewd remarks on the circumvention of justice, and his anticipation of the fun to be had at Shallow's expense —all are entirely in keeping with his own character.

DAVY—Shallow's serving man who indeed has become much like his master in many ways, as Falstaff observed.

BARDOLPH—Falstaff's serving man.

THE PAGE—Falstaff's diminutive servant.

CHARACTERS NOT PRESENT BUT MENTIONED

WILLIAM—Shallow's cook.

WILLIAM VISOR OF WONCOT—One of the principals in a suit to be tried before Justice Shallow.

CLEMENT PERKS—The second principal in a suit to be tried before Justice Shallow.

PRINCE HARRY—Prince Henry, or Hal.

PURPOSE OF THE SCENE

1. To develop the comic character of Justice Shallow, particularly as it is revealed in the dialogue with Davy and in Falstaff's soliloquy.

2. To advance the comic subplot wherein Falstaff continues to be pre-eminent.

SUGGESTED QUESTIONS

1. In what ways does Dave prove to be much like his master?
2. What is ironical in Falstaff's observation that "It is certain that either wise bearing or ignorant carriage is caught, as men take diseases, one of another" (lines 83-85)?

A C T   V — S C E N E   2

SYNOPSIS

In the palace at Westminster, Warwick greets the Lord Chief Justice of England. Learning that Henry IV has died, the latter expresses the wish that he had not outlived the King, in whose service he inevitably made some enemies. Warwick, aware of what the Justice has in mind, agrees that Henry V will be strongly prejudiced against him. The Chief Justice can add only sad words of resignation to fate.

The Princes Lancaster, Clarence, and Gloucester enter with Westmoreland. Observing them, Warwick expresses regret that the new King has not the temper of even the least favored of his three brothers. If young Henry were like any one of his brothers, nobles who flourished when Henry IV was alive would not have reason to expect the worst. "Oh, God, I fear all will be overturned!" exclaims the Chief Justice.

After greetings are exchanged, Gloucester and Lancaster express sympathy for the Chief Justice. In the words of Lancaster, he stands "in coldest expectation." Clarence is sure that the Justice will now have to approve of Falstaff. The Chief Justice states that he had performed the duties of his high office honorably and impartially and that if the truth did not prevail he will join the late King in death.

Henry V enters with his attendants and is greeted by the Chief Justice. He notes the evidence of fear as well as sorrow and reassures his brothers. None, he says, should expect cruelty in his Court. His brothers properly grieve for their father as he does; but they have no other reason to be sad, for he will be both father and brother to them. Their replies are rather perfunctory ones, and Henry V is aware of their lack of confidence in him. Especially he knows that the Chief Justice expects to be castigated. To him young Henry now turns. When the Justice insists that the King has no just cause to hate him, Henry reminds him of how he, the immediate heir of England, had been rebuked and imprisoned by the Chief Justice. Can this be forgotten?

With dignity and eloquence the Chief Justice states his case. He had been the instrument of the King's justice; Prince Henry had dared to strike him in court, the "very seat of justice." If the new King wishes to reject the edicts of his father, let him have a son who will spurn the royal image in the same way. The Justice concludes by inviting Henry V to bring his charges against him.

Now Henry speaks with no less eloquence and dignity. He has only praise for the amazed legal official. He approves of every word the latter had said and bids him to continue to serve—to wield the sword of justice boldly, justly, impartially. Moreover, Henry V welcomes the wise counsel of this man whom he addresses as the "father of his youth."

Henry then assures his brothers that his wildness had died with his father—that is, as King he no longer would conduct himself in a manner which would invite censor. He points out that he had survived to prove how wrong were the doleful prophets who foresaw disorder and misrule when he came to the throne. He then gives the order for the assmebly of the high court of Parliament and announces his intentions of selecting the best counsellors. With them and the help of the Chief Justice he will provide England with a government unsurpassed for order and effectiveness. Neither Prince nor peer, he concludes, will ever have occasion to pray for a new ruler.

CHARACTERS IN SCENE 2

HENRY V—The now completely reformed Prince of the earlier scenes, who, to the surprise of all others present in this scene, is the personification of magnanimity and dedication to duty. It is to be recalled that from the very beginning of the two-part chronicle history Shakespeare prepared the way for this important scene in which the apparently wayward heir to the throne embraces order and justice.

THE LORD CHIEF JUSTICE—England's leading legal official who understandably expects to be severely reprimanded and removed from office. In his longest speech he succeeds in emphasizing his absolute dedication to royal service and order within the realm.

GLOUCESTER—Humphrey, Duke of Gloucester, youngest son of Henry IV.

CLARENCE—Thomas, Duke of Clarence, second son of Henry IV.

LAN CASTER—John, Duke of Lancaster, third son of Henry IV.

WARWICK—Richard de Beauchamp, Earl of Warwick, famous warrior and favored counsellor of Henry IV.

WESTMORELAND—Ralph Neville, Earl of Westmoreland.

CHARACTERS NOT PRESENT BUT MENTIONED

FALSTAFF—Sir John, who is identified implicitly as the symbol of wildness and disrespect for the law.

HENRY IV—The deceased father of the new King, in this scene referred to as Harry (by Henry V and by Warwick) and as His Majesty (by the Lord Chief Justice).

PURPOSE OF THE SCENE

1. To present the newly crowned Henry V as the youth who made good his promise to amaze the world by his reformation—or, better perhaps, showing himself publicly in his true colors. In this sense, he does "falsify men's hopes," to use the words he had spoken in soliloquy at the end of Act I, Scene ii, of the earlier play.

2. To provide the admirable Lord Chief Justice full opportunity to make the case for law and order in the State.

3. To complete the preparation for the rejection of Falstaff.

SUGGESTED QUESTIONS

1. What image is evoked when Henry V makes reference to the "balance and the sword" (line 103)?

2. What line or lines specifically point to the impending rejection of Falstaff?

3. In what political sense can Henry V be a father to the Princes?

ACT V – SCENE 3

In this fine comic scene, Shallow flourishes as the always amusing yet gracious country squire conducting Silent, Falstaff, Bardolph, and the page to his apple orchard, where everyone enjoys the pleasures of merry old rural England. Despite Shallow's insistence that all is barren and beggarly, there is obviously plenty, and especially plenty of good wine, of which all partake. Justice Silent, the man who had hardly a word to say in the earlier scene, is irrepressible as he bursts forth with one drinking song after another and is completely unrestrained in his remarks. Falstaff, already well fortified with sack, commends Shallow on his hospitality and Silent on his unexpected conviviality. Davy, now the ubiquitous serving man, darts in and out, seeing to it that everyone is served. "Lack nothing. Be merry," are the words of Shallow. And indeed all have an abundance and all are merry.

Davy announces the arrival of Pistol, who has hurried from the Court with momentous news. Falstaff, instantly alert, instructs Davy to admit him at once. Pistol indeed has important intelligence, but takes his time in conveying it. Sir John, he announces, is now "one of the greatest men of the realm." Silent, now very deep in his cups, expresses the opinion that one Goodman Puff is greater. And this gives Pistol the cue to explode as he denounces the harmless Silent as a "most recreant coward base." Still ranting, he finally manages to inform Falstaff that he has "happy news of price." Sir John, adopting the bombastic style, urges him to report it. Silent revives to sing lines from a Robin Hood ballad, and Justice Shallow interrupts to adjudicate. He says that there are two courses to follow – either reveal the news or conceal it. And he adds that he has "some authority under the King." "Which King?" demands Pistol. "Speak, or die." And Falstaff at last learns that Hal, his "tender lambkins," now rules England.

Sir John has visions of grandeur. He orders Bardolph to saddle his horse and excitedly promises Shallow and Pistol high honors. At this climactic moment, Silent, having passed out, is carried to his bed. Then Falstaff, announcing that he is "Fortune's Steward," commands Bardolph to take any available horse, for he, Sir John, "holds all the laws at his commandment." Blessed are his friends, he concludes, but woe to the Lord Chief Justice! Pistol, in his own extravagant style, adds his malediction on England's custodian of law and order as all leave the stage.

CHARACTERS IN SCENE 3

FALSTAFF – Sir John, completely at ease in a situation where he is afforded good food and an abundance of wine. He reaches the highest point in his career when he learns that Hal is King of England.

SHALLOW – Justice-of-the-Peace and squire of Gloucestershire, now flourishing as the expansive, affable host.

SILENT – Kinsman of Shallow and himself a justice-of-the-peace. Thanks to the virtues of wine, he becomes the life of the party.

BARDOLPH – Falstaff's serving man.

THE PAGE – Falstaff's little servant.

DAVY – Shallow's serving man.

PISTOL – One of Falstaff's cronies, here functioning as the messenger in the comic subplot. He is given a fine chance to employ startling expressions culled from the more sensational plays of the era.

PURPOSE OF THE SCENE

1. To bring to a climax the action of the comic subplot.

2. To provide, at the comic level, significant elements of contrast in relation to the main plot, notably the action in the preceding scene.

SUGGESTED QUESTIONS

1. Why is Falstaff so sure that the new King is "sick" for him?

2. What is implied by Falstaff's identification of himself with King Cophetua (line 106)?

3. Is there any special significance in the words of Silent's third ballad (line 77-79)?

A C T   V – S C E N E   4

SYNOPSIS

Two beadles draw the loudly protesting Hostess Quickly and Doll Tearsheet across the stage, not without difficulty. The Hostess insists that the Second Beadle has dislocated her shoulder and says that she would die to see him hanged. From the words of the First Beadle it is learned that Doll is to receive the punishment of a convicted prostitute – a public whipping. Already established as the mistress of invective, she has a choice collection of scurrilous epithets for him and claims that, as a result of his rough handling, she may lose her unborn child. The Hostess fervently expresses the wish that Sir John Falstaff were present: "He would make this a bloody day to somebody." But she also hopes that Doll does miscarry. The First Beadle scornfully remarks that, if Doll did so, she would have a full dozen cushions. Doll adds more invective and, ordered to move along, she demands to be brought to justice. The Hostess has not remained silent by any means. She deplores the alleged fact that such righteous people should suffer. Her last words inevitably include a malapropism.

CHARACTERS IN SCENE 4

HOSTESS QUICKLY—Owner of the disreputable Boar's-Head Tavern in Eastcheap. Now in dire straits, she continues to mix up words in a comic fashion.

DOLL TEARSHEET—Prostitute at the Boar's-Head, as voluble and scurrilous as ever.

BEADLES—Minor correction officers, responsible to local constables.

CHARACTER MENTIONED BUT NOT PRESENT

SIR JOHN—Falstaff, hero of Mistress Quickly and Doll Tearsheet.

PURPOSE OF THE SCENE

1. To contribute to the resolution of the comic subplot.
2. To show how order is being restored at all levels of society.

SUGGESTED QUESTIONS

1. Why should Hostess Quickly express the wish that Doll Tearsheet miscarry?
2. What does the First Beadle mean when he says to Doll: "If you do, you shall have a dozen cushions again" (lines 16-17)?
3. Why does the First Beadle call Doll a "she knight errant" (line 25)?

ACT V – SCENE 5
SYNOPSIS

Near Westminster Abbey, two grooms strew rushes on the streets, evidence that an important event impends. It is to be the Coronation of Henry V, as one of the grooms states. Falstaff enters with Shallow, Pistol, Bardolph, and the Page. He is all confidence as he assures the gullible Shallow that Henry will be overjoyed to see his old companion. He regrets that he had not had time to use part of the one thousand pounds he had gotten from Shallow: he and members of his group, stained by travel, need new liveries. But, he says, he had ridden hard day and night to prove his affection for the new King. At this point in the action Shallow is the complete yes-man as far as Falstaff is concerned, for he expects at least to be knighted. When Pistol reports that Doll Tearsheet is in prison, the confident Sir John promises to arrange for her prompt release.

Shouts and the sound of trumpets announce the arrival of King Henry V. Prominent among his followers is the Lord Chief Justice. Falstaff and Pistol greet the King effusively. Seeing the knight, Henry instructs the Chief Justice to reprove him. Falstaff, incredulous, again addresses Henry: "My King! My Jove! I speak to thee, my heart!" And then Henry speaks the chilling words: "I know thee not, old man." He lectures his old companion of earlier, carefree days severely, making reference to Falstaff's buffoonery, so indecorous in a white-haired old man; his gluttony; and his neglect of his soul. Warning Sir John not to reply to him "with a fool-born jest," he pronounces sentence, instructing the Lord Chief Justice to see that it is carried out. Falstaff is banished. He is not to come within ten miles of the King on pain of death. But Henry informs Falstaff that he will provide a competence so that the knight will not resort to trickery to raise money. Further, he states, Falstaff will not lack advancement if he truly reforms.

After the King and others leave, Falstaff and Shallow converse. Sir John admits that, so far at least, he has failed to earn the one thousand pounds his friend had given him. But he insists that he will arrange to see the new King privately and that Shallow will be given royal preferment. Shallow, however, is now completely disillusioned. Although Falstaff declares that the King was merely pretending to dismiss his old friend, Shallow remains unconvinced.

As the group are about to leave for dinner, Prince John and the Lord Chief Justice enter, accompanied by officers of the Crown. On the orders of the Chief Justice, Falstaff and his companions are led away to prison. Pistol, in character to the last, revives a Latin tag he had used on an earlier, happier occasion: fortune having deserted him, hope alone remains.

At the end of the scene, Prince John and the Lord Chief Justice hold the stage. Both express their approval of the King's actions. Finally, the audience learns that Henry has called for the assembly of Parliament and, in all probability, will soon lead an invasion of France.

CHARACTERS IN SCENE 5

FALSTAFF—The roistering companion of Henry's madcap days, described by the new King as "The tutor and feeder of my riots." The fat knight at last learns that his wit will not serve him. His basic lack of good judgment and, for that matter, his vanity, are clearly set forth in this scene.

HENRY V—The now completely reformed and dignified ruler of England. Here he is presented as the public justicer passing sentence on a leading representative of disorder in his kingdom. If he appears to some to be unduly cold and severe, it is to be recalled that he does not leave Falstaff destitute, nor does he close the door on the knight's possible restoration.

THE LORD CHIEF JUSTICE—Now one of the strong supports of a King determined to uphold the law, he remains the very symbol of order in the realm.

LANCASTER—Prince John, Duke of Lancaster, brother of Henry V.

SHALLOW—Robert Shallow of Gloucestershire, who has paid a steep price for his trust in Sir John Falstaff and for his own ambition to gain social advancement.

PISTOL—Falstaff's crony and "lieutenant."

CHARACTER NOT PRESENT BUT MENTIONED

DOLL—Doll Tearsheet, the unfortunate prostitute of the Boar's-Head Tavern and one of Falstaff's great admirers.

PURPOSE OF THE SCENE

1. To provide the resolution of the entire action, main plot and sub-plot, in a play the basic theme of which is disorder versus order.
2. To complete the picture of a reformed young Henry,

who now justifies himself by acts, not merely by promises.

3. To prepare the way for *The Life of King Henry the Fifth,* the next English chronicle history written by Shakespeare.

SUGGESTED QUESTIONS

1. Why does Henry V call for the prompt meeting of Parliament?

2. What does the King mean when he says to Falstaff: "...I do despise my dream" (line 55)?

3. What is the implication of the varied terms Falstaff uses successively in his address to the King (44-50)?

SUMMARIES OF LEADING CHARACTERS

HENRY IV — In this play the titular hero, who does not make his appearance until late in the play, although frequent reference is made to him, is much as he was in Act I, Scene 1, of the earlier play. He is a man worn by the cares and troubles of ruling an England torn by civil dissension. He is also a man who is tortured by the knowledge that he himself had been a rebel — that he had deposed Richard II and been responsible for his death. There is abundant evidence that he had been a strong leader, one gifted with the "specialty of rule," to use the sixteen-century term. This is apparent in the counsel he gives to Thomas of Clarence and more particularly to Prince Henry, and in the latter's words to his dying father. If he had aroused the animosities of Northumberland, Scroop, Mowbray and others, he nevertheless had attracted the unwavering loyalty of men like Westmoreland and Warwick. Henry is anything but the cold politician in this play. His concern for the welfare of England is very real and is reflected especially in his worry about the character of his son and heir. He has earned the affection and respect of Henry the younger, as of his three other sons. Nor must one ignore the import of the Lord Chief Justice's words of tribute to the man he long had served. But it is particularly as the grief-stricken father of a son whom he believes to be ungrateful and undisciplined that Henry IV makes his strongest appeal.

PRINCE HENRY — Although Hal appears chiefly in the scenes of the comic subplot, he is never the madcap youth who ignores responsibility. Instead, he is an unusually poised and gifted young man, the breadth of whose character is emphasized again and again. The key to understanding his behavior is, in large part, to be found in the Earl of Warwick's comforting words addressed to the despairing King (IV. iv. 67 ff.). The Prince chose to associate with Falstaff, Poins, and the rest of the riotous crew who made the Boar's-Head their headquarters as a part of his education for kingship. For this is the man who, as Henry V, will move freely among his encamped soldiers in France, conversing easily and understandingly with them. It comes as no surprise to the audience that he should honor the Lord Chief Justice and banish Falstaff. Nor were these actions intended as surprises. Even before Hal made his appearance in this play, the words of the Hostess point to the fact that he would tolerate no disrespect for the King. It will be recalled that he struck Falstaff for making derogatory remarks about Henry IV. In so doing, Hal was acting not only as a dutiful son but as a loyal subject. King Henry IV, convinced that his eldest son's "headstrong riot" will have no curb, acknowledges elements of superiority in Hal's character: the heir-apparent is gracious, sympathetic, charitable. Further evidence of his breadth is his capacity to criticize himself. Just as he is always aware of Falstaff's intentions, so he knows what are the implications of his own actions. Intellectual depth is apparent in his philosophical reflections on what the Crown entails, which are to be taken at their face value. Finally, the all-encompassing virtue of magnanimity in Hal's character is revealed in his solemn promise to his dying father and in his gracious speech to the Lord Chief Justice.

SIR JOHN FALSTAFF—The credits in Falstaff's character are sufficiently impressive, and one can understand why Prince Hal found him so entertaining. His brilliant wit and contagious high spirits make it altogether too easy, perhaps, to ignore the debits. Who is likely to forget such comic descriptions as those of the Gloucester recruits and of Justice Shallow, or such sparkling verbal exercises as his soliloquy on the virtues of wine? He cannot be dismissed as merely a buffoon. For one thing, he has a great fund of knowledge. In his spontaneous discourse he shows close familiarity with the Bible, secular literature, formal logic, music—indeed all the subjects appropriate to a member of the upper classes in Shakespeare's day. It is to be remembered that, as Justice Shallow said, Falstaff had been a page in the household of the first Duke of Norfolk, and that was one of the ways in which the sons of aristocrats were educated. Further, he had attended one of the law schools in London, the pre-requisite for which was university training. And he is *Sir* John Falstaff, a knight of the realm.

Yet Falstaff has chosen to close his eyes on the fact that rank has its obligations. If he indeed possesses much knowledge, he lacks wisdom, basic sound judgment. It has been said that he is a "knave without malice." But malice, or something very close to it, is apparent in his boastful exclamation after learning that Hal is now King of England: "...woe to my Lord Chief Justice!" Contempt for public justice is basic in his character, and it manifests itself not only in his attitude toward the Lord Chief Justice but in his capitalizing on the credulity of such lowly individuals as Mistress Ursula and Hostess Quickly. In the Bible, which Falstaff knew sufficiently well to include many allusions in his discourse, he may have read:

...he who possesses justice lays hold of her and she meets him as an honorable mother. With the bread of life and understanding she feeds him, and gives him the water of wholesome wisdom to drink...

(Ecclus. 15, 1-3)

But Falstaff preferred sack; he cared nothing for the water of wholesome wisdom. Little wonder, then, that he should be completely incredulous when Henry V denounces and banishes him.

Glutton, lecher, parasite, braggart, liar, "great fool," — each of these terms of opporbrium are applicable to Falstaff. However amusing he may be as, for a time, he flourishes as the privileged jester to the Prince, one cannot ignore this fact. It is typical of him that, while officers of the Crown wait for his leadership, he sends Bardolph to fetch Doll Tearsheet to him. For Falstaff, the incomparably amusing Falstaff, is a rebel — a traitor to law and order.

PRINCE JOHN, DUKE OF LANCASTER — The role of this third son of Henry IV is not one which invites the sympathy of modern audiences. But, like the Lord Chief Justice, in a different way, he is presented as the relentless foe of disorder in the kingdom. His determined attitude toward the northern insurgents and his sound estimate of Falstaff's behavior mark him as one devoted to public duty. He is not depicted as a warm, human person like his gifted elder brother, Prince Hal. But he must be recognized as a pillar of law and order. In this respect he fulfils his function in the play.

THE EARL OF WESTMORELAND — He is one of the characters who, in his capacity as Prince John's emissary to the rebels, functions as the voice of political orthodoxy in this play: no subject, however exalted, has the right to "lift an angry arm" against God's representative on earth, the King. Unflinchingly he carries out the order of his superior; it is he who places the rebels under arrest for treason at the end of the parley at Gaultree Forest in Yorkshire.

MOWBRAY — The second Duke of Norfolk is an astute and courageous warrior who had proved his worth. From one point of view his action contrasts with that of the pusillanimous Earl of Northumberland, who fears to commit himself in the struggle against

Henry IV. From another point of view, he provides a contrast to the unrealistic Lord Hastings and even the Archbishop of York, who in his optimism, rejects Mowbray's sound counsel.

THE EARL OF NORTHUMBERLAND—The elder Henry Percy is depicted as one who is at first determined to avenge himself upon Henry IV after the defeat at Shrewsbury and the death of his son. But he emerges as one who is concerned primarily about his own safety and welfare. His action of abandoning the Yorkshire rebels is consistent with his convenient absenting himself from the conflict at Shrewsbury, as dramatized in *Henry IV, Part I*.

THE ARCHBISHOP OF YORK—Richard Scroop is a man who owed his advancement to high ecclesiastical office to Richard II and who never forgets that Henry IV was the one who ordered the execution of his brother. He is the determined leader of the active rebel force in the north parts. But it is not merely personal grievances that motivate his bold challenge of the Crown. His consideration and acceptance of the terms offered by Prince John indicate that basically he is a man of good will, anxious to bring a just settlement to issues which have led him to rebel against the King.

LORD CHIEF JUSTICE OF THE KING'S BENCH—He is not without mellow good humor, as is evident in his first exchange with Falstaff in this play. Indeed, some commentators go so far as to say that he really enjoys plump Jack as much as anyone else. Yet basically he is the noble, serious pillar of the law, properly devoted to the execution of justice. That he had not hesitated to punish Prince Hal is sufficient proof of his moral courage. It will be noted that the newly crowned Henry V repeats the essential charges against Falstaff that the Lord Chief Justice had made earlier in the play. His courage is no less apparent in his apologia, spoken in the belief that the new King was about to excoriate him and remove him from office. Of all the characters in the play he is the one eminently fitted to be the "father" of King Henry V's youth.

WARWICK—Richard de Beauchamp, Earl of Warwick, remains almost constantly at the side of Henry IV, serving as the trusted and capable counsellor and attendant. In this play he is remembered especially for his insight into the character of Prince Hal when he seeks to reassure the troubled King. Yet late in the play he joins those who fear that Hal will not follow the wise path of his father.

LORD HASTINGS—One of the representatives of the northern aristocrats who actively opposed the rule of Henry IV, he proves to be a bad counsellor to the Archbishop of York, for he is over-confident and easily deceived by the royalist leaders. He thus provides an interesting contrast to the sagacious Mowbray.

BARDOLPH – Falstaff's serving man proves his worth to his master in numerous ways. Under instructions, he attempts to underwrite the knight's credit with tradesman; he is ready to draw his sword when Fang, the sheriff's officer, declares Falstaff to be under arrest; and he expertly carries out the business of accepting bribes from the Gloucestershire recruits. But his greatest contribution is his physical appearance. His flaming nose continues to inspire witty comment as it did in *Henry IV, Part I*.

PISTOL – A "humours" character, that is, one who has a special idiosyncrasy which makes him ridiculous, he serves as emissary to Falstaff, who ironically addresses him as "Captain Pistol." Perhaps some find his ranting rather monotonous, but there is sufficient evidence that Elizabethans were vastly amused by this broad satire on the verbal excesses in popular tragedies and melodramas. He reappears in *Henry V*. Doll Tearsheet, whose favors he had enjoyed, has the best epithets for him: he is "a swaggering rascal," a "fustian rascal," a "bottle-ale rascal." And, of course, he is a coward.

POINS – One of the regulars at the Boar's-Head Tavern, with whom Prince Hal chooses to associate for a time, he functions in this play much as he did in *Henry IV, Part I*. It is he who devises the plot to entrap Sir John Falstaff, who is jealous because the Prince shows Poins some favor. Poins is sufficiently skilful in witty conversation, but it is primarily his ingenuity in devising practical jokes that has attracted the Prince.

SHALLOW – Master Robert Shallow, Esquire, the Gloustershire justice-of-the-peace, is essentially a caricature – and a good one. He does share two things with Falstaff. He had been a student at one of the London law schools; and he is ambitious to capitalize upon his friendship. But there identity with Sir John ends. He indeed is a shallow man. One does not laugh with him, as one often does with Falstaff, but at him. The poverty of his mind is revealed time and again. For example, it is he who boasts of wild escapades in his youthful days, who is impelled to explain Falstaff's joke on Ralph Mouldy's name, and who pontificates when Pistol arrives with important news for Sir John. His vanity is no less apparent, again with reference to his alleged youthful wildness and in his reminding all present that he has some authority from the King. His garrulity, his uncertain memory of times past, and his tendency to introduce irrelevancies contribute notably to the comedy in this play. In his person Shakespeare also satirizes the country justice who makes the most of his local authority and is easily influenced by any close associate to modify legal decisions.

SILENT – Kinsman of the wispy Shallow, the bare-bones

Silent, himself a justice-of-the peace, provides an amusing contrast to the loquacious squire. At first he contributes nothing but unspoken admiration of Shallow. But later the wine extolled by Falstaff works its wonders, and Silent distinguishes himself as the singer of popular ballads and the frank commentator on Sir John himself.

MISTRESS QUICKLY—Hostess of the Boar's-Head Tavern and, according to Falstaff, a widow, she is among those victimized by Sir John. She endears herself to the audience chiefly because of her genius for misusing big words of which she is so fond. Despite the fact that the audience first meets her in this play in the act of demanding the arrest of Falstaff, the latter remains her hero. And her affection for him actually points to the fact that she also embraces disorder. Among other things, she is a procuress, and her protestations of respectability are rather pathetic. It is from this point of view that one should interpret the action in her last scene, wherein she is dragged off to prison.

DOLL TEARSHEET—Falstaff's Helen of Troy, as Pistol calls her, is another representative of unlicensed behavior. Prince Hal and Poins describe her accurately enough at the end of Act II, Scene 3. Indeed she "should be some road," one "as common as the way between St. Albans and London." If she reserves a special place in her affections for Falstaff, her favors remain for hire even to the likes of Pistol. She is generally depicted as a harridan addicted to shrill vocal outbursts.

GENERAL NOTES

DURATION OF THE ACTION

Shakespeare, the poet-dramatist, telescopes the events of history in this play as in the other chronicle-histories. If he did not do so he would not have achieved drama. Henry IV endured troubles with the Welsh and with France, which are referred to but not dramatized in this play, and with the Lollards (native religious protestants), and with Scotland. But he confines his attention for dramatic purposes to the northern insurgents. The following brief summary of the actual time schedule of historical events may give a good insight into the dramatist's method of adapting historical material to his purpose.

Rumors and authentic reports of what happened at Shrewsbury belong to the year 1403. Two years later the rebellion led by the Archbishop of York occurred. It was not until 1409 that, as recorded by Holinshed, Owen Glendower, leader of the belligerent Welsh, died. The meeting at Gaultree Forest in Yorkshire, followed by the arrest of the rebel leaders, took place in 1405. Three years later the Earl of Northumberland and Lord Bardolph were defeated by the royalists and sent to their deaths. King Henry IV fell ill in 1412 and survived until 1413. Shakespeare, obviously, compresses the events of years into a few weeks and days for "the two hours traffic" of his stage.

MEDIUM: VERSE AND PROSE

Shakespeare employs verse almost entirely in the serious parts of the play, and prose almost entirely elsewhere. Out of a total of 3446 lines, 1860 are in prose. This is a clear indication that, in contrast to *Henry IV, Part I,* the comic scenes are dominant, at least in playing time, in the later play which concerns us.

Blank verse, that is, unrhymed iambic pentameter, belongs especially to the main plot wherein the very fate of the realm is the issue. Such verse is necessarily formal, an idealization of ordinary discourse. One way in which the poet emphasizes the high rank of a given speaker and the seriousness of the immediate action is to employ this medium. Often it is highly rhetorical, as when the Earl of Northumberland gives way to grief and rage in Act I, Scene i. To apply the standrads of realistic and naturalistic discourse to such lines is to miss the point entirely. So elsewhere in the plot. Such formalization and idealizing are especially apparent in such speeches as those by Westmoreland and Prince John when they address the rebel leaders. Nor would it do to reject blank verse in the scenes in which Henry IV appears. But if such verse is often highly rhetorical, Shakespeare avoids the excesses which, indeed, he satirized, in the bombastic outbursts of Pistol. Moreover, at this advanced state in his creative life, he used blank verse with increasing freedom so as to provide a more natural tone to speeches. One way of doing this is to write lines which admit no pause at the end of the line. And this run-on effect is made possible especially by the use of terminal words which are not accented on the last syllable. Compare the following lines (IV. iv. 3-6):

We will our youth lead on to higher fields
And draw no swords but what are sanctified.

So far the pause is at the end of each line, and the last word is accented on the final syllable.

Our Navy is addressed, our powers collected,
Our substitutes in absence well invested...

In these lines, which immediately follow the first two, the final syllables are unaccented so that, despite the punctuation, the sense runs on from the first to the second line naturally, as in ordinary discourse.

A second way of avoiding excessive formality recommended itself to Shakespeare. Frequently a speech ends short of a complete line of verse, and the opening words of the next speaker complete the line. Consider the lines at the very beginning of the play:

> *L. Bar.* Who keeps the gate here, ho?
> Where is the Earl?
> *Por.* What shall I say you are?
> *L. Bar.*   Tell thou the Earl
> That the Lord Bardolph doth attend him here.

Rhymed iambic pentameter couplets are used eighty-four times in the play. They occur at the end of many speeches, as when Prince Henry refers to the crown in reply to his father (IV. v. 221-225):

> My gracious liege,
> You won it, wore it, kept it, gave it me.
> Then plain and right must my possession be,
> Which I with more than with a common pain
> 'Gainst all the world will rightfully maintain.

Typically, rhyming couplets are used at the end of the last speech in scenes of the main plot. Thus at the end of Act I, Scene I, Northumberland says:

> Get posts and letters, and make friends with speed.
> Never so few, and never yet more need.

The couplets provide special emphasis, a particular kind of climax; often they are epigrammatic.

By the time he came to write the *Henry IV* plays, Shakespeare habitually used prose for comic scenes. Falstaff, appropriately, is a speaker of prose. And when it is the comic element which is to the fore, Prince Hal and all others speak in prose. Since Falstaff is hardly the conquering hero, it would not do to have him use blank verse as the chief medium even in Act IV, Scene 3, wherein Sir John "captures" Colevile of the Dale; and addressing the knight, Prince John also speaks in prose. But, it will be noted, when the Prince turns to the Earl of Westmoreland, he shifts to blank verse. So elsewhere in the play, whenever serious matters relating to the main action are introduced. At the end of the comic tavern scene, Act II, Scene 2, Peto enters with important news for Prince Hal and Falstaff. He speaks lines of blank verse, as does Prince Hal in reply.

One should recognize that there is a wide range in the kinds of prose used in this play. Falstaff can be as colloquial as anyone. "Whose mare's dead?" he asks when he makes his first appearance in Act II, Scene 1. And he can more than hold his own with Prince Hal in sparkling prose that has the very rhythm and sophistication of upper class discourse. The fact that he often calls a spade a spade should not blind one to this fact. Take the following dialogue, for example (II. iv. 352 ff.):

> *Prince.*   See now whether pure fear and entire cowardice doth not make thee wrong this virtuous gentlewoman to close with us. Is she of the wicked? Is thine hostess here of the wicked? Or is thy boy of the wicked? Or honest Bardolph, whose zeal burns in his nose, of the wicked?
>
> *Poins.*   Answer, thou dead elm, answer.
>
> *Fal.*   The Fiend hath pricked down Bardolph irrecoverable, and his face is Lucifer's privy kitchen, where he doth nothing but roast maltworms. For the boy, there is a good angel about him, but the Devil outbids him too.

The ranting of Pistol, the billingsgate of Doll Tearsheet, and the simple, realistic talk of Shallow and Silence further illustrate the wide range in the prose style. So great is Shakespeare's reputation as premier poet that perhaps not enough credit is given to him as a writer of superior prose at all levels.

SIXTEENTH - CENTURY POLITICAL THEORY

Since *Henry IV, Parts I and II,* are political plays, it is necessary to understand the political doctrine behind them if one is to do justice to Shakespeare's intentions. Elizabeth I, the fifth Tudor to rule England, had come to a throne which was in many ways insecure because of rival claims. Henry VIII, her father, had found it especially necessary to inculcate the doctrine of absolute obedience to the Crown after the break with Rome in 1536. During his reign he had experienced the Pilgrimage of Grace, a rebellion in northern England; and later the Exeter Conspiracy, an alleged attempt to depose Henry VIII and to place a Yorkist on the throne of England. After Henry VIII's death, England endured the Western Rebellion of 1549. And during Elizabeth's reign there occurred the Rebellion of 1569, as well as plots against the Queen's life, notably the Babington Plot, which led to the trial, conviction, and execution of Mary, Queen of Scots. Throughout the century and beyond,

England had reason to fear an invasion and the rising of native Catholics: the danger was by no means restricted to the year 1588, when Philip II of Spain sent his Armada to subdue England. In view of such challenges to Tudor supremacy, there was a need of a political philosophy which would prevent challenges to royal authority and devastating civil war. The basic arguments were developed during the reign of Henry VIII and augmented as new crises arose during the reigns of Edward VI and Elizabeth I. It found expression in officially approved pamphlet and tract, and in belletristic literature, notably drama and non-dramatic poetry. Especially it was emphasized in official sermons, the first group of which was introduced in the year 1549. These included strongly worded instruction on the subject of obedience. They were augmented in 1570, following the Rebellion of 1569 and the papal decree of excommunication of Queen Elizabeth I. Every Englishman was required to hear the sermons on obedience three times during the year. The gist of the doctrine was this: the ruler was God's lieutenant on earth; no subject, however exalted, had the right actively to oppose him. To do so was a sin against religion, punishable by suffering here and now and by eternal damnation after death. Even if the ruler is a tyrant, the subject had no right to oppose him, for the head of the state was the anointed representative of God on earth. In support of this doctrine, appeals were made primarily to Biblical authority. Texts such as Romans xiii and Proverbs viii, as well as ones in the Gospel according to St. Matthew, were cited repeatedly. John of Gaunt, Duke of Lancaster, summed up the doctrine concisely in his response to his sister-in-law, the Duchess of Gloucester, who reminded him that the reigning King, Richard II, had been responsible for the death of her husband and Gaunt's brother:

> God's is the quarrel, for God's substitute,
> His deputy anointed in His sight,
> Hath caused his death. The which if wrongfully,
> Let Heaven revenge, for I may never lift
> An angry arm against his minister.
>   (*Richard II,* Act II, Scene 2, lines 37-41)

That Henry IV should so suffer is to be explained by the fact that he, son of John of Gaunt, did "lift an angry arm against [God's] minister." He endures rebellion; he sees the apparent waywardness of Prince Hal as part of his punishment; he does not live to lead a new crusade against the foes of Christianity and thus do penance for his grievous sins. But, according to sixteenth-century Tudor political theory, he wore the crown on God's sufferance, no one had the right to oppose him. All this should make understandable the words of indictment spoken first by the Earl of Westmoreland and later by Prince John to a high church dignitary who had turned rebel, the Archbishop of York. It should illuminate further the apparently despicable behavior of Prince John, who, after tricking the rebel leaders, sends each to death — even the admirable Sir John Colevile of the Dale. In Prince John's words, "God, and not we, hath safely fought today."

QUESTIONS AND ANSWERS

1. QUESTION: How would you describe the character of Henry V as he appears in Act V?

ANSWER: He is now the ideal ruler. In Scene 5 he assures his brothers that he will surround himself with wise counsellors and that his reign will be second to none in its reputation for justice and wisdom. It is his reconciliation with the Lord Chief Justice of the King's Bench, a man with whom he had had difficulties earlier, which is the dramatic representation of his avowed intentions. In his rejection of Falstaff, we have complete evidence that he will indeed govern in accordance with the principles of law and order.

2. QUESTION: What evidence do we have of Shallow's ambitions to become at least a knight of the realm?

ANSWER: He is first presented as the local big-wig, now in his dotage, who boasts of his youthful exploits and who is something of a name-dropper. He speaks of his comradeship with Sir John Falstaff, who was once a page in the household of the eminent first Duke of Norfolk. On Falstaff's testimony we know that he speaks glibly of John of Gaunt, son of Edward III and father of Henry IV. He is indeed the affable host, but he obviously has an axe to grind. The dead give-away is the snatch of song sung by Silent (V. iii. 77-79):

Do me right,
And dub me knight.
Samingo.

And it is Shallow himself who assures Silent that it is well to have a friend who is influential at Court, and he is at pains to make it clear that he is "under the King, in some authority."

3. QUESTION: What is Falstaff's defense of himself and of his way of life?

ANSWER: At least an entire chapter could be written on this subject, but in brief the following are essential points. First, he correctly states that he is "not only witty in [himself] but the cause of wit in other men." To the Lord Chief Justice he insists that he is indeed old, but only in wisdom and judgment, the fruits of long experience. As the intimate of the heir-apparent, he knows how to amuse the Prince. Reflecting on how he will gull Justice Shallow and how he will use this experience to regale the Prince and thus maintain his status as privileged jester, Falstaff reflects that "a lie with a slight oath and a jest with a sad brow will do with a fellow that never had an ache in his shoulders"—that is, a young man unafflicted with rheumatism.

4. QUESTION: What are the functions of the soliloquies in this play and who speaks them?

ANSWER: The soliloquy is one of the long-lived conventions of drama which Shakespeare found particularly useful. The term itself comes from the Latin word *solus,* meaning "alone." A character in a play may occupy the stage alone and speak his thoughts for the benefit of the audience. Thus the audience may be given a penetrating insight into the character of the speaker or may learn the motives for an action. Again it may provide a commentary on the character of others in the play or give details relating to antecedent action.

Both Falstaff and Prince Hal deliver soliloquies. Sir John's first one appears at the end of Act I, Scene 1, and is just six lines long. But from it we get a good insight into his character: he is a man who is confident that his wit will make it possible for him to capitalize even on afflictions. Elsewhere (III.ii.323 ff. and V.ii. 69-95), his prose soliloquies tell us a great deal about Shallow and just as much about himself. His greatest and longest soliloquy occurs near the end of Act IV, Scene 3 (lines 92-135). This is his rilliant discourse on the virtues of wine, in which Falstaff contributes much to the understanding of Prince Hal and Prince John.

Prince Hal's memorable soliloquy occurs in Act IV, Scene 5, as he contemplates the crown resting on a pillow near his sleeping father. From his words we understand his true motive for removing the crown and placing it on his head and an insight into the serious side of the Prince's character. Further, we are made increasingly aware of the great responsibilities which he must face when he becomes King of England.

5. QUESTION: What does Prince Hal mean when he says to Poins: "Let the end try the man" (II. ii. 50)?

ANSWER: A man must be judged by the final outcome of his actions. In this line Shakespeare gives the audience a clear indication of the Prince's intentions. It is one of the passages which look forward to the rejection of Falstaff.

6. QUESTION: What is the purpose of the epilogue to the play?

ANSWER: Traditionally, an epilogue is the last division of a formal speech. In plays it is usually added as the plea of an actor for sympathetic treatment by the audience. Shakespeare used seven epilogues; but the one in *Henry IV, Part II,* is unique because it contains an apology. From the lines spoken by the Dancer, it is apparent that an unidentified play had given offense by introducing the name of Sir John Oldcastle, an actual historical personage whose descendants survived. This was Falstaff's earlier name, and it survives, in a sense, when Prince Hal addresses Sir John as "my old lad of the castle" *(Henry IV, Part I,* Act I, Scene 2, lines 47-48). Of interest also is the fact that, according to the Epilogue, Shakespeare originally planned to find a place for Falstaff in his next chronicle history play, *Henry V.* When he came to write that play, however, he did no more than to report Falstaff's death.

7. QUESTION: What reason had Henry IV to be now confident, now disconsolate as regards his successor?

ANSWER: He takes comfort in the knowledge that his son will inherit the crown from the father. He is convinced that those who personally opposed him, knowing that Richard II had willed the throne to Edmund Mortimer, will not oppose a king who was not guilty of usurpation. But in view of Prince Hal's lapses in conduct after the Battle of Shrewsbury and his return from Wales, he feels that his son will make mistakes as fatal as those which cost Richard II life and crown.

8. QUESTION: What is the meaning of the following lines of advice spoken by King Henry IV to Thomas of Clarence (IV.iv.41-48):

> Learn this, Thomas,
> And thou shalt prove a shelter to thy friends,
> A hoop of gold to bind thy brothers in,
> That the united vessel of their blood,
> Mingled with venom of suggestion—
> As, perforce, the age will pour it in—
> Shall never leak, though it do work as strong
> As aconitum or rash gunpowder.

ANSWER: The King has urged Thomas of Clarence to study the complex character of the heir-apparent, who particularly favors him. The image in this passage is that of a cask. Thomas' other brothers are the staves and Thomas himself is the hoop which holds them together. The "venom of suggestion" is the malicious accusations and slanders of the envious. Such "venom" will test the strength of the cask, which should be able to withstand weather, poison, or discharge from weapons.

9. QUESTION: Compare the characters of the Earl of Northumberland and the Archbishop of York.

ANSWER: The Earl breaks forth in stormy passion when he learns of the defeat and his son's death at Shrewsbury, and it would seem that nothing will stop him from seeking revenge at once. Actually, however, he is a man who talks bravely enough on occasion but fails miserably when put to the test. Shakespeare followed Holinshed in suggesting that the Earl remained "crafty sick" at Warkworth Castle rather than joining his son and his brother at Shrewsbury. Although he had given his solemn pledge to lead forces in support of those raised by the Archbishop of York, he is easily persuaded to fly to Scotland and to remain there until he learned how the Yorkist rebels fared. The inescapable conclusion is that the Earl of Northumberland depends upon outward show and lacks basic integrity.

In contrast, the Archbishop of York, however mistaken he may be in his efforts and wrong in his judgment as regards Prince John's intentions, is a courageous and honest man. It is true that he had a personal grievance against King Henry IV, who had been responsible for the execution of his brother. But as Shakespeare depicts him, the Archbishop's reasons for leading an armed revolt transcend personal issues. This is evident in the fact that he had prepared articles of grievances and endeavored to get redress prior to the rising, and that he readily accepted the terms offered by Prince John. There is no indication that lack of confidence in the strength and ability of the rebel force led him to capitulate. He received the news of Northumberland's flight without thought of retreat. Finally, he had won and held the loyalty of such men as Mowbray, Lord Hastings, and Sir John Colevile of the Dale.

10. QUESTION: What is the meaning of Shallow's reference to himself as once having been "Sir Dagonet in Arthur's show"?

ANSWER: Arthur's show was an archery exhibition put on by a group of men who assumed the names of King Arthur's knights. Since Sir Dagonet was the court fool in the Arthurian stories, it is only fitting that Shallow should have had that name.

NOTES

NOTES

NOTES

NOTES

HENRY V

NOTES

including
- *Life of Shakespeare*
- *Background of* Henry V
- *Genealogical Tables*
- *Plot Summary of* Henry V
- *List of Characters*
- *Summaries and Commentaries*
- *Sixteenth-Century Political Theory*
- *Questions for Review*
- *Selected Bibliography*

by
Jeffery Fisher, M.F.A.
University of Tennessee

INCORPORATED

LINCOLN, NEBRASKA 68501

Editor

Gary Carey, M.A.
University of Colorado

Consulting Editor

James L. Roberts, Ph.D.
Department of English
University of Nebraska

Cliffs Notes, Inc.   Lincoln, Nebraska

CONTENTS

HENRY V NOTES

LIFE OF SHAKESPEARE

Many books have assembled facts, reasonable suppositions, traditions, and speculations concerning the life and career of William Shakespeare. Taken as a whole, these materials give a rather comprehensive picture of England's foremost dramatic poet. Tradition and sober supposition are not necessarily false because they lack proved bases for their existence. It is important, however, that persons interested in Shakespeare should distinguish between *facts* and *beliefs* about his life.

From one point of view, modern scholars are fortunate to know as much as they do about a man of middle-class origin who left a small English country town and embarked on a professional career in sixteenth-century London. From another point of view, they know surprisingly little about the writer who has continued to influence the English language and its drama and poetry for more than three hundred years. Sparse and scattered as these facts of his life are, they are sufficient to prove that a man from Stratford by the name of William Shakespeare wrote the major portion of the thirty-seven plays which scholars ascribe to him. The concise review which follows will concern itself with some of these records.

No one knows the exact date of William Shakespeare's birth. His baptism occurred on Wednesday, April 26, 1564. His father was John Shakespeare, tanner, glover, dealer in grain, and town official of Stratford; his mother, Mary, was the daughter of Robert Arden, a prosperous gentleman-farmer. The Shakespeares lived on Henley Street.

Under a bond dated November 28, 1582, William Shakespeare and Anne Hathaway entered into a marriage contract. The baptism of their eldest child, Susanna, took place in Stratford in May, 1583. One year and nine months later their twins, Hamnet and Judith, were christened in the same church. The parents named them for the poet's friends Hamnet and Judith Sadler.

Early in 1596, William Shakespeare, in his father's name, applied to the College of Heralds for a coat of arms. Although positive proof is lacking, there is reason to believe that the Heralds granted this request, for in 1599 Shakespeare again made application for the right to quarter his coat of arms with that of his mother. Entitled to her father's coat of arms, Mary had lost this privilege when she married John Shakespeare before he held the official status of gentleman.

In May of 1597, Shakespeare purchased New Place, the outstanding residential property in Stratford at that time. Since John Shakespeare had suffered financial reverses prior to this date, William must have achieved success for himself.

Court records show that in 1601 or 1602, William Shakespeare began rooming in the household of Christopher Mountjoy in London. Subsequent disputes between Shakespeare's landlord, Mountjoy, and his son-in-law, Stephen Belott, over Stephen's wedding settlement led to a series of legal actions, and in 1612 the court scribe recorded Shakespeare's deposition of testimony relating to the case.

In July, 1605, William Shakespeare paid four hundred and forty pounds for the lease of a large portion of the tithes on certain real estate in and near Stratford. This was an arrangement whereby Shakespeare purchased half the annual tithes, or taxes, on certain agricultural products from sections of land in and near Stratford. In addition to receiving approximately ten percent income on his investment, he almost doubled his capital. This was possibly the most important and successful investment of his lifetime, and it paid a steady income for many years.

Shakespeare is next mentioned when John Combe, a resident of Stratford, died on July 12, 1614. To his friend, Combe bequeathed the sum of five pounds. These records and similar ones are important, not because of their economic significance but because they prove the existence of a William Shakespeare in Stratford and in London during this period.

On March 25, 1616, William Shakespeare revised his last will and testament. He died on April 23 of the same year. His body lies within the chancel and before the altar of the Stratford church. A rather wry inscription is carved upon his tombstone:

> Good Friend, for Jesus' sake, forbear
> To dig the dust enclosed here;
> Blest be the man that spares these stones
> And curst be he that moves my bones.

The last direct descendant of William Shakespeare was his grand-daughter, Elizabeth Hall, who died in 1670.

These are the most outstanding facts about Shakespeare the man, as apart from those about the dramatist and poet. Such pieces of information, scattered from 1564 through 1616, declare the existence of such a person, not as a writer or actor, but as a private citizen. It is illogical to think that anyone would or could have fabricated these details for the purpose of deceiving later generations.

In similar fashion, the evidence establishing William Shakespeare as the foremost playwright of his day is positive and persuasive. Robert Greene's *Groatsworth of Wit*, in which he attacked Shakespeare, a mere actor, for presuming to write plays in competition with Greene and his fellow playwrights, was entered in the *Stationers' Register* on September 20, 1592. In 1594 Shakespeare acted before Queen Elizabeth, and in 1594 and 1595 his name appeared as one of the shareholders of the Lord Chamberlain's Company. Francis Meres in his *Palladis Tamia* (1598) called Shakespeare "mellifluous and hony-tongued" and compared his comedies and tragedies with those of Plautus and Seneca in excellence.

Shakespeare's continued association with Burbage's company is equally definite. His name appears as one of the owners of the Globe in 1599. On May 19, 1603, he and his fellow actors received a patent from James I designating them as the King's Men and making them Grooms of the Chamber. Late in 1608 or early in 1609, Shakespeare and his colleagues purchased the Blackfriars Theatre and began using it as their winter location when weather made production at the Globe inconvenient.

Other specific allusions to Shakespeare, to his acting and his writing, occur in numerous places. Put together, they form irrefutable testimony that William Shakespeare of Stratford and London was the leader among Elizabethan playwrights.

One of the most impressive of all proofs of Shakespeare's authorship of his plays is the First Folio of 1623, with the dedicatory verse which appeared in it. John Heminge and Henry Condell, members of Shakespeare's own company, stated that they collected and issued the plays as a memorial to their fellow actor. Many contemporary poets contributed eulogies to Shakespeare; one of the best known of these poems is by Ben Jonson, a fellow actor and, later, a friendly rival. Jonson also criticized Shakespeare's dramatic work in *Timber: or, Discoveries* (1641).

Certainly there are many things about Shakespeare's genius and career which the most diligent scholars do not know and cannot explain, but the facts which do exist are sufficient to establish Shakespeare's identity as a man and his authorship of the thirty-seven plays which reputable critics acknowledge to be his.

THE BACKGROUND OF *HENRY V*

Since *Henry V* is the last play of Shakespeare's tetralogy, the earlier three plays shed some light upon the present play. The Elizabethan audiences which Shakespeare was writing for would have known these earlier plays and, of course, they would have been familiar with many of the characters in this play. Therefore, since *Henry V* is the play which shows King Henry V as the ideal Christian monarch, the earlier plays leading up to this figure of perfection are enlightening. For example, when Henry prays just before the Battle of Agincourt, he says:

> Not to-day, O Lord,
> O, not to-day, think not upon the fault
> My father made in compassing the crown.
> (IV.i.310-12)

He is referring to the manner in which his father, Henry IV, became king. The *fault* referred to is the deposition and murder of Richard II, a theme which runs throughout all of the plays in this tetralogy. Henry V, therefore, is the Christian king who wears a crown gotten by questionable means. Furthermore, characters like Bardolph and

Pistol and Hostess Quickly had appeared in some of these earlier plays, and there are many references to the famous Sir John Falstaff, one of Shakespeare's greatest comic creations. Therefore, a brief knowledge of the earlier plays will clearly enhance the reading, enjoyment, and understanding of *Henry V*.

RICHARD II (Synopsis)

The play opens with a dispute between Henry Bolingbroke, Duke of Hereford, and Thomas Mowbray, Duke of Norfolk. Bolingbroke has accused Mowbray of treason, and the two of them exchange insults in the presence of King Richard. After attempts to reconcile them fail, Richard orders them to take part in a traditional chivalric trial by combat. On the field of combat, the king changes his mind and banishes the two men—Bolingbroke for ten years (commuted to six) and Mowbray for life. Then the king makes plans to leave for the wars in Ireland.

Before departing, Richard visits the ailing father of Bolingbroke, John of Gaunt, Duke of Lancaster. Gaunt warns Richard with his dying words that he is flirting with danger and doing great harm to the country by allowing himself to be influenced by his sycophantic courtiers. When the old man dies, Richard takes possession of all of Gaunt's wealth and sets out for Ireland.

Unhappy with Richard's incompetence as a ruler and worried by his seizure of the Duke of Lancaster's wealth, a number of nobles rally support for Henry Bolingbroke. When Bolingbroke and his army decide to return from exile in France, the rebel forces prepare to confront Richard on his return from Ireland.

The rebel noblemen force the king to abdicate, and Bolingbroke is crowned as Henry IV. Richard is imprisoned in Pomfret Castle, where he faces his death alone, philosophically contemplating the meaning of his fall from grandeur. Sir Pierce of Exton decides solely on his own to execute the deposed king; as a result, he is banished by King Henry. The play ends with Henry IV planning a penitential pilgrimage to the Holy Land.

HENRY IV, PART I (Synopsis)

When the play opens, King Henry has called the Percies—Northumberland, Worcester, and Hotspur—to the palace. He demands to know why the ranking Scottish prisoners taken by Hotspur have not been turned over to him. The Percies are furious with Henry's seeming arrogance; they deeply resent the fact that this man whom they helped to the throne should demand absolute obedience from them. Thus, they begin to plot their revolt.

Meanwhile, in the comic subplot, Prince Hal and his boon companions make plans to rob a group of travelers in order to play a practical joke on their beloved, blustering cohort, Sir John Falstaff. The joke almost backfires, but Falstaff manages to barely escape and back at the tavern, he emerges triumphantly as the comic hero of the escapade. The merrymaking is interrupted, however, when Prince Hal is called back to court on urgent business.

Hotspur's threats were serious; meeting with Worcester, Mortimer, and Glendower at the residence of the Archdeacon in North Wales, the men plan a campaign against the royal forces; afterward, they plan to divide England into three parts. Momentarily, Hotspur is dejected that he cannot count on Northumberland's troops, but he reasons that perhaps the populace will be even more impressed when they realize that Hotspur accomplished his *coup* without Northumberland's help.

When he learns that Henry's royal army has set forth for battle, Hotspur is again worried—this time about the news that Prince Hal accompanies his father's troops as second in command. But deciding that his victory will seem even more miraculous if he can dispose of Hal personally, Hotspur vows to kill Hal himself, and his ardor and impetuosity is rekindled.

When the plot returns to the comic characters, Falstaff is arrayed as a military commander, leading a group of pitiful, physically unfit "soldiers" who vow they will fight for England. Both Prince Hal and Westmoreland remark on the company's unfitness, but they decide to let them continue to march. In the meantime, the Archbishop of York is alarmed to learn of the Percies' plot and about the fact that neither Mortimer nor Northumberland will be accompanying Hotspur's men; he fears reprisal from King Henry if Hotspur is defeated.

In parley at the king's camp at Shrewsbury with two of Hotspur's allies, Worcester and Vernon, Prince Hal speaks words of praise for Hotspur, modestly concedes that he himself has been derelict, and he offers to fight his rival in single combat, in place of an all-out battle between the two opposing forces. The two rebel leaders depart, ostensibly to report to Hotspur what has been said by the king and the prince.

Hotspur impatiently decides to engage in total combat. During the course of the battle, most of Falstaff's men are killed; Hal heroically rescues his father from the sword of Douglas, a Scottish Earl; and he slays his rival, Hotspur. Worcester and Vernon are captured and later put to death, but Douglas is released by a generous Prince Hal. The rebel forces have been badly defeated, and King Henry sends another of his sons, John of Lancaster, to the North, where John will oppose Northumberland and Archbishop Scroop; Henry himself will leave with Prince Hal to fight the forces led by Glendower and Mortimer.

HENRY IV, PART II (Synopsis)

When Part I closed, Henry IV was dispatching his son John of Lancaster to the north to fight Northumberland and Archbishop Scroop; this play now opens with Northumberland receiving conflicting news about the results of the Battle of Shrewsbury. When he hears of the defeat and death of his son Hotspur, he flees to Scotland to await further developments. Meanwhile, Falstaff becomes involved with Mistress Quickly, and he uses his royal commission to avoid being imprisoned for debt. He continues his riotous feasting and drinking and joking with Prince Hal. Prince Hal, however, while tolerating the unrestrained behavior of Falstaff, nevertheless shows some concern for his royal father and for the affairs of the realm. Since the prince has already shown his valor and honor at the Battle of Shrewsbury, we are now more receptive to his comic behavior with Falstaff, as he once more endorses the precept that life should have its lighter moments—as we will see in *Henry V*, when King Henry plays a practical joke on Williams, a common soldier.

Meanwhile, Prince John moves against the rebel forces and is able to subdue them and arrest the leaders for high treason. This news, however, does not gladden the dying King Henry IV because his main concern is with the conduct of Prince Hal, who at this moment is dining with Poins and other lowly associates. Henry ponders the fate of England when Prince Hal becomes king, and he hopes, above all, for unity among his sons. Prince Hal is defended by the Earl of Warwick, who argues that the prince is schooling himself to understand even the lowliest subject, and he predicts that Prince Hal will turn "past evils to advantage."

Prince Hal enters at this point and learns that his father is gravely ill. Everyone leaves except the heir-apparent, who says that he will keep watch at his father's bedside. Observing his father's crown, he philosophizes about it as a symbol of care and anxiety. Noticing his father in a stupor, he concludes that he is dead, and he lifts the crown and places it on his head, reflecting still further about the responsibilities that the crown encompasses. After he leaves the room, the king awakens, sees the crown on his son's head, and immediately assumes that Prince Hal is anxious to see him dead. In a touching speech, he speaks to Prince Hal and reproves him for being impatient to wear the crown; he accuses the prince of having no love for his father and laments that the prince's years of unruly behavior have culminated in such a conclusion.

Prince Hal convincingly asserts his love and respect for his father; he says that he wishes him to live for a long time yet. Obviously affected by Prince Hal's love for him, the king admits that he came to the throne by "bypaths and crooked ways," and he implores God to forgive him for deposing an anointed ruler (Richard II). Prince Hal promises that he will defend the crown against all the world.

For some time, everyone has expected total misrule and chaos when Prince Hal would finally become King Henry V. Especially concerned has been the Lord Chief Justice of England, who had, only a short time before, banished Falstaff and, upon the late king's order, briefly imprisoned the prince. Contrary to all expectations, Henry V approves of all of the actions of the Lord Chief Justice and bids him to continue to serve the crown in his present capacity. The new king then assures his brothers that his life of wild living ended with his father's death, and he is now a completely reformed prince. To the surprise of all present, the king begins to personify immense magnanimity and dedication to duty. It is to be recalled from the very beginning of the two-part chronicle history that Shakespeare has prepared the way for this important order and justice; at last, in *Henry V*, Henry becomes the ideal Christian ruler.

With the ascension of Prince Hal to the throne, Falstaff immediately envisions all types of grand rewards for himself, and he also expects high honors for Hal's other comrades from the tavern. Expecting to reap extravagant benefits, Falstaff immediately leaves for the coronation. When Falstaff approaches the king, however, Henry orders the Lord Chief Justice to reprove the old fellow. Falstaff is incredulous and addresses Henry directly, calling "My King! My Jove! I speak to thee, my heart!" In chilling words, Henry answers, "I know thee not, old man." He then lectures Falstaff about his lifestyle, admonishing him to reform, and if amends are made, then Falstaff can return by slow degrees to the king's favor.

Everyone is amazed and all approve of Henry's actions. At the close of the play, we learn that Henry has called for the assembly of Parliament and that he will soon lead an invasion into France to claim it for England, as we will see in the first act of *Henry V*.

GENEALOGICAL TABLES

The following tables chart the descendants of Edward III, whose grandson Richard II was the last of the Plantagenet line of kings. Reference is made by the Duchess of Gloucester in *Richard II* (I.ii.11) to Edward's seven sons. Of these, only four had descendants who figured later in contests for the throne, forming two new lines of kings, the Lancastrian and the Yorkist, contending with varying success in the Wars of the Roses until Richard III was killed in the battle of Bosworth in 1485 and his niece Elizabeth of York married the Lancastrian heir Henry Tudor, founding the Tudor line. Names of kings are in capitals; "m." indicates "married."

EDWARD III, reigned from 1327 to 1377

Edward, the Black Prince	William of Hatfield	Lionel of Clarence	John of Gaunt	Edmund of York	William of Windsor	Thomas, Duke of Gloucester

Edward, the Black Prince
m. Joan Plantagenet; by 1st husband Thomas Holland

RICHARD II
m. (1) Anne of Bohemia
(2) Isabella of France   Duke of Surrey   Thomas, Earl of Huntingdon

Joan Holland, Duchess of York

Hence we learn that the Earl of Surrey and the Duchess of York were step-nephew and step-niece of Richard II

Lionel of Clarence

Philippa m. Edward Mortimer

Roger, Earl of March

Edmund, Earl of March

Lionel, the 3rd son had only a daughter ineligible for the throne, but her grandson Edmund Mortimer, Earl of March, lays claim to it in the rebellion under Henry IV.

14

John of Gaunt, Duke of Lancaster
m. Blanche of Lancaster and Catherine Swynford

Bolingbroke, HENRY IV	John Beaufort
HENRY V	John Beaufort
HENRY VI	Margaret Beaufort m. Henry Tudor
	HENRY VII (Tudor) m. Elizabeth of York

The Lancastrian kings were Henry IV, 1399-1413, Henry V, 1413-22, and Henry VI, 1422-71.

Henry VI's incompetence led to Wars of the Roses, the murder of Henry in 1471, and seizure of the throne by the Yorkist Edward IV.

Edmund, Duke of York
m. Isabella of Castile and
Joan Holland,
Duchess of York

Aumerle   Richard, Duke of York

EDWARD IV   RICHARD III

EDWARD V   Elizabeth
m. HENRY VII

The Yorkist kings were Edward IV, 1471-83, Edward V, 1483-83, and Richard III, 1483-85. Richard murdered his nephew Edward V and seized the throne.

In 1485, Henry Tudor, the great-great-great grandson of Edward III and leader of the Lancastrian line, ended the Wars of the Roses by killing Richard in the Battle of Bosworth. To unite the Lancastrians and Yorkists, he married Elizabeth, the Yorkist heiress and the great-great granddaughter of Edward III.

Thus was founded the House of Tudor, of which Elizabeth was the reigning queen during most of the life of Shakespeare. His purpose in writing the plays of the Henrys, *Henry IV, Parts I* and *II*, *Henry V*, and *Henry VI, Parts I, II*, and *III*, was to glorify the monarchy of England and instruct the nation in patriotism and in pride of their political institutions.

GENERAL PLOT SUMMARY OF *HENRY V*

As indicated at the close of *Henry IV, Part II*, King Henry V is planning on entering into a war with France over some disputed lands and titles. He has instructed the Archbishop to be sure that his claims are valid. When the play opens, the Archbishop explains to his Bishop how he plans to convince the king to enter into a war with France, thus protecting the church's property, which might otherwise be placed in the hands of the state rather than left it in the church's control.

After the king is convinced of the validity of his claims, an ambassador from France arrives with a rejection of the claims; he also delivers an insulting barrel of tennis balls from the French Dauphin, who still considers King Henry to be the silly and rowdy Prince Hal.

As they are on the verge of leaving for France, King Henry is tending to some business—releasing a prisoner for a minor offense—and then he turns to three of his trusted advisors and has then executed for conspiring with the French to assassinate him. Meanwhile, in the French court, no one seems to take Henry seriously. The entire court is contemptuous of his claims and of his abilities. They are so overconfident that they do not send help to the town of Harfleur, which Henry easily conquers. After this victory, Henry gives strict instructions that all the citizens are to be treated with mercy and that his soldiers are not to loot, rob, or insult the native population. However, a companion from Hal's youth, Bardolph, an inveterate thief, steals a small communion plate, and, as a result, he is executed.

In spite of the English victory, the French still do not express concern, even though the Princess Katharine is involved; if Henry is victorious, she will become the Queen of England; as a result, she feels the necessity to learn the English language, and so she begins taking instructions in that language. Meanwhile, the reports that the English are sick and tattered allow the French to prepare for the battle with complete confidence, especially since they outnumber the English 60,000 to 12,000 troops.

Just before the crucial Battle of Agincourt, an emissary once again approaches King Henry with demands that he immediately surrender his person. His demands are rejected, and King Henry, in a patriotic speech, urges his troops to fight for "Harry, England, and St. George." By miraculous means, the English are victorious and the French are shamed into submission. At the end of the play, King Henry's demands are granted, and he is seen wooing and winning Princess Katharine as his future queen.

LIST OF CHARACTERS

THE ENGLISH

King Henry V

The ruling monarch, who is presented in the play as the ideal Christian king. The main purpose of the play is to convey the idea that Henry V represents in all aspects the model of the ideal ruler. (For a summation of Henry's character, see pp. 69-72).

The Duke of Exeter

He is the uncle of Henry V and a trusted advisor; he functions as both a statesman and as a warrior. Even though he is left in charge of the city of Harfleur, where he is instructed to rule with leniency, he turns up at the Battle of Agincourt, and later he acts as the English ambassador and mediator of the treaty between Henry V and the King of France.

The Duke of Bedford

A brother to Henry, he is used to suggest the close familial bonds between the two brothers. (Historically, he was not present at the Battle of Agincourt, since Henry had appointed him as Regent of England during his absence in France.)

The Duke of Gloucester

Henry's youngest brother. Although he is present in most of the scenes where Henry appears, he has little function in the drama except to illustrate, as Bedford does, familial loyalty. He is placed in charge of some military operations, and he is gently chided by his brother Henry for hoping that the French will not attack while the army is tired. His remark allows Henry to speak on the necessity of relying on the Divine Providence of God: "We are in God's hand, brother, not in theirs."

The Duke of York

Henry's cousin, whom he is very fond of; upon learning of his death during the Battle of Agincourt, Henry is moved to tears when he hears of the duke's courage and his last words of loyalty to the king.

The Archbishop of Canterbury

He is a man of great learning and a master of the English language. He is one of the first persons who brings forth Henry's claim to the French lands, and by so doing, he protects the church's own property from being taken for royal expenditures. He is an extremely astute man, supporting Henry's army with heavy levies from the church; because of this, he is able to retain for the church the basic lands from which the levies are derived.

The Bishop of Ely

An assistant to the Archbishop, he functions mainly as a sounding board for the Archbishop's ideas.

The Earl of Cambridge, Lord Scroop, and Sir Thomas Grey

The conspirators who accept money from France to assassinate Henry V. They are discovered and immediately executed for treason. Their betrayal of Henry evokes from the king a bitter denunciation of their intentions and causes him to wonder whom he can trust. Lord Scroop and the Earl of Cambridge had been especially good friends and confidants of the king.

The Earl of Westmoreland

Another of Henry's administrators who, early in the play, urges him to press for his claims in France.

The Earl of Salisbury

His only function in the drama is to give a patriotic speech in Act IV, when it is discovered that the French armies far outnumber the English forces. He gives a six-line speech and is heard of no more.

The Earl of Warwick

Like the Earl of Salisbury, he plays no particular role in the drama. He appears in several scenes, but speaks only one line in the entire play. He is sent along with Gloucester to make sure that Fluellen and Williams do not get into a real fight; otherwise, he has no function.

Captain Fluellen

An intensely loyal Welshman who provides much of the humor in the play by his eagerness to argue and to show off his knowledge of the classics, even though he gets most things mixed up. He is a very proud, opinionated, conceited, testy person who is willing to argue with anyone about anything.

Captain Gower

A friend of Fluellen's, he often serves merely to draw out Fluellen's eccentricities. He is a good soldier who is actually more perceptive about human nature than is Fluellen, and he realizes quickly that Pistol is a cowardly braggart.

Captain Jamy

A Scotsman who appears only briefly in Act III, Scene 2, and seems to immensely enjoy arguing.

Captain Macmorris

He appears only in Act III, Scene 2, when he gets into an argument with Fluellen concerning the Irish.

Bardolph

This character is retained from the earlier *Henry IV* plays, where he was distinguished by having a bad complexion, a fiery red nose, and carbuncles on his cheeks. For some reason, he is now a lieutenant in this play, but he is still a coward and a thief. He is hanged during the course of the play for stealing a communion plate from a French church.

Pistol

Like Bardolph, Pistol also appears in the *Henry IV* plays and thus would be a character that the audience would be familiar with. He is a ranting and raving coward, a "swaggering rascal," a "fustian rascal," and a "bottle-ale rascal." At the end of Act V, Scene 1, Pistol is finally dispensed with, thus bringing to a close a series of characters that began three plays earlier in *Henry IV, Part I.*

Nym

A corporal who is as much of a coward as Bardolph and Pistol are, and he is also an accomplice in their thefts. Like Bardolph, Nym ends up on the gallows.

The Boy

One of Shakespeare's magnificent minor characters, he is younger than the others, and yet he has the quick wit and intelligence to discern the cowardice of Bardolph, Nym, and Pistol. When they try to teach him how to pick pockets, he is outraged and threatens to leave their service. Unfortunately, he is killed when the French raid King Henry's supply area during the Battle of Agincourt.

Hostess Quickly

A simple, uneducated woman who is married to Pistol, but has an unabashed admiration for Sir John Falstaff. She dies of the French malady (syphilis) just before Pistol is to return to England.

Michael Williams

One of the three soldiers whom King Henry, in disguise, meets the night before the Battle of Agincourt. He questions the king's rightness to wage this war, but he never questions his own obedience to the crown. He wonders if the king doesn't have a heavy moral obligation for the souls of those who die in battle. Williams even wonders if the king could not use himself for ransom so that the rest of them will not get killed. When Henry, in disguise, challenges Williams, Williams accepts and they promise to fight each other if they are both alive after the Battle of Agincourt. They exchange gloves so as to recognize each other. Afterwards, when it is discovered that he was arguing and challenging the king, Williams defends himself in such an honest and straightforward manner that the king rewards him with a glove filled with money.

John Bates and Alexander Court

Along with Williams, these two men represent the average or common English soldier. Court has only one line, but Bates has a slightly larger role; for example, he does not share Williams's concern as to whether or not the king's cause is a just one; it is sufficient enough for him to know his duty, and his duty is to fight for the king.

THE FRENCH

Charles VI

The quiet and dignified King of France, who is able to sense the impending danger caused by the approaching English forces, but whereas he grasps the significance, he cannot communicate his fears to the French nobility. He orders his son, the Dauphin, not to go to battle, but apparently this order is ignored since the Dauphin is at the Battle of Agincourt. In the final scene of the play, Charles delivers a gentle speech which is conciliatory as he looks forward to a time of peace and a prosperous union with England through the son whom he hopes his daughter Kate will provide King Henry.

The Dauphin

Next in line for the throne of France, the Dauphin is insolent, opinionated, and stubborn. He knows of Henry's wild, youthful escapades, but he is not perceptive enough to realize that Henry has changed. He still thinks of Henry as a mere wastrel, a young man to whom no attention should be paid. Therefore, he sends Henry a barrel of tennis balls, implying that Henry should content himself with playing ball and not waging war. At the Battle of Agincourt, the Dauphin is more concerned with singing the praises of his horse than he is with the serious business of war. After the defeat of the French, he bitterly feels the shame of it, and he does not appear again in the play.

The Constable of France

The official commander-in-chief of the French forces, he stands out as one of the most capable of the French forces. Yet ultimately, he too succumbs to the temptation of not taking the English seriously; as a result, he is soundly beaten by them.

The Duke of Burgundy

One of the powerful French noblemen and one of the officials of the court, he is responsible for drafting the treaty at the end of the play; he delivers a splendid speech on the virtues of peace.

The Duke of Orleans

Like the other French lords, he is boastful and contemptuous of the English forces, but he does defend the Dauphin when the Constable suggests that the Dauphin might not be as brave as he would like people to believe.

The Duke of Bourbon

One of the French lords who is terribly ashamed about the "ready losses" of the French to the English: "Shame and eternal shame, nothing but shame."

Montjoy

The French herald, or messenger, in charge of delivering the various ultimatums from the French to the English. After the defeat of the French, he comes humbly to ask for peace and request permission for the French to be allowed to collect their dead.

Rambures and Grandpré

Two French lords who appear only briefly.

The Duke of Bretagne and The Duke of Berri

Two noblemen who are onstage only briefly and receive orders from the King of France.

Queen Isabel

The French queen who joins in the negotiations for peace in the hope that her feminine voice will help soothe certain matters in the negotiations. She is pleased with the union between Henry and her daughter Kate and hopes for a strong union of the two kingdoms as a result of the marriage.

Katharine

A young girl of fourteen who accepts the fact that she will be given to Henry as his bride; consequently, she is beginning to learn English for that day when she will be Queen of England.

Alice

Katharine's lady-in-waiting; she is the well-mannered companion of the young princess.

SUMMARIES AND COMMENTARIES

ACT I—PROLOGUE

Summary

The Chorus (one person) enters and calls upon the "Muse" to help in presenting this play since it deals with such a lofty subject matter. The Chorus explains that the small Elizabethan stage can hardly transform itself into the fields of France, or into an English court, or into a battlefield upon which thousands of horses and soldiers fight; with imagination, however, when "we talk of horses . . . you [can] see them" moving across the landscape. Thus the greatness of the subject matter—a subject dealing with England's ideal king, Henry V—requires that the audience exert its greatest imagination to be able to see in their minds the vastness and the splendor that the play recalls. The audience must also be tolerant of the actors who attempt to portray personages of such high estate. And finally, the audience must be prepared for "jumping o'er times" back and forth, from England to France.

Commentary

Because of the ambitions of the playwright and the limitations of the Elizabethan stage, an introduction is in order and the Prologue serves as that introduction. Chronologically, this is only the second time in Shakespeare's career that he has used the device of a Chorus to introduce a drama (the first time he used a Chorus, it introduced *Romeo and Juliet*).

One of Shakespeare's purposes in using the Chorus is to be able to celebrate the greatness of Henry V directly; for that reason, he does not have to rely solely on the other characters to sing the king's praises. The Chorus also sets the time and place for the drama and excites the imagination of the audience. The audience, of course, must use its imagination in any type of drama, but now Shakespeare is demanding that they extend even further their imagination and create large battlefields and countries across the sea and hordes of horses charging up and down the landscape. This demand to the audience is partly an answer to the classicists who complained that Shakespeare took too many liberties with the Elizabethan stage and violated the classical sense of the unities of time and place. It is, nonetheless, effective.

Before each of the subsequent acts, Shakespeare will also use the Chorus as a device to compensate for the limitations of the stage and to continually remind the audience of a need for imaginative cooperation.

ACT I—SCENE 1

Summary

The opening scene is set in the ante-chamber of the king's palace in London. The Archbishop of Canterbury and the Bishop of Ely are discussing a bill that is still pending, one that was to be passed during King Henry IV's reign. The bill would have divested the church of more than half of its lands and wealth—in fact, it "would drink the cup and all." Because of civil strife at that time, the bill was forgotten, but now it is once again being discussed. Fortunately, King Henry V is a true lover of the church and, it is believed, can be dissuaded from supporting the bill. Canterbury describes the changes that have overtaken Prince Hal since he became King Henry V:

> Never was such a sudden scholar made;
> Never came reformation in a flood,

> With such a heady currance, scouring faults.
>
> (32-34)

While still a prince, Hal and his "unlettered, rude and shallow" companions spent their time indulging in riotous living. The wildness of his youth seemed to have left him the moment his father died:

> The breath no sooner left his father's body,
> But that his wildness, mortified in him,
> Seem'd to die too.
>
> (25-27)

Henry V is now a sober, wise and beloved king; in the same way that "The strawberry grows underneath the nettle/ And wholesome berries thrive and ripen," so did Prince Hal conceal his real worth as a youth and then emerge fully ripened into a magnificent monarch.

Canterbury then discusses how he has been trying to sway the king against the bill. He has suggested to the king that instead of taking so much from the church's holdings, the king should regain some of France's domains which would yield much more revenue. He maintains that Henry has a claim on the French crown derived from his great-grandfather, King Edward III. The Archbishop of Canterbury then explains that he and the king were earlier interrupted by the French ambassador, and that he is to meet again with the king to further explain the matter to him. He has an appointment to see the king at four o'clock and must be on his way. Ely expresses his eagerness to know the outcome of the meeting.

Commentary

For a full understanding of King Henry in *Henry V*, it is essential that one knows something about him as Prince Hal, as Shakespeare conceived of him in the earlier plays, *Henry IV, Part I*, and *Henry IV, Part II*. (See the summaries of these plays, pp. 9-13, and also the section on sixteenth-century political theory.) This background information is necessary because Shakespeare probably conceived of the series as a related group of plays leading up to presenting Henry V as England's ideal king. Certainly, the traits and qualities which are attributed to Henry are a result, in part, of what he has learned from his past life and past experience.

Scene One opens with a discussion of Henry's qualities and his past escapades, emphasizing the differences between the wild youth he once was and the wise and prudent king that he has become. The discussion between the Archbishop of Canterbury and Bishop Ely reminds the audience of the tremendous changes that have taken place in Henry since his coronation. Upon the death of Henry IV, the wild behavior of Prince Hal's past was immediately rejected and replaced by the sober duties of kingship. Thus the opening scene begins the essential theme of the play—that is, the "miraculous" transformation of a wild, impetuous, and dissolute prince into an ideal, perfect Christian monarch, yet one who is also fully aware of various, earthly political intrigues. After due praise of the new king, the churchmen bring into focus the political intrigue in terms of the bill which will deprive the church of a major portion ("the better half") of her wealth and revenues. The Archbishop's interest lies first in the preservation of both the state and the church, and thus, he must be diplomatic when he ensures that neither church nor state be deprived; he is, of course, willing to make large levies on church revenues for the sake of the state, but he also must see to it that the church retain control of her revenues. As a result, with diplomatic cunning and political intrigue, the Archbishop hopes to convince King Henry to seek additional revenues in France; to do this, he cleverly advances the theory that Henry is entitled to certain domains in France. If he is successful in this stratagem, the church will not be deprived of her revenues. The Archbishop's chances of success in persuading King Henry are enhanced by the fact that King Henry is "full of grace and fair regard," and he is also a "true lover of the holy church." Consequently, this ideal monarch, through his love of the church and through his spiritual virtue, will be manipulated into a political conflict with France. Consequently, the theme of King Henry's moral growth will be presented against a background of moral political choices and political intrigues instigated by representatives of the spiritual church.

ACT I—SCENE 2

Summary

Scene Two takes place in the "presence chamber" of the palace. The king wants to hear from the bishops concerning the rightness of his claims in France before he sees the ambassadors from France. The Archbishop of Canterbury and the Bishop of Ely enter to explain to the king his rightful claim to the French throne. But before they begin, the king warns them to tell the truth. Henry understands that a legitimate claim would mean a war with France and would cost thousands of lives. He wants more information about the "Salic law" which France is using to disprove Henry's claim. Therefore, he urges Canterbury to begin and to speak with "your conscience wash'd/ As pure as sin with baptism."

In a very long and involved speech, Canterbury explains that the king has a legitimate claim to the French crown. The Salique (Salic) laws were once applied to a small area in Germany (not even France) called Salique Land. There was, long ago, a decision made by the settlers of the area that decreed that the family's inheritance would not pass on to the women. This law "was not devised for the realm of France," for several of the kings of France obtained their right to the throne through their mothers' line. What is more, Canterbury explains, the French are simply using this law to keep Henry from the French throne.

King Henry asks if he can in good conscience make the claim. The Archbishop of Canterbury responds with a biblical quote from the Book of Numbers: "When a man dies, let the inheritance/ Descend unto the daughter." He then urges the king to fight for his claim by remembering the great exploits of his great-grandfather, Edward III, whose mother was Isabella, the daughter of Phillip IV of France.

Here, the Bishop of Ely, Exeter, and Westmoreland all implore the king to remember his noble ancestry and his regal blood. They remind the king of his courageous heritage and the unswerving loyalty of his subjects. The Archbishop of Canterbury promises him that not only his subjects, but the clergy as well, will financially support him in his fight for the French throne:

> In aid whereof we of the spiritualty
> Will raise your Highness such a mighty sum
> As never did the clergy at one time
> Bring in to any of your ancestors.

(132-35)

Henry expresses his fears for the Scottish defenses if he were to leave, recalling that every time that English kings have gone off to war, the Scots "come pouring like the tide into a breach." While Canterbury believes there is nothing to worry about, Ely and Exeter seem to agree with the king. Canterbury responds, then, using the metaphor of a bee colony in which he compares the working of a kingdom to that of a beehive: every bee has an assigned task to perform, and they all work to accomplish a common goal for the total good. Therefore, he urges Henry to divide up his forces into quarters and, with one quarter, he can conquer France and leave the other three-fourths to defend the homeland:

> If we, with thrice such powers left at home
> Cannot defend our own doors from the dog,
> Let us be worried, and our nation lose
> The name of hardiness and policy.
>
> (217-20)

The king seems satisfied with this suggestion and pronounces that he and his forces are going to France. He then summons the ambassadors from France. They are sent by the Dauphin (the king's son) and not by the King of France. Henry assures the ambassadors that they can speak freely and safely because "We are no tyrant, but a Christian king," and he urges them to speak frankly about what is on the Dauphin's mind.

They say that the Dauphin is aware of Henry's claim upon the French throne, but that the Dauphin believes Henry to be young and immature and worthy only of the gift which he sent with his ambassadors: tennis balls. King Henry, with dignity and clarity, responds that he will go to France to play a match that will "dazzle all the eyes of France." The tennis balls, he says, will be transformed into cannonballs, and many will "curse the Dauphin's scorn." Granting the ambassadors safe conduct, Henry bids them farewell. After their exit, he says that he hopes that he will make the "sender [the Dauphin] blush at it," and then he begins to prepare for war with France.

Commentary

In Scene One, we only heard about King Henry V; now, in Scene Two, the praise we heard is justified with Henry's appearance. Here is the ideal Christian king who has rejected the depraved companions of his youth. King Henry is seen as a prudent and conscientious ruler; that is, he has apparently already decided to wage war against France, and now he seeks from the Archbishop a public statement justifying his actions. And furthermore, he is fully and conscientiously aware of the loss of lives that this struggle will entail. To the Archbishop, he admonishes:

> Therefore take heed how you impawn our person,
> How you awake our sleeping sword of war:
> We charge you, in the name of God, take heed;
> For never two such kingdoms did contend
> Without much fall of blood. . . .
>
> (21-25)

With this speech emerges the theme which will be carried forth to the battlefield later in the play—the theme of the horrors of war and the loss of many lives which this encounter will entail and, thereby, the heavy responsibility which it places upon the *conscience* of the king who decides to wage such a war.

Consequently, the king commands the Archbishop to consult his *own* conscience before speaking and justifying such an undertaking. Here is the mature Christian king, concerned not with just matters of state, but with the conscience of the entire state (or nation) as well. The Archbishop explains the justification for Henry's actions in a speech that has to be one of the most garbled, confused, and tedious speeches in all of Shakespeare's works (in dramatic productions, this speech is usually cut and altered severely). When the Archbishop, the head of the church of England, pleads with Henry to let "the sin [be] upon my head" if there be any wrongdoing, Henry resolves to proceed; he has full assurance that he can go to war with a clear conscience.

When Henry expresses concern about an invasion from Scotland (it has happened before when the king and his army are absent from England), the Archbishop answers with the now-famous beehive comparison. This elaborate comparison of the state or human society to a beehive is a familiar Renaissance idea which supports the idea that all classes (royalty, workers, drones, and fighters) are necessary for the welfare of the perfect state.

Another facet of Henry's character is revealed during his handling of the ambassadors from France. The Dauphin has apparently heard a great deal about the wildness and immaturity of the young Prince Hal and is openly insulting to the newly reformed king. (By the Dauphin's assumptions about Henry's past life, Shakespeare also assumed that his audience was familiar with his earlier plays about Prince Hal.) But Henry is not rankled by the Dauphin's insults; instead, he responds with an evenness of temper, amazing self-control, and complete courtesy:

> We understand him well,
> How he comes o'er us with our wilder days,
> Not measuring what use we made of them.
>
> (266-68)

Henry means, as was indicated in Scene One by the Archbishop, that the "wilder days" were a part of the king's training and have been put to good use in his present knowledge of human nature.

In this scene, the Archbishop is presented as a person of great learning and one who is a master at garbling the English language in a serious manner. He is completely dedicated to England, to the king, and, last but not least, to the church. He is an admirable diplomat in the manner in which he is able to inspire and convince the king of the rightness of the engagement against France. We, however, must always keep in mind that the Archbishop's insistence upon the rightness of the claims against France are due, in part, to his desire to retain the church's revenues—with this in mind, he even promises more revenues for the war than any clergy has ever before provided.

With all the noblemen, kinsmen, and churchmen united behind the king, the first act ends with a perfect sense of unity of state and church and citizenry.

As the following genealogical chart shows, and as the confusion of the Archbishop's speech attests to, there is total and utter confusion concerning how *anyone* could make a strong, legitimate case for Henry's claim to the French throne. Henry's claim is based on a flimsy assertion that his great-great-grandmother, who was in line for the French throne, married his great-great-grandfather, Edward II of England. Yet as the chart shows, there were many in the male line of descendants who are much more entitled to claiming a legitimacy to the French throne. And aside from all other matters, King Edward III renounced forever any claim by any of the sovereigns of England to the throne of France. In conclusion, King Henry V has absolutely no claim whatsoever, and the Archbishop's speech simply obscures all these issues.

THE CLAIM OF HENRY V TO THE FRENCH THRONE

ACT II—PROLOGUE

Summary

The Chorus appears on stage again telling the audience that England has been preparing to go to war. Young men are leaving their farms and joining forces with the king; England is "like a little body with a mighty heart." The French are frightened upon hearing of England's plans to wage war. The Earl of Cambridge, Lord Scroop, and Sir Thomas Grey have been paid by France to kill the king; they plan to accomplish this when the king and his forces are in Southampton, ready to sail for France. Finally, the Chorus tells the audience again to use their imaginations and suppose that they are to be transported first to Southampton and "thence to France."

Commentary

The Prologue, or the Chorus, informs the audience of the length of time which has passed since Henry's decision to invade France and the present, actual time. All of the preparations for war have been made, and enough time has elapsed for the French to learn of the plans for war and, as a counter measure, to enter into a conspiracy to have Henry assassinated.

The Chorus also reminds the audience that they must continue to use their imaginations as the scene will soon shift from London to Southampton and then to France.

ACT II—SCENE 1

Summary

This scene introduces several of Shakespeare's comic characters whom Elizabethan audiences were already familiar with from *Henry IV, Parts I* and *II*. On a street in London, Corporal Nym and Lieutenant Bardolph meet. Bardolph tells of the marriage between Pistol and Hostess Nell Quickly, a woman who had apparently once promised to marry Corporal Nym.

No sooner do Pistol and Hostess Quickly enter than Nym and Pistol draw swords and launch into a verbal match. Efforts by Bardolph and Quickly do not calm them, but a Boy enters and urges Hostess Quickly to come quickly to tend an ailing Falstaff. She exits, and Bardolph draws his sword and threatens to use it on both Nym and Pistol if they don't settle their feuding. They are hesitant, but after Bardolph threatens again, they agree to shake hands. Pistol agrees to pay Nym the eight shillings he owes him, and Pistol then says that he has a position in the army as a seller of provisions and the three of them can share in the profits.

Quickly reenters to tell the men that Falstaff is dying, and they all go off to see him, explaining on the way that the changes in the king's behavior brought about Falstaff's downfall.

Commentary

The characters introduced in this scene have no real purpose in the play. Bardolph, Pistol, and Hostess Quickly are included only because they were in the earlier *Henry IV* plays, and Shakespeare's audience would expect to see them again. Furthermore, Shakespeare lets the audience know that Sir John Falstaff—one of Shakespeare's greatest comic creations—is not totally forgotten. Yet since the king has undergone a complete transformation, these comic characters, once his old drinking cronies, will never appear in scenes in which the king appears; they have very little or nothing to do with the main story. They simply provide the comic relief from the serious plot developments, and as noted, these characters were well known and well loved by the audience. However, this scene stresses that this is *not* the world of *Henry IV*, and the mere absence of Sir John Falstaff reinforces this idea. Even the humor has changed; the quarreling between these characters is more of the snarling type and thus loses much of the gusto of the earlier plays.

In *Henry IV, Part I*, Bardolph was Falstaff's servant and held the rank of corporal. He is usually presented as having a large, flaming red nose, facial blemishes, and carbuncles on his cheeks, and as was true earlier, he is often the butt of many jokes because of his physical appearance. In *Henry IV, Part II*, he was still a corporal; Shakespeare never reveals how Bardolph received his present rank of lieutenant in this play, and critics who suggest that it could have been through Falstaff's influence miss the point that Henry's vow to be mature and responsible would not allow Falstaff to be in his presence, much less to have any influence over him. But even though Bardolph has been promoted, he is still just as much a coward as he was earlier; however, with his promotion, he has learned to conceal his cowardice better. His purpose of remaining in the army is that it provides him with a good opportunity to loot.

Pistol and Nym also provide comic relief through their worldly boasting, their blustering and swaggering, and their constant misuse of the English language. Many of their expressions are absurd, alliterative nonsense. Hostess Quickly is the same good-hearted, simple person that she was in the earlier plays. She has always had a great admiration for Sir John Falstaff, and presently she is deeply concerned over his serious illness.

ACT II—SCENE 2

Summary

Now in Southampton, Bedford (the king's brother), Exeter (the king's uncle), and Westmoreland are discussing the conspirators—Scroop, Cambridge, and Grey—who, for a price, are planning to kill the king. The king, however, is aware of the plot and those behind it.

Henry, Scroop, Cambridge, and Grey enter and begin to discuss the support and loyalty which the king has among his subjects. And as if to illustrate Henry's deserved loyalty to his goodness and wisdom, Shakespeare has Henry order a man who committed a minor offense the day before to be released from prison. Scroop, Cambridge, and Grey argue that the king must set an example and prosecute the offender to the full extent of the law, but the king argues for mercy and pardons the offender, explaining that if he punishes severely for petty crimes, how shall he punish major crimes? Henry then shows the three men some papers which prove that he knows about their plot. Cambridge, Scroop, and Grey each confess and ask him for mercy.

Henry, answering them in a moving and bitter speech, says first that these three who expressed no compassion for the minor lawbreaker deserve none now for themselves; he then speaks of the ideal of loyalty and the crime of betrayal. The treachery of Lord Scroop, who "knew'st the very bottom of my soul,/ That almost mightst have coined me into gold" and who betrayed Henry for a price, is the most incredible. Henry cannot understand why these three so-called old friends have plotted against him for nothing more than French gold. He questions how he can trust *any* man if these three whom he thought were most loyal could betray him. But compassionately he says:

> I will weep for thee;
> For this revolt of thine, methinks, is like

Another fall of man.

(140-42)

He then orders their arrest for high treason against the crown.

Exeter arrests the three, and they tell the king they are ready to die for their crimes; they ask him to forgive them, and each asserts that he is glad that their plan has been uncovered. Henry, in words that suggest his greatness as a magistrate, says that he holds no personal grudge ("Touching our person seek we no revenge"), but the safety of the nation is at hand. He therefore pronounces the sentence:

> Hear your sentence.
> You have conspired against our royal person
> Join'd with a proclaimed enemy and from his coffers
> Received the golden earnest of our death . . .
>   Therefore, get you hence,
> Poor miserable wretches, to your death.

(166-78)

Then, exhibiting further the qualities of mature kingship, he turns his attention immediately to matters of state and prepares for the embarkation to France.

Commentary

The treason that the Chorus speaks of in the Prologue is now discovered and resolved by King Henry in a very calm and reasoned manner. This scene emphasizes many of Henry's admirable qualities. In the first part of the scene, he shows great mercy in forgiving a person whose offense was unintentional. It is also ironic that the three traitors argue for exceedingly harsh punishment: "Let him be punished, sovereign, lest example/ Breed, by his sufferance, more of such a kind." Ironically, King Henry allows the offenders to convict themselves.

The treasonable actions of Cambridge, Grey, and Scroop emphasize the many cases of duplicity that a true king must contend with, and Henry's treatment of the conspirators is firm, just, and decisive; yet in Henry's long speech of denunciation, there is also a note of deep personal tragedy. All of these conspirators have been the recipients of special favors from the king. The treachery of Lord Scroop is the most difficult for Henry to understand since Lord Scroop knew Henry's innermost person: Lord Scroop "knewest the very bottom of my soul." Thus as Henry contemplates the contrast between appearance and reality, between the inner duplicity of the traitors and their outward show of loyalty, he is faced with not so much a political tragedy as he is faced with a *personal* tragedy. But however much the tragedy is personal, he must transcend it, and for the sake of England, he must send the traitors whom he has believed to be loyal friends to their deaths.

At the end of his speech of denunciation, he feels the betrayal so personally that he accounts for it in terms that would imply that man is sometimes simply born depraved and evil. At least Lord Scroop's betrayal is, for Henry, deep-rooted enough to be compared with the original fall of man:

> I will weep for thee;
> For this revolt of thine, methinks, is like
> Another fall of man.
>
> (140-42)

But the mark of a great king is that he must rise above personal tragedy, and thus Henry does as he tells the conspirators:

> Touching our person seek we no revenge;
> But we our kingdom's safety must so tender,
> Whose ruin you have sought, that to her laws
> We do deliver you. Get you therefore hence,
> Poor miserable wretches, to your death.
>
> (174-78)

Here, Henry sets aside his personal views and calmly sends the traitors to their deaths for the safety and welfare of the entire nation, a nation which could have been destroyed if the treachery had been successful. After dealing with the traitors, then, Henry turns his attention immediately to the duties at hand—the war with France.

Historically, both Cambridge and Lord Scroop wanted to replace Henry on the throne with Edmund Mortimer, who also had a claim to the throne and who, in the earlier *Henry IV* plays, had support from Lord Scroop's father for the throne.

ACT II—SCENE 3

Summary

In front of a tavern on a London street, Hostess Quickly tells her husband, Pistol, that she wants to accompany him to Staines on his way to Southampton. Pistol says no; they (Pistol, Bardolph, and Nym) are mourning Falstaff's death. Hostess Quickly describes for them the death of Sir John Falstaff, whom she attended until the end, and as they make ready to leave for Southampton, Pistol gives Hostess Quickly advice about running the inn. Then he kisses her, as does Bardolph, but Nym refuses. She bids them all adieu.

Commentary

The main purpose of Scene Three is to announce the death of Sir John Falstaff, and the manner of that announcement by Hostess Quickly contains as much humane feelings from these comic characters as we are to find from them in the entire play. We should remember from the earlier plays that Hostess Quickly did have a strong admiration for the marvelous fat knight. Her misused words and phrases are comically absurd, but they nevertheless possess a charm that is missing in the rest of the drama that concerns them.

Once Sir John's death is announced, Pistol expresses the common concern for greed and gain which the lower characters in this play have and their decision to join their king:

> Come, let's away. . . .
>   Yoke-fellows in arms
> Let us to France; like horse-leeches, my boys,
> To suck, to suck, the very blood to suck!
>
>   (49-58)

As noted earlier, the low characters will now function mainly as looters or bloodsuckers.

ACT II—SCENE 4

Summary

In the palace of the French king, the king expresses his fear of the approaching English forces. He tells the Dauphin to prepare for war "with men of courage and with means defendant." But the Dauphin maintains that the English will be easy to defeat and that Henry is a "vain, giddy, shallow, humorous youth."

The Constable of France believes the Dauphin is mistaken and has misjudged the character of the English king. The French king agrees and urges the Dauphin to remember that "King Harry" comes from the line of Edward, the Black Prince of Wales, a fierce warrior who won the Battle of Cressy. "This is a stem/ Of that victorious stock; and let us fear/ The native mightiness and fate of him."

Exeter enters, as the ambassador from King Henry, asking the French king to give up his crown and give it to King Henry, the rightful heir; if he refuses, bloodshed and war will follow. He warns the Dauphin that his gift of tennis balls was not appreciated and that he shall have to answer to King Henry for the insult.

The French king tells Exeter that he shall have to wait until the next day for his answer.

Commentary

The basic purpose of this scene is twofold: first, to show that the French court is not prepared for war, and second, to show the disunity which is prevalent in the court. The French king, Charles VI, is not characterized as an impressive king. Even though he is correct in his appraisal of King Henry, he does not possess a commanding presence.

The Dauphin, as was indicated by his insulting gift of the tennis balls in the first act, is characterized as a rather insolent, self-opinionated young man who will function as a direct contrast to the more noble Henry. The Dauphin believes that the French should have good defenses but not because of the approach of young King Henry; he is guided not by fear but only by the general principle that one should always have good defenses.

Of more direct concern in this scene are the words of Exeter, the English ambassador; he echoes the king's determination, and he anticipates the spirit of the scenes to come in his reference to the horrors of war which can be avoided only by the French king's submission to the will of King Henry V. Exeter warns:

> . . . if you hide the crown
> Even in your hearts, there will he rake for it.
> Therefore in fierce tempest is he coming,
> In thunder and in earthquake, like a Jove,
> That, if requiring fail, he will compel.
>
> (97-101)

ACT III—PROLOGUE

Summary

The Chorus enters with a flourish and once more urges the audience to imagine the king and his troops setting sail for France and also to imagine an England emptied of all her stalwart soldiers, defended only by "grandsires, babies, and old women." The English ambassador has returned; the French king has offered his daughter, Katharine, and some minor dukedoms, but he has refused to give up his throne. Henry has rejected the offer and he now sails to France to do battle.

Commentary

As with the previous Prologues, this one serves to explain a lapsed time period, and again it reminds the audience that they must continue to use their imaginations—this time, however, the language of the Prologue is more elaborately descriptive. The king embarks on a "fleet majestical" which bears the English forces to France, and the entire "brave fleet" is adorned and lighted by dawn:

> . . . behold the threaden sails,
> Borne with the invisible and creeping wind,
> Draw the huge bottoms through the furrow'd sea,
> Breasting the lofty surge.
>
> (10-13)

ACT III—SCENE 1

Summary

This scene, consisting solely of a soliloquy by King Henry, contains many famous passages; in fact, this speech is probably the best known speech in the entire play. The scene is Harfleur, where Henry, surrounded by his troops, urges them on to one more supreme effort. Henry's speech proves that he knows his men well; speaking plainly and to the point, he appeals to their manhood, their ancestry, and their love of England:

> Follow your spirit, and upon this charge
> Cry, "God for Harry! England and Saint George!"
> (33-34)

Commentary

This speech confirms for the audience the personal and inspiring leadership of King Henry V. Even though some critics have dissected the speech and found it lacking, it is nevertheless one of the most inspiring war speeches ever uttered, and apparently it is very successful in spurring the soldiers on to make one more supreme effort. Lines 6-17 seem to suggest that in terms of the various passions of man, his spiritual emotions are directly dependent upon his physical state. In times of peace, the manly virtues are quite proper and will suffice, but in times of war, man must put aside manly virtues and become a virtual beast. It is the duty of the soldier to become a beast and his actions should be in imitation of a wild beast—the blood is to be "summoned" and the sinews are to be "stiffened."

ACT III—SCENE 2

Summary

In another part of the Harfleur field, Bardolph, apparently inspired by Henry, calls, "On, on, on, on, on! To the breach, to the breach!" But Nym and Pistol remind him that they might be killed;

they have no intention of dashing "to the breach." The Boy wishes that he were back in London. Fluellen, a Welsh officer in the English army, enters and commands them to fight. He drives them forward and leaves the Boy to reflect on the pickpocket schemes that Nym, Pistol, and Bardolph are involved in.

Fluellen reenters with another Welsh officer, Gower, who tells Fluellen to come with him, that the Duke of Gloucester wants to speak to him. Gloucester, along with the Irish Captain Macmorris, is "mining"—that is, digging tunnels under the city. Fluellen does not think highly of the captain.

Captain Macmorris and Captain Jamy, a Scotsman, enter then, and Fluellen compliments Captain Jamy on his military knowledge. Meantime, Captain Macmorris is angry that work on the mines has stopped and he will not be able to blast the walls of Harfleur with his mines. Fluellen tries to goad Macmorris into an argument, but the captain is unwilling to waste words, so Fluellen makes a remark about the Irish, a remark which Macmorris immediately resents. A fight is about to ensue when Captain Gower steps in before swords are actually drawn. A trumpet announces that a parley has been called, and Fluellen promises to resume the argument when a break in the action occurs.

Commentary

This scene, placed between Henry's charge to his armies and his confrontation with the Governor of Harfleur (and the surrender of the town), is Shakespeare's now familiar means of using a comic interlude to comment upon the serious scenes. In contrast to the nobility of Henry's inspired charge in the preceding scene ("Once more unto the breach, dear friends, once more . . ."), Bardolph repeats the charge in a bit of low, echo-like comedy: "On, on, on, on on! To the breach," thus connecting the two scenes and also showing that not all of Henry's soldiers are inspired by his valiant and heroic leadership.

The behavior of Nym, Bardolph, and Pistol is a negative counterpoint to Henry's stress on the model Englishman's patriotic virtues. These low characters would prefer to be "in an alehouse in London . . . [and] would give all . . . for a pot of ale and safety." This comic scene, however, lacks the force of the scenes in the *Henry IV* plays, where Sir John Falstaff imparted more pertinent observations about the situation. The Boy's earlier comments remind us of Falstaff, but they are, nonetheless, a poor substitute for the original.

Behind the comic aspects, however, even here Shakespeare seems to insert into these interludes something new, a deep concern about the serious waste of human lives. Nym doesn't have "a case of lives" to spare, and Pistol, in spite of his obvious cowardice and striking flamboyance, reflects: "knocks go and come; God's vassals drop and die."

When the Boy is left alone on the stage, we see another view of King Henry's inspired Englishman. In contrast to the young Boy, Bardolph is "white-livered and red-faced," Pistol has a vicious tongue but a "quiet sword," and Nym has never hurt anyone except himself—when he was drunk. Yet together, they will "steal anything and call it purchase." For the Boy, their combined "villainy goes against my weak stomach." His inexperienced and untried manhood is admirable as he deserts the three and goes off to do "some better service."

The Welsh officer Fluellen, introduced in this scene, is one of the more interesting characters in the play. While he is eager to argue and quick to show off his knowledge on almost any subject, and while he is opinionated and conceited, he is also a good soldier who shows great courage and loyalty to Henry. Ultimately, in spite of all his flaws, he will become one of the more lovable characters in the play due to his quaint and amusing ways. His antagonist in this scene, Captain Macmorris, the Irishman, is seen no more, and the long argument presented in a heavy dialect is often severely cut or omitted from many productions since it does not move the plot forward.

ACT III—SCENE 3

Summary

Scene Three opens before the gates of Harfleur, where King Henry is warning the Governor and the local citizens of the dreadful things that will happen if the city does not surrender. The king and his men are prepared to show no mercy and will reduce the town to ashes if the Governor does not surrender. The Governor replies that the Dauphin, whom he entreated to come and defend the town, sends word that his forces are not yet ready "to raise so great a siege." He therefore surrenders Harfleur to King Henry and asks for mercy. The king responds by entrusting the town to Exeter and charging him to be merciful to all the people of the city and to fortify it. He will then lead the army to ⌐alais.

Commentary

Here, in the capitulation of Harfleur, we have the first significant surrender, and we see Henry as a victor for the first time. In this role, he is stern and undeviating in his demands that the Governor surrender the town peacefully. He depicts vividly the many horrors which could result if his demands are not met; yet, in contrast, he is willing to show great mercy if his demands are met. A new note, however, is introduced in Henry's closing speech. Winter is coming, and there is a growing sickness among the men. This problem will remain a constant concern throughout their encampment at Calais, when Henry's men will be seen as only tatters of their former selves.

In the Governor's surrender, we hear that the Dauphin refused to send help. We can assume that the Dauphin has still not taken Henry's threats seriously.

ACT III—SCENE 4

Summary

In a room of the French palace at Rouen, Katharine, the king's daughter, and Alice, the old gentlewoman, have an English lesson. Alice knows only a little English and Princess Katharine is trying to learn the language. All of the dialogue is in French except the few words (hand, nails, arm, and elbow, etc.) that she learns from Alice during the lesson.

Commentary

Katharine, the future Queen of England whom Henry will woo and become betrothed to in the final scene of the play, is here introduced as a girl of fourteen whose destiny has already been decided. The purpose of the scene is to give the audience some light-hearted relief from the battle scenes and also to show that Katharine, by her statement that "it is necessary" that she learn English, is already reconciled to the idea that she is to be Henry's queen.

In this scene, the French words and phrases that appeared in the early editions of the play were filled with errors and have been corrected by successive editors. Even though the content is trivial and hardly needs a translation, a loose translation follows:

Kath. Alice, you have been to England, and you speak the language well.

Alice. A little, my lady.

Kath. I beg you to teach me because it will be necessary that I learn it. How does one say *la main* in English?

Alice. *La main*? It is called de hand.

Kath. De hand. And *les doigts*?

Alice. *Les doigts*? O my goodness, I have forgotten *les doigts*; but I shall soon remember it. *Les doigts*? I think that they are called de fingres; yes, de fingres.

Kath. *La main*, de hand; *les doigts*, de fingres. I think that I am a good student; I have quickly learned two English words. How does one say *les ongles*?

Alice. *Les ongles*? They are called de nails.

Kath. De nails. Listen and tell me if I speak well: de hand, de fingres, and de nails.

Alice. You have spoken well, my lady; it is very good English.

Kath. Tell me the English for *le bras*.

Alice. De arm, my lady.

Kath. And *le coude*.

Alice. De elbow.

Kath. De elbow. I will now repeat all of the words that you have taught me up to now.

Alice. I think that it will be very difficult, my lady.

Kath. Excuse me, Alice; listen: de hand, de fingres, de nails, de arma, de bilbow.

Alice. De elbow, my lady.

Kath. O my goodness, I forgot. De elbow. How does one say *le col*?

Alice.	De nick, my lady.
Kath.	De nick. And *le menton*?
Alice.	De chin.
Kath.	De sin. *Le col*, de nick; *le menton*, de sin.
Alice.	Yes. To your honor, in truth, you pronounce the words as though you were a native English lady.
Kath.	I do not doubt it at all that I shall be able to learn it in a little more time.
Alice.	Have you yet forgotten what I have already taught you?
Kath.	No, I shall recite to you promptly: de hand, de fingres, de mails,—
Alice.	De nails, my lady.
Kath.	De nails, de arm, de ilbow.
Alice.	With your permission, de elbow.
Kath.	That is what I said; de elbow, de nick, and de sin. Now how do you say *le pied* and *la robe*?
Alice.	De foot, my lady, and de coun.
Kath.	De foot and de coun! O my Lord! These are very bad words—evil, vulgar and immodest, and not for ladies of honor to use. I would never pronounce these words before French gentlemen—not for the whole world. Foo! Le foot and le coun! Nevertheless, I am going to recite my entire lesson together one more time: de hand, de fingres, de nails, de arm, de elbow, de nick, de sin, de foot, de coun.
Alice.	Excellent, my lady!
Kath.	It is enough for this time; let's go to dinner.

ACT III—SCENE 5

Summary

In another room of the Rouen palace, the King of France is worried about the presence of King Henry and his soldiers in France. The Dauphin is upset by the ladies of the court, who are, in turn, disgusted with the lack of manliness exhibited by the French officers of the army. According to the Dauphin, their wives think that

> Our mettle is bred out and they will give
> Their bodies to the lust of English youth
> To new-store France with bastard warriors.
>
> (28-30)

The Duke of Bourbon and the Constable speak with disdain about England and her forces, and they note that Henry's army must be stopped quickly. The king calls on all of the French nobility to fight at once against Henry but commands the Dauphin to stay with him. The Constable remarks that such a battle between Henry's sick and hungry forces and all of the French nobility will be uneven enough to convince Henry to surrender.

The king then sends all of the French nobility to battle against Henry—with the exception of the Dauphin, whom he orders to remain with him.

Commentary

Since the English audience of Shakespeare's day would have known that the English were indeed victorious in their encounter with the French forces, this scene is therefore filled with dramatic ironies. The French are so certain of victory that they are arrogant and overconfident. Rather than being apprehensive about Henry's forces, they hold his army in contempt: "His soldiers sick and famish'd in their march . . . when he [Henry] shall see our army,/ He'll drop his heart into the sink of fear." Dramatically, the audience will take pleasure in seeing the insufferable pride of the French brought low by Henry's yeomen.

Dramatically, the Dauphin is presented as a worthy opponent of Henry, even though his father, Charles VI, is still in charge. (Historically, Charles was actually insane at this time, and the Dauphin was in charge of the royal council; this is only one of many examples of the way in which Shakespeare alters history for dramatic purposes.) The Dauphin, even though he is ashamed of the French army's fighting record is still shown here as being contemptuous of the English army; yet still, apparently, he does not take Henry seriously.

ACT III—SCENE 6

Summary

In the English camp in Picardy, Fluellen meets Gower and tells him that they have saved the bridge which they were fighting for, and he extravagantly extols the Duke of Exeter's bravery and leadership. He also mentions that Pistol fought courageously. Pistol enters then and asks Fluellen to intercede for Bardolph, who is to be hanged for stealing a pax from the church. (A pax was a small plate, usually with an engraved picture of Christ or a saint, and it was used in the communion service to hold the wafers. In Holinshed's *History*, the object was a "pyx"—the vessel used to hold the consecrated communion host and, consequently, an object of much more value and, from a mercenary viewpoint, the offense would be much greater. Thus again, Shakespeare alters history to lessen Bardolph's crime in order to allow Pistol to pun that Bardolph's death is "for a pax of little price." Actually, the intrinsic value of the object does not matter since theft from the church was punishable by death.) Fluellen refuses, saying discipline must be maintained and that he would not interfere—even for his brother. Angry, Pistol leaves, hurling insults at Fluellen. Gower tells Fluellen about Pistol's true character lest he be misled, and Fluellen pretends to understand; he promises to deal with him.

Henry and the Duke of Gloucester enter. Fluellen tells them how heroically the Duke of Exeter performed. When the King asks about the casualties, Fluellen tells him that there was only one—Bardolph is soon to be hanged for robbing a church. Henry reiterates his orders that the French populace is to be dealt with fairly; there is to be no plundering. He hopes in this way to win the people's loyalty and respect.

The French herald, Montjoy, enters and says that the French king demands that "Harry" pay for the damage which his troops have caused. Henry recognizes Montjoy's rank and admits that his English army is indeed small and tired; he would like to avoid a confrontation, but they will fight if harassed. Henry tells his brother Gloucester that God is on the side of the English army and then orders the march to the bridge.

Commentary

Historically, the events related by Fluellen refer to the fact that King Henry had to march fifty miles out of his chosen path in order to find a bridge to cross the river. They discover a suitable bridge at a place called Teroune, but the French are on the verge of destroying it when the Duke of Exeter bravely drives them back. The additional fifty-mile march was an additional hazard on King Henry's men and further weakened them.

Fluellen, as a comic character, is further developed in this scene. Comically, he is totally mistaken about Pistol and is actually a terrible judge of character. In his speech about Fortune, we see once again his propensity for trying to show off his knowledge on any subject. But, as King Henry later points out, though Fluellen "appears a little out of fashion/ There is . . . much valour in this Welshman"; particularly in his rejection of Pistol's pleas to intercede for Bardolph's life, Fluellen shows that he is a strong advocate for absolute discipline.

For students of Shakespeare, King Henry's actions are often puzzling. On the one hand, he is the exemplary, impeccable king who pronounces:

> We give express charge, that in our marches
> through the country, there be nothing compelled
> from the villages, nothing taken but paid for, [and]
> none of the French upbraided or abused in disdainful
> language; for when lenity and cruelty play for a
> kingdom, the gentler gamester is the soonest winner.
>
> (115-20)

In other words, he tells his soldiers to conduct themselves in the most respectable manner possible—even no abusive words are to be spoken. In contrast, when Fluellen casually announces that the only casualty from the encounter with the French is that Bardolph is to be executed for robbing a church, King Henry expresses no concern for, nor even recognition of, this old companion from his youthful days of tavern living. (In both of the *King Henry IV* plays, Bardolph, as noted earlier, was, along with Pistol and the late Sir John

Falstaff, the drinking companion of King Henry when he was the "madcap Prince Hal.") It is difficult for some critics to understand how King Henry can so easily forget his past relationship with Bardolph that he can send him to his death with only the cursory comment: "We would have all such offenders so cut off." The contrast between Henry's order for lenity and mercy for the captured French and the strict enforcement of discipline among the English forces appears contradictory. Furthermore, Bardolph is to be put to death for stealing a small plate from the church, and yet King Henry himself has deprived the church of large sums in order to wage his wars with the idea of taking not a small plate, but a large crown— the French crown. Thus the subplot here, involving Bardolph's theft, is also a comment on the main plot of Henry's war against France.

With the arrival of the French emissary, Montjoy, we see still another side of Henry—his concern for his men and the honesty with how he appraises his situation: "My people are with sickness much enfeebled,/ My numbers lessen'd." Shakespeare is dramatically creating a situation in which the English will have to overcome tremendous odds to be victorious—all for the glory of "Harry, England, and Saint George."

ACT III—SCENE 7

Summary

It is the night before the battle in the French camp near Agincourt. The Constable, the Duke of Orleans, Lord Rambures, and the Dauphin (who is present against his father's orders) are boasting about who has the best armor and the best horses. When the discussion turns from the wonders of the Dauphin's horse to the splendors of the others' mistresses, the Dauphin exits to ready himself for the battle. The Constable then has a discussion with the Duke of Orleans concerning the Dauphin's bravery. A messenger enters to announce that the English are camped only fifteen hundred yards away. The Constable and Orleans contend that the small English army cannot be very smart if they mean to fight them, but Rambures reminds them of the courageousness of the English. Nevertheless, the Constable and Orleans are certain that it will be an uneven battle and that by 10 o'clock they each will have captured a hundred Englishmen.

Commentary

In this scene, Shakespeare continues his satirical presentation of the French nobility by contrasting the seriousness and sobriety of the English with the superficiality and pretentiousness of the French. By doing so, Shakespeare continues to make the French appear rather ridiculous. On the night before a major battle, the French nobility join in an absurd banter concerning the value of their horses. The contrast between Henry, King of England, and the Dauphin, heir to the throne of France, is made obvious in the conversation of each man before the major battle. The Dauphin's main concern is with the beauty and perfection of his horse—a "beast for Perseus; he is pure air and fire; the dull elements of earth and water never appear in him. . . ." When the Dauphin then goes on to remind his comrades that he once wrote a sonnet to his horse, which began with the words "Wonder of nature," the Duke of Orleans sarcastically says that he has "heard a sonnet begin so to one's mistress." The Dauphin, however, is not even aware of the subtle reversal of values. Furthermore, to continue the contrast between Henry and the Dauphin, Shakespeare introduces the subject of the Dauphin's bravery; the Constable wonders if the Dauphin will stand and fight, or if he will be like a hawk who, when released, will take flight.

Throughout the scene, therefore, the French nobility reveal a rather fundamental moral carelessness which will be reflected in their resounding defeat at Agincourt. The Duke of Orleans and the other nobility speak of King Henry with utter contempt and of Henry's English soldiers as the king's "fat-brain'd followers" who, if they had any wits, must have "left their wits with their wives." In other words, Shakespeare is preparing his audience with reasons why the French nobility, outnumbering the English five to one *and* on horseback, are soon to be defeated by English yeoman who are "with sickness much enfeebled." The French, believing in and relying on their inherent aristocratic superiority, will go to battle incompetently prepared and will meet their deaths at the hands of English soldiers who are inspired by the noble spirit of their king and thus, by perseverence, discipline, and a belief in "Harry,

England, and Saint George" will win the battle against overwhelming odds.

ACT IV—PROLOGUE

Summary

The Chorus gives us a picture of the two opposing camps on the night before the battle; there are the whispers of the sentinels, the firelight from each camp, the neighing of the horses, the sounds of armor, some roosters crowing, and clocks striking in two nearby villages. Inside the French camp, the confident soldiers play dice while waiting anxiously for dawn; meanwhile, the English, aware of their small number and of their weakened condition, contemplate the morning's danger. The Chorus describes King Henry's walking from tent to tent talking to his soldiers ("a little touch of Harry in the night"), calling them "brothers, friends, and countrymen." He looks strong and confident, and he is a comfort to his men.

The Chorus then apologizes once again for the inadequacies of the stage and urges his audience to be ready to imagine the battle of Agincourt in their minds.

Commentary

As before, the Chorus makes another apology for the limitations of the stage and the need for imagination on the part of the audience. In conformance with the Elizabethan tradition and Shakespeare's custom, there is no absurd effort to present a battle on the stage. Throughout Shakespeare's history plays, a few soldiers represent entire armies, but here, where England's ideal king is being presented, Shakespeare resorts to using the Chorus, urging and reminding the audience that they must imagine the two opposing camps at nighttime on the eve of the crucial Battle of Agincourt.

Shakespeare continues to depict the contrasting mood of the two camps. Again, as in the last act, the Chorus informs us that the French are overconfident and high spirited, whereas the English are so dejected that the king himself must wander through the camp, offering encouragement.

In the last scene of Act III, we saw how frivolous the French were with their light-hearted talk of horses, mistresses, and love poetry. Now, Act IV will open by contrasting the situation in the English camp.

ACT IV—SCENE 1

Summary

In the English camp on the night before the battle, the king tells his brother Gloucester that he is worried about the outcome of the battle. When Sir Thomas Erpingham enters, the king, on an impulse, borrows Erpingham's cloak and is thus no longer identifiable as the king. He sends the others out to "commend [him] to the princes in our camp" and, since he wishes "no other company," he asks to be left alone to "debate" with himself.

Pistol enters and does not recognize Henry; he extols the king and asks the "young man" his name, and Henry tells him that his name is "Harry, le Roy." When Pistol discovers that he is a Welshman and knows Fluellen, he tells him that he plans to fight Fluellen. "Harry" warns him he might be defeated and Pistol becomes so incensed that he insults "Harry" with a vulgar gesture and leaves. As Henry steps aside, Fluellen and Gower enter, unaware of the king's presence. Fluellen is angry with Gower for speaking his name too loudly, afraid that the French might have overheard it. Gower maintains that "the enemy is loud" and cannot hear him; in order to end the argument, Gower promises to speak lower and they exit. The king remarks that Fluellen is odd, but that he is a good soldier.

Next, three common soldiers, John Bates, Alexander Court, and Michael Williams, enter. Henry, unrecognized, tells them he serves under Sir Thomas Erpingham. Bates asks him if he thinks that the king should be told how bleak the situation really is. Henry says no, that the king is "but a man," as they are, and if he exhibited fear, he would discourage the army. Bates personally thinks that the king would prefer to be back in London, but Henry disagrees; he believes that the king is content to be where he is. Then Bates says that the king should be ransomed to save the lives of the men in the army. Henry responds by saying that he himself would not want to leave his king alone to fight the battle because of the king's "cause being just and his quarrel honorable."

Williams is unsure of the justness of the king's claim. Bates does not think it matters; if it is unjust, the guilt is upon the king's head and they will not have to share in the blame. When Williams suggests that those who die "unprovided" (unrepentant) will be a burden upon the king's conscience, Henry responds by saying that all who go to battle should be spiritually prepared, but that the king is *not* responsible to God for their deaths.

When the discussion returns to the king's ransom, Henry says he overheard the king say it would never happen; Williams jokes that it could happen after they are all killed and they would not know the difference. After another exchange of quips, in which Henry intimates that if times were different, he might be angry at Williams, Williams takes up the idea and challenges "Harry" to a fight if they should both survive the battle. They agree to exchange gloves and wear them in their caps so they can find each other the next day. Bates calls them both fools and urges them to be friends for there are plenty of Frenchmen for them to fight.

After the three soldiers leave, Henry is left alone with his thoughts. He talks about the custom of blaming everything upon the king and concludes that a slave has a better life than a king, for he can sleep soundly at night and not worry about affairs of state.

Sir Erpingham enters and finds the king and tells him that his associates are waiting for him. He leaves, and alone once more, Henry prays to God, asking Him to fill his soldiers with courage. He also asks God not to recall the guilt of Henry's father concerning the death of Richard II because he has already made reparations and plans to do more.

Henry's brother Gloucester enters, and the king leaves with him.

Commentary

As noted above in the commentary to the Prologue, this scene serves, first, to emphasize the contrasting attitudes between the French camp—their joviality and overconfidence and superficiality—with the prevailing seriousness of the English camp. In contrast to the frivolity of the French, the entire scene in the English camp is essentially serious. Yet, there is an anticipation of great humor when the disguised king exchanges gloves with Williams and promises to meet him in a duel if they both survive today's battle; we anticipate Williams finding out that he was arguing with the very monarch for whom he is fighting.

The main purpose of this scene is to further illuminate the character of King Henry on the night before the significant and decisive Battle of Agincourt. Any time that a king wraps himself in a cloak and goes among his men incognito, talking with the common soldiers, we have a very dramatic situation. Continuing a dramatic device of the earlier *Henry* plays, the rowdy and rebellious Prince Hal had to, at first, disguise himself to become a king; now as king, he disguises himself to become a common man. Now wrapped in the obscurity of a commoner's cloak and further obscured by the darkness of night, the king is able to learn the feelings of his common soldiers, represented not by the comic Pistol (who knew the king as Prince Hal) and not by the dedicated, if peculiar, Fluellen (and Gower), but as seen in the personages of John Bates, Alexander Court (even though this character speaks only eleven words in the entire play), and Michael Williams. Even the names "John Bates" and "Williams" suggest something of the basic nature of these good English soldiers—that is, this is the stuff of which an ideal Englishman is made of and which will help Henry win military glory for England.

Most critics value this scene as proof of the greatness of Henry as a king—that is, it exhibits the simplicity and modesty, the democracy and the deep religious nature of the king. But Shakespeare no doubt hoped that his audience would be aware of some ambiguity in a situation where the king is in darkness and is in disguise, suggesting that a man's actions by day are different from his words concealed by night. In the first act, the king was ready to place the responsibility for the war on the shoulders of the Archbishop; here, when a common soldier suggests that the responsibility for the deaths of many Englishmen must rest on the conscience of the king, Henry vehemently denies this possibility. Williams maintains:

> If the cause be not good, the king himself hath a heavy
> reckoning to make, when all those legs and arms and heads,
> chopped off in a battle, shall join together at the latter day
> and cry all "We died at such a place . . ." it will be a black
> matter for the king that led them to it.
>
> (140-44)

(Yet, at the same time that Williams makes this assertion, he also fully believes that it is the duty of the subject to obey: "To disobey were against all proportion of subjection.") To answer Williams, Henry eludes taking blame by this analogy: "So, if a son that is by his father sent about merchandise do sinfully miscarry upon the sea, the imputation of his wickedness, by your rule, should be imposed upon his father that sent him. . . ." He further adds that "every subject's duty is the king's; but every subject's soul is his own." We see also that Henry believes that "the king is but a man, as I am; the violet smells to him as it doth to me . . . his ceremonies laid by, in his nakedness he appears but a man, and though his affections are higher mounted than ours, yet, when they stoop, they stoop with the like wing." In other words, the king is like the common man except that he has more concerns, and when disaster or grief strikes, one man is the same as another.

In his soliloquy, Henry expresses the suffering he endures, and he pours forth his anguish and his sense of guilt for the crown that his father usurped; particularly, we sense his sorrow when he utters a final prayer, beginning "God of battles. . . ." The sense of guilt which he feels for his father's crime against the preceding king (Richard II) is carefully scrutinized:

> Not to-day, O Lord,
> O, not to-day, think not upon the fault
> My father made in compassing the crown!
>
> (310-12)

This passage alone, given in a soliloquy, ultimately attests to the deep religious nature of Henry V.

ACT IV—SCENE 2

Summary

The scene shifts to the French camp where everyone is ready to go to battle. The sun has risen and it is time to begin. There follows a brief scene in French, loosely translated as follows:

> Orl.   The sun doth gild our armour; up, my lords!
> Dau.   Mount me on my horse; you, my valet, my lackey. ha!
> Orl.   Oh noble spirit!

Dau. Begone, water and earth.

Orl. Nothing more? only air and fire.

Dau. Heaven also, my cousin Orleans.

(This scene is a continuation or a conclusion of the last scene in Act III, when the Dauphin was discussing the merits of his horse which, according to him, possesses only fire and air; he now adds to those qualities that of heaven also.) A messenger enters and says that the English forces are also ready, and the Constable gives the call to mount up. He and the others pity the small, beleaguered English forces and hope that they have said their prayers. He has so much confidence in his superior force that he is sure that the mere appearance of his army will cause the English to "crouch down in fear and yield." A French lord, Grand-pré, enters and continues to ridicule the poor "bankrupt" and "beggar'd" condition of the Englishmen. Impatient for battle, the Constable grabs his banner and cries to his men to take the field.

Commentary

The remainder of this act reads, in part, like a pure chronicle— that is, Scene Two is set in the French camp, and then we shift to the English camp in Scene Three, and then we have a comic interlude, and then we return to the French forces on the battlefield, and then to the English forces. As noted earlier, the frivolity of the French is contrasted with the seriousness of the English. The extended insults heaped upon the English by the arrogant French officers prepare the audience to relish even more the defeat of the French forces which have shown such utter contempt for the English. The dramatic irony is that the audience knows what is going to happen, and the French forces are totally ignorant of their fate.

In the beginning of this scene, the Dauphin still speaks of his horse as being possessed of no such common elements as earth and water, but of being made of pure air and fire, the same sentiments that he expressed in his last speech. In doing so, we now realize that the night has passed and, with the dawn, the battle is about to begin, and the French are still overconfident.

ACT IV—SCENE 3

Summary

In the English camp, Gloucester, Bedford, Exeter, Westmoreland, and Salisbury discuss the battle. There are five times as many French soldiers as there are Englishmen, and the French are fresh and rested. The Earl of Salisbury bids his friends goodbye, saying they may not meet again until they meet in heaven; he then exits to do battle.

The king enters and hears Westmoreland wish for ten thousand more English troops. In answer to Westmoreland, Henry says that if God plans for them to win, there will be greater glory with no more troops than these to share the honors with. He urges anyone who does not wish to fight to leave. Today is a day set aside for the celebration of the "Feast of Saint Crispian," and all of those English soldiers who survive the battle will be honored and remembered every Saint Crispian's Day. Henry promises that all of their names shall become household words and their deeds remembered "to the ending of the world." Every Englishman who fights with him shall be his brother, and all Englishmen who do not take part in the battle will hold their manhoods cheap on Saint Crispian's Day.

The Earl of Salisbury enters and warns the king that the French are ready to charge. Henry asks Westmoreland if he still wishes for more help. Westmoreland, inspired by the king's speech, is now willing to fight the French with only the king at his side.

The French herald, Montjoy, sent from the Constable, asks King Henry to surrender now, before the slaughter begins. The king is impatient and his speech is meant more for his troops than for the French herald: Henry and his troops will either defeat the French or die. Montjoy exits, taking the king's message back to the Constable. King Henry grants his cousin, the Duke of York, the privilege of leading the troops into battle.

Commentary

The opening of this scene reestablishes for the audience the great odds against which the English are confronted. There are about sixty thousand French soldiers matched against somewhat less than twelve thousand Englishmen—five-to-one odds—and Westmoreland's wish for another ten thousand "of those men in England/ That do no work to-day" (the battle was fought on a Sunday, and the majority of Englishmen would not be working on that day) allows Henry to enter and make his famous Saint Crispian's Day speech. (The battle was fought on the day set aside to honor two fourth-century saints—Saint Crispian and Saint Crispin—and both names are used by Henry during the course of his speech.) Henry's speech contrasts strongly in its dignity and manliness with the boastful frivolity of the French nobility.

In his speech, which is a superb rhetorical vehicle for theatrical declamation, Henry is able to rouse his soldiers to a high pitch of patriotism. He would not want to share the honor of this day with other men. The fewer men there are, the greater the honor will be to those who do fight. Furthermore, if any man does not want to fight, then:

> Let him depart . . .
> We would not die in that man's company . . .
> We few, we happy few, we band of brothers;
> For he to-day that sheds his blood with me
> Shall be my brother. . . .
>
> (36/38/60-62)

Westmoreland then expresses this response to Henry's rousing speech: "Would you and I alone,/ Without more help, could fight this royal battle."

Henry is again given the opportunity to give a rousing speech when the French herald demands that Henry surrender himself for ransom. Henry reminds the envoy of the man who sold a lion's skin in advance but was subsequently killed while hunting the lion. Likewise, this very day might provide his English soldiers with new coats of lion skins.

> And my poor soldiers tell me, yet ere night
> They'll be in fresher robes, or they will pluck
> The gay new coats o'er the French soldiers' heads
> And turn them out of service.
>
> (116-19)

He assures the herald that the only ransom which the French will receive will be his bones ("joints"). On this note, the famous Battle of Agincourt begins.

ACT IV – SCENE 4

Summary

On the battlefield, Pistol enters with a captured French soldier who mistakes Pistol for a gentleman of high quality. When Pistol asks for the Frenchman's name, he hears only "*O Seigneur Dieu!*" (Oh, Lord God). Pistol mistakes the French word "Dieu" for the Frenchman's name—"Dew." Pistol then rants and raves, causing the Frenchman to say: "*O, prenez miséricorde! ayez pitié de moi!*" (Oh, take mercy on me! Have pity for me.) Again, Pistol is confused; he thinks that the word "moi" means "moy," a coin of some denomination, and he asserts that he wants at least forty "moys" or else he will cut the Frenchman's throat. After further misunderstanding, Pistol calls for the Boy to come and translate. He then finds out that the man's name is Monsieur le Fer, and Pistol makes several puns on the English words "fer," "firk," and "ferret." Pistol then tells the Boy to tell the Frenchman that he is about to cut the Frenchman's throat immediately unless he is highly paid with English crowns. The Frenchman begs for mercy and his life, saying that he is from a good family who will pay well for his ransom—at least two hundred crowns. Pistol makes more threats and finally says that that amount will abate his passion. The Boy, however, translates Pistol's speech as follows: "[Pistol] says that it is against his oath to pardon any prisoner; however, for the sake of the two hundred crowns you have promised him, he is willing to allow you your freedom and your liberty." The French prisoner then responds: "I thank him on bended knees, a thousand thanks, and I consider myself lucky to have fallen into the hands of such a courtly gentleman—one who, I believe, must be the bravest, the most valiant, and the most distinguished nobleman in England." Pistol is satisfied and exits with his prisoner. Alone, the Boy comments upon the empty bravery and the hollow courage of Pistol, who roars like some devil from an old stage play. From the Boy, we also hear about the deaths of Nym and

Bardolph, and the prediction that his own fate is precarious since only boys like himself are left to guard the equipment.

Commentary

This is the first scene we have that deals directly with the battle that is taking place. Four more scenes dealing with the battle will follow. It is ironic, therefore, that our first knowledge of this key battle comes in the form of a comic interlude—that is, if some braggart so low, incompetent, cowardly, and as rascally as Pistol can capture a French soldier, then we must assume that the French are in total disarray and that the English are initially successful. It is further ironic that one of the greatest of cringing cowards is praised so highly by the French captive and is able to extort two hundred crowns; one wonders what the other soldiers, truly brave soldiers, are accomplishing. This scene, a comic interlude, is inserted here apparently because Shakespeare wanted to further emphasize the poetic irony of the French officers' having viewed the entire battle in such a frivolous manner and their looking upon the English so derisively.

ACT IV—SCENE 5

Summary

In another part of the field, the Constable of France, the Dukes of Orleans and Bourbon, Lord Rambures, and the Dauphin realize that although they greatly outnumber the English forces, they are being defeated. There is much confusion on the battlefield, but they continue fighting, declaring their utter shame, realizing that in mere numbers, "We are enough yet living in the field/ To smother up the English."

Commentary

This short scene is the second one dealing with the battle itself. It shows that the French are indeed being dispersed in spite of their great number. As is obvious, the main intent of the scene is to show the shame of the once boastful and arrogant French as they are being defeated by those "wretches that we played at dice for." The entire day, then, is nothing but "shame, and eternal shame, nothing but shame!"

ACT IV—SCENE 6

Summary

In another part of the battlefield, Henry notes that they seem to be winning ("Well have we done, thrice valiant countrymen."), and he asks about his kinsman, the Duke of York, whom he saw fighting and covered with blood. Exeter repeats York's last words and tells him in a moving speech how bravely York died. The Duke of York, wounded and dying, stumbled upon his noble cousin, the Earl of Suffolk, who lay dying. York took his cousin "by the beard, kissed the gashes," and called upon Suffolk to tarry for a moment so they could die together. Then:

> So did he turn and over Suffolk's neck
> He threw his wounded arm and kiss'd his lips;
> And so espoused to death, with blood he seal'd
> A testament of noble-ending love.

> (24-27)

Exeter tells how he wept like a woman at the sight, and King Henry is about to join "with mistful eyes" when, hearing an alarm, he realizes that the French have reinforced their armies, and he orders his men to kill all of the French prisoners.

Commentary

First, this scene functions to announce the beginning of the English successes. Then it shifts its emphasis to narrate the deaths of the Duke of York, who has played only a small role in the drama, and the death of the Earl of Suffolk, who has not even appeared in the drama. This might seem confusing to the modern viewer, but from our knowledge of many of Shakespeare's history plays, some of the greatest moments are associated with a description of love and death; added to this is the bloody gore of the battlefield. Thus, in order to give a depth to the deaths of two who have played virtually no role in the development of the drama, this scene must be rendered within the context of a grim battle atmosphere.

Shakespeare's main purpose, here, is to show another aspect of Henry the King – one who can mourn and weep for his kinsmen and fellow soldiers fallen in battle, and then, in the next moment, put aside all sense of personal loss and sternly command the deaths of all the French prisoners in order to ensure the safety of the English soldiers. This quality of decisiveness is the stuff that all great field commanders are made of (at least Shakespeare seems to be saying this). We see evidence of the complete presence of mind and control that Henry has in the midst of a raging battle and in the throes of passion because of the deaths of his kinsmen.

For many modern readers, Henry's command to kill all the French prisoners might seem extremely cruel and barbaric or savage, but unless Henry wants to be defeated and have all of his men put to death, he must execute the prisoners before they are freed or before they revolt. In terms of historical accuracy, Henry did not reportedly issue this order until he discovered that the French had massacred all of the young boys and lackeys left in charge of the English equipment in the camp. This massacre is covered in the next scene.

ACT IV – SCENE 7

Summary

In another part of the battlefield, Fluellen and Gower discuss Henry's order to kill all the French prisoners. Gower is delighted, and Fluellen compares the king to Alexander the Great.

The king and several associates enter, along with the French herald, Montjoy, who admits the French defeat and describes the carnage of the battlefield in great detail. The king declares that this victory will be remembered as the Battle of Agincourt. Fluellen expresses his love and loyalty to the king, and Williams enters and explains to the king that he is looking for his glove in someone else's cap; he is ready to fight the rascal if only he can find him. The king mischievously hands Fluellen his glove, telling him that he took it from the French Duke of Alençon. To make sure that there is no

serious trouble, Henry sends Gloucester and Warwick to watch
Fluellen and Williams; he will follow to observe the fun.

Commentary

This scene is rather diverse and diffused in structure. The opening discussion by Fluellen and Gower over the senseless and
unheard of slaying of the sick, the unarmed, the wounded, and,
worst of all, the slaughter of the innocent young boys by the French
soldiers causes Henry's men to remark upon the king's sense of
justice. Both Fluellen and Gower feel that such measures are absolutely justified, and in justifying them, Fluellen compares King
Henry to Alexander the Great, one of the most bloody conquerors of
the ancient world. Here, however, we should remember that whereas
Henry is trying to establish an imperialism, Alexander was at a loss
to know what to do when there were no more lands to conquer; for
that reason, the analogy to Alexander is not necessarily a flattering
one.

King Henry's appearance on the stage shows his incensed rage
over the massacre of the young English boys.

> I was not angry since I came to France
> Until this instant.
>
> (58-59)

His anger leads him to utter threats of harshness and inhumanity,
and he threatens to kill those not yet captured if his orders are not
obeyed. However, when he is assured of victory, his humility is restored in the moment when he gives full and complete credit for the
victory to God:

> *Mont.*   The day is yours.
> *K. Henry.*   Praised be God, and not our strength, for it.
>
> (89-90)

At this point in the battle, Henry is still willing to carry on his
private joke with Williams, the character he promised to do battle
with if they were both alive after the day's battle. Instead, however,
he gives the glove to Fluellen, a man whom he admires greatly, and
then sends others to see that no real harm ensues. A director would

do well, perhaps, to cut this entire scene since it does not advance the plot, does not illuminate King Henry's character too favorably, and because it basically detracts from the drama itself.

ACT IV – SCENE 8

Summary

In another part of the field, Williams and Gower enter and then Fluellen enters and tells Gower of the king's order concerning him and suggests the possibility of a promotion. At the same time, Williams recognizes his glove in Fluellen's cap and strikes him. Examining the glove in Williams's hand, he recognizes it as the match to the glove of the French Duke of Alençon which King Henry has just given to him. He therefore assumes that Williams is some sort of traitor in league with Alençon, and they are about to fight when the Earl of Warwick and the Duke of Gloucester enter and stop the fight. The king and Exeter appear also, and Henry admits his part in the charade. Williams bravely confronts the king by saying it was the king's fault since the king was in disguise. Henry orders Williams's glove to be filled with coins.

An English herald enters with the casualty reports. Ten thousand French soldiers, including an exceptionally large number of French noblemen, have been slain. The English loss is miraculously light. Henry repeatedly gives all of the credit to God and orders a mass to be said. Afterward, he says, "To England then/ Where ne'er from France arrived more happy men."

Commentary

This scene concludes the comic incident involving King Henry's encounter with the common soldier Williams before the battle when they swapped gloves and promised to fight. Many prudish critics, forgetting what a penchant for a practical joke Prince Hal formerly possessed, criticize Henry for his handling of this situation. After all, there was a *promised* rendezvous between Henry and Williams; if they both were alive after the battle, they would fight, and Williams is willing to uphold his promise, but King Henry makes light of his own promise. Those who object to Henry not living up to his word of honor have no sense of comedy, or the Renassiance, or no sense of the concepts of honor as they were understood by the Elizabethan audience. It would be completely out of character for the king to enter into combat with one of his own soldiers; furthermore, it would be treasonous for a soldier to enter into combat with the king. When the king accuses Williams of abusing the person of the king, Williams boldly defends himself before the king saying:

> Your Majesty came not like yourself; you appeared
> to me but as a common man; witness the night,
> your garments, your lowliness; and what your
> Highness suffered under that shape, I beseech
> you take it for your own fault and not mine.
>
> (53-57)

For such an honest answer, Henry awards the soldier a glove filled with crowns. Fluellen, who has just been struck by Williams, now realizes that the soldier "has mettle enough in his belly" and offers some additional money, but his offer is refused by the good, honest Williams.

When the French and English dead are numbered and the tally is brought to King Henry, consistent with his character as Shakespeare has presented it, Henry once again takes no glory for himself but, instead, he dedicates his miraculous victory to the will of God. Here, then, is the Christian king, proud of his human victory, but still humble before God as he, in a single speech, gives all credit to God, four times:

> O God! thy arm was here. . . .
>   Take it, God,
> For it is none but thine. . . .
> And be it death proclaimed through our host
> To boast of this or take the praise from God
> Which is His only. . . .
>   God fought for us.
>   (111/116-17/119-21/125)

In this scene, we again see King Henry as a multi-dimensional man— a man among men enjoying a good jest, as a royal king receiving the miraculous news of his overwhelming victory, and as a model Christian ruler, placing his honors subservient before the might of God.

ACT V—PROLOGUE

Summary

As in the other four acts, the Chorus enters and asks the audience once again to imagine certain events. After the last act, Henry left France, crossed the English Channel, and set out for London. Many of his lords tried to convince him to let "his bruised helmet and his bended sword" go before him as was the custom of the ancient Caesar upon returning victorious. Henry refused, believing that it might detract from the glory of God, to whom he attributes the victory. All of London poured out to acclaim him. The Holy Roman Emperor even came to England to try and arrange a peace, but he was unsuccessful, and now the audience must use its imagination once again and picture Henry now in France.

Commentary

For many critics, Act V is not an integral part of the drama of *King Henry V.* Many see the real intent and the true action of the play as having ended with the victory of the Battle of Agincourt and find the entire last act to be superfluous, an anticlimax to the real intent of the play. However, Shakespeare was approaching the very heights of his dramatic powers, and the act should be read for his intention and not for mere "plot."

ACT V—SCENE 1

Summary

In the English camp, Gower asks Fluellen why he is wearing a leek when the Welsh national day to do so has passed. Fluellen explains that he is looking for that "rascally, scurvy, beggarly, lousy" Pistol, who made derogatory insinuations about the Welsh people's national custom of wearing leeks to commemorate "Davy," their patron saint. Pistol enters, and Fluellen immediately begins to berate him in fierce language; he orders him to eat the leek and when Pistol refuses at first, he is roundly beaten by Fluellen until he agrees to eat it. When he falters, Fluellen spurs him on with more wallops, until Pistol has eaten the entire leek. After Fluellen leaves, Pistol says of him: "All hell shall stir for this." Gower then verbally scathes him and leaves in disgust. Alone, Pistol is dejected because he has just heard that his wife, Hostess Quickly, has died of "the French malady" (syphilis), and Pistol has no place to go—he is finished, he says, and decides to turn to a life of stealing.

Commentary

For the critics who object to the final act, one can only quote the famous eighteenth-century critic Dr. Samuel Johnson, who says of this scene: "The comic scenes of the history of Henry the Fourth and Fifth are now at an end, and all the comic personages are now dismissed. Falstaff and Mrs. Quickly are dead; Nym and Bardolph are hanged; Gadshill was lost immediately after the robbery; Poins and Peto have vanished since, one knows not how; and Pistol is now beaten into obscurity. I believe every reader regrets their departure." Seemingly, Shakespeare knew that his audience would feel suspended if he did not give an account of the last of the group, bringing to a conclusion his story of a group of the most delightful and some of the most depraved low people in all of his dramas. The final picture of Pistol makes us *not* want to see this surly braggart any more, and yet we feel some compassion toward him because of the depths to which he has fallen. He is left empty of purse and devoid of friends, contemplating a career of masquerading as a wounded veteran in order to cheat and wheedle and steal.

ACT V—SCENE 2

Summary

This scene takes place in the French palace. King Henry and his court greet the King and Queen of France, Princess Katharine, and other French nobility. The queen urges that they talk of love and not of war. The Duke of Burgundy makes a long speech about the virtues of peace, to which Henry responds that only if all his demands are met is such a peace possible. Henry appoints a group to discuss his conditions with the King of France: Exeter, Clarence, Gloucester, Warwick, and Huntingdon. The queen volunteers to go along to help with the settlement, leaving King Henry alone with Katharine and her gentlewoman, Alice.

In this love scene where Henry woos Katharine, the king's tone is gently mocking, and yet it is apparent that he is quite serious in his courting. He tells Katharine that he is an athlete and a soldier, but he is not a poet who can speak cleverly to win her love. Katharine seems hesitant, so Henry tells her that they will rule all of England and France and bear a son. When Katharine finally agrees, Henry tries to kiss her hand, which she claims is unworthy. He then tries to kiss her lips but is told that it is not the custom for maids to kiss before marriage. The king tells Katharine that they will *set* the customs—not *follow* them—and with that, he kisses her lips.

The French king and his advisors reenter. After some bantering exchanges between the Duke of Burgundy and Henry over Katharine's blushing, Henry asks if Kate shall be his wife. The acquiescence to this first demand must be met before any other aspects of the treaty can even be discussed. The French king agrees to the marriage, noting that Kate will bear sons to rule England and France. Henry seals the agreement by kissing Kate in front of all and orders preparations for the marriage to be made. Then there will be a gathering of all the other lords in order to work out the details of the treaty.

Commentary

Depending upon the mood of the reader or viewer, this love scene between Henry and Kate can either be the most charming reason for the existence of the fifth act or it can be an absurd travesty on the theme of love. One possible objection to the scene is that the conditions for the treaty between France and England depend on Henry's insistence that Kate must first be his wife. No other terms are to be even considered until it is agreed that she will be his wife, and therefore, the wooing of Kate is an artificial pretense since it is a foregone conclusion before the wooing that Kate will be Henry's wife.

Yet, for most people, this is one of the most delightful love scenes that Shakespeare ever wrote. Theater conventions demand that we forget that all sorts of political intrigues and machinations are going on; Burgundy, the French king and queen, and the English counselors are tending to the political aspects, leaving Henry on stage to expose the audience to another side of his personality. We have seen Henry as a common man moving among men, as an administrator, as a judge both merciful and strict as the occasion demanded, and we have also seen him (or heard of him) as a superb warrior. Now, we see him in a new light—as the lover who woos and sues for the hand in marriage of the lovely young Katharine, Princess of France.

Even if Henry knows that all conclusions are foregone in regard to Katharine, yet the thrill is in the lovemaking itself. He will win her to him regardless of the political affiliations, and it is to this purpose that he begins his direct and simple wooing, filled with charm and wit and good-natured teasing. He pretends that he is not the person to speak fancifully of love, and yet he wins the lady's heart with his fanciful speaking.

Henry maintains that if Katharine's love depends on his performing some physical feat, then he would quickly win her, but he cannot muster up the proper words for doing so; yet his very words *do* win her over. Finally, he pretends to be plain spoken, and yet he uses language and ideas that dazzle the young lady. In conclusion, the final aspect of Henry which is presented to the audience is that of the successful lover. If the theater critics and drama analysts object to the fifth act, the audience leaves the theater wholly delighted with Henry's success in love.

ACT V—EPILOGUE

Summary

The Chorus enters and ends the play, explaining that the events on the stage were mightier than could be actually portrayed. Henry and Katharine did produce a son, Henry the Sixth, whose story is told in other plays.

Commentary

The Chorus in the Epilogue simply reminds the audience once again that the stage has not been adequate for the subject matter, but then no stage could be large enough for an adequate presentation of the man who is the ideal king, the mirror of all Christian kings.

A CHARACTER SUMMATION: KING HENRY V

While *Henry V* is not Shakespeare's best play, all of the three preceding history plays—*Richard II* and *Henry IV, Parts I* and *II*—lead up to *Henry V* and its depiction of Henry as the idealized Christian king. Whereas the earlier plays had shown Henry as the "madcap Prince Hal," a chap who was constantly in the company of lower-class types and who was constantly in some trouble of one sort or another, yet this earlier life ultimately becomes a preparation for his kingship, and his earlier knowledge of these low types allows him to understand his common subjects and to measure his own sense of worth by their lack of noble qualities.

Each scene in *Henry V* is constructed either to illustrate some aspect of Henry V's character or to present some of the low characters as comic relief. Consequently, various scenes depict his religious nature, his mercy, pity, and compassion, his absolute sense of justice, his administrative skill, his fighting ability, his innate nobility, his ability to communicate with the common class of soldiers and people, and, in the final scene, his role as a romantic lover in the suit of Katharine's hand in marriage.

In the opening scenes, he is characterized as being troubled over the religious rightness of his claim to the French lands and the French crown. He relies heavily on the advice of the Archbishop, with the idea that his (the king's) conscience will be clear. He charges the Archbishop "in the name of God" to "religiously unfold" the means by which he can lay claim to these lands. Throughout the play, Henry V's religious nature is constantly emphasized, and after the crucial Battle of Agincourt, he is the first to give all the credit of the victory to God. At his triumphant return to London, we hear that he is frightened that too many people will praise him and not give full credit to God.

In one scene, Henry is presented in a situation where he must be a judge. First, we see him as merciful and forgiving as he releases a prisoner for a minor offense; he then turns to three conspirators and, with a sense of just majesty, he dispenses stern justice to them.

And even here, although he feels a deep personal insult because of the conspirators' plot, it is ultimately the threat to the peace of England that allows Henry to put aside personal feelings and execute the men for the sake of "the health of England."

He can, then, in the same scene turn immediately from feeling a sense of personal betrayal and instantly administer to the needs of the kingdom and the conduct of the war. In addition, during the war, he demands that the conquered French be treated with respect while, at the same time, he allows one of his boon companions of his madcap days to go to his death because he stole from a church.

Even though we never see King Henry actually fighting on the stage, we are told repeatedly of his fighting prowess and of his battered armor and sword; in other scenes, we see him as the inspirational orator and leader of men, exhorting them to rise to the great demands put upon them by the nature of the wars.

Due to his associations during his youth, Henry is also able to communicate well and naturally with the common soldiers and even, because of the carefree tenor of his youth, he still possess a penchant for a practical joke, as we see when he allows Williams and Fluellen to almost come to blows because of the gloves in their hats. Finally, as would be appropriate with the ideal king, we see Henry dressed in all his regal regalia, as the witty and urbane lover who is courting the charming princess Kate.

Therefore, in the above scene and others, many and various aspects of Henry's character are presented so as to demonstrate Shakespeare's point that here, indeed, is the ideal Christian king.

SIXTEENTH-CENTURY POLITICAL THEORY

Since the *Henry* plays are basically political ones, it is necessary to understand the political doctrine behind them if one is to do justice to Shakespeare's intentions. Elizabeth I, the fifth Tudor to rule England, had come to a throne which was in many ways insecure because of rival claims. Henry VIII, her father, had found it especially necessary to inculcate the doctrine of absolute obedience to the crown after the break with Rome in 1536. During his reign he had experienced the Pilgrimage of Grace, a rebellion in northern England, and, later, the Exeter Conspiracy, an alleged attempt to depose Henry and place a Yorkist on the throne of England. After Henry VIII's death, England endured the Western Rebellion of 1549; during Elizabeth's reign there occurred the Rebellion of 1569, as well as plots against the queen's life, notably the Babington Plot, which led to the trial, conviction, and execution of Mary, Queen of Scots. Throughout the century and beyond, England had reason to fear an invasion and the rising of native Catholics. The danger was by no means restricted to the year 1588, when Philip II of Spain sent his Armada to subdue England.

In view of such challenges to Tudor supremacy, there was a need for a political philosophy which would prevent challenges to royal authority and devastating civil war. The basic arguments were developed during the reign of Henry VIII and augmented as new crises arose during the reigns of Edward VI and Elizabeth I. It found expression in officially approved pamphlets and tracts, and also in drama and non-dramatic poetry. Especially it was emphasized in official sermons, the first group of which was introduced in the year 1549. These included strongly worded instructions on the subject of obedience. They were augmented in 1570, following the Rebellion of 1569 and the papal decree of excommunication of Queen Elizabeth I. Every Englishman was required to hear the sermons on obedience three times during the year. The gist of the doctrine was this: the ruler was God's lieutenant on earth; no subject, however exalted, had the right to actively oppose him. To do so was a sin against religion, punishable by suffering here and now and by eternal damnation after death. Even if the ruler were a tyrant, the subject had no right to oppose him; the head of state ruled with God's sufferance. In support of this doctrine, appeals were made primarily to biblical authority. Texts such as Romans 13 and Proverbs 8, as well as ones in Matthew, were cited repeatedly. John of Gaunt, Duke of Lancaster, summed up the doctrine accurately and concisely in his response to his sister-in-law, the Duchess of Gloucester, who reminded him that the reigning king, Richard II, had been responsible for the death of her husband and Gaunt's brother:

> God's is the quarrel, for God's substitute,
> His deputy anointed in His sight,
> Hath caus'd his death; the which if wrongfully,
> Let Heaven revenge; for I may never lift

An angry arm against His minister.
(*Richard II*, I.ii.37-41)

That Henry IV should so suffer is to be explained by the fact that he, son of John of Gaunt, did "lift an angry arm against [God's] minister." He endures rebellion; he sees the apparent waywardness of Prince Hal as part of his punishment; he is not permitted to lead a crusade against the foes of Christianity and do penance for his grievous sins. But, according to Tudor political theory, he wore the crown by God's authority; no subject had the right to oppose him. All this should make understandable the Percies' position and make unacceptable the view that Henry IV is a hypocrite.

QUESTIONS FOR REVIEW

1. Comment upon the many different attributes of Henry V that are brought out in the various scenes in the play.

2. Why is Henry so much more lenient, apparently, with the captured French than he is with the English soldiers who are caught violating his instructions?

3. How does the Chorus function? How would the play be different if it were left out completely?

4. In a famous movie version of *Henry V*, starring Sir Laurence Olivier, the Battle of Agincourt is presented with both armies costumed in a splendid array of armor and filled with pageantry. How does this presentation romanticize Shakespeare and contradict the text?

5. Comment on how Shakespeare alters historical fact for the sake of dramatic appeal.

6. How does Fluellen function in the drama? How would the drama be altered if a director omitted this role from the drama?

7. What is the dramatic appeal of the king when he is in disguise, moving among his common soldiers?

8. Analyze Shakespeare's purpose in having a common soldier, such as Williams, stand up to the king and speak his views so forthrightly.

9. How do Pistol and the Boy function in the play?

10. How can we account for the total success of the English against such overwhelming odds at the Battle of Agincourt?

SELECTED BIBLIOGRAPHY

ADAMS, J. Q. *A Life of William Shakespeare.* Boston: Houghton Mifflin Co., 1923.

ALEXANDER, PETER. *Shakespeare.* Oxford: Oxford University Press, 1964.

BERMAN, RONALD, ed. *Twentieth Century Interpretations of Henry V.* Englewood Cliffs, N. J., Prentice-Hall, Inc., 1968.

BEVINGTON, DAVID. *Shakespeare.* Arlington Heights, Ill.: A.H.M. Publications, 1978.

BRADLEY, A. C. *Shakespearean Tragedy.* London: The Macmillan Co., 1904.

FARNHAM, WILLARD. *The Medieval Heritage of Elizabethan Tragedy.* Berkeley, California: University of California Press, 1936.

GIBSON, H. N. *The Shakespeare Claimants.* New York: Barnes & Noble, Inc., 1962.

KNIGHT, G. WILSON. *The Wheel of Fire.* London: Oxford University Press, 1930.

LEAVIS, F. R. *The Common Pursuit.* Hardmonsworth, Middlesex: Penguin Books, Ltd., 1963.

74

QUINN, MICHAEL, ed. *Shakespeare: Henry V, A Casebook.* New York: The Macmillan Co., 1969.

SEWELL, ARTHUR. *Character and Society in Shakespeare.* Oxford: Clarendon Press, 1951.

SPIVACK, BERNARD. *Shakespeare and the Allegory of Evil.* New York: Columbia University Press, 1958.

STIRLING, BRENTS. *Unity in Shakespearean Tragedy: The Interplay of Theme and Character.* New York: Columbia University Press, 1956.

TRAVERSI, DEREK. *Shakespeare: From Richard II to Henry V.* Stanford: Stanford University Press, 1957.

NOTES

NOTES

NOTES

NOTES

NOTES

NOTES

HENRY VI, PARTS 1, 2, 3

NOTES

including
- *Life of Shakespeare*
- *Brief Summary of the Trilogy*
- *List of Major Characters*
- *The Historical Background*
- *A Chronology of English Monarchs*
- *The Shakespearean Background*
- *Summaries and Commentaries*
- *Questions for Review*
- *Suggested Essay Topics*
- *Select Bibliography*

by
W. John Campbell, Ph.D.
University of Wisconsin

Cliffs Notes
INCORPORATED
LINCOLN, NEBRASKA 68501

Editor

Gary Carey, M.A.
University of Colorado

Consulting Editor

James L. Roberts, Ph.D.
Department of English
University of Nebraska

ISBN 0-8220-0032-6
© Copyright 1985
by
C. K. Hillegass
All Rights Reserved
Printed in U.S.A.

Cliffs Notes, Inc.   Lincoln, Nebraska

CONTENTS

HENRY VI, Part 3

QUESTIONS FOR REVIEW

SUGGESTED ESSAY TOPICS

SELECT BIBLIOGRAPHY

HENRY VI, Parts 1, 2, 3
Notes

LIFE OF SHAKESPEARE

Many books have assembled facts, reasonable suppositions, traditions, and speculations concerning the life and career of William Shakespeare. Taken as a whole, these materials give a rather comprehensive picture of England's foremost dramatic poet. Tradition and sober supposition are not necessarily false because they lack proved bases for their existence. It is important, however, that persons interested in Shakespeare should distinguish between *facts* and *beliefs* about his life.

From one point of view, modern scholars are fortunate to know as much as they do about a man of middle-class origin who left a small country town and embarked on a professional career in sixteenth-century London. From another point of view, they know surprisingly little about the writer who has continued to influence the English language and its drama and poetry for more than three hundred years. Sparse and scattered as these facts of his life are, they are sufficient to prove that a man from Stratford by the name of William Shakespeare wrote the major portion of the thirty-seven plays which scholars ascribe to him. The concise review which follows will concern itself with some of these records.

No one knows the exact date of William Shakespeare's birth. His baptism occurred on Wednesday, April 26, 1564. His father was John Shakespeare, tanner, glover, dealer in grain, and town official of Stratford; his mother, Mary, was the daughter of Robert Arden, a prosperous gentleman-farmer. The Shakespeares lived on Henley Street.

Under a bond dated November 28, 1582, William Shakespeare and Anne Hathaway entered into a marriage contract. The baptism of their eldest child, Susanna, took place in Stratford in May, 1583. One year and nine months later their twins, Hamnet and Judith, were christened in the same church. The parents named them for the poet's friends, Hamnet and Judith Sadler.

Early in 1596, William Shakespeare, in his father's name, applied to the College of Heralds for a coat of arms. Although positive proof is lacking, there is reason to believe that the Heralds granted this request, for in 1599 Shakespeare again made application for the right to quarter his coat of arms with that of his mother. Entitled to her father's coat of arms, Mary had lost this privilege when she married John Shakespeare before he held the official status of gentleman.

In May of 1597, Shakespeare purchased New Place, the outstanding residential property in Stratford at that time. Since John Shakespeare had suffered financial reverses prior to this date, William must have achieved success for himself.

Court records show that in 1601-02, William Shakespeare began rooming in the household of Christopher Mountjoy in London. Subsequent disputes over the wedding settlement and agreement between Mountjoy and his son-in-law, Stephen Belott, led to a series of legal actions, and in 1612 the court scribe recorded Shakespeare's deposition of testimony relating to the case.

In July, 1605, William Shakespeare paid four hundred and forty pounds for the lease of a large portion of the tithes on certain real estate in and near Stratford. This was an arrangement whereby Shakespeare purchased half the annual tithes, or taxes, on certain agricultural products from parcels of land in and near Stratford. In addition to receiving approximately ten per cent income on his investment, he almost doubled his capital. This was possibly the most important and successful investment of his lifetime, and it paid a steady income for many years.

Shakespeare is next mentioned when John Combe, a resident of Stratford, died on July 12, 1614. To his friend, Combe bequeathed the sum of five pounds. These records and similar ones are important, not because of their economic significance but because they prove the existence of William Shakespeare in Stratford and in London during this period.

On March 25, 1616, William Shakespeare revised his last will and testament. He died on April 23 of the same year. His body lies within the chancel and before the altar of the Stratford church. A rather wry inscription is carved upon his tombstone:

Good Friend, for Jesus' sake, forbear
To dig the dust enclosed here;
Blest be the man that spares these stones
And curst be he who moves my bones.

The last direct descendant of William Shakespeare was his grand-daughter, Elizabeth Hall, who died childless in 1670.

These are the most outstanding facts about Shakespeare the man, as apart from those about the dramatist and poet. Such pieces of information, scattered from 1564 through 1616, declare the existence of such a person, not as a writer or actor, but as a private citizen. It is illogical to think that anyone would or could have fabricated these details for the purpose of deceiving later generations.

In similar fashion, the evidence establishing William Shakespeare as the foremost playwright of his day is positive and persuasive. Robert Greene's *Groatsworth of Wit,* in which he attacked Shakespeare, a mere actor, for presuming to write plays in competition with Greene and his fellow playwrights, was entered in the *Stationers' Register* on September 20, 1592. In 1594 Shakespeare acted before Queen Elizabeth, and in 1594-95 his name appeared as one of the shareholders of the Lord Chamberlain's Company. Francis Meres in his *Palladis Tamia* (1598) called Shakespeare "mellifluous and hony-tongued" and compared his comedies and tragedies with those of Plautus and Seneca in excellence.

Shakespeare's continued association with Burbage's company is equally definite. His name appears as one of the owners of the Globe in 1599. On May 19, 1603, he and his fellow actors received a patent from James I designating them as the King's Men and making them Grooms of the Chamber. Late in 1608 or early in 1609, Shakespeare and his colleagues purchased the Blackfriars Theatre and began using it as their winter location when weather made production at the Globe inconvenient.

Other specific allusions to Shakespeare, to his acting and his writing, occur in numerous places. Put together, they form irrefutable testimony that William Shakespeare of Stratford and London was the leader among Elizabethan playwrights.

One of the most impressive of all proofs of Shakespeare's authorship of his plays is the First Folio of 1623, with the dedicatory verse which appeared in it. John Heminge and Henry Condell, members of Shakespeare's own company, stated that they collected and issued the plays as a memorial to their fellow actor. Many contemporary poets contributed eulogies to Shakespeare; one of the best-known of these poems is by Ben Jonson, a fellow actor and, later, a friendly rival. Jonson also criticized Shakespeare's dramatic work in *Timber: or, Discoveries* (1641).

Certainly there are many things about Shakespeare's genius and career which the most diligent scholars do not know and cannot explain, but the facts which do exist are sufficient to establish Shakespeare's identity as a man and his authorship of the thirty-seven plays which reputable critics acknowledge to be his.

BRIEF SUMMARY OF THE TRILOGY

Henry VI, Part 1

Part 1 deals primarily with the conflicts between **Lord Talbot**, general of the English armies, and **Joan la Pucelle**, more commonly known as Joan of Arc. Talbot has been in France leading the English attempts to gain the French crown, a goal which Henry V had placed high among his priorities. Talbot is shown to be an excellent soldier and very loyal to the English crown. But his king, Henry V, has just died, and messengers arrive at Henry's funeral to announce that the English have been defeated in France. **Charles, the French Dauphin**, took advantage of Henry V's critical illness to raise a fearsome army against the attacking English forces. In addition, Joan of Arc lent hope to the French armies since she was apparently gifted with visionary powers.

As a result, dissension immediately arises in England between the **Duke of Gloucester** (young Henry VI's uncle and Protector of England) and the **Bishop of Winchester** (also known as Henry Beaufort); their disputes arise from personal ambition to influence the young king and gain control of the throne. Moreover, there is additional disagreement between **Richard Plantagenet** (the future Duke of York) and the **Earl of Somerset** (also known as John Beaufort), who will don, respectively, the symbols of the white rose and the red rose as the disastrous Wars of the Roses begin. It is Richard Plantagenet's goal as a Yorkist to wrench the crown away from the Lancastrian Henry VI and restore the Yorkists to the throne.

Meanwhile, the youthful Henry VI is taken to France in order to be crowned King of France. He tells Somerset and York to resolve their differences by being friendly toward one another; thus, York is made Regent of France and, along with Somerset, is ordered to supply Talbot with the necessary supplies to win the English/French battle.

Due to the feud between Somerset and York, however, each man attempts to discredit the other by failing to send Talbot the required assistance. Talbot and his son struggle valiantly against the stronger French army at Bordeaux, but after many skirmishes they are killed. Accordingly, the English armies suffer defeat and enormous losses, but they converge in one last attempt to rout the French. During this battle, York takes Joan of Arc prisoner and berates her as a strumpet and a she-devil. Shortly thereafter, Joan is condemned and burned at the stake.

In a sub-plot, we learn that the **Earl of Suffolk** convinced Henry VI to take **Margaret of Anjou** as his wife; she had no dowry (virtually unheard of in those days—especially for a woman who would marry a king), but she had courage and spirit, and this made for a promising combination in their offspring. Suffolk realized that his success in bringing Henry and Margaret together set him up for a more advantageous position with the king. It was an excellent opportunity for him to rule the young Henry and, indirectly, the whole country.

Part 1, then, covers a period of about eighteen years, from Henry's infancy to his proposed marriage to Margaret of Anjou.

Henry VI, Part 2

Suffolk returns to England with Margaret of Anjou and a peace treaty; the latter is ironic for when Suffolk returns to England, he finds Henry surrounded by a number of threatening lords who are attempting to undo the kingdom and set themselves up as virtual dictators. Gloucester, the good Lord Protector, deeply regrets both the marriage and the peace treaty, but he remains bound to his duty as a loyal subject. More important than anything else to Gloucester is his maintaining absolute protection of the royal authority.

Only the Nevilles—the new **Earl of Salisbury** and the **Earl of Warwick**—are prepared to support Gloucester, and very soon, several

English nobles put aside their animosity for one another in order to join forces against Gloucester. For example, **Cardinal Beaufort** (formerly Bishop of Winchester), Somerset, and York cooperate with Suffolk and Margaret against Gloucester, the Lord Protector: once they can get rid of Gloucester, they think that they will be able to accomplish their individual, greedy goals. Gloucester has been an obstacle to them all. This, then, is the main story of Part 2: the destruction of Gloucester and the collapse of order after his death.

Gloucester's enemies are unable to turn the king or the English people against him, so they decide to murder the Lord Protector. Anarchy follows: Suffolk is banished and will soon be murdered, York is hiding in Ireland gathering his rebellious armies, and Cardinal Beaufort dies. And there is also an entire act of this part of the trilogy (Act IV) devoted to the rebellion of Jack Cade, a romantic who has been encouraged by York. Cade organizes a mob, scorns all authority other than his own, is lifted into power by a fickle mob and is soon tossed out of power by them. The play concludes with the flight of Henry and Margaret after their defeat by York and his three sons at St. Albans. Royal authority is lost in the smolder of heated factions against the crown.

Henry VI, Part 3

Part 3 is considered to be the least successful play of the trilogy primarily because it is one long array of fighting and feuds. It chronicles the final phase of Henry's reign, a time of great anarchy for England and a time of great struggle between the fierce Queen Margaret and the equally fierce house of York. Shakespeare seems to have built Part 3 around the idea that disloyalty and faithless ambition serve no purpose other than to create chaos and disharmony.

York is shown to be unscrupulous, but perhaps the best candidate for the throne. He has argued his case in both Parts 1 and 2 as the legitimate heir to the throne and as England's best hope for peace. He offers Henry a compromise: Henry may remain king for the rest of his life provided that he recognize the Yorks as the legitimate heirs to the throne upon his death. Margaret rejects this proposal angrily, and the fighting begins again. She and her ally Lord Clifford capture York and behead him, leaving behind his young sons who are clearly unfit to rule. York's son Edward, who is king at the moment, sends Warwick to France to request in marriage the hand of Lady Bona, the sister-in-law of the king of France. Shortly thereafter, however, Edward falls in love with Lady Grey and creates enemies of King Lewis of France, Warwick, and Edward's own brother Clarence. All of the latter join forces with Margaret in an effort to dethrone Edward, and the fighting begins again.

The result of this turmoil is that England is confronted with a situation in which the crown has been violated by both sides: the choice between Henry and Margaret or Edward is equally treacherous. The country is ripped to pieces.

The major focus of Part 3 is to trace the events of the final phase of Henry's reign and to show the evolution toward the reign of Richard III. Richard is the strongest of York's sons, though by no means admirable. He opens Part 3 by hurling Somerset's severed head to the floor and then, midway through the play, he reveals his own bloody plans for the throne. At the end of the play, Richard kills Henry and becomes King Richard III. He is a cruel, unsuitable king and is no solution to England's woes. But we have seen in Act IV of the third part of the trilogy that Edward's queen is able to flee the war and escape to a hiding place; she is pregnant with the infant Elizabeth, who will eventually marry Richmond and, by so doing, will unite the houses of York and Lancaster into a union of peace and harmony.

LIST OF MAJOR CHARACTERS

Henry VI

Infant king at the beginning of Part 1; son of Henry V and the grandson of Henry IV; Henry belongs to the House of Lancaster, the "red roses," and he is killed at the end of Part 3.

John, Duke of Bedford

Uncle of Henry VI; younger brother of Henry V; Regent of France.

Humphrey, Duke of Gloucester

Uncle of Henry VI; younger brother of Henry V; Lord Protector of England while Henry is an infant; is arrested for treason and murdered in Part 2; Humphrey by name.

Henry, Duke of Exeter

Great-uncle of Henry VI.

Bishop of Winchester (Cardinal Beaufort)

Great-uncle of Henry VI; very ambitious; becomes Cardinal Beaufort; uses religion to suit his own purposes; lifelong enemy of Gloucester, he conspires in the Lord Protector's death and dies unrepentant; illegitimate son of John of Gaunt; prelate of the Church.

Richard Plantagenet

Son of the late Richard, Earl of Cambridge; becomes Duke of York; belongs to the House of York, the "white roses." He claims to be the rightful heir to the throne occupied by Henry VI; he is killed in Part 3; his sons Edward and Richard become kings after his death, thus restoring the Yorkists to the throne.

John Beaufort

Earl of Somerset; later Duke of Somerset; illegitimate; supporter of Henry VI.

Earl of Salisbury

Military leader of the English armies in France alongside Lord Talbot; killed in Part 1.

Earl of Warwick

Named Richard Neville; son of the Earl of Salisbury; known as "the king maker," he supports the Duke of York's attempts to capture the throne.

Lord Talbot

A central figure in Part 1; general of the English armies in France; opponent of Charles the Dauphin and Joan of Arc; killed in Part 1.

Edmund Mortimer

The Earl of March; uncle of Richard Plantagenet; spends most of his adult life in jail after his supporters try to place him on the throne as the rightful heir; the Duke of York will pledge to carry out Mortimer's request that the Yorkists have the throne restored to them.

Sir John Fastolfe

A cowardly soldier who deserts Talbot's army in France; the early editions of *Henry VI* call him Sir John Falstaff, but he should *not* be confused with the Falstaff of *Henry IV* and *The Merry Wives of Windsor*.

Charles, the Dauphin

Dauphin of France, made king during Part 1; initially skeptical about Joan of Arc's visionary powers, then welcomes her, then fails to save her from being burned to death.

Lewis XI

King of France in Part 3.

Reignier

Duke of Anjou; titular King of Naples; father of Queen Margaret, who marries Henry VI.

Joan la Pucelle

Joan of Arc; French peasant whose vision inspires her to protect France from the English; burned at the stake by the English in Part 1.

Margaret

Daughter of Reignier, Duke of Anjou; marries Henry VI.

Eleanor

Duchess of Gloucester; condemned as a witch.

Margery Jordan

A witch.

Lady Grey

Queen of Edward IV; afterward, mother of Elizabeth (*not* Elizabeth I).

Earl of Suffolk

He arranges for Henry VI's marriage to Margaret of Anjou; becomes the king's favorite, and in Part 2 he is elevated to the rank of duke; named William de la Pole; falls in love with Margaret in Part 2, and ultimately he dies at sea, the victim of pirates.

Lord Clifford

A supporter of Henry VI and Queen Margaret; killed by the Yorkists in Part 2.

Young Clifford

Son of Lord Clifford; becomes Queen Margaret's favorite in Part 3; determined to avenge the death of his father.

THE HISTORICAL BACKGROUND

Shakespeare's *Henry VI, Parts 1, 2, & 3* cover the events leading from the beginning of Henry VI's reign in 1422 until his death in 1471. By the end of Part 3, Shakespeare has led us to the midway point in the Wars of the Roses (1455–87). In *Richard III*, he focuses on the latter years of these Wars – that is, from the attainder and execution of George, Duke of Clarence, in 1478 to the defeat of Richard III at Bosworth Field in 1485. That war, a prolonged, intermittent conflict between the two noble houses of Lancaster and York, was closer to Shakespeare and his contemporaries than are the Napoleonic wars to the present generation.

On the throne of England when Shakespeare wrote, Elizabeth I ruled; she was the granddaughter of Richmond, the first of the Tudors, who, it was firmly believed, was the God-chosen savior of an England long torn by dissension and civil war. Throughout the sixteenth century, in particular, England had reason to fear civil strife as well as foreign invasion, and thus Elizabethans manifested a keen interest in the historical events of the preceding century. As has now been well established, Shakespeare's generation viewed history as a mirror in which could be read lessons important to ruler and subject alike. Moreover, the chronicle histories which provided materials for Shakespeare's "history plays" were written with a Tudor bias, presenting and interpreting characters and events from the point of view accepted as orthodox in sixteenth-century England.

Since Henry VI reigned in the period immediately prior to the Wars of the Roses and during the first years of these Wars, it is desirable to review briefly the story of this epoch which lasted for thirty-some years, during which many princes, many members of the nobility, and at least 100,000 commoners were slain. This was the dynastic struggle between the house of York and the house of Lancaster. Actually, the Lancastrians never adopted the red rose as their symbol, for it was used first by Henry Tudor (Richmond) in 1485, but because of historical precedent, a red rose is associated with the Lancastrians.

At the head of the White Rose party was Richard Plantagenet, third Duke of York, whose claim to the throne was an impressive one. On his mother's side of the family, he was descended from Lionel, Duke of Clarence, the elder brother of John of Gaunt—from whom the Lancastrians were descended. Unfortunately for Richard, however, Parliament had declared for the younger line, which had the advantage of uninterrupted descent through the males.

Richard of York (that is, Richard Plantagenet) was able to capitalize upon Henry VI's notorious weakness as a ruler and on his many misfortunes. Following Jack Cade's Rebellion (1450), Richard was hailed as a popular champion, particularly because of his opposition to the Duke of Somerset, who conducted affairs for the king (King Henry). There was even a proposal that Richard be recognized as the heir to the throne, the first suggestion of the devastating quarrel which became later known as the Wars of the Roses. Taking some liberty with history, Shakespeare dramatized the origin of these two hostile parties in *Henry VI, Part 2* and continued the story of these events into *Part 3*, wherein the Yorkists emerged triumphant.

By the year 1453, when Henry VI became quite ill, the Duke of York had succeeded in getting control of the government, and he was appointed "Protector and Defender of the Realm" by Parliament in 1454. But the king recovered late in the next year, and York was replaced by his rival, Somerset. York did not remain quiet for long. When a council was summoned to make provisions "for the safety of the king against his enemies," the duke led a force of his supporters in a march on London. Somerset, joined by the king and a host of nobles, led an army from London to meet the threat, and the two forces met at St. Albans. The Wars of the Roses had begun. Somerset was killed, and Margaret of Anjou, Henry's energetic queen, emerged as head of the Lancastrian party. During the next four years, England experienced a period of restiveness before warfare broke out again. Although York was supported by the powerful Earl of Warwick, head of the house of Neville, the Yorkists were defeated and York himself fled to Ireland.

King Henry's government, now controlled by Margaret and her council, proved anything but efficient. Faced with poverty and disaster, the average Englishman yearned for the return of Richard of York. In June 1460, Warwick and Edward, Richard's eldest son, moved on London and were joined by Richard, who again claimed the crown (October, 1460). This time, Parliament ruled that the head of the house of York should be heir to the hapless Henry VI. But Margaret was not to be repressed. She succeeded in mustering a strong force in the north and met the Yorkists at Wakefield. In this battle, Richard lost his life. And, since Edward (his son) was just a youth of eighteen, Warwick became the head of the White Rose party. In the next year, the Yorkists were defeated in the second Battle of St. Albans. Nevertheless, Warwick did manage to join forces with Edward and to occupy London. Thus, Margaret eventually lost the fruits of her victory. Young Edward, son of Richard, was declared king by the citizens and by the lords of Yorkshire, and this time, he did not hesitate to take the throne, although this did not constitute a legal election.

Subsequent events worked in Edward's favor. Margaret's Lancastrian forces were defeated near Towton in York on March 29, 1461. Henry VI and his son Edward fled to Scotland. By 1464, the Yorks' Edward was full master of England. Nevertheless, his position was jeopardized by his marriage to Elizabeth, a widowed daughter of Richard Woodville. Warwick, his chief supporter, was enraged, not only because the Woodvilles were of Lancastrian connection, but because Warwick himself had all but completed a plan for the English monarch to marry the sister-in-law of Louis XI of France. Edward IV further aggravated matters by favoring his wife's relatives at the expense of the Nevilles. Meanwhile, Henry VI had returned to England in 1464 and had been placed in the Tower of London (1465). Not long afterward, however, the king was released, and Edward IV was forced to flee to Holland. But because of the support of Charles of Burgundy, Edward was able to assemble a force and return to England. Once more the unfortunate Henry was imprisoned, and Warwick's army was defeated, Warwick himself being slain. To cap all this, the Lancastrians suffered a devastating defeat at Tewkesbury on May 4, 1471. Margaret was taken prisoner and her son, Edward, the young Prince of Wales, was put to death. Henry VI was reported to have died "of pure displeasure and melancholy," but in all probability, Edward IV ordered that he be put to death.

A CHRONOLOGY OF ENGLISH MONARCHS

THE NORMAN CONQUEST

1066–87	William the Conqueror
1087–1100	William II
1100–35	Henry I
1135–54	Stephen

PLANTAGENETS

1154–89	Henry II
1189–99	Richard I
1199–1216	John
1216–72	Henry III
1272–1307	Edward I
1307–27	Edward II
1327–77	Edward III
1377–99	Richard II (mother a Plantagenet; father a Lancastrian)

HOUSES OF LANCASTER AND YORK

1399–1413	Henry IV (Lancaster)
1413–22	Henry V (Lancaster)
* 1422–61	Henry VI (Lancaster) (1455–87 Wars of the Roses)
1461–70	Edward IV (York)

* 1470–71   Henry VI (Lancaster)
  1471–83   Edward IV (York)
  1483–85   Richard III (York)
    Henry VI had a split reign

THE TUDORS

1485–1509	Henry VII
1509–47	Henry VIII
1547–53	Edward VI (father Henry VIII; mother Jane Seymour)
1553–58	Mary I (father Henry VIII; mother Catherine of Aragon)
1558–1603	Elizabeth I (father Henry VIII; mother Anne Boleyn)

THE EARLY STUARTS

1603–25	James I
1625–49	Charles I
1649–60	The Civil Wars and Interregnum

THE LATER STUARTS

1660–85	Charles II
1685–88	James II

THE REVOLUTION SETTLEMENT OF 1688

1689–1702	William III
1689–94	Mary II
1702–14	Anne

THE HANOVERIAN KINGS

1714–27	George I
1727–60	George II
1760–1820	George III
1820–30	George IV
1830–37	William IV
1837–1901	Victoria
1901–10	Edward VII

THE HOUSE OF WINDSOR

1910–36	George V
1936	Edward VIII (abdicated)
1936–52	George VI
1952–	Elizabeth II

THE SHAKESPEAREAN BACKGROUND

The three five-act parts of *Henry VI* date from the earliest phase of Shakespeare's career. The Shakespearean critic Francis Fergusson has divided this career into four major periods: (1) *apprenticeship* to the London theater (which began with Shakespeare's arrival in London around 1586 and lasted until he joined the Lord Chamberlain's Men in 1594); (2) *growing mastery*, from 1594 to 1599, when the Globe Theatre was opened; (3) *maturity*, during which time the great tragedies were written; this period began with the acquisition of the Globe Theatre and continued until the acquisition of the Blackfriars Theatre in 1609; and (4) *the final retrospect*, from 1610 until Shakespeare's death in 1616.

The *Henry VI* plays belong to the first of these four periods, along with *Titus Andronicus, The Comedy of Errors, Two Gentlemen of Verona, Richard III, Love's Labour's Lost*, and probably *King John*. Shakespeare learned very early in his career that it was valuable to use history as a basis for his plays. He was not so much interested in teaching history, however, as in presenting it poetically in the form of stories. The genre of the history play was extremely popular when Shakespeare arrived in London. It was an outgrowth of the English people's deep faith in their monarchy (at that time, Elizabeth I was on the throne). In his book *Shakespeare's History Plays*, E. M. W. Tillyard describes how the Tudor chroniclers believed that their monarch was the only one capable of maintaining peace and justice in the kingdom. Divine Providence was ultimately responsible for selecting the correct monarch, and citizens were convinced that the history of their country would unravel within this system of Providence. The monarch was someone whom they looked up to for guidance and direction, and this is one of the reasons why Shakespeare often used royalty as subjects for his plays: historical figures almost always found a receptive audience in the England of his time. The

Tudor success was seen as the final happy ending of the Wars of the Roses and the beginning of a new era in England. *Henry VI* and *Richard III* are sometimes referred to as "the Tudor epic" since they are set in this period of the Wars of the Roses. *Richard II* (set in the period of Richard's reign from 1377 to 1399) and the *Henry IV* plays chronicle the beginnings of the English civil wars; and *Henry V* is a bit of an afterthought. *Henry VIII*, considered to be Shakespeare's last play, has essentially nothing to do with the other history plays, nor does *King John*, which is widely acknowledged to be one of Shakespeare's weakest dramas; it is rarely performed on the stage, and when it is, audiences are usually unimpressed.

Shakespeare disliked the style and manner of the history plays which were in vogue at the time of his arrival in London, and he decided to adapt history to his own vision of the world, highlighting the personal and human drama of his subjects and focusing on the conflicts which tormented royalty. It made little sense to him to see royalty glorified beyond all means of recognition; if audiences were unable to identify with a drama, then there was no point in presenting it to them. Shakespeare was not concerned with publishing his plays, but rather with the successful staging of them for his contemporaries. It is for this reason that the English director Michael Langham argues that Shakespeare should be seen on the stage before he is read and studied: his dramas speak directly to the heart, and the communication comes to life when one sees the plays in the flesh.

Shakespeare returned to historical subjects throughout his career, with a history play (*Henry VIII*) as his last dramatic work. His subjects include King John (a Plantagenet), Richard II (also a Plantagenet), Henry IV (a Lancastrian), Henry V (also a Lancastrian), Henry VI (another Lancastrian), Richard III (a Yorkist), and Henry VIII (a Tudor). Shakespeare's history plays capture the evolution of the British monarchy from the Middle Ages (Plantagenets) through to the Renaissance (Tudors). They were not written in chronological order; the *Henry VI* plays came first, followed by *Richard III*, *King John*, *Richard II*, the *Henry IV* plays, *Henry V*, and *Henry VIII*. There is a total of ten history plays in the Shakespearean canon.

Because the *Henry VI* plays belong to Shakespeare's earliest period of writing, when we compare them with what will come later, we discover that they are less poetic and, dramatically, less satisfying. But as a trilogy, they can be very effective on the stage and constitute an impressive epic sweep. Scholars still debate the exact dates of their production and the order in which they were written. The important point is: Shakespeare was able to turn Henry's disastrous reign into a flowing, intelligent drama which is not devoid of interest. Henry's reign was a complicated one; as a weak king, he was surrounded by dozens of people determined to take advantage of him and to accomplish their own goals at his expense. Shakespeare uses only that information from the period which serves to highlight his drama. He is not concerned with total accuracy or with including all of the historical details from the period. Rather, his is a selective approach to history and, because of this method, we are not weighed down with subject matter which is irrelevant to the primary drama. Most significantly, it is the *crown of England* which interests Shakespeare, *not* Henry VI as a man or ruler. To be sure, Henry VI is often at the center of the action, and the trilogy focuses on the events during his reign, but it is the crown, and the English people's unshakable faith in the crown as a symbol of stability in their country, that Shakespeare is concerned with in this trilogy. Each of the three parts may be treated as an entity since each deals with a separate struggle for the crown. And as each struggle is resolved, Shakespeare sketches the beginnings of a new effort to dethrone Henry VI, and this new effort becomes the subject of the next part. Shakespeare apparently thought that Henry VI was not fit to serve as king, and the trilogy depicts the various weaknesses which expose him to the many and varied assaults on his throne.

When reading *Henry VI,* it is helpful to recall the historical events which occurred in the years prior to Henry's reign. His ancestor Henry IV had come to the throne after the murder of Richard II, and through his immense prestige as a "conquering hero," Henry IV succeeded in earning the confidence of his people. They felt that Henry IV was the man to safeguard their country, and this made it very difficult for Richard II's heirs to protest his murder. When Henry V became king, England had entered into an intensely patriotic period which paralleled Henry V's near-success at claiming the crown of France for England. *Henry VI, Part 1* begins at the moment of Henry V's death – a time when Henry VI is still an infant and the country is being run by Gloucester, the Lord Protector. Due to the absence of a mature king, the gates of protest are flung open for challengers to the throne. This sets the stage for the evolution of Henry VI's monarchy and for the drama at hand.

SUMMARIES AND COMMENTARIES

HENRY VI, Part 1

ACT I

The play opens in Westminster Abbey at the funeral of Henry V, once the shining Prince Hal, "this star of England." Henry V leaves behind him the boy Henry VI, who is too young to reign. Several of the principal characters of this trilogy are present at the funeral, including Humphrey (the good Duke of Gloucester), an uncle of Henry VI, who has been designated to reign in Henry VI's place as Lord Protector until Henry is old enough to assume an active role. Also present is another of Henry VI's uncles, the Duke of Bedford, who is Regent of France; and present also is Warwick, who (as an Earl) has significant influence in the kingdom and is known as "the king maker." Also present is a great-uncle of Henry VI, Henry Beaufort (who will soon become the Cardinal of Winchester), and others.

The Duke of Bedford and the Duke of Gloucester bemoan the passing of their late king: "England ne'er lost a king of so much worth." As early as the first speech of the play, then, Shakespeare sets the tone for trouble: a beloved king has died, and there is no one to take his place. Henry V had virtue, was an excellent soldier, and was a fearless competitor: "He ne'er lift up his hand but conquered." Now the throne risks being conquered by outsiders. The Duke of Exeter (another great-uncle) suggests that some wicked "French sorcerers" conspired to bring about Henry V's end, and this prepares us for the eventual role played by Joan la Pucelle (more commonly known as Joan of Arc, or the Maid). Winchester states that part of Henry's glory was due to the Church, which aided Henry's victories because Henry always fought "the battles of the Lord." Gloucester, however, retorts that the Church had *nothing* to do with Henry's glorious reign. Rather, the churchmen did not pray sufficiently – if at all – for the king; they preferred to have a monarch who was an "effeminate prince," one whom they could dominate. Shakespeare sets Gloucester up, therefore, as being the defender of the throne, of the royal family, and of the country: Gloucester will become the prime obstacle for several ambitious nobles, and this struggle will unravel dramatically in Part 2 of the trilogy. Gloucester represents a set of beliefs contrary to those held by such people as Winchester. Whereas Gloucester is the Lord Protector of England and has the country's best interests at heart, many of his peers seek to aggrandize themselves at the expense of the monarchy. They wish to have influence at the royal court and see their personal, ambitious desires brought to fruition. A major conflict, then, is drawn in this first scene: there will be a struggle between opposing factions for the monarchy. The old order will be called upon to defend itself from those who see themselves as legitimate heirs, those who feel that they should be on the throne.

Bedford finally puts an end to the arguing and calls upon the ghost of Henry V to keep the realm from "civil broils" – or else "our isle be made a marish of salt tears." A messenger enters then with news from France: the English have suffered enormous losses and have been defeated at Rheims, Orleans, Champagne, and other French towns in their quest for the French throne. The English losses, he says, were due to a lack of manpower and money – not because of any French "sorcery"; moreover, the English soldiers are aware of various divisive factions at work back in England. They realize that there is confusion in the court and that the English generals do *not* have the necessary support at court in order to make victory possible. The messenger warns the nobles to resolve their petty arguments and realize that many human lives are at stake abroad: "Let not sloth dim your honours new-begot." He says that "England's coat is half cut away." Bedford proclaims his patriotism and states his intention to fight for "the cause"; he says that he intends to conquer France for England ("Wounds will I lend the French.").

Another messenger enters and announces that Charles, the Dauphin of France, has been crowned king in Rheims and that the Bastard of Orleans is with him, as well as the Duke of Anjou. The nobles are seemingly unanimous in their desire to fight France, but Gloucester and Bedford exchange sharp words about Bedford's true dedication to the cause. The seeds of dissent are present, then, even in an otherwise "unified" cause.

A third messenger enters with the news that Lord Talbot, general of the English armies, has been overthrown: he was surrounded by a French army of 23,000 men, almost four times the size of the English army (6,000 soldiers). Talbot fought valiantly for three hours and would have won, but Sir John Fastolfe "played the coward" and fled the battle scene, damaging morale and bringing about a general massacre. Talbot was wounded (a spear in his back) and taken prisoner, but his life was spared; most of his men, however, were slaughtered. Bedford vows to revenge the act by wrenching the Dauphin's crown: he will take ten thousand soldiers with him to France and aid the weak forces of the Earl of Salisbury. Exeter recalls the oath which they all took to the late King Henry: "To quell the Dauphin utterly/ Or bring him in obedience to your yoke." Gloucester hastens to the Tower so that he can examine the artillery available, stating that he will proclaim young Henry the new king of England. Exeter says that he plans to go to Eltham, where Henry VI is, so that he can prepare for the king's safety. When Exeter is gone, Winchester is left alone. He reveals his plan to steal the young king and "sit at [the] chiefest stern of public weal." In other words, he wishes to have power over everyone.

The scene shifts to Orleans, France, where the Dauphin (Charles) is in conversation with the Duke of Alencon and Reignier (Duke of Anjou). Charles is pleased that fate is on the side of the French and that they have defeated the English. Spontaneously, he and Reignier decide that there is no point in waiting to attack the English again: "Let's raise the siege; why live we idly here?" Talbot has been captured and only the "mad-brained Salisbury" remains. Thus, they sound the alarum, but, later, they are surprised to find themselves driven back by the English. Charles concludes that his men are cowards; they abandoned him amidst the enemy. They discuss the English courage and audacity.

Just as they are about to leave the English behind them, the Bastard of Orleans enters with news: he has brought with him "a holy maid," Joan la Pucelle, or Joan of Arc, who has been allegedly ordained by heaven to raise the siege against the English and drive them out of France. Seemingly, the maid is gifted with prophecy exceeding even that of "the nine sibyls of old Rome." Charles consents to speak with her, but he first decides to test her skill: he asks Reignier to stand in his place as Dauphin. When Joan enters, however, she identifies the trick immediately: "Reignier, is't thou that thinkest to beguile me?" She then insists on speaking privately with the Dauphin.

Joan tells Charles how she was seated in the field one day and was greeted with a vision from "God's mother" (Mary). Mary instructed Joan to leave her "base vocation" and save her country from calamity.

Charles agrees to take Joan to battle with him and, if she is successful, he will place all his confidence in her word. But first, he challenges her to a duel; if, in single combat she "vanquishes" Charles, he will know that her words "are true." They spar with swords, and Joan bests him. Charles is impressed: "Thou art an Amazon. . . . 'Tis thou that must help me. . . . Let me thy servant and *not* sovereign be." Joan argues that France must fight till the end and never surrender. She predicts that England's glory is at an end because Henry V is dead. Reignier urges haste; she must drive the English from Orleans "and be immortaliz'd."

The scene moves once again to London; as is typical of the *Henry VI* plays, Shakespeare jumps back and forth from country to country. In London, Gloucester arrives to survey the Tower of London, but is told by the guards that he is unable to enter: Winchester (Henry Beaufort) has forbidden it: Gloucester and his people have been black-listed by Winchester. This is the first unmistakable proof that we have that Winchester intends to seize control of the kingdom, despite *any* possible consequences. Winchester enters then and gloats in the presence of Gloucester, who boldly calls Winchester a "manifest conspirator" and states that Winchester sought to murder Henry V. Gloucester insists on being allowed in the Tower or else he vows to drive Winchester back.

A skirmish breaks out between their men, and the Mayor arrives, demanding that everyone return home. His officer commands them to put away their weapons—or be executed. Winchester warns Gloucester to be careful, and Gloucester warns Winchester that he will stamp Winchester's hat (his religious symbol) beneath his feet. The conflict between the two men is drawn: Winchester, as a representative of the Church, desires power, and he will try to impose himself through the authority of the Church, even if his intentions have nothing to do with religion or God. Gloucester, on the other hand, is the rightful Protector of England, and he is prepared to bring force to bear whenever necessary in his attempts to protect both Henry VI and the English people. Thus, it is clear that religion, law, and politics all disappear into the background as personal ambition and a drive for power consume Winchester. The Mayor himself even exclaims that Winchester is "more haughty than the devil."

At Orleans, in France, Salisbury welcomes Talbot back to the action, asking him questions about his treatment while he was a

French prisoner (Talbot was released from jail through an arrangement with the Duke of Bedford, who exchanged another prisoner for Talbot). Talbot says that he was publicly humiliated by the French, exposed in the market place and mocked as the "terror of the French,/ The scarecrow that affrights our children."

As the two men are talking, Salisbury is shot from somewhere in the town; one of his eyes is destroyed and he dies. Then a messenger announces that the Dauphin has joined forces with Joan la Pucelle and that the French are gathering strength.

Talbot drives back the Dauphin, then Joan enters, driving back some Englishmen. Joan and Talbot duel, while Talbot curses her, claiming that she is a witch and that he will send her back to "him thou serv'st." They exchange more sharp words, and she taunts him to action. Then she announces that she will rescue Orleans. She dares Talbot to follow her and attempt to overtake her army. Her confidence is unfailing: she believes that divine strength is on her side. Talbot is confused by her; he believes that her "witch powers" are responsible for defeating the English. He bemoans the fact that the English soldiers lack courage and that Joan will reclaim Orleans – despite his efforts to hold her back. In the next scene, Charles confirms that Joan has indeed recovered Orleans.

Act I, then, sets up the major conflict of the play; it is a struggle for power on a number of levels:

(1) personal ambition (that is, Gloucester vs. Winchester);
(2) monarchic ambition (Gloucester attempting to protect the young king's interests); and
(3) international ambition (England at war with France).

Chaos and disorder reign in the place of a stable monarchy, and this idea will be further developed as the drama unfolds.

ACT II

This act opens outside Orleans with a French sergeant instructing his sentinels (guards) to alert him if there are any signs of the English. Talbot enters then with Bedford and Burgundy; the Duke of Burgundy's father has been murdered by the Dauphin, and this has caused Burgundy to become an ally of the British. The three men discuss the French army's brazen attitude of celebration, and Talbot suggests that they enter the city, where the French lie asleep.

The French sentinel sounds the alarum, and the French soldiers are clearly caught off-guard. Charles scolds Joan for deceitful planning; he claims that she flattered the French with minor gains, but set them up for major losses. She replies that her powers cannot work *all* of the time, that they are unable to prevail when she is *sleeping*. She blames the attack on unreliable watchmen.

The next day, Talbot orders that the body of Salisbury is to be brought into the marketplace so that the French can see *why* Talbot revenged Salisbury (". . . hereafter ages may behold/ What ruin happened in revenge of him."). The English armies, we learn, having fought all night, successfully revenged themselves on their enemies. And it seems now that Joan and the Dauphin fled the scene when they realized how serious a threat the English actually were.

But there is a French plan afoot to recapture Talbot: the Countess of Auvergne invites him to visit her castle, and Talbot accepts. Burgundy and Bedford fear chicanery on the part of the Countess, but Talbot decides to see her anyway. Before going, he whispers something in his captain's ear.

Once inside the castle, Talbot becomes the Countess' prisoner: she wishes to prevent him from causing any more damage to the French. Talbot does not take her seriously. Through a refined manipulation of irony, he dodges her insults and succeeds in alerting his men. She quickly acquiesces and apologizes for her abuse of him. The sudden strength of Talbot and his men makes her realize with whom she is dealing.

Back in London, Richard Plantagenet (who will become the Duke of York) meets with Warwick ("the king maker"), the Duke of Somerset, the Earl of Suffolk, and others in the Temple Garden. An argument has taken place inside the Temple Hall between Richard and Somerset, and the group has withdrawn into the garden where things are more private. Somerset calls upon Warwick to decide who is right in the argument, but both Warwick and Suffolk decline to pass judgment since they feel unequipped to assess the subtle points of the dispute. Their argument concerns the throne of England, which will eventually be the cause of the Wars of the Roses: Richard Plantagenet and his followers choose a white rose as their symbol, while Somerset and his group opt for a red rose. Warwick dons a white rose and sides with Plantagenet. Suffolk takes a red one. Already, in this initial discussion, there is a clear suggestion of the bloodshed and

SELECTED YORK-LANCASTER GENEALOGY

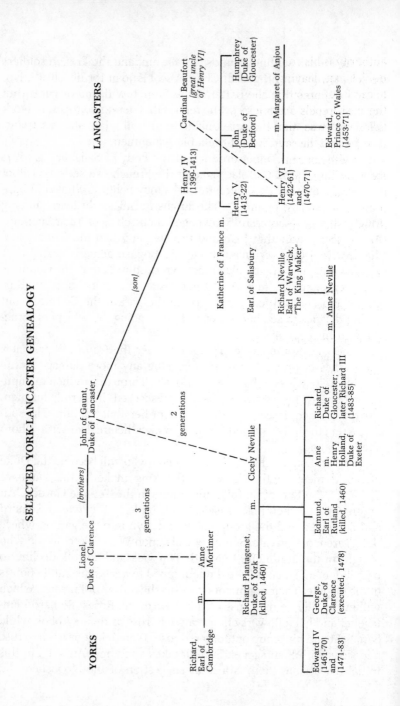

sorrow ahead. Somerset warns: "Prick not your finger as you pluck it off,/ Lest bleeding you do paint the white rose red." So the Yorks, on the side of Richard Plantagenet, are set against the Lancasters, supported by Somerset. The young king Henry VI is conspicuously absent from this colloquy; this shows to what extent the future of the English monarchy is being decided by factions which do not involve the king directly. Henry is brought into the conflict only because of his bloodline, and it is not significant that he appear at this point in the play. Rather, it is the *crown* of England which is of importance, *not* the *person* of the young king. But Henry's ultimate weakness as a ruler is already foreshadowed in his absence from this serious debate.

A lawyer present at the discussion claims that Somerset is wrong in his belief that the "red roses" are the legitimate heirs to the throne of England. He sides with Plantagenet and the white roses. Warwick interrupts and informs Somerset that he is in error about Plantagenet: the latter's grandfather was Lionel, Duke of Clarence, third son to Edward III, King of England. This royal link surely justifies Richard's claim to the throne. Shakespeare, however, errs in the genealogy of Richard since there are actually four generations between Platagenet and Lionel. But the lineage *is* genuine, and Richard does have a legitimate claim to the crown. Somerset argues that Richard's father was executed for treason, but the young Plantagenet counters with: "Condemn'd to die for treason, but no traitor . . . I'll note you in my book of memory/ To scourge you for this apprehension." The scene ends with Warwick declaring his allegiance to the white rose faction.

Richard meets then with his aging uncle, Edmund Mortimer, Earl of March, in the Tower of London, and Mortimer relates his story to Richard in a weak, dying voice: Henry IV, grandfather to the present king, deposed his nephew Richard, Edward's son, who was also the first-born son and the lawful heir to the throne. The Percies of the North found this usurpation unjust and attempted to advance Mortimer to the throne, reasoning that he was the legitimate heir to the throne since Richard II had no children.

Mortimer reasons that he was, by birth, derived from Lionel, Duke of Clarence, the *third* son of King Edward III, whereas Henry IV was the son of John of Gaunt, the *fourth* son of Edward III. But when Henry V came to the throne, Mortimer was thrown in jail. Thus, Mortimer now pronounces his nephew Richard Plantagenet to be his heir, but warns him to be careful in his attempt for the monarchy: "Be thou politic./ Strong-fixed is the house of Lancaster/ And like a mountain, not to be remov'd." Mortimer dies, and Richard vows to revenge his lineage.

Act II advances the plot by explaining in detail the reasons behind Richard Plantagenet's rebellion: he believes himself to be the rightful heir to the throne and shall proceed to confront the Lancasters with this fact.

ACT III

This act opens at the Parliament House in London during an open conflict between Gloucester and Winchester about a bill, which Gloucester attempts to submit and which Winchester rips apart. Gloucester accuses Winchester of having designs on the king: "If thy thoughts were sifted,/ The King, thy sovereign, is not quite exempt/ From envious malice of thy swelling heart." Winchester retorts that his uncle, Gloucester, seeks to be the only one in the kingdom with power over Henry VI. Then Warwick speaks up in favor of Gloucester: "Is not his Grace Protector to the King?"

At this point, Henry enters and attempts to reconcile the two men in a speech which depicts him as a precocious young man (in point of actual fact, Henry would be only five years old). Furthermore, Henry pleads for family unity and peace, and he hints that this kind of internal struggle augurs badly for the country: "Believe me, lords, my tender years can tell/ Civil dissension is a viperous worm/ That gnaws the bowels of the commonwealth."

The mayor enters and a skirmish follows: the supporters of Gloucester and Winchester have begun stoning one another and have wrought havoc in the town. Significantly, Henry calls upon Gloucester, *not* Winchester, to quell the strife: it is as if he has greater trust and faith in his Lord Protector.

Henry's first speeches portray him as a weak and fearful king, and although he is young, he is of royal blood and is expected to emulate the greatness of his ancestors. But from the very beginning, he shows no signs of strength or power; he defers to others and laments his sorrowful plight: "O, how this discord doth afflict my soul!" It should be remembered that the conflict in the streets between Gloucester's and Winchester's men has nothing to do with the Wars of the Roses, yet eventually, both conflicts will combine into a rising torrent of terror and bloodshed.

Winchester and Gloucester strike a begrudging agreement, and the skirmish is called off. When the two factions leave, Henry is offered a scroll by Warwick, and he re-establishes Richard Plantagenet to his royal bloodline, thereby making Richard Duke of York. Richard pledges an ironic allegiance to the young king: "Thy humble servant vows obedience/ And humble service till the point of death." In other words, Richard will remain faithful until Henry's death – at which point, he intends to assume the throne himself.

Gloucester suggests that Henry leave for France in order to be crowned king, and Henry reveals his dependence on his uncle: "When Gloucester says the word, King Henry goes." Exeter, in a monologue, predicts that the feigned love of the peers for one another will break out into vicious dissension: "Till bones and flesh and sinews fall away,/ So will this base and envious discord breed." He predicts that an old-time prophecy uttered in the time of Henry V will come true – namely, that Henry V would *win* all and that Henry VI would *lose* all. This is another indication that the reign of Henry VI promises to be less than glorious.

Back in Rouen, France, Joan is in disguise; she plans to enter the city with four soldiers dressed like peasants. Her plan succeeds, and once inside the gates, she reasons that it will be possible to give notice to the French troops and that Charles will be able to launch an attack. This capture of Rouen has no basis in historical fact: the city actually remained under English control until 1449, and this was eighteen years after Joan of Arc had been burned there.

Once inside the city, Joan sets a torch ablaze and flashes it for Charles to see. She is elated at the possibility of conquering the English inside the town and at restoring French rule to Rouen: "Behold! this is the happy wedding torch/ That joineth Rouen unto her countrymen,/ But burning fatal to the Talbotites!" Charles and his men storm the city, and Talbot flees, promising revenge and blaming the French treachery on Joan, "that witch, that damned sorceress."

Talbot invites the Frenchmen to fight the battle on the field, but Alencon refuses. So Talbot beseeches Burgundy to help restore the town to the English. Burgundy replies, "My vows are equal partners with thy vows," but this vow will soon prove to be devoid of meaning since Burgundy will betray the English and commit himself to supporting his native Frenchmen. Bedford, who is dying, resolves to remain close to the front so as to inspire courage in his soldiers. Talbot and Burgundy leave to gather up their forces in preparation for a renewed attack on the French. Once again, Fastolfe flees camp in order to save his life. Left alone, Bedford dies.

Talbot and Burgundy re-enter with the news that Rouen has been taken back from the French: "Now will we take some order in the town." It seems that Joan, Charles, and the Bastard had all fallen asleep.

The scene shifts then to Joan and the two men, somewhere between Rouen and Paris; they are discussing the fall of Rouen to the English. Joan advises that they should not be worried about it: "Let frantic Talbot triumph for a while/ And like a peacock sweep along his tail./ We'll pull his plumes and take away his train,/ If Dauphin and the rest will be but rul'd." She recommends order and discipline, and Charles agrees to support her. She vows furthermore to sway the allegiance of the Duke of Burgundy; Talbot, she says, would be weakened by such a desertion.

In an impassioned, persuasive speech to Burgundy, Joan argues the virtues of her homeland under threat by a foreign invader: "See, see the pining malady of France!/ Behold the wounds, the most unnatural wounds,/ Which thou thyself has given her woeful breast." She convinces Burgundy to support the French effort against the English. As with the recapturing of Rouen, this episode did *not* take place as such in reality: Burgundy's abandonment of the English did not take place until several years after Joan's death. But in the play, Joan uses patriotism as a leverage to lure Burgundy back into the French camp: "When Talbot hath set footing once in France/ And fashion'd thee that instrument of ill,/ Who then but English Henry will be lord/ And thou be thrust out like a fugitive?" Burgundy is portrayed as a man entranced by the language of persuasion; he does not appear as one who is invincible in his convictions or whose allegiance to a group of people is unbending. Whatever suits his needs of the moment is what determines Burgundy's affiliation. Shakespeare weaves a touch of irony into Joan's response to Burgundy's conversion: "Done like a Frenchman: turn, and turn again!"

At the palace in Paris, Talbot takes a break during his war activities and presents himself to the king. He says that he is the epitomy of loyalty through and through; he is proud to recite the sites of his conquests in France: fifty fortresses, twelve cities, and seven walled towns of great strength. Henry has grown older than the last time we saw him, but he is still a young king; Shakespeare does his best to hurry the aging process so that we are not dealing with an irresponsible youth. Instead, we are dealing with a vulnerable young adult. Henry lauds Talbot for his many years of devotion to the country, and in recognition of Talbot's faithfulness to the royal family, Henry elevates him to the rank of Earl of Shrewsbury. The act ends with a minor skirmish between Vernon and Basset – the former is a supporter of Richard Plantagenet, while the latter is faithful to Somerset. The skirmish serves to remind us, symbolically, that the Wars of the Roses are imminent and that the York-Lancaster conflict is nowhere near to being settled.

ACT IV

As the act opens, Henry is being crowned by Winchester in Paris. Fastolfe enters with the news that Burgundy has betrayed the English, and Talbot, in turn, rails at Fastolfe for having deserted the English forces at the battle of Patay. Henry banishes Fastolfe, on pain of death, and Fastolfe scurries from the room.

The letter from Burgundy, which Fastolfe brought with him, discloses Burgundy's new allegiance to Charles, "the rightful king of France." Henry, in his naiveté, orders Talbot to confer with Burgundy about the desertion and to chastise him for his conduct – another sign that the young king has little understanding of the politics of power.

York (Richard Plantagenet) and Somerset bring their quarrel to the king, who addresses them as "good cousins both." Henry commands a peace between them. He claims that there is no room for argument among the English, particularly as they are in France and must present a facade of unity. In an attempt to reconcile the two factions, Henry plucks a red rose and puts it on his uniform, claiming that "Both are my kinsmen, and I love them both." Then he sends the Duke of York (Richard Plantagenet) off to be a regent in France and instructs Somerset to provide auxiliary support to York's forces.

Outside the gates of Bordeaux, Talbot announces that the French should give themselves up to the English and proclaim Henry their king. Talbot is then met head-on by a general who asserts that the town is well fortified and prepared for a fight. Talbot discovers that the general means business: an enormous troop of Frenchmen descend on the meager English forces. Motivated by his feud with York, Somerset has refused to send the horses which Talbot requires.

A messenger blames the English slaughter at Bordeaux on the discord between York and Somerset: "Whiles they each other cross,/ Lives, honours, lands, and all hurry to loss." Sir William Lucy rages at Somerset for withholding necessary support from Talbot: "The fraud of England, not the force of France,/ Hath now entrapp'd the noble-minded Talbot." Somerset dispatches the horsemen, but it is too late: the English are losing the battle and nothing will help.

In an emotional scene between Talbot and his son John, Talbot orders the young boy to flee the battlefield lest he be killed. The son refuses to abandon his father, so the two remain together in their fight for England's victory. After a number of skirmishes, the two of them are slain, and the English suffer tremendous losses. In a mocking, naturalistic style, Joan permits Sir Lucy to remove the corpses of the two Talbots: "For God's sake, let him have them;/ To keep them here,/ They would but stink, and putrefy the air." Sir Lucy proclaims that their ashes shall become a phoenix which shall cause holy terror.

ACT V

In London, Gloucester tells the king of the pope's message – that peace must be achieved between England and France so that the bloodshed can end. As a means to this end, Gloucester informs the king that the Earl of Armagnac, a man of great authority in France, has offered his only daughter to Henry as his future wife. Henry summons the royal ambassadors and promises to go along with their advice on the matter.

Winchester enters, dressed as a cardinal, and Exeter remarks that Henry V's prophecy is about to be fulfilled: "Henry the Fifth did sometime prophesy/ If once he come to be a cardinal,/ He'll make his cap co-equal with the crown." In other words, Winchester has advanced one step further in his quest for absolute power.

Henry informs the group of ambassadors that he shall indeed marry the Earl of Armagnac's daughter. He sends as a symbol of agreement a jewel for the French woman. In a brief aside, Winchester establishes his contention to be inferior to none, especially to Gloucester: "I'll either make thee stoop and bend thy knee,/ Or sack this country with a mutiny."

On the plains of Anjou, a scout announces to Charles (the Dauphin) and Joan that the English armies are headed in their direction and shall presently launch an attack on the French. Joan requests help from the spiritual bodies on whom she has depended, but when they appear before her, she finds them unwilling to cooperate with her. This means trouble for France, and Joan prepares for defeat: "See, they forsake me! Now the time is come/ That France must vail her lofty-plumed crest/ And let her head fall into England's lap." Burgundy and York (Plantagenet) fight hand to hand, and the French soldiers flee the scene, leaving Joan in York's power. They exit, and Suffolk and Margaret enter. Suffolk, who is married, admires Margaret of Anjou's beauty. She is a daughter of the King of Naples, and Suffolk decides to win her for Henry. The only problem is that her father is poor, but Suffolk wagers that the youthful Henry will nonetheless be drawn to her beauty. Her father agrees to the proposition provided he be allowed to enjoy peace and quiet in the territories of Anjou and Maine.

At Anjou, York orders that Joan be brought forth. He heaps insults on her, and she denies her earthly lineage. In fact, she denies *all* blood relationship with her shepherd father. Her forefathers, she says, were "kings,/ Virtuous and holy; chosen from above . . ./ To work exceeding miracles on earth." She denies that she ever had anything to do with "wicked spirits." She tells York and the others that they – and not she – are "polluted . . . and stained . . . and corrupt." She has been "chaste and immaculate" since infancy. And when the English will not listen to her defense, Joan announces that she is pregnant and defies them to murder not only her but "the fruit within [her] womb." The English scoff, but Joan is adamant. The child's father, she says, is Reignier (who will soon become the father-in-law of Henry). York tells Joan that her "words condemn thy brat and thee." Joan is led away, but not before she utters a curse upon England: "May never glorious sun reflex his beams/ Upon the country where you abode."

Winchester (Henry's great-uncle) announces that a peace treaty has been struck between England and France. York, outraged at the idea of surrendering everything that England has fought for, foresees with grief the loss of France. Charles (the Dauphin) is insulted at Henry's suggestion that he be named viceroy to the King of England and that he become a liege to the English crown. Alencon, however, advises Charles to accept the truce in order to bring peace to an otherwise torn-apart country, adding that Charles can always break the truce when it serves his purposes. So Charles accepts the proposal.

At the palace in London, Suffolk spares no effort to persuade Henry to marry Margaret. But Gloucester reminds Henry that he is already engaged to someone else, a lady of esteem and a daughter of a man whom England cannot afford to offend – meaning the influential Earl of Armagnac. Exeter argues that Armagnac is wealthy, whereas Margaret's father is poor; surely it would be more advantageous to marry a woman of wealth. But Suffolk prevails, and Henry decides in Margaret's favor. He asks Suffolk to sail for France and bring her back to be his queen. Part 2 of the trilogy will begin with the arrival of Margaret in England.

Suffolk, left alone at the end of Part 1, acknowledges to himself that he has won an important victory with the king. He realizes that he now has power in the royal circle and can set himself up as someone to be reckoned with: "Margaret shall now be queen, and rule the king;/ But I will rule both her, the king, and realm." Alongside the other nobles in pursuit of this influence (Gloucester, Winchester, and Plantagenet, the rebellious Duke of York), Suffolk completes the tableau of a vicious, bitter struggle in the making. Part 2 will advance this struggle to the point of action and will show even further the disintegration of a weak king's monarchy into a state of growing chaos.

HENRY VI, Part 2

ACT I

Part 1 of *Henry VI* was centered largely around the conflict for power in England and Joan la Pucelle's role in the defense of France against the English; Part 2 is devoted to an examination of the mounting conspiracy against the extremely unselfish and noble Gloucester and the resultant chaos which ensues after his murder.

The play opens in a stateroom at the palace in London. Suffolk has arrived back in England with the new queen, Margaret of Anjou, who will not only come to despise Henry, but who will actually take matters in her own hands and rule the kingdom as she pleases. At this point in the drama, however, Margaret meets Henry for the first time, and he is instantly infatuated with her "beauteous face."

As a part of the marriage contract, a peace treaty with France is announced, one which calls for an eighteen-month period of peace. Moreover, England will relinquish to Margaret's father, the King of Naples, the duchy of Anjou and the county of Maine, and Henry agrees to marry Margaret despite the fact that she has *no* dowry. These terms of marriage are *extremely* unsatisfactory to Gloucester, Henry's uncle, who is so stunned that he drops the marriage contract on the floor while he is reading it in disbelief. But King Henry is quite happy with his new bride and, as a gesture of appreciation, he elevates Suffolk to the rank of duke. At the same time, the Duke of York (Richard Plantagenet) is relieved of his title as Regent of France until the eighteen-month period of truce is over.

In particular, Gloucester resents the fact that his own brothers, King Henry V and the Duke of Bedford, worked so hard to conquer France for England, only to have their efforts now tossed aside by an inexperienced youth smitten with love:

> O peers of England, shameful is this league,
> Fatal this marriage, cancelling your fame,
> Blotting your names from books of memory,
> Razing the characters of your renown,

Defacing monuments of conquer'd France,
Undoing all, as all had never been!

(I.i.98–103)

The nobles then discuss amongst themselves the pro's and con's of their king's marriage: Cardinal Beaufort (formerly Winchester), a great-uncle of Henry's, is critical of Gloucester's opposition to the king; Warwick reminds them of his personal efforts on the battlefield, which helped to win the duchies of Anjou and Maine for England, and he is clearly infuriated that Henry has frivolously given them over to the King of Naples. York has no sympathy for France and holds Suffolk in disdain: "For Suffolk's duke, may he be suffocate,/ That dims the honour of this warlike isle!" The situation, then, is this: Henry has opted for a marriage based solely on physical attraction; his marriage has no monetary or political advantages, and Henry's nobles (with the exception of Suffolk, who sees personal gain in the marriage, and Cardinal Beaufort, whose attitudes always fall on the opposite side of the coin from Gloucester's) are dissatisfied with the conjugal union. Gloucester prophesies that England will lose France entirely before long.

Beaufort attempts to persuade the other nobles that they should not trust Gloucester because of his "smoothing words" and his "flattering gloss"; obviously, he has designs on the throne. Accordingly, Buckingham suggests that they get rid of Gloucester, and Beaufort leaves immediately to put matters in motion. Somerset, however, warns the nobles that Cardinal Beaufort is not to be trusted either: "His insolence is more intolerable/ Than all the princes in the land beside." Basically, the situation develops because of a conflict between pride and ambition; none of the nobles is exempt from these emotions, and survival will depend on a combination of integrity and strength.

The Earl of Salisbury then appeals to Warwick and to the Duke of York, asking them to put the public good before personal gain and to stamp out the ambitions of Somerset, Buckingham, Suffolk and Cardinal Beaufort: they should respect and "cherish Duke Humphrey's [Gloucester's] deeds/ While they do tend the profit of the land." So there are now two opposing factions, even if only tenuous: Beaufort, Suffolk, Somerset, and Buckingham, who oppose Gloucester and support Henry's marriage, versus Salisbury, Warwick, and York, who support Gloucester. York supports Gloucester because it is convenient to do so: were he to support Beaufort, Suffolk, or anyone else, he would have more obstacles in *his* way to the crown. As it is, Gloucester is a known commodity and is more easily handled than a completely new "regime." This is what prompts York to say in a monologue:

> A day will come when York shall claim his own;
> And therefore I will take the Nevils' [Warwick's and
>   Salisbury's] parts
> And make a show of love to proud Duke Humphrey;
> And when I spy advantage claim the crown,
> For that's the golden mark I seek to hit.
>
> (I.i.239–43)

Note that York has *no love* for Henry, whom he calls "proud Lancaster," and who, York says, holds the sceptre "in his childish fist."

For the first time, we meet Gloucester's wife, Eleanor, a woman who will cause a great deal of trouble for both her husband and for the country. She is an ambitious woman, anxious to be queen, and she intends to push Gloucester closer and closer to the throne:

> What seest thou there? King Henry's diadem [crown],
> Enchas'd with all the honours of the world?
> If so, gaze on, and grovel on thy face
> Until thy head be circled with the same.
>
> (I.ii.7–10)

As Duchess of Gloucester, Eleanor provides a parallel to the ambitious Margaret: her husband becomes an instrument of her own desires and, as a human being, he counts for little – in her estimation. Gloucester is aware of this tendency in his wife, and he beseeches her to dispense with it: "O Nell, sweet Nell, if thou dost love thy lord,/ Banish the canker of ambitious thoughts!" The fact that she will do precisely the opposite of what her husband wishes should tell us something of her love for him. He is no more than a means to an end, and this fact reinforces the tragedy of Gloucester's position: Gloucester does *not* wish to be king, yet he wishes to prevent others from obtaining the crown. He tells Eleanor of a dream he had in which "on the pieces of the broken wand/ Were plac'd the heads of Edmund Duke of Somerset,/ And William de la Pole, first Duke of Suffolk." Eleanor interprets her husband's dream as meaning that whoever attempts to harm Gloucester will have his head cut off. Eleanor then relates a dream wherein Henry and Margaret kneeled before her and placed the crown on *her* head. Gloucester scolds her openly for such presumptuousness.

Gloucester is called away to Saint Albans, and in his absence, Eleanor receives Sir John Hume, a priest, whom she will entrust with her secret desire to use witches and spirits in her quest for the throne. Hume is a flatterer and does not hesitate to accept Eleanor's money for his "services," even though unbeknownst to her, Hume has *already* been hired by Suffolk and Cardinal Beaufort to work *against* her. Eleanor, meanwhile, asks Hume whether he has conferred with Margery Jordan, a "cunning witch," and Roger Bolingbroke, a "conjurer." Hume replies that they have promised to bring Eleanor in contact with "a spirit" who will answer her questions.

Inside the palace, Queen Margaret and Suffolk encounter a group of petitioners, one of whom incorrectly assumes that Eleanor is accompanied by Gloucester – and not by Suffolk. He wishes to present complaints to Gloucester, their Lord Protector, about certain goings-on in the township. They are surprised and somewhat fearful when Suffolk glances at the names of the men charged with the complaints: one of the complaints is directed against Suffolk himself for "enclosing the commons of Melford"; another is directed against Thomas Horner for claiming that the Duke of York is the rightful heir to the throne, etc. The queen rips up the supplications and chastises the petitioners for wanting to be "protected" by Gloucester. It is clear that *she* is among those who would do away with the Lord Protector.

In a speech to Suffolk, Margaret questions the English system of monarchy whereby Henry must still defer to a Protector; in particular, she dislikes the fact that she herself is "subject to a duke." She is also critical of Henry's religious devotion and of the fact that he is not more courageous and more manly. She delineates the other nobles whom she holds in disdain (Beaufort, Somerset, Buckingham, and York), but none of them bothers her as much as does Eleanor, Gloucester's wife: "Shall I not live to be aveng'd on her?" Suffolk tells Margaret that he has laid a snare for Eleanor and that, though they dislike Beaufort, they must join forces with him and the other nobles in bringing about the downfall of Gloucester; "So, one by one, we'll weed them all at last,/ And you yourself shall steer the happy helm."

The king enters, surrounded by his nobles, and an argument develops immediately over who should be appointed to the regentship of France – York or Somerset. Gloucester states that it should be the king's decision and no one else's. Immediately, several of the nobles and Margaret, as well, heap insults on Gloucester. Then, Margaret drops her fan and, when Eleanor refuses to pick it up, Margaret boxes her on the ear. A few nasty quips are tossed back and forth between the women before the king interrupts them. Suffolk then introduces Horner, a man whose apprentice (Peter) has stated that Horner said that York felt he was the rightful heir to the throne. York denies such a claim and asks for Peter's execution. Gloucester says that he believes that Peter's charge casts some doubt on York's reputation; York, therefore, should *not* be chosen Regent of France. The king thus chooses Somerset in his place. A combat is then scheduled between Thomas Horner and his apprentice, Peter, the two who are involved in the alleged claims made by York.

Meanwhile, in Gloucester's garden, the witch Margery Jordan meets with the two priests, Hume and Southwell, as well as with Roger Bolingbroke, a scholar and a conjurer. Eleanor is seated in her chair, and a spirit is conjured up, one who welcomes their questions. First, they ask what shall become of the king, and they are told that the king will outlive a certain duke who would depose him and that this duke will die a violent death. The spirit reports further that Suffolk will die "by water" and that Somerset should "shun castles," that he will be safer on sandy plains. The spirit vanishes as York and the Duke of Buckingham arrive on the scene. Eleanor and the others are arrested, and York congratulates Buckingham on being so efficient.

ACT II

At St. Albans, an argument breaks out amongst the various political factions: Gloucester versus his uncle Beaufort (Winchester), Margaret versus Gloucester, and so on. This scene makes for exceedingly poor drama since there is neither poetic stamina to the verse nor is there any suspense about plot development. In fact, it is often annoying and tedious. These nobles are grown men who have been fighting since the beginning of Part 1, and it seems highly unlikely that their feud would continue for so long without some form of violence or royal ultimatum. In short, there is nothing new on any front – simply more of the same. In fact, Henry sums up the situation quite nicely: "How irksome is this music to my heart!"

Buckingham arrives then to report that Eleanor (Gloucester's wife) has conspired with witches *against the state* and has been arrested. Gloucester is dismayed and hurt, and he states that if his wife is guilty, he will banish her from his household. Henry decides that he will return to London in the morning and look into the matter more carefully.

In London, York (Plantagenet) relates his claim to the throne in a conversation with Salisbury and Warwick. The scene is best read with a family genealogy on hand; it resembles those sections of the Old Testament which flow with "he begat so and so," and another person "begat so and so," etc. Warwick, known as "the king maker," sees York's point of view: "Till Lionel's issue fails, his [John of Gaunt's] should not reign./ It fails not yet, but flourishes in thee [that is, York]." When he is finished, York tells Salisbury and Warwick to tolerate Suffolk and Winchester and the others until they have "snared" Gloucester; then, as they meet the king's wrath, York will seize the throne. Warwick says that he will make York king, and he proclaims his fidelity to the rightful king: Long live our sovereign Richard, England's king!" Richard Plantagenet, Duke of York, promises to reward Warwick well.

In a Hall of Justice in London, Henry assembles various members of state (his queen, York, Salisbury, Gloucester, etc.) for the purpose of banishing Gloucester's wife, Eleanor, from England. Margery Jordan, Hume, Southwell, and Bolingbroke are also brought in. Eleanor is banished to the Isle of Man, and the four others are sentenced to be executed. This is a major blow to Gloucester, who is now torn between his loyalty to his wife and his loyalty to his kingdom. He recognizes his wife's wrongdoings, and he believes that the hardship of his remaining Protector to the king would be too stressful, given the circumstances. So he resigns his position, with the ready encouragement of Margaret, and Henry gives him permission to go with Eleanor to the Isle of Man. Then Henry states that he will be his own "Protector" and that God will be his "hope and guide."

York, meanwhile, is eager to have the combat begin between Thomas Horner and his apprentice, Peter Thump. It is a scene of mild comedy because Horner and his neighbors arrive drunk. Peter slays his master, but just before he falls dead, Horner utters: "I confess,

I confess treason." This reflects badly on York since suspicions are now even more strongly aroused concerning Peter's testimony that York has ambitions for the throne.

In a street scene, Gloucester watches as Eleanor is escorted to the place where she must do three days' penance before beginning her term of exile. Eleanor, barefoot in a white sheet, scorns her husband for allowing her to be treated so basely. She warns him about his death, which she says is imminent, and she relates the names of all those who have "lim'd bushes to betray thy wings." In a moment of surprising naïveté, Gloucester answers that he is safe. He says that he is absolutely guiltless, and he would have to do something truly vile before anyone would attempt to kill him: "All these [men] could not procure me any scath/ So long as I am loyal, true, and crimeless." He advises his wife to remain quiet and to expiate her sins through patience. Eleanor is led away by Stanley, and she proudly tells him to lead the way: "I long to see my prison."

ACT III

Act III is the beginning of Gloucester's final downfall. It opens at the Abbey at Bury St. Edmund's with the king and his entourage at Parliament. The king notes that Gloucester is not present, an unusual characteristic of the former Protector. Margaret attempts to sour Henry on Gloucester: "Will ye not observe . . . How insolent of late he is become,/ How proud, how peremptory, and unlike himself?" Suffolk claims that Gloucester instigated Eleanor's treasonous acts and that he desired the downfall of the king. Beaufort and York each voice complaints about Gloucester. Henry, however, will have nothing to do with their gossip. He remains faithful to Gloucester.

Somerset arrives with the news that all is lost in France. Then Gloucester enters, and Suffolk arrests him for treason. This is an unsteady scene with little dramatic development; there was no "scene of decision" to arrest Gloucester before his arrival, and Suffolk's dramatic action to do so comes as a complete surprise. Gloucester defends himself systematically against their charges and, in doing so, he gains much sympathy from us. He shows no signs of moral or ethical weakness, nor is there any evidence in the play to support the accusations levied against him. Suffolk pronounces that Gloucester shall be put under the control of his old nemesis, his uncle, Cardinal Beaufort

(Winchester), and this is a moment when Henry's spinelessness comes through very clearly: he makes absolutely *no* attempt to defend his former Lord Protector, nor does he substantiate his earlier claims that Gloucester is "virtuous, mild, and too well given/ To dream on evil." Henry is clearly an impotent pawn whose usefulness as a king is limited by his inexperience and his lack of courage.

In a long and searing speech, Gloucester exposes the motivation of his enemies, pointing the finger at each of them for their vicious plotting: "Beaufort's red sparkling eyes blab his heart's malice,/ And Suffolk's cloudy brow his stormy hate. . . ." Gloucester shows himself to be astute of judgment and wise in the ways of human psychology. He knows that Henry will never survive in their midst, but he is prepared to die in order to defend the principle of truth: "Good King Henry, thy decay I fear."

When Gloucester is taken away, Henry hastens to give the nobles total liberty for taking action against Gloucester: "My lords, what to your wisdoms seemeth best,/ Do or undo, as if ourself were here." He is, to the end, a grief-stricken wimp. He knows that Gloucester's enemies are about to do him wrong, yet he cannot muster sufficient courage to act against them. After he leaves, his wife, Margaret, assesses her husband's abilities as a king: "Henry my lord is cold in great affairs,/ Too full of foolish pity." The problem of Gloucester, in effect, can be understood from both sides: on the one hand, Gloucester has been a strong protector of Henry and the country, so it is clear why Henry feels so close to his uncle; on the other hand, Gloucester has been an obstacle to the nobles in their quest for greater authority, and from their point of view, no advances are possible until he is out of the way. Henry is guilty of weakness and of a lack of insight, while the nobles are guilty of devising various plans for bloody violence. When all is said and done, we have a microcosmic vision of evolution and survival: the strongest and most conniving of the court is the one who will dominate the rest of them. Margaret, York, Beaufort, and Suffolk agree unanimously that Gloucester *must* die.

A messenger arrives from Ireland to report that rebels are killing the Englishmen in that country and that help is badly needed. Cardinal Beaufort (Winchester), who quickly assumes the power which Gloucester once possessed, nominates York (Plantagenet) to serve as the nation's leader against the rebels. Suffolk confirms Beaufort's recommendation, adding that they represent the will of the king: "Our authority is his consent,/ And what we do establish he confirms." The nobles exit, leaving York behind. In a long monologue, York vows to carry out his *own* plan: the men whom he has been given to conquer the Irish rebels are *precisely* the forces needed to seize the English throne: "'Twas men I lack'd and you will give them me." While he is in Ireland, he says, he intends to stir up a "black storm" in England which will not cease to rage until "the golden crown" sits on his head. He has chosen John Cade of Ashford as the one to incite a rebellion in England. Cade is a headstrong Kentishman who will act for York under the name of John Mortimer, whom he resembles. York plans to use Cade to fire York's popularity with the commoners. If Cade is caught, it is highly unlikely that he will confess to the nature of York's plan. Thus, with Gloucester dead, only Henry VI will stand between York and the throne.

In the next scene, the murderers of Gloucester run through a room in the palace, reporting to Suffolk that the deed is done. When the king enters, ignorant of Gloucester's death, he orders that Gloucester be summoned and that a fair trial to judge his treason be held. Suffolk returns, pale and trembling, with the news that Gloucester has been found "dead in his bed." Henry faints, and Margaret shouts: "Help, lords! the king is dead!" When Henry is revived, he pierces Suffolk with accusations that the latter is a vicious, evil man: "Hide not thy poison with such sug'red words./ Lay not thy hands on me; forbear, I say! Their touch affrights me as a serpent's sting." The first prophecy of the sorcerers, then, is fulfilled: that is, a king (Henry) *did* outlive a duke (Gloucester), who died a violent death.

In a long and hypocritical speech, Margaret bemoans the death of Gloucester, claiming that she will now be looked upon as an accomplice in his murder. She tries to win Henry's faithfulness to her, but she gets nowhere with him. She concludes, "Ay me, I can no more! Die, Margaret!/ For Henry weeps that thou dost live so long."

Warwick enters to report that Gloucester was murdered by Suffolk and Beaufort (Winchester). The citizens have formed a mob and are lusting for revenge, regardless of their object. Henry asks Warwick to examine Gloucester's corpse in an effort to determine *how* he was killed. Warwick then wheels the deathbed into the king's room for all to behold. What they witness is a ghastly, sordid sight which proves that the duke was indeed murdered:

> His face is black and full of blood,
> His eyeballs further out than when he liv'd
> Staring full ghastly like a strangled man;
> His hair uprear'd, his nostrils stretch'd with struggling.
>
> (III.ii.168–71)

Warwick exchanges harsh words with Suffolk, accusing him of involvement in the murder and promising to "cope with" him. Salisbury enters then to report that the crowd outside demands the death of Suffolk. Henry replies that his thoughts have centered more and more on Suffolk as the murderer. Suffolk is thus banished from the country. This is the first time that Henry asserts himself powerfully as king; it demonstrates the depth of his love for Gloucester and, in an indirect way, it shows that he is capable of enforcing his will when moved to anger. Left alone, Margaret and Suffolk declare their love for one another and bid one another painful farewells.

Vaux, a gentleman of the court, arrives to report that Cardinal Beaufort (Winchester) is on the point of death: "For suddenly a grievous sickness took him,/ That makes him gasp and stare and catch the air,/ Blaspheming God and cursing men on earth." In Beaufort's bedchamber, the Cardinal confesses to having conspired toward the murder of Gloucester, but when the king invites him to make a signal of hope concerning life after death, Beaufort makes no sign. He dies unrepentant.

ACT IV

By the end of Act III, Shakespeare has gotten rid of Gloucester, Eleanor, Suffolk, and Beaufort – four pivotal characters surrounding the king. Now we are left with York (Plantagenet) and his supporters, and the king and his entourage. The conflict of personal ambition gives way to that of a more sustained struggle for the throne. It is at this point that the Wars of the Roses occupy the forefront of the action, with the white roses of the house of York in opposition to the red roses of the house of Lancaster.

Suffolk, who was banished in Act III, disguised himself in rags and left the country onboard a ship. Pirates at sea captured the ship and beheaded him for his evil doings, thus fulfilling another aspect of the sorcerers' prophecy. A gentleman close to Suffolk returns his body to England, where the Queen, or Suffolk's friends, he assumes, may revenge his death.

The beginning of the York protests (the faction of the white roses) takes place in Scene 2, at Blackheath, with various supporters of Jack Cade: George Bevis, John Holland, Dick the Butcher, and Smith the Weaver, along with Cade himself. Cade announces that his father was a Mortimer and his wife a Plantagenet; therefore he is heir to the throne of England. And as he declaims about how he will rule the kingdom when he becomes king, Sir Humphrey Stafford enters and instructs Cade and his followers to drop their plans. The king will be merciful, he claims, and Cade will not suffer if he gives up his plan to revolt. Cade has been speaking to his men as if he were Sir John Mortimer, but Stafford knows his true identity and scoffs at his intentions: "Villain, thy father was a plasterer,/ And thou thyself a shearman." Stafford and his brother realize that they cannot stop Cade from proceeding, so they order that the king's army be brought in to overcome the rebel and his supporters. Cade is not worried: he stands for liberty, and he will not be deterred. In the fight which ensues, both the Staffords are slain, auguring well for the rebellion. Cade dresses himself in one of the Staffords' armor, and the two men leave for London to free all the prisoners.

At the palace in London, the queen is caressing Suffolk's severed head just as the king walks in with a supplication from the rebels. Henry decides to talk directly with Jack Cade instead of having the rebel's supporters put to death. A messenger enters and announces that Cade's men are savagely destroying anything in their path, that they have captured London Bridge, and that Cade intends to crown himself in Westminster. Moreover, the fickle mob has joined forces with Cade "and they jointly swear/ To spoil the city and your royal court." Henry and Margaret flee to Killingworth until an army can be raised to defend them.

The Cade rebellion is in full force, with its men running all over London. The rebels capture the Tower of London, and Cade, disguised as Mortimer, claims that he is "lord of the city." Absolute chaos is the result, with men being murdered for any reason whatever. Cade orders that both London Bridge and the Tower of London be set on fire; he orders the burning "of all the records of the realm." The melee resembles a proletariat revolution, where everything is "by and for the people." As Cade says, "Henceforward all things shall be in common."

As a representative of Henry, Buckingham proclaims a royal pardon to the populace; if they will abandon Cade and his rebellion, Henry will *not* punish them. The mob then shouts out in favor of the king, showing their fundamental fickleness. After Cade makes a speech to them, however, they swing back to his side. This see-sawing continues for a while, and then Cade flees, disgusted with them all. Buckingham offers a thousand crowns to anyone who brings him Cade's head.

At the Killingworth Castle, Henry regrets aloud that he is a king and *not* a subject. Buckingham enters with a repentant mob, and Henry "redeems" Cade's followers and praises them for having decided to support the monarchy.

It is learned that York is back from Ireland with a force of heavily armed Irish soldiers. Their intention, supposedly, is *not* to overthrow the king, but to get rid of Somerset, whom they believe to be a traitor. Henry asks Buckingham to meet with York and "ask him what's the reason of these arms." He instructs Buckingham to tell York that Somerset has been sent to the Tower, and that he will release Somerset once York's troops have disbanded.

Cade finds himself in a country garden in Kent after having been in hiding for five days. The proprietor of the garden, Alexander Iden, comes upon him and, after a brief discussion, they begin to fight. Iden slays Cade and drags him to a dunghill, "which shall be thy grave." He cuts off Cade's head and prepares to show it triumphantly to the king, leaving Cade's body "for crows to feed upon."

ACT V

The act opens in some fields between Dartford and Blackheath. York and his army of Irishmen plan to "pluck the crown from feeble Henry's head." Buckingham arrives and asks York why he has assembled such a great army in a time of peace and in a location so close to the court. York is outraged, but he quells his anger and replies that his purpose is to get rid of Somerset, whom he considers to be seditious and a threat to Henry. Buckingham reports that Somerset is already in the Tower as a prisoner, so York abruptly and surprisingly dismisses his army. The two men are then greeted by the king, who is scarcely able to say a word before Iden enters with Cade's head.

Iden is knighted for his efforts and, at this point, the queen enters with Somerset. York discovers the ruse and is furious with Henry for being so dishonest: "False king! why has thou broken faith with me,/ Knowing how hardly I can brook abuse?/ King, did I call thee? No, thou are not king,/ Not fit to govern and rule multitudes." This is the first time that York has openly declared his hostility to Henry: "Thy hand is made to grasp a palmer's staff/ And not to grace an awful princely sceptre." He informs Henry that, by heaven, Henry shall rule no longer over him who is the rightful heir. Somerset makes a move to arrest York for treason, but York demands that his sons be present; they will bail him out of his present situation. His sons, Edward and Richard, arrive and vow to defend their father. York asserts openly to all present that *he* is king, and he requests that Warwick and Salisbury be brought to him.

Warwick enters, but he does not bow before the king, and Henry realizes that the Nevilles do *not* support him. Salisbury states his belief that York is the rightful heir to the throne. Henry calls for Buckingham and requests that he arm himself. This leads directly to the Battle of Saint Albans.

At Saint Albans, Warwick challenges Clifford of Cumberland to fight with him. But York too wishes to slay Clifford and does this in short order. Clifford's son sees what has happened and swears that he will spare "no York" in battle (young Clifford will reappear in Part 3 of the trilogy).

Richard (York's son) and Somerset begin fighting, and Somerset is killed. Margaret and Henry arrive on the scene, with Margaret urging that they flee. Henry seems indecisive and unable to decide whether to fight or flee: it is a classic psychological phenomenon described by Freud as the fight/flight syndrome. Ultimately, Henry opts for flight, a suitable option for a hopeless fighter.

The play ends when Salisbury arrives on the scene from the battle. Despite his age, he has fought valiantly and is a fitting model for younger soldiers in the camp. Young Richard Plantagenet helped him three times during the battle, and Salisbury pays tribute to him. But he cautions that they have not won *yet,* and York adds that the Lancasters should be pursued before the writs go forth. The spirit of battle is re-ignited by Warwick:

> Saint Alban's battle won by famous York
> Shall be eterniz'd in all age to come.
> Sound drum and trumpets, and to London all;
> And more such days as these to us befall!
>
> (V.iii.30–33)

The play ends on this note of optimism for the Yorks: they are the legitimate heirs to the throne, and they intend to make this a reality. In Part 3, we shall witness the conclusion to this pursuit.

HENRY VI, Part 3

ACT I

Part 3 of this trilogy might aptly be subtitled: "Crown, crown, who's got the crown?" The English crown is taken and won several times throughout the drama, and it is sometimes difficult to remember precisely *who* is on *which* side of the struggle.

The play begins as the Duke of York, his sons (Edward and Richard), and Warwick have returned to Parliament in London, and Warwick wonders how Henry escaped from the Yorkists after the Battle of Saint Albans. York explains that Henry slyly stole away during the battle and deserted his men, who were soon slaughtered.

York's sons then recount their triumphs in battle, and each brags about whom he killed; Richard proudly displays Somerset's head. As we said earlier in these Notes, Part 3 is not the most theatrically satisfying of the three dramas; it is a panorama of egos, challenges, and bloody fights-to-the-death, and, on stage, this often makes for tiresome, difficult scene changes.

Young Richard has gained the approval of his father by beheading Somerset, York's longtime enemy, and Warwick vows that he will kill Henry unless Henry renounces his crown in favor of York and his heirs. Warwick then escorts York to the throne, just before the entrance of the king, Clifford (Margaret's favorite), Northumberland, Westmoreland, Exeter and others. Henry immediately realizes that York, backed by Warwick, means to have the throne, and when Northumberland and Clifford impulsively vow to avenge their fathers' deaths at the hands of York, Henry stops them, reminding them that the people of London support the rebels. For his part, Henry says that he refuses to fight "in the parliament-house" (another sign of weakness in this appeasing, peace-seeking young king). Instead of using weapons, Henry says, "frowns, words, and threats/ Shall be the war that Henry means to use." Then he states that *his* right to the throne comes from his father, King Henry V, who seized France. He asserts that York is merely the son of a duke and the grandson of an earl. Warwick, in turn, accuses Henry of having lost France, but Henry retorts that it was the Lord Protector (Gloucester) who lost it – and not Henry – because Henry was but an infant of nine months when that happened.

York's sons urge their father to "tear the crown" from Henry's head; they are willing to fight. Henry grows impatient; he threatens a war which will "unpeople" his realm before he allows his crown to be taken from him, arguing that *he* is the true heir to the throne. York, in turn, argues that Henry IV rebelled against Richard II, and got the throne "by conquest." Henry admits that this is true, but he does so *only* in an aside. Openly, he maintains that Henry IV was Richard II's *heir*. Thus, what might otherwise have seemed like a very straightforward matter is converted into an impossible imbroglio, resolvable only on the battlefield.

At this point, Exeter, who had been on the king's side earlier, decides that York is the "lawful king." Clifford, however, refuses to kneel to York, the man who killed his father. Warwick demands that Henry resign and, in order to appear more threatening, he stamps his foot, and soldiers appear, ready to take away the prisoners. Henry, seeing that he is outnumbered, begs Warwick to allow him to remain king for at least the rest of his life. York *agrees* to this idea, but *only* on the condition that Henry name him and his sons as *direct heirs*. He does so, and Westmoreland, Northumberland, and Clifford chastise the king for disinheriting his only son (calling him a "faint-hearted and degenerate king"), and then they depart to inform Queen Margaret. Henry regrets his decision to compromise, but he is more concerned about the present – not the future. He wants to take an oath to cease the civil war. Again he repeats his wish to be treated as king and sovereign by York and his followers, and so York pledges his loyalty and returns to his castle. Warwick, however, stays behind in London with his soldiers to guard the city. Seemingly, the houses of York and Lancaster are reconciled.

Exeter and Henry are ready to depart when they see Margaret and young Prince Edward approaching. She rails against Henry for what she considers to be an extremely foolish concession on his part. And Edward, of course, questions Henry's decision; as Henry's son, he has just lost his claim to the throne. Henry replies that he had *no choice:* he was forced by circumstances to act as he did. Margaret warns him that he has forfeited his safety and honor, and she refuses to see him again until their son is restored as Henry's heir to the throne. She announces plans to enlist the aid of the northern lords in the fight against the Yorkists, and although Henry begs them to stay, young Edward vows not to see his father until such time as he, Edward, returns victorious from the battlefield. Henry can do nothing but let them fight, while he tries to regain the favor of Westmoreland, Northumberland, and Clifford.

On a plain before Sandal Castle near Wakefield, York enters to hear his sons arguing. Edward urges him to seize the crown now, and young Richard explains that the oath which their father took has no meaning since it did not take place before a magistrate. His argument with his brother, he says, arose over who should plead the case to York; both believe that their father is the rightful heir, and both wish to see him disregard his oath *not* to claim the throne during Henry's lifetime. York is convinced of the truth of his sons' arguments, and so he dispatches them to gather support for an uprising. He is interrupted, however, by a messenger who warns him that Margaret and "all the northern earls and lords" plan to lay siege to the York castle. Moreover, Margaret and Edward have 20,000 men with them, so they present a very real threat to the Yorkist position. York decides to keep his sons with him and sends his brother Montague to London to warn the nobles of the upcoming events. York's uncles, Sir John and Sir Hugh Mortimer, arrive and set off to meet the queen in the field. They have only 5,000 men in contrast to Margaret's 20,000, but York is nonetheless confident of success ("A woman is general; what should we fear?").

An alarum sounds, and York's young son Rutland enters with his tutor, looking for a means of escape. Instead, they are captured by Clifford, and the tutor is taken away by soldiers. Rutland begs for his life, but he is cruelly slaughtered by Clifford as an act of revenge for York's having murdered Clifford's father. This only serves to intensify York's eventual wrath, of course.

York enters, tired and faint, mourning the death of both his uncles and the success of Margaret's army. Unable to escape or fight, the exhausted York is taken prisoner by Northumberland and Clifford, but he vows that success will ultimately come from his death. As Clifford, the queen's favorite, prepares to execute York, Margaret stops him in order to insult York with one final humiliation. She has him led to a molehill and taunts him about his desire to rule England, and she mocks his "mess of sons" who are incapable of helping him now. Then she offers him a handkerchief soaked in Rutland's blood, and she puts a paper crown on York's head, saying, "Off with the crown; and with the crown, his head." Then she orders York's execution. But before Margaret and Clifford stab him, York tears off the crown and curses her. Then he is beheaded, and his head is set on the gates of the castle so that it "may overlook the town of York."

ACT II

Several days later, York's sons, Edward and Richard, march onto a plain in Herefordshire, fearful of their father's fate, which is as yet unknown to them. A messenger dashes in with the story of York's humiliation and his murder, and Edward dissolves into grief. Richard, however, is fired with anger and calls for revenge. Then Edward rallies and claims the title of Duke of York. But Richard encourages his brother to demand more – demand Henry's *throne*.

Warwick and his men enter and are told of York's death. Warwick, however, has already heard about it and says that he gathered together an army in London and marched to Saint Albans for the purpose of intercepting Queen Margaret. He had been told that she intended "to dash" the pledge given by York concerning Henry's right to reign during York's lifetime. Since Margaret intends to nullify York's oath in favor of her own son's succession, Warwick committed himself to defending the oaths taken by Henry and York. But when his soldiers were assembled, Warwick discovered that they were not really interested in fighting, even with the promise of higher pay. He conjured several reasons: the king's gentleness or rumors of Margaret's fierceness, or the fear of Clifford.

Richard derides Warwick for retreating, but explains to Warwick that it is only out of frustration that he is critical of Warwick ("In this troublesome time, what's to be done?"). Warwick then tells the young men that the queen, Clifford, and Northumberland have gone to London to defy the king's oath to deliver his throne, eventually, to Richard's heirs. Thirty thousand soldiers have gone in support of them, and so Warwick urges that York's sons try to assemble at least 25,000 men in an attempt to counterattack Margaret and claim the throne. Richard and Edward promise to help, and Edward is assured by Warwick that in every borough they pass through on their way to

London, he will be named king. And those who do not support him will forfeit their heads.

Margaret and Henry arrive at the York castle with the Prince of Wales (Edward, their son), Northumberland, and Clifford. Margaret delights in showing York's impaled head to Henry, but Henry pleads to God that this bloody deed was not his fault. Clifford reminds the king that York has made him disinherit Edward, his son, but Henry argues that perhaps the crown is not his to give, because it was "ill-got." Margaret then urges Henry to steel his "soft courage" and give Edward his promised knighthood *immediately*. Henry obeys her.

A messenger enters to warn of the enormous Yorkist march and of the Yorkists' gaining men as they progress toward London. Clifford and Margaret urge Henry to withdraw from the battlefield because of his indifference to war, but the Yorkists enter, and York's son Edward immediately challenges Henry to surrender the crown. Henry tries to speak, but he is shouted down by an exchange of insults. Both sides part ways and group their troops for battle.

Edward, Warwick, and George (another of York's sons) withdraw from the battlefield in Yorkshire since the ranks of their soldiers are broken and "Edward's sun is clouded." Richard (York's son) enters to report the death of Warwick's brother at the hands of Clifford, and this sufficiently angers Warwick, Edward, and George to return to the battle. Revenge *must* be sought.

Henry enters alone, having been forced by Margaret and Clifford to leave the battle; they told him that they were more successful in battle if he was absent. Henry sits down and reflects on his condition, as he has done in other parts of this trilogy; he wishes that he were a "homely swain" rather than a king. As he sits alone, a young man enters, one who has just killed his father by mistake in battle; and moments later, a father enters who has mistakenly killed his son. Henry cries out in anguish, and he sympathizes with them deeply, but his horror of this kind of slaughter is impotent, suggesting Henry's fundamental inadequacy throughout the battle. Despite his desire to help bring peace to England, there is not much he can do to influence matters. Margaret, Edward, and Exeter urge Henry to escape with them since the battle has turned against them. Henry, indifferent to his safety, does as he is told.

A wounded Clifford enters, sensing a Lancastrian defeat, and faints. The Yorkists arrive and hear a groan from Clifford as he dies.

Warwick has the Duke of York's head removed from the castle gate and has it replaced with Clifford's. He announces that they will proceed to London for Edward's coronation and then he will depart for France, where he will ask the king for the hand of Lady Bona, sister of the French queen, for Edward. This will assure French support for the Yorkist efforts. Edward then names Richard as the Duke of Gloucester, and George as the Duke of Clarence.

ACT III

This act opens in a forest in the northern part of England, where two gamekeepers are hiding themselves under a thick bush; they are stalking a deer. A disguised Henry enters, carrying a prayer book and counting his sorrows. One of the keepers recognizes the king and makes a move to capture Henry, but he is stopped by the other so that they may hear more of the king's story, which Henry relates aloud to himself. He confesses that Margaret and his son have gone to France for aid, but he fears that she will be unsuccessful. The keepers corner him and lead him away to the authorities. They state that their loyalties lie with King Edward.

Lady Grey appears then before King Edward in order to win back the lands of her husband, who was slain in battle at Saint Albans in the cause of the Yorkists. Edward's brothers comment upon the exchange between their brother the king and Lady Grey, in which he attempts to woo her as his queen in exchange for the lands. Edward is pressing his suit to marry her when he is interrupted by a messenger, who announces that Henry VI has been taken prisoner. Edward orders that Henry be taken to the Tower while he and his brothers question the man who arrested him. Richard stays behind and, in a long soliloquy, he reflects on his desire that Edward should produce *no heirs* if he marries Lady Grey; if there are no heirs, this would make it easier for Richard to claim the throne after Edward's death. He bemoans his unsightly, hunchbacked appearance and vows to do whatever is necessary in order for him to become king.

In France, Margaret secures an audience before King Lewis. He listens to her eloquent plea for help against the Yorkists, then he asks her to be patient. Warwick enters suddenly with his request that Lewis' sister-in-law, Lady Bona, be allowed to marry Edward, the new King of England. Lewis asks Margaret to leave him alone with

Warwick. Warwick immediately assures King Lewis that Edward is honorable in his love and is the rightful King of England. Lady Bona, who is present, agrees to the marriage proposal, and so Lewis informs Margaret of his change of heart: he has opted to help a *strong* monarch (Edward) instead of a weak one (Henry). He will not be able to do anything political for her.

A messenger enters with letters for Margaret, Lewis, and Warwick, which contain news of King Edward's sudden marriage to Lady Grey. An enraged Warwick renounces King Edward and returns to Henry VI's side. He tells Margaret that he is her "true servitor," and he vows to "replant Henry in his former state."

At this point, the machinations of the plot resemble the melodrama of a soap opera. Warwick volunteers to land French soldiers on England's coast in an effort to unseat King Edward. Thus, the messenger is sent back to England to announce the imminent arrival of French forces. Lewis vows to send 5,000 soldiers with Warwick and a fresh supply with Henry's son Edward, the Prince of Wales. Warwick, to further prove his loyalty, gives his eldest daughter in marriage to Henry's son, ending the act on a firm note that he and King Lewis seek revenge on Edward, who would mock England's throne and who would renounce a proposed marriage to a lady of the French court. Furthermore, Edward's fickle choice of wife has made Warwick look ridiculous.

ACT IV

In London, Gloucester (Richard, the hunchbacked son of Plantagenet) and Clarence (George, Richard's brother) argue over their brother Edward's marriage to Lady Grey. Clarence confronts Edward, who has just entered, with the fact that France and Warwick will not willingly submit to such humiliation as Edward has dealt them. Gloucester warns Edward that a "hasty marriage seldom proveth well," but he says that he does not ultimately oppose his brother's marriage to Lady Grey. Montague (Warwick's brother) and Lord Hastings warn Edward that England *must* be prepared to fight. In addition, both Clarence and Gloucester are jealous of the wives whom Edward has bestowed on his new wife's brother and son. Discontent reigns in the house of York. Clarence even announces his decision to leave the court and find a wife for himself. The queen (Lady Grey) tries to intervene and make peace among the brothers, and Edward warns them that they *must* bend to his will—or experience his *wrath*.

The messenger from France enters with the message from Lewis, Margaret, and Warwick regarding the imminent arrival of French troops on English soil. Edward is not unduly upset; he states that he will meet them in war. Clarence then decides to marry Warwick's younger daughter (thereby joining Warwick's camp), and he challenges his supporters to go with him. Somerset follows him. Gloucester (Richard) remains behind, but not for love of Edward; instead, for love of the crown. Edward announces that preparations for war are to begin immediately.

Warwick welcomes Clarence and Somerset into his camp and vows that Clarence shall marry his younger daughter. He then informs them that King Edward's camp may be easily taken. Only three watchmen guard the king, who has vowed not to sleep until either he or Warwick is killed. He has chosen to stay in the field with only a small guard ("carelessly encamp'd") since " 'Tis the more honor, because more dangerous."

Warwick, Clarence, Oxford, Somerset, and several French soldiers enter, and Edward's watchmen, followed by Richard and Hastings, flee when they realize they are outnumbered. Edward is then brought out of his tent, and Warwick announces that Edward is not the Duke of York and seizes the crown from him. He orders that Edward be conveyed to Warwick's brother, the Archbishop of York, and that the rest of them shall march to London to seat Henry once again on his rightful throne.

Queen Elizabeth (the former Lady Grey) has heard that Edward was taken prisoner, and she tells this news to Rivers, her brother, revealing that she must be strong since she carries Edward's heir. She asks Rivers to help her escape in order to save the unborn child.

Gloucester (Richard) meets with Hastings and Sir William Stanley in a park in Yorkshire where he hopes to rescue Edward, his brother. Edward is encountered along with his huntsman, and he is told that he is to go to Flanders for his own safety; his huntsman is to accompany him. Warwick, Clarence, Somerset, Oxford, Montague, and young Henry (Earl of Richmond) free Henry from the Tower, and since Warwick made it all possible, he announces that he will be in charge of the government even though Henry shall remain king.

Warwick chooses Clarence as Protector and says that he and Clarence will govern jointly so that Henry can, as he wishes, lead a quiet, private life.

Warwick then proclaims that Edward is a traitor, and he ordains that all of Edward's lands and goods must be confiscated. Henry requests that Margaret and their son, Prince Edward, be sent for so that his joy may be complete. Then he notices the young Earl of Richmond, Henry, and says that he is England's hope for the future: "His head by nature [is] fram'd to wear a crown." A messenger suddenly announces that Edward (York) has escaped, and Warwick blames the Archbishop of York for the carelessness. He withdraws to plan strategy with the others while Somerset and Oxford remain with the young Earl of Richmond. They decide that he must be sent to Brittany for safety's sake, "till storms be past of civil enmity."

Edward (York), his brother Gloucester (Richard), and Hastings approach the gates of York with soldiers from Burgundy, only to find the gates locked. The Mayor appears on the walls and explains that he and his colleagues are loyal to Henry. Hastings claims that *they* are Henry's friends, and Edward says that he is still Duke of York. Therefore, the Mayor (deceived) lets them enter, and Edward "vows" to defend the town.

Sir John Montgomery marches up with soldiers and offers to help Edward regain the crown. Edward tells Gloucester that he will not stake his claim until he is stronger, and the latter replies that he will proclaim Edward as king, which will bring many supporters to the cause. Edward is therefore proclaimed king, and Montgomery throws down his gauntlet as a challenge to anyone who usurps the position.

In London, at the palace, Warwick announces that Edward is marching toward London with many supporters and that troops must be gathered in order to oppose him. King Henry, meantime, will remain in London. Later, Henry and Exeter discuss the reasons for which people chose Edward over him and also discuss their chances. Suddenly, Edward, Gloucester, and soldiers break in and seize Henry and order him to the Tower. Then they begin their march toward Coventry to meet Warwick.

ACT V

In Coventry, Warwick receives reports from messengers about the location of his commanders. He hears a flourish, which heralds the arrival of Edward, Gloucester (Richard), and their men, and, unaware that they were so close by, Warwick is taken by surprise and has no defense plan in motion. Within minutes, Oxford, Montague, and Somerset arrive with reinforcements. Clarence also arrives, but he takes the red rose of Lancaster from his hat and pledges his allegiance to the side of his brother Edward, who orders Warwick and his troops to prepare for battle. Warwick shouts that he will not defend Coventry but that he will meet Edward at Barnet, and the latter responds by leading the way.

On a field near Barnet, King Edward (Plantagenet) enters, dragging a wounded Warwick. He exits to find Montague since he intends to kill him too. Somerset and Oxford enter to inform Warwick of the queen's arrival from France with reinforcements. Just before Warwick dies, they tell him that Montague has also been killed.

King Edward celebrates his victory, but he knows that Margaret must yet be defeated. Margaret tells Oxford and Somerset that they will replace Warwick and Montague as the anchors of the quest to get Henry back on the throne. Edward arrives, and the battle begins.

Shortly afterward, Margaret, Somerset, and Oxford are taken prisoners by King Edward and Gloucester (Richard). Oxford is sent as a prisoner to Hames Castle, and Somerset is beheaded. The captured Prince Edward is brought in, resolute in his demands that King Edward must yield up the throne. King Edward, Gloucester, and Clarence all stab the young prince. Margaret faints, and Gloucester tells Clarence that he is off to London "on a serious matter" in the Tower. Margaret is led away to prison. Edward asks for Gloucester, and Clarence tells him that he has gone "to make a bloody supper in the Tower." Thus, Edward makes plans to return to London also.

At the Tower, Gloucester and Henry walk along the walls, talking. Henry suspects that his death is at hand and, as Gloucester stabs him, Henry warns him that more slaughter will follow. Evil omens, he says, were abroad when Richard, the "indigested and deformed lump" was born. Gloucester stabs him one more time in order to send him to hell, and then, talking to himself, he plots a scheme to poison Edward's mind against Clarence: "Clarence, beware! Thou keep'st me from the light,/ But I will sort a pitchy day for thee;/ For I will buzz abroad such prophecies/ That Edward shall be fearful of his life,/ And then, to purge his fear, I'll be thy death." Gloucester, of course, hopes to be the future Richard III, and he will stop at nothing to obtain the crown for himself.

In London, Edward recounts a list of men who have died because they desired the throne. Then he calls forth his queen with their son, for whose sake he fought the war. He asks Gloucester (Richard) and Clarence to kiss the child but, as Gloucester does so, he mutters in an aside that his kiss is a "Judas kiss," which will bring harm to the child. Edward then orders that Margaret be sent back to France, desiring that the time now be spent "with stately triumphs, mirthful comic shows,/ Such as befits the pleasure of the court."

When we recall that *Henry VI* was written early in Shakespeare's career, we realize that the drama's shortcomings are often compensated for by the hint of what is to come in future works. In conjunction with *Richard III,* this trilogy constitutes the first series of history plays which Shakespeare wrote, and it is a genre which he will develop considerably as he matures. The three parts of *Henry VI* can be read separately or as parts of a whole, but it must be remembered that the dramas are *not* an accurate presentation of history. Shakespeare contorts and bends historical reality to suit his dramatic purposes, and this often causes confusion if one attempts to follow their plots along strictly historical lines. The historical chroniclers of that era, especially Holinshed and Halle, document an ongoing series of battles and feuds which run through the fifteenth century. Shakespeare, in turn, chooses those events which interest him most and uses them as a backbone for his human drama – one of overpowering ambition, courage, and energy.

Henry VI, whose reign spanned the period from 1422 to 1471, was a weak and disastrous king. He was ill-equipped to control the turbulent forces at work in his own country, and he was in no way prepared to lead a defense against the invasion of foreigners. As England sinks deeper and deeper into trouble, Henry's reign unravels as a desperate, insecure tenure. Gloucester represents the old spirit of England, one of faith and courage, of determination and honor. But even Gloucester is unable to stand undaunted by the disintegration of the monarchy, and he is killed in Part 2, the turning point in the trilogy. Without Gloucester, Henry is exposed for what he is: immature, unschooled, and doomed. The chaos of the mob is the most obvious sign of this confusion and represents the low point from which the kingdom must build itself anew. The murder of Gloucester signals the end of an epoch and the beginning of a period which will lead to the relatively more stable reign of the Tudors. Gloucester is one of the few characters for whom we have sympathy and deep feeling; most of the other characters are cold, steel-like caricatures of politically hungry vultures, or else they are one-dimensional, singularly ambitious beings. It causes us no real pain to witness Suffolk's murder. To be sure, it is a tragedy of sorts, but in the overview of the country's situation, this seems like a necessary, inevitable event.

The trilogy presents constant problems of character identification, family lineage, and so on. But when one grasps the notion that there are a handful of central, key figures, one ceases to worry unduly about the occasional minor characters who float in and out of the drama; a list has been included in these *Notes* to aid in this process of identification. Insofar as the characterization is concerned, Shakespeare has obviously done better work. But there are glimmerings of interesting people and of conflicts which stimulate good drama, and the *Henry VI* plays may be considered as essential groundwork for the study of Shakespearean psychology.

It is the pursuit of the crown which primarily intrigues Shakespeare in these dramas and, within this context, his trilogy makes for many gripping moments. The individual characters may suffer at the expense of the general effect, but when one remembers that this was one of Shakespeare's initial attempts at professional drama, it can be seen as a fortunate event in the history of theater.

QUESTIONS FOR REVIEW

1. Describe the style employed by Shakespeare in *Henry VI*.
    - the beginnings of a poetic style are evident, but it is still rough, undeveloped and likely a re-working of another dramatist's play from the same period; it is not typical of Shakespearean verse, particularly of the kind found in his great plays of the 1599–1608 period.
    - very little use of metaphor or rhetorical devices.
    - frequent references to historical events, but often in an inaccurate framework.
    - very abrupt changes from scene to scene; unlike the smooth mastery of the later plays.

2. What gave rise to the Wars of the Roses?
   - the Wars began at the Battle of Saint Albans.
   - they were the manifestation of the conflict between the Yorkists (led by Richard Plantagenet) and the Lancasters.
   - the Yorkists were the *legitimate* heirs to the throne, but the Lancasters ruled because of the usurping of power by their ancestor, Henry IV.
   - the Yorkists chose as their symbol the white rose, and the Lancasters chose the red rose; an easy way to remember which family had which rose is to recall that the letters *W* and *Y* are close to each other in the alphabet (*White Yorks*).

3. What are the various kinds of love found in *Henry VI?*
   - love of truth (Duke of York in his quest for the monarchy)
   - love of country, honor, justice (Duke of Gloucester in his role as Lord Protector of England)
   - love of power (Cardinal Beaufort, Suffolk, Margaret, Gloucester, Jack Cade, Richard Plantagenet, Buckingham, Warwick, Eleanor)
   - physical/emotional love (Margaret and Suffolk, Henry's love for Margaret, etc.)

4. What is the value of *Henry VI* in a course on Shakespeare?
   - generally considered to be among Shakespeare's first plays; represents his early attempts at stylized drama, at incorporating history into a narrative plot, at maintaining a high level of dramatic intensity while exposing certain deep human emotions

SUGGESTED ESSAY TOPICS

Long Essays

1. Using the *Henry VI* plays as examples of the history plays, show how Shakespeare uses fact and fiction to suit his dramatic purpose.

2. Trace the evolution of character in Henry VI, Gloucester, and the Duke of York, and explain the interplay of duty vs. ambition in each of these characters.

3. Show how Talbot, Gloucester, and Richard Plantagenet are pivotal figures in each of Parts 1, 2, and 3 of *Henry VI*.

4. Write an essay on the role of good and evil in *Henry VI*. To what extent could Gloucester in Part 1 be considered to be an agent of "good" and Queen Margaret in Part 2 a force of "evil"?

Short Essays

1. What is the symbolism of the red and white roses in the Wars of the Roses? What gave rise to these wars?

2. Write a short essay on the language of Shakespeare in this early group of plays.

3. Using *Richard II*, or *Henry IV, Parts 1* or *2*, or *Henry V*, show by contrast that *Henry VI* is indeed an early Shakespearean effort, both in terms of style and dramatic effect.

4. What is the principal idea of each section of *Henry VI*, and how does Shakespeare develop this idea?

SELECT BIBLIOGRAPHY

ALEXANDER, PETER. *Shakespeare*. Oxford: Oxford University Press, 1964.

BENTLEY, GERALD EADES. *Shakespeare, a Biographical Handbook*. New Haven: Yale University Press, 1961.

BEVINGTON, DAVID. *Shakespeare*. Arlington Heights, Ill.: A.H.M. Publications, 1978.

BRADLEY, A. C. *Shakespearean Tragedy*. London: Macmillan, 1904.

CAMPBELL, LILY BESS. *Shakespeare's Tragic Heroes*. Cambridge University Press, 1930.

CLEMEN, WOLFGANG. *The Development of Shakespeare's Imagery*. Cambridge: Harvard University Press, 1951.

CURRY, WALTER CLYDE. *Shakespeare's Philosophical Patterns*. Baton Rouge, 1937.

DRIVER, T. F. *The Sense of History in Greek and Shakespearean Drama*. New York: Columbia University Press, 1960.

FERGUSSON, FRANCIS. *Shakespeare: The Pattern in His Carpet*. New York: Delacorte, 1970.

MARRIOTT, J. *English History in Shakespeare*, 1918.

TILLYARD, E. M. W. *Shakespeare's History Plays*. London, 1956.

WEBSTER, MARGARET. *Shakespeare Without Tears*. Cleveland: World Publishing Company, 1965.

NOTES

NOTES

NOTES

NOTES

NOTES

NOTES

NOTES

RICHARD II

NOTES

including
- *Life of Shakespeare*
- *General Plot Summary*
- *List of Characters*
- *Summaries and Commentaries*
- *Sixteenth-Century Political Theory*
- *Character Summations*
- *Questions for Review*
- *Selected Bibliography*

by
Denis Calandra, Ph.D.
Department of Theater
University of South Florida

INCORPORATED

LINCOLN, NEBRASKA 68501

Editor

Gary Carey, M.A.
University of Colorado

Consulting Editor

James L. Roberts, Ph.D.
Department of English
University of Nebraska

ISBN 0-8220-0068-7
© Copyright 1982
by
C. K. Hillegass
All Rights Reserved
Printed in U.S.A.

1990 Printing

Cliffs Notes, Inc.   Lincoln, Nebraska

CONTENTS

RICHARD II NOTES

LIFE OF SHAKESPEARE

Many books have assembled facts, reasonable suppositions, traditions, and speculations concerning the life and career of William Shakespeare. Taken as a whole, these materials give a rather comprehensive picture of England's foremost dramatic poet. Tradition and sober supposition are not necessarily false because they lack proved bases for their existence. It is important, however, that persons interested in Shakespeare should distinguish between *facts* and *beliefs* about his life.

From one point of view, modern scholars are fortunate to know as much as they do about a man of middle-class origin who left a small English country town and embarked on a professional career in sixteenth-century London. From another point of view, they know surprisingly little about the writer who has continued to influence the English language and its drama and poetry for more than three hundred years. Sparse and scattered as these facts of his life are, they are sufficient to prove that a man from Stratford by the name of William Shakespeare wrote the major portion of the thirty-seven plays which scholars ascribe to him. The concise review which follows will concern itself with some of these records.

No one knows the exact date of William Shakespeare's birth. His baptism occurred on Wednesday, April 26, 1564. His father was John Shakespeare, tanner, glover, dealer in grain, and town official of Stratford; his mother, Mary, was the daughter of Robert Arden, a prosperous gentleman-farmer. The Shakespeares lived on Henley Street.

Under a bond dated November 28, 1582, William Shakespeare and Anne Hathaway entered into a marriage contract. The baptism of their eldest child, Susanna, took place in Stratford in May, 1583. One year and nine months later their twins, Hamnet and Judith, were christened in the same church. The parents named them for the poet's friends Hamnet and Judith Sadler.

Early in 1596, William Shakespeare, in his father's name, applied to the College of Heralds for a coat of arms. Although positive proof is lacking, there is reason to believe that the Heralds granted this request, for in 1599 Shakespeare again made application for the right to quarter his coat of arms with that of his mother. Entitled to her father's coat of arms, Mary had lost this privilege when she married John Shakespeare before he held the official status of gentleman.

In May of 1597, Shakespeare purchased New Place, the outstanding residential property in Stratford at that time. Since John Shakespeare had suffered financial reverses prior to this date, William must have achieved success for himself.

Court records show that in 1601 or 1602, William Shakespeare began rooming in the household of Christopher Mountjoy in London. Subsequent disputes between Shakespeare's landlord, Mountjoy, and his son-in-law, Stephen Belott, over Stephen's wedding settlement led to a series of legal actions, and in 1612 the court scribe recorded Shakespeare's deposition of testimony relating to the case.

In July, 1605, William Shakespeare paid four hundred and forty pounds for the lease of a large portion of the tithes on certain real estate in and near Stratford. This was an arrangement whereby Shakespeare purchased half the annual tithes, or taxes, on certain agricultural products from sections of land in and near Stratford. In addition to receiving approximately ten percent income on his investment, he almost doubled his capital. This was possibly the most important and successful investment of his lifetime, and it paid a steady income for many years.

Shakespeare is next mentioned when John Combe, a resident of Stratford, died on July 12, 1614. To his friend, Combe bequeathed the sum of five pounds. These records and similar ones are important, not because of their economic significance but because they prove the existence of a William Shakespeare in Stratford and in London during this period.

On March 25, 1616, William Shakespeare revised his last will and testament. He died on April 23 of the same year. His body lies within the chancel and before the altar of the Stratford church. A rather wry inscription is carved upon his tombstone:

> Good Friend, for Jesus' sake, forbear
> To dig the dust enclosed here;

> Blest be the man that spares these stones
> And curst be he that moves my bones.

The last direct descendant of William Shakespeare was his granddaughter, Elizabeth Hall, who died in 1670.

These are the most outstanding facts about Shakespeare the man, as apart from those about the dramatist and poet. Such pieces of information, scattered from 1564 through 1616, declare the existence of such a person, not as a writer or actor, but as a private citizen. It is illogical to think that anyone would or could have fabricated these details for the purpose of deceiving later generations.

In similar fashion, the evidence establishing William Shakespeare as the foremost playwright of his day is positive and persuasive. Robert Greene's *Groatsworth of Wit*, in which he attacked Shakespeare, a mere actor, for presuming to write plays in competition with Greene and his fellow playwrights, was entered in the *Stationers' Register* on September 20, 1592. In 1594 Shakespeare acted before Queen Elizabeth, and in 1594 and 1595 his name appeared as one of the shareholders of the Lord Chamberlain's Company. Francis Meres in his *Palladis Tamia* (1598) called Shakespeare "mellifluous and hony-tongued" and compared his comedies and tragedies with those of Plautus and Seneca in excellence.

Shakespeare's continued association with Burbage's company is equally definite. His name appears as one of the owners of the Globe in 1599. On May 19, 1603, he and his fellow actors received a patent from James I designating them as the King's Men and making them Grooms of the Chamber. Late in 1608 or early in 1609, Shakespeare and his colleagues purchased the Blackfriars Theatre and began using it as their winter location when weather made production at the Globe inconvenient.

Other specific allusions to Shakespeare, to his acting and his writing, occur in numerous places. Put together, they form irrefutable testimony that William Shakespeare of Stratford and London was the leader among Elizabethan playwrights.

One of the most impressive of all proofs of Shakespeare's authorship of his plays is the First Folio of 1623, with the dedicatory verse which appeared in it. John Heminge and Henry Condell, members of Shakespeare's own company, stated that they collected and issued the plays as a memorial to their fellow actor. Many contemporary poets contributed eulogies to Shakespeare; one of the best known of these poems is by Ben Jonson, a fellow actor and, later, a friendly rival. Johnson also criticized Shakespeare's dramatic work in *Timber: or, Discoveries* (1641).

Certainly there are many things about Shakespeare's genius and career which the most diligent scholars do not know and cannot explain, but the facts which do exist are sufficient to establish Shakespeare's identity as a man and his authorship of the thirty-seven plays which reputable critics acknowledge to be his.

GENERAL PLOT SUMMARY

The play opens with a dispute between Henry Bolingbroke, Duke of Hereford, and Thomas Mowbray, Duke of Norfolk. Bolingbroke has accused Mowbray of treason, and the two of them exchange insults in the presence of King Richard. After attempts to reconcile them fail, Richard orders them to take part in a traditional chivalric trial by combat. On the field of combat, the king changes his mind and banishes the two men – Bolingbroke for ten years (commuted to six) and Mowbray for life. Then the king makes plans to leave for the wars in Ireland.

Before departing, Richard visits the ailing father of Bolingbroke, John of Gaunt, Duke of Lancaster. Gaunt warns Richard with his dying words that he is flirting with danger and doing great harm to the country by allowing himself to be influenced by his sycophantic courtiers. When he dies, Richard takes possession of all of Gaunt's wealth and leaves for Ireland.

Unhappy with Richard's incompetence as a ruler and worried by his seizure of the Duke of Lancaster's wealth, a number of nobles rally support for Henry Bolingbroke. When Bolingbroke and his army decide to return from exile in France, the rebel forces prepare to confront Richard on his return from Ireland.

The rebel noblemen force the king to abdicate, and Bolingbroke is crowned as Henry IV. Richard is imprisoned in Pomfret Castle, where he faces his death alone, philosophically contemplating the meaning of his fall from grandeur. Sir Pierce of Exton decides solely on his own to execute the deposed king, and then, as a result, he is banished by King Henry. The play ends with Henry IV planning a penitential pilgrimage to the Holy Land.

LIST OF CHARACTERS

King Richard

Historically, he is said to be the handsomest man of his time; in the play, he has great charm and a love for beautiful things. His court is characterized outwardly by its luxury and refinement, but Richard's own particular favorites are greedy men who are interested primarily in the profits made from usurping land, excessive taxation, and fraud. Richard allows himself to be used by these men and, as a result, he is deposed by one of his noblemen whom he sends unfairly into exile.

Bolingbroke

Henry, Duke of Hereford and Lancaster; he takes revenge on Richard after the king unfairly banishes him from England and, moreover, claims all of Henry's family lands and wealth after Henry's father, John of Gaunt, dies. Bolingbroke is a "model" Englishman and, for that reason, he is not entirely convinced that he has the right to usurp the crown from a man who *seems* corrupt even though he is supposed to be God's deputy on earth.

York

He is Richard's most powerful supporter, and when Richard leaves with his forces to fight in Ireland, he leaves York in charge of England. York is honest and good throughout the play and because of these qualities, he finally cannot condone Richard's unprincipled actions; thus he changes his allegiance to Bolingbroke and his supporters.

Aumerle

York's headstrong son remains loyal to Richard throughout the play, despite the fact that this loyalty threatens his relationship with his father. He even becomes involved in a plot to assassinate Bolingbroke, but at the pleading of his mother, he confesses his deed and is pardoned by Bolingbroke.

Queen Isabella

She appears four times in the play and, each time, she is characterized by her gentleness and her devotion to Richard. Moreover, there is a feeling of helplessness about her. Her grief becomes despair when she realizes that her husband has been deposed. She tries, however, to goad him into at least a *show* of valor and resistance when she speaks with him on his way to prison.

Mowbray

Clearly, he had a hand in the murder of Gloucester, even though he denies it. Richard exiles him for life, probably in order to remove this hand-chosen assassin from the country. Mowbray dies abroad, during one of the Crusades.

Northumberland

A powerful and aggressive character; his allegiance is early aligned with Bolingbroke. He fights alongside Bolingbroke and arranges for Richard's surrender. It is he who breaks up the last of Richard's conspirators.

Percy

Northumberland's son. He is an eager soldier, chivalrous, and an active supporter of Bolingbroke.

Duchess of Gloucester

It was the murder of her husband which caused Bolingbroke to accuse Mowbray of assassination and treason. She begs old Gaunt to take revenge on Richard; her anger is fiery and passionate. She dies of grief for her husband.

Duchess of York

Her loyalty is, foremost, to her son, who is loyal to Richard. Her whole character revolves around Aumerle's safety. She herself is fearless before Bolingbroke, but she fears the latter's power to silence her son's seemingly treasonous words and deeds.

Surrey

He is sympathetic with Aumerle and refutes Fitzwater's claim that Aumerle, in Fitzwater's presence, did take credit for Gloucester's death.

Carlisle

He is ever-loyal to Richard because he sees Richard's role as one that was heaven-ordained. He rails against Bolingbroke but, importantly, he also chides Richard for the kind of king he has been. In the end, Bolingbroke pardons him because of his unusually high character.

Abbot of Westminster

He hears Aumerle's wish to revenge himself on Bolingbroke and, therefore, he invites Aumerle home so that the two of them can make further plans.

Ross and Willoughby

Representatives of the followers of Bolingbroke.

Fitzwater

He swears that he heard Aumerle take full credit for Gloucester's murder. Surrey takes issue with this statement, and Fitzwater challenges him to a duel.

Exton

Believing that Bolingbroke wishes him to kill Richard, he does so; immediately afterward, however, he is sure that he acted rashly. Bolingbroke banishes him.

Salisbury

Richard leaves him in charge of the military forces while he fights in Ireland. He is upset when he discovers that he has no Welsh support for Richard when he knows that Bolingbroke and his supporters are ready to attack Richard.

Scroop

He announces to Richard that the common people have championed Bolingbroke as their favorite. He appears only in Act III, Scenes 2 and 3.

Berkeley

In charge of the troops guarding Bristol Castle, he is rebuked when Bolingbroke confronts him, and he refers to Bolingbroke as Hereford – and not as Lancaster.

Bushy and Green

They are followers of Richard, but they are neither heroic nor staunch in their loyalty. They plot, connive, and flee at the approach of danger. Bolingbroke corners them finally and has them killed. They are representative of the low-class of flatterers whom Richard surrounds himself with.

Bagot

He has a part only slightly larger than Bushy and Green; otherwise, he is not distinguishable from them.

SUMMARIES AND COMMENTARIES

ACT I – SCENE I

Summary

King Richard II opens the play by asking old John of Gaunt if he has brought John's son, Henry Bolingbroke, to substantiate charges of treason which he has made against Thomas Mowbray, Duke of Norfolk. After asking Gaunt if he has already questioned his son on the matter, Richard asks that the two men be brought before him; Richard greets them formally, and then he asks Henry Bolingbroke to clarify his case against Mowbray. Bolingbroke charges Mowbray with being a "traitor and a miscreant," but before he can finish speaking, Mowbray breaks in and offers a counter-accusation: "I do defy him and I spit at him,/ Call him a slanderous coward and a villain." Mowbray suggests that they settle their quarrel by dueling at Coventry, and Bolingbroke throws down his glove as a symbol of his counter-challenge, according to the rites of knighthood. After Mowbray retrieves the glove and accepts the challenge, the king asks Bolingbroke to explain his accusation against Mowbray. Bolingbroke levels the charges: "All the treasons of these eighteen years" have their origin in Mowbray; he did plot the murder of the Duke of Gloucester. Mowbray responds that he committed *one* grave sin in the past – laying an ambush for old Gaunt's life, but he has since repented it. He denies killing Gloucester. The king tries to calm them both with the words "Forget, forgive; conclude and be agreed," and he appeals to old Gaunt for help in the matter. Gaunt cannot decide what to do, and so he exits. Meanwhile, Mowbray refuses to withdraw the challenge. "The purest treasure," he says, which "mortal times afford/ Is spotless reputation. . . ." Therefore, he tells Richard, the king can command his life, but not his shame; Bolingbroke's reply is similar: "Shall I seem crestfallen in my father's sight?" Richard seemingly cannot determine which of the men is lying and, therefore, he refuses to arbitrate any longer; he orders that the duel shall take place at Coventry on Saint Lambert's Day (September 17): "There shall your swords and lances arbitrate."

Commentary

As is the case with Shakespeare's other history plays, this play has as its central concern a civil strife which threatens a country with a weak government. Thus, *Richard II* opens with a scene that graphically illustrates the point: two nobles are locked in bitter argument over who is most loyal to the crown, and the only logical outcome would seem to be a physical struggle, even to the death. The best that the king can do is agree to let them fight.

The character of old Gaunt is important here because he is referred to several times as an "old" man and is therefore supposed to be a "sage" man. Richard appeals to Gaunt to help settle the argument, but with no success; neither the ruler nor he who possesses the wisdom of age can calm the troubled waters in this first scene; only a decision based on formal violence will decide the issue.

Note in particular the chivalric atmosphere of this scene. When the challengers speak to the king and to each other, they use a very formal style of address. For example, Bolingbroke first speaks to his king:

> In the devotion of a subject's love,
> Tend'ring the precious safety of my prince,
> And free from other misbegotten hate,
> Come I appellant to this princely presence.
>
> (31-34)

And Mowbray, when he accepts the challenge, also speaks in a formal manner:

> I take it up; and by that sword I swear
> Which gently laid my knighthood on my shoulder,
> I'll answer then in any fair degree
> Or chivalrous design of knightly trial.
>
> (78-81)

The formal speech patterns and the chivalric code of behavior here act as metaphors for order and control. These men are preparing to kill each other, but they are going about it in a gentlemanly way. Such formal patterns exist, according to Shakespeare's orthodox belief, in the world of government too. There is always an attempt—even when it becomes a struggle—to keep the most violent passions regulated within a pattern.

Speaking of formal patterns, we must not ignore the real passion and invective in some of the remarks which the opponents hurl at each other. Take, for example, Bolingbroke's promise to tear out his own tongue and "spit it bleeding" in Mowbray's face rather than withdraw from the fight. This is naked, unbridled passion. But it is spoken within the formal context of a verbal tournament, preluding the tournament at Coventry. And, in reference to passion, there is an important, implicit clue as to the murderer of Gloucester in this scene. Mowbray has indeed had a hand in killing him (and that's what Bolingbroke accuses him of), but Mowbray did it at Richard's request. When Bolingbroke utters the words, "the death," Mowbray says, "I slew him not; but, to my own disgrace/ Neglected my *sworn duty* in that case" (italics mine). Mowbray swore, without a doubt, to Richard to see to it that Gloucester was either killed by his hand or by Mowbray's order.

One more matter that should not be neglected in any discussion of language in this scene includes the fact that the language, besides being mostly chivalrous and formal, suggests a religious theme in several places: such words as "miscreant," "innocent souls," "rites of knighthood," and "our sacred blood" occur frequently. This language will be of even more importance later in the play.

ACT I – SCENE 2

Summary

The scene takes place at the London palace of John of Gaunt; old Gaunt is talking to the Duchess of Gloucester, who is paying him a visit. The duchess is very upset; she wants revenge and she hopes that old Gaunt will see to it that revenge is exacted because Gloucester, her husband, was Gaunt's brother. Gaunt advises his sister-in-law that they can't do anything against the "butchers of [Gloucester's] life." They had best leave the "quarrel to the will of Heaven." The duchess is shocked at Gaunt's apparent lack of will to take vengeance for her "dear lord." Her husband's blood was Gaunt's own blood, she emphasizes. Likewise, she tells Gaunt that her murdered husband and Gaunt shared the same womb, but Gaunt refuses to submit to her tactics. The duchess, however, continues; she argues that "to safeguard thine own life/ The best way is to venge my Gloucester's death." Gaunt explains that his hands are tied; the king, "God's deputy," caused the murder, hence revenge must be left to heaven. One cannot defy God's appointed deputy in England, he insists. The duchess appears to acquiesce and bids Gaunt goodbye. She hopes that at least right will triumph when Bolingbroke and Mowbray fight at Coventry, and that Bolingbroke's spear "may enter butcher Mowbray's breast!" Weeping, she bids Gaunt farewell.

Commentary

Shakespeare's plays were written for performance without any breaks between the scenes or the acts. The flow of the scenes, their placement, and the effect which was created by contrasting elements in the scene constitutes his chief technical resource. In the first scene, for example, Richard tries to arbitrate a dispute between two peers of his realm. The issue is one of state – loyalty to the king – and also a personal matter of honor between two men of arms. The tone of the opening scene tells us that something is *wrong* in the state of England. Scene 2, appropriately, personalizes this *wrongness*, this grief, by showing us a woman lamenting aloud both the loss of her husband *and* the fact that she is likely not to see proper vengeance done. That she is suffering personally is certain, and her confusion is clear in her last speech, for she finds it difficult to say farewell to old Gaunt.

> Commend me to thy brother, Edmund York.
> Lo! this is all: nay, yet depart not so;
> Though this be all, do not so quickly go.
> I shall remember more. Bid him . . . Ah! What?
> With all good speed at Plashy visit me.
>
> (62-65)

The phrasing – "Lo! . . . nay, yet depart not. . . . Bid him . . . Ah! What?" – tells more about her distraught state of mind than the words themselves.

At the beginnings of the scene, when the duchess tries to play on Gaunt's feelings for his murdered brother, her language echoes Christian and biblical phrases. She refers to the patriarch:

> Edward's seven sons, whereof thyself art one,
> Were as seven vials of his sacred blood,
> Or seven fair branches springing from one root.
>
> (11-13)

As she continues, her emotion wells up.

> But Thomas, my dear lord, my life, my Gloucester,
> One vial full of Edward's sacred blood, ...

. . . is hacked down . . .
Ah! Gaunt, his blood was thine!

(16-22)

The effect of this speech is to reinforce her feelings of loss by emphasizing the "sacredness" of their common father's blood. The irony, and a serious religious and political problem for Shakespeare's age, is that another father-figure, one who is also "sacred," is Richard II, the king, and he has had a hand in perpetrating the crime. Gaunt has relatively few lines in this scene, and for good reason. He, like others around him, feels impotent before this impossible dilemma. This old and sage Gaunt, in his helplessness in the face of personal and public grief, is an important early theatrical image in the play. He can only lamely repeat the formula:

God's is the quarrel; for God's substitute,
His deputy anointed in His sight,
Hath caused his death. . . .

(37-39)

ACT I – SCENE 3

Summary

Richard and his knights arrive at Coventry, on a field prepared for single combat, and enter to the sound of trumpets. Then Mowbray enters with a herald. The king bids the Marshal to "demand of yonder champion" the cause of the present quarrel. After Mowbray is asked the cause of his being here, he repeats his case, promising to prove himself true and, furthermore, promising to prove Bolingbroke "a traitor to my God, my King, and me." Trumpets are heard again, and Bolingbroke, armed like his counterpart, enters the scene. Richard asks the Marshal once again to inquire the cause of complaint. The Marshal does so, and Bolingbroke repeats his previous accusation: Mowbray is a traitor, "foul and dangerous." Bolingbroke then asks permission to bid farewell to the king by kissing his ring. The king acknowledges the request and descends from his seat to "fold him in our arms." Richard states that despite whose blood will be shed, no revenge will be taken.

Bolingbroke then takes leave of the king, his kinsmen, his followers, and finally his father. He bids them to shed no tears and promises to perform valiantly for his father's sake. His father, in turn, bids him to "be swift like lightning" in the fight.

Mowbray then has his turn to bid farewell to the king, claiming to be a "loyal, just, and upright gentleman" who will fight without boasting about it. "As gentle and as jocund as to jest/ Go I to fight," he says, for "truth hath a quiet breast."

Before the fight begins, however, King Richard throws his baton to the ground as a signal to halt the proceedings. "Let them lay by their helmets and their spears," he says "and both return to their chairs again." Richard explains that he does not wish to see blood spilled by his countrymen, as in civil war, and therefore will banish the two contestants from England. Bolingbroke is not to return for ten years, while Mowbray is banished for life. The two men accept their sentences gracefully, though Mowbray, who is never to return, expresses a deep sadness that he will not be able to speak the English language again; he feels condemned to a "speechless death."

As the two turn to leave, Richard stops them and makes them lay their hands on his royal sword and promise never to come into contact with one another again nor to engage in any treasonous act; never are they "to plot, contrive, or complot any ill." Both swear accordingly, but Bolingbroke has a parting word with Mowbray; he asks him—now that he is banished and free from other punishment—to confess the crime against the state which he has commit ted. Mowbray replies that he'd rather be "from heaven banished" than admit to such a thing. He exits then.

Richard turns to Gaunt and immediately reduces old Gaunt's son's sentence from ten years to six years because Gaunt's old eyes betray a "grieved heart." Bolingbroke gratefully accepts the commutation of his sentence and muses on the ease with which Richard can change the course of another man's life: "Such is the breath of kings." Gaunt also thanks the king, but remains saddened because he is an old man who may not live the six years before his son returns. When the king cheerfully reminds him that he is in good health and will live many more years, Gaunt stops him short by saying that even the king "cannot buy my breath." The king questions Gaunt, wondering why he did not defend his son more vehemently. Gaunt replies that he was urged to speak as a judge and not to argue "like a father." His duty to the judgment process forced him to remain as objective as possible, and now he must suffer privately for it.

In the last minutes of the scene, Bolingbroke and his father take leave of each other. Gaunt tries to cheer up his son by saying that it won't be too long before he returns and that if he keeps his mind on other things, the time of exile will pass quickly. Bolingbroke, however asks:

> . . . who can hold a fire in his hand
> By thinking on the frosty Caucasus?
> Or cloy the hungry edge of appetite
> By bare imagination of a feast?
> Or wallow naked in December snow
> By thinking on fantastic summer's heat?
>
> (294-99)

He departs, swearing that wherever he wanders he can at least boast that "though banished, [he is] yet a trueborn Englishman."

Commentary

Notice the progression of this scene. It begins as a highly formal, almost ritualistic display in the chivalric tradition. The accused and the accusing parties are announced; they state their cases, make their farewells, and prepare to fight. It ends with a father and a son, Gaunt and Bolingbroke, saying goodbye for six years, or, considering Gaunt's age, maybe for the last time in their lives. The scene moves from the affairs of state in a public ceremony to the intimate details of personal, familial relationships. That very pattern, you will recall, was the pattern of scenes one and two. Here it is repeated, with continuous focus on the principals in the drama.

When Richard pronounces the words "orderly proceed" at the start of the scene, he is, of course, sounding the keynote to all of Shakespeare's history plays again. The ritual of this hand-to-hand combat, though it is enacted to resolve a passionate dispute and may end in bloodshed, will be carried out according to mutually acknowledged rules. One must imagine the start of this scene as being filled with suggestions of the spectacle of a medieval tournament. Representatives of the opposing camps march in, present themselves to the king, speak their pieces, and take up positions on an elaborate stage tableau. The picture on stage and the accompanying regular trumpet blasts are clear metaphors for a kind of *order*. And at the center of this ordered world is, of course, King Richard, who is stationed upstage to observe the proceedings. When he descends from his raised platform (which was traditional) and walks downstage to stop the proceedings later in the scene, he travels quite a distance (the depth of Shakespeare's stage was about 25 feet), reinforcing his pivotal place on the stage and in the political picture.

The language of Bolingbroke, describing himself and Mowbray as two men who "vow [to take] a long and weary pilgrimage," continues the religious imagery which is germane to the subject of this play. Bolingbroke wants to take a long farewell with his father because it may be their last farewell. But before he launches into his private farewell, he is embraced by the king, a poignant moment when one considers the scene later in the play when the two of them meet again – when Richard renounces his throne to Bolingbroke. Richard hands him the crown then. Here, the father of the nation, as it were, embraces one of his "sons"; later, that "son" will depose him. Bolingbroke bids farewell to his faithful followers, then to his actual father, Gaunt.

Notice, too, the way that Shakespeare contrasts the characters of these opponents by suggesting a difference in their bearing in these scenes. When they first encountered one another in the first scene of this act, Mowbray made a point of contrasting his own response to the situation with Bolingbroke's. Implicitly, he is claiming that Bolingbroke is somewhat hot-headed and, therefore, less creditable than himself. There he said:

> Let not my cold words here accuse my zeal.
> 'Tis not the trial of a woman's war,
> The bitter clamour of two eager tongues,
> Can arbitrate this cause betwixt us twain;
> The blood is hot that must be cooled for this.
>
> (I.i.47-51)

He has apparently listened to Bolingbroke's enraged words and has decided to respond with a posture of perfect reasonableness. In this scene, he strikes the same theme when he says, "Truth hath a quiet breast." The reason for this relatively calm bearing might be his quiet confidence that the king is on his side and, therefore, he shall come to no harm. Whatever the reason, the posture of one combatant being more feverish than the other is important for dramatic reasons. Besides adding variety in characterization, this contrast prepares for a similar contrast later during the deposition scene (IV.i). Notice there how quietly Bolingbroke endures the lengthy diatribes of King Richard II.

An important dramatic facet in this scene is Richard's decision to stop the combat and to exile the opponents. All of the spectacle and verbal exchange in the scene is leading up to a violent combat which never takes place. Why does Shakespeare have Richard stop the fight? For one thing, Richard is, in fact, indebted to Mowbray for being instrumental in eliminating a potential enemy (Gloucester). For another, to allow the combat to go forward and risk the life of the apparently popular Bolingbroke would be a poor political move. It seems best to appear the wise and kind ruler by preventing any civil bloodshed at all. Notice that Richard also manages to banish Mowbray, the one who has evidence against him, for life, while commuting the sentence of Bolingbroke from ten years to six years, further mollifying his potential political opponents. Rulers in Shakespeare's age would have been familiar with Machiavelli's famous *Prince*, a popular and rather cynical manual for rulers, and would have known that it is always wiser to appear harsher at first, making severe punishments all at once, and then to soften one's stance with mercy. The mercy, however, is not received quite as Richard had expected, and this irritates him.

There is a serious undertone of antagonism between Richard, on the one hand, and Gaunt and his son, on the other. Richard knows very well what he is doing in commuting the sentence as he does, and he is hoping that Gaunt will receive this lordly gesture appropriately. When Gaunt takes up his son's cue on the words "such is the breath of kings" and tells the king that though he can easily send a man into exile or even cut a man's life short, he *still* does not have the power to add one minute to a man's life, he is raising a very sensitive issue and one very important to a central theme of this play. In a play in which the deposition of God's appointed minister, the king, is a central action, it is a highly charged dramatic moment when the matter of the limitation of the power of the king is raised. None of this by-play is openly acknowledged by the speakers, but their words are certainly spoken with an awareness of all connotations. What Gaunt is saying, in effect, is that although Richard may be God's anointed and appointed deputy, he is certainly *not* God Himself. One wonders if the conversation which he had with his sister-in-law in the previous scene, coupled with the present sorrow of saying goodbye to his son, has given him some of the courage which the Duchess of Gloucester found wanting. That Gaunt's remarks have the desired effect on Richard is clear from the way in which the king exits, with two clipped lines reiterating the sentence just meted out:

> Cousin, farewell, and uncle bid him so;
> Six years we banish him, and he shall go.
>
> (247-48)

The last moments of the scene are especially important for their emotional tone. There is speed in the delivery of the lines between Gaunt and his son, Bolingbroke, that belies the feelings underneath. Bolingbroke is silent at first, until his father urges him to speak.

> *Gaunt*:   O, to what purpose dost thou hoard thy words,
>   That thou return'st no greeting to thy friends?
> *Bolingbroke*:   I have too few to take my leave of you,
>   When the tongue's office should be prodigal
>   To breathe the abundant dolour of the heart.
> *Gaunt*:   Thy grief is but thy absence for a time.
> *Bolingbroke*:   Joy absent, grief is present for that time.
> *Gaunt*:   What is six winters? They are quickly gone.
> *Bolingbroke*:   To men in joy; but grief makes one hour ten.
> *Gaunt*:   Call it a travel that thou tak'st for pleasure.
>
> (255-64)

This seems a very genuine scene, psychologically. Gaunt's distress is shown by the fact that he is using "arguments" to make his son feel better, which he had, just a few minutes before, rebuked the king for using—that is, that the exile really won't be so long, that it really is only a temporary absence. In addition, it is as if the rush of words they exchange is a way of covering up feelings they would rather not have to cope with. There is an irony in the remark which Gaunt makes to his son, telling him that his absence will serve as a foil to his coming home, and make the coming home that much more joyous. In a way, this is true, for Bolingbroke's return will eventually lead to his becoming king, albeit reluctantly. His return *will* seem greater because of the absence. Also, Richard's behavior, by comparison, will make Bolingbroke seem greater. Interestingly, this metaphor of a *foil* carries on into the *Henry IV* plays. There, we find Bolingbroke an older and a wearier man, now the king himself, having to deal with a recalcitrant son, Prince Hal. Throughout the play, Hal's escapades with the lower orders of society are described in such a way that they can be seen as setting his "true" (princely) self off as a jewel is set off by the less precious metal leaf which serves as backing for it in a setting.

There is superb humaneness in old Gaunt as he gives his son some conventional fatherly advice at the end of the scene. He is trying to be perfectly reasonable and allay his son's fears: don't think that the king has banished you, but rather think that you have banished the king; try to think that a foul pestilence sits in the land and you are better off out of the country. In a sense, there *is* a truth in this, in that there is a less than perfect king on the throne, but Bolingbroke can answer only from his heart, and none of his father's arguments make him feel any better. Who can "wallow naked in December snow/ By thinking on fantastic summer's heat?" he asks. The reality of banishment will be so painful that he won't be able to delude himself for a minute into believing otherwise. At the very last, however, Bolingbroke exits with an important, manly, and patriotic flourish:

> Where'er I wander, boast of this I can,
> Though banish'd, yet a trueborn Englishman.
>
> (308-9)

These, undoubtedly, are the words of a hero.

ACT I – SCENE 4

Summary

The scene opens shortly after the last. Richard is subtly trying to test the loyalty of Aumerle, the son of the Duke of York, and, at the same time, to find out from him what Bolingbroke said on his departure, for Aumerle escorted Bolingbroke away. Aumerle says that Bolingbroke said only "Farewell." Clearly, he does not like Bolingbroke and did not enjoy escorting him away, feigning feelings of fond farewell. Richard does not want to seem villainous, and so he reminds Aumerle that Bolingbroke is "our cousin." He then explores another avenue of conversation; he says that he has had certain of his men – Bushy, Bagot, and Green – observing the country people, and they report that the banished Bolingbroke is popular among the commoners. He ponders,

> How he did seem to dive into their hearts
> With humble and familiar courtesy,
> What reverence he did throw away on slaves,
> Wooing poor craftsmen with the craft of smiles. . . .
>
> (25-28)

To Richard, it seems "as were our England in reversion his."

Green then speaks up and reminds Richard that, at least, Bolingbroke is out of the way; now they must turn their attention to the pressing problem of the Irish rebellion. Richard decides to go into battle himself against the rebels, and he plans to do so with the greatest assurance of success. To that end, he decides that he must first fill his coffers with riches borrowed from (and demanded from) his country's nobles. At that point, Bushy rushes in with the news that Gaunt is extremely ill, probably dying. Richard wishes the old man "good speed" (to death). In fact, his comment is quite mercenary:

> The lining of his coffers shall make coats
> To deck our soldiers for these Irish wars.
>
> (61-62)

They all exit then to go to Gaunt's bedside.

Commentary

Here we see Richard in close-ups; he is a man who is accustomed to exploiting his countrymen, and in this scene he is a marked contrast to the "true-born Englishman" who bade us farewell in the previous scene. Not only does Shakespeare show Richard quite openly preparing to take his country's wealth to spend on a foreign war, but also hoping for an early death for the venerable old Gaunt. This is rather bold characterization, somewhat melodramatic, and more typical of Shakespeare's early plays than his later ones. There is no question at this point where an audience's sympathies lie.

Note also the character of Aumerle in this scene. He is a young man, the son of the Duke of York, and naturally enough he shows loyalty to his king. He is proud of having successfully feigned grief at Bolingbroke's departure, and he happily joins Bagot and Green at the king's side. Shakespeare will later sound this note of feigned grief when Richard gives up the crown. There, it will be Bolingbroke who sarcastically commends Richard for putting on a good show of suffering. The matter of loyalty to the king is important, with regard to Aumerle, because of his actions later in the play when he is chided by his father for behavior disloyal to the new king, Bolingbroke. In the end, of course, Bolingbroke pardons Aumerle, but that pardon will seem all the more magnanimous because of the memory of this early scene in which Aumerle is quite clearly a loyal ally of Richard's and a foe of Bolingbroke's.

Consider the dramatic effect when Richard sarcastically bids his followers to come with him to the dying Gaunt's bedside: "Come, gentlemen, let's all go visit him;/ Pray God we may make haste and come too late!" And they reply, to a man: "Amen!" The contrast with the closing of the previous scene is a powerful one.

ACT II – SCENE 1

Summary

This scene takes place at Ely House in London, where Gaunt lies ill. His first speech forms a sort of "bridge" between the end of the last scene and this act. Speaking to his brother, the Duke of York, Gaunt asks, "Will the king come that I may breathe my last/ In wholesome counsel to his unstaid youth?" Clearly, Gaunt is worried about conditions in England. York, however, has no easy words of consolation; he thinks that the king is beyond listening ("all in vain comes counsel to his ear"); he thinks that the king listens only to young men who are more concerned with aping Continental fashions than coping with England's political troubles. Still, however, Gaunt hopes that his advice won't be wasted. He reasons that dying men are listened to more carefully because it is recognized that their words are precious because they are so scarce.

Acknowledging that he probably sounds like an Old Testament prophet, Gaunt charges Richard with the sin of wasting himself in a "rash fierce blaze of riot" which "cannot last." He is determined to convert the erring Richard to a better life worthy of his role as king. He appeals strongly to the patriotic sentiments of the audience as he rhetorically describes England:

> This royal throne of kings, this sceptred isle,
> This earth of majesty, this seat of Mars,
> This other Eden, demi-paradise. . . .
>
> (40-42)

Then Gaunt reverses the imagery and speaks of the shame which has been brought to England of late, how Richard turned this paradise into a shameful place and turned this fortress-like isle into a prison. As the king enters, York hastily warns Gaunt to temper his rage, saying that "young hot colts being raged do rage the more."

Richard, with his favorite courtiers, approaches Gaunt and is amazed at the old man's invective. Gaunt charges that Richard is the sicker of the two men, and he extends the idea of sickness and infection to include England itself: "Thy deathbed," he says, "is no lesser than thy land,/ Wherein thou liest in reputation sick. . . ." He points to the covey of political sycophants which the king surrounds himself with; the crown of England cannot encompass all these "thousand flatterers," Gaunt warns. Richard is no king; Richard is no more than a greedy landlord to his country.

Richard loses his composure and abruptly stops the old man: if Gaunt were not the brother to great Edward's son, he would soon have his head separated from his body. Gaunt is not impressed. He reminds the company that that sort of scruple didn't bother Richard when he ended Gloucester's life. As Gaunt is taken out, he turns and hopes that "these words hereafter thy tormentors be!"

Gaunt's death is announced shortly thereafter by Northumberland, and the Duke of York is distressed to hear Richard almost gloat over "the plate, coin, revenues, and moveables . . ." of old Gaunt. What is to become of the entire system of allegiance and inheritance, he asks, if Richard can so capriciously take the lands and property of Gaunt, which rightfully belong to Gaunt's son, Bolingbroke? If Richard does this, York warns him that he "plucks a thousand dangers on [his] head." Richard is unmoved; he means to immediately "seize into our hands/ His plate, his goods, his money, and his lands," and to that end he orders Bushy to arrange the transfer of possessions.

When the king is gone, Northumberland, Willoughby, and Ross discuss the state of the nation. Northumberland fears that banishment will be the punishment if one of Richard's flatterers chooses to decide to denounce him. Ross points to the grievous, unjust taxes now levied on commoners and nobles alike, and Willoughby mentions the plethora of "blank checks" and "forced loans." The three men see no hope for England; ". . . unavoided is the danger now." The times demand revolt, and Ross urges Northumberland to lead the revolt. Northumberland then gives them the news that already he has had news from Bolingbroke; Gaunt's son has gathered a large number of highly placed sympathizers who have ships and some "three thousand men." As soon as Richard leaves for Ireland, Bolingbroke means to fight to reclaim what is his. Moreover, Northumberland promises them that they personally will soon have a chance to "redeem . . . the blemished crown,/ Wipe off the dust that hides our sceptre's gilt,/ And make high majesty look like itself."

Commentary

This long scene begins with the individual rage of an esteemed old man who is soon to breathe his last, and it ends with the suggestion that the rage has spread to large numbers of people who are prepared to do something about it. The situation is a potentially revolutionary one, and Shakespeare traces the development of political turmoil by first allowing one man to speak his frustration and bear the insults of a capricious ruler, and then showing the effect of this scene of humiliation on those who have witnessed it. When Northumberland, Ross, and Willoughby conspire at the very end of the scene to join forces with the rebellious army of Bolingbroke, we have a feeling that there is a rightness to their decision. We not only hear *about* Richard's ill-treatment of deserving countrymen, but we witness that ill-treatment. Shakespeare's dramatic strategy is at its most effective here.

In the first conversation between York and Gaunt, Gaunt is perhaps a symbol for the sickly state of the nation, for there is the suggestion that what is symbolically best about the nation is languishing at the moment. Then after York prepares the ground with references to corrupt foreign influences and herds of flatterers, it is Gaunt who delivers the rousing patriotic speech which is the emotional center of the entire scene. By the end of the speech, it is as though Gaunt is identified with all that is good and noble and blessed about England. The scene gains further dramatic significance by the fact that these are the words of a dying man. Point for point, the features of England which Gaunt mentions in his rousing speech are those features which are being misshapen by the actions of the king and his court. "This seat of Mars" – England – a proud, warring nation, we are soon to learn, has become so craven that it gains more and spends more from its cleverly concluded truces than it does from the actual spoils of war. And when Northumberland and his friends speak at the end of the scene, it is clear that they *loath* the new set of priorities that Richard has set for the nation. Even the war fought in Ireland is fought on borrowed, extorted, and stolen money, and it is fought for a purely *imperialistic* purpose – that is, to fill the coffers of the profligate king. Gaunt's charges are keen and forceful: "This fortress built by nature for herself," "this precious stone set in the silver sea" has become instead a prison "bound in with shame" and an object to be pawned, "now leased out." Gaunt is responding to the corruption of his England in the interests of the private indulgence of a bad king, and Shakespeare, for his part, like many of his contemporaries, is here making unhappy reference to changes in the economic system which was taking place in Elizabethan England. The new order for England would be the order of a profit-oriented world. Shakespeare also sounds the religious note of the play anew in this scene when he makes reference to the "Christian service and true chivalry" of the former "royal kings" of England. At the end of Gaunt's speech, one can imagine the old man being somewhat exhausted, especially when he utters the lines,

> Ah! would the scandal vanish with my life,
> How happy then were my ensuing death!

(67-68)

His own strength is diminishing in strong contrast with the swift and lively entry of Richard and his queen and courtiers. Richard, true to his reputation, always travels "in style," as it were. Whenever he comes onto the scene, it is always with a verbal flourish and an entourage. He is a man who likes "entrances," a man with a special penchant for acting. Consider the situation when Gaunt utters his last tired breath at the end of his patriotic tirade, and Richard bursts onto the scene. Notice the way in which Richard speaks to the old man. His speech is short and clipped, and his treatment of Gaunt is disrespectful, to say the least. First, there is the exchange between them on the subject of Gaunt's punning comment on the state of his health and the meaning of his name – gaunt, sickly, and thin. Richard's words are, at first, questions, one after the other – "What comfort, man? How is it with aged Gaunt?"; "Can sick men play so nicely with their names?"; "Should dying men flatter . . . those that live?" But when Gaunt loses patience, as an old man deprived of the comfort of having a son near him as he himself nears death, he launches a direct attack on the king and his court. The king, in turn, responds viciously. Gaunt's reference to the "thousand flatterers [who] sit within thy crown" and more specifically to the fact that Richard is dangerously close to deposing himself strikes a raw nerve within Richard. Earlier, he entered the scene self-assured and confident that Gaunt was no threat to him because of his illness; he has come to Ely House in the first place to collect the old man's wealth, but now he loses his composure at these words and suddenly attacks the old man:

> A lunatic, lean-witted fool,
> Presuming on an ague's privilege,
> Dar'st with thy frozen admonition
> Make pale our cheek, chasing the royal blood
> With fury from his native residence.
>
> (115-19)

This attack adds cowardice and foolhardiness to the list of Richard's faults. One should remember, however, that Richard's response to any attack on himself is, in orthodox terms, justified; he *is* the king and, therefore, an entity apart from ordinary mortals. The complication in this scene, and indeed in the play as a whole, is that this king seems unworthy of the divine office he occupies. His attacker, old Gaunt, especially after the emotional "this other Eden" speech, is much more the "kingly" figure to be identified with England's virtues than the actual king himself.

Before Gaunt exits, he virtually accuses the king of the murder of Gloucester, and he warns him that these words will later haunt him:

> Live in thy shame, but die not shame with thee!
> These words hereafter thy tormentors be!
>
> (135-36)

The words will haunt him, and we should recall them when we witness the last scenes of the play, when the king faces death and despondency – as old Gaunt now does.

One reason for Shakespeare's writing the next part of the scene, between Richard and York, is that it offers a point of contrast between the two "old" men (York and Gaunt) in their responses to the king. We have already witnessed the conversation between York and Gaunt, and we know that York is unhappy with the state of England, though he is less likely to become infuriated and risk any treasonous act or statement. He tried to conciliate old Gaunt, tried to calm him in the face of the king, and now he uses the words of a diplomat to quell the king's anger toward Gaunt:

> I do beseech your Majesty, impute his words
> To wayward sickliness and age in him. . . .
>
> (141-42)

York has a careful nature here; clearly, he knows just how explosive the situation is and doesn't want anyone to risk upsetting whatever equilibrium prevails. He will retain this role throughout the entire play, even after the rebels prove successful in deposing Richard.

It is significant that this "normative" figure, York, has his patience tried when Gaunt's death is announced, and the king, without the least trace of remorse, makes plans to immediately collect the booty he came for in the first place. The king's words, ironically, point to his own future situation: "The ripest fruit first falls, and so doth he;/ His time is spent, our pilgrimage must be. So much for that" (153-55). The king himself is "ripest" in the sense that he is most near-ly "rotten"; and the king will indeed follow Gaunt on a "pilgrim-age" – to humiliation and death. Richard breaks off these thoughts in mid-sentence and turns his mind to Gaunt's "plate, coins, and revenues." It is here that York approaches exasperation: "How long shall I be patient?" he asks and begins a lengthy discourse on the falseness of Richard's conduct. One must imagine Richard's de-meanor through all this long speech of York's. His interrupting words are: "Why, uncle, what's the matter?" The tone is almost cer-tainly sarcastic because it couldn't fail to be clear to anyone exactly *what* the matter *is*. York continues his desperate argument, com-pletely unaware that, at best, the king is merely tolerating his words. York concludes his argument about succession: since Richard is violating rights of inheritance and succession by seizing Gaunt's goods, he is putting the very idea of succession in jeopardy:

> Take Hereford's rights away, and take from Time
> His charters and his customary rights;
> Let not tomorrow then ensue today;
> Be not thyself.
>
> (195-98)

Indeed, in being a bad king, Richard is *not* being himself, kingship being by definition divine and therefore good. Richard is totally un-moved by this speech and, single-mindedly, he repeats his inten-tions:

> Think what you will, we seize into our hands
> His plate, his goods, his money, and his lands.
>
> (209-10)

York departs in despair, a mood which will change to hope in the rebellious persons of Northumberland, Willoughby, and Ross.

Remember that these three men have been present for most of the foregoing scene and have witnessed the behavior of the king – both to Gaunt and to York. At first, their plight seems to be the same as York's. They dare not open their mouths for fear of the re-percussions. That foul injustice has been done to Gaunt and to his son Bolingbroke is without doubt, but they must tread lightly when considering what action to take. The dialogue is written in such a fashion as to emphasize the volume of wrongs which the king has done. One after another of his deeds is catalogued, all those things we have already heard Gaunt and York accuse him of. The reason for the repetition is to indicate just how widespread the discontent with the king is; in addition, it serves as a way of allowing these individual nobles to garner the courage to decide to commit what will be, after all, treasonable acts. They list all the wrongs, then they pause to consider their weight, and Northumberland speaks for them all when he expresses fear at his own thoughts: he "dares not say" what they can do to set things right in England. It is important to realize that there is something conspiratorial about this scene, in that the three nobles are aware of the gravity of the situation. But when they decide at the end to join forces with Bolingbroke's forces, they do so with conviction.

> . . . we shall shake off our slavish yoke,
> Imp out our drooping country's broken wing,
> Redeem from broking pawn the blemish'd crown [and]
> Wipe off the dust that hides our scepter's gilt. . . .
>
> (291-94)

Note in these words of Northumberland's the reference to Richard's financial dealings ("redeem from broking pawn") and the pun on the word "gilt," which refers to both the golden scepter, the symbol of the crown which has become besmirched by the king's behavior, and to the actual "guilt" which lay on Richard's head, presumably for the murder of Gloucester. The irony is heavy with significance.

ACT II – SCENE 2

Summary

At Windsor Castle, deep in conversation with Bushy, one of the king's favorites, the queen is trying to discover the source of her deep depression. The king has departed for Ireland, and the queen feels that something ominous is about to occur:

> Yet again, methinks
> Some unborn sorrow, ripe in Fortune's womb
> Is coming towards me. . . .
>
> (8-10)

Her "inward soul" persuades her that there is something amiss causing her anxiety, something more than mere separation from the king, although that separation is indeed a source of pain to her.

Green hurries onstage as they are talking and proves the queen's premonition correct by delivering the news that Bolingbroke has landed with his army in the north of England. York enters then and laments the fact that he was left by Richard to uphold the royal forces, to "underprop the land." There is no money left to fight a successful campaign against the rebels, and even if there were, it seems apparent that the popular figure in the country is *not* the king but his adversary – Bolingbroke. Adding to the general woe which has befallen the present company, a messenger enters with the news that the Duke of York's sister-in-law, the widow of the late Duke of Gloucester, has died. "God for his mercy! what a tide of woes/ Comes rushing on this woeful land at once," cries York in despair. He is thoroughly confused; he is duty-bound (by conscience and kinship) to defend the nation against the rebels, but his sympathies are with his nephew Bolingbroke, whom the king has wronged.

The queen and York leave, and Bushy, Bagot, and Green remain behind to discuss their plans. Bagot decides to go to Ireland and join the king, while Bushy and Green decide to seek refuge at a sympathetic castle in Bristol. The three of them are convinced that the Duke of York's chances of repelling the rebels are slim. The task of defending Richard's crown, Green likens to "numbering sands, and drinking oceans dry." Convinced that they "may never meet again," they exit.

Commentary

The dramatic strategy of this scene is similar to that which Shakespeare uses elsewhere and which he will bring to its most perfect execution in *Macbeth*. He builds suspense and tension by having a figure of some importance in the play, here the queen, articulate her *premonition* of evil things to come, then after a suitable interval in which another character, Bushy, tries to dissuade her from her gloomy thoughts, he has the news announced that her *intuition* was *correct*; shortly thereafter, woe upon woe is to be visited upon all present. It is interesting to note that in the queen's immediate response to Green's information about the rebel forces that she even uses a form of imagery which Shakespeare will later have Lady Macbeth use to great effect:

> So, Green, thou art the midwife to my woe,
> And Bolingbroke my sorrow's dismal heir;
> Now hath my soul brought forth her prodigy,
> And I, a gasping, new-delivered mother,
> Have woe to woe, sorrow to sorrow, joined.
>
> (62-66)

The image of giving birth in the context of sorrow and political intrigue (birth given to a monster-prodigy) and all as if first conceived in the imagination (the soul brought forth the monster) is of special importance to this play. First, there is the general theme of legitimacy and inheritance to consider: the play is about a deposition and an unlawful succession to the throne, and for all of its consideration of the inadequacy of the king in question, the process shall bring forth *misery* as its *heir*. Another motif, which Shakespeare makes much of in the last acts of the play, is that of the relationship between one's experience of suffering and the imagination. Later, Richard is isolated in his prison cell and will meditate on the "populous" world of his thoughts and how they breed:

> My brain I'll prove the female to my soul,
> My soul the father; and these two beget
> A generation of still-breeding thoughts. . . .
>
> (V.v. 6-8)

After Bushy's advice to "despair not," the queen continues with her theme and uses phrases which relate the current state of sorrow to their immediate causes:

> Who shall hinder me?
> I will despair and be at enmity

> With cozening hope. He is a flatterer,
> A parasite, a keeper-back of death,
> Who would gently dissolve the bands of life,
> Which false hope lingers in extremity.
>
> (67-72)

Hope, she says, is a flatterer and a parasite and keeps even death at bay; she is speaking these lines to the very characters in the play who have been identified (by most of the sympathetic characters) with the flattery and corruption which will drag Richard down to his doom.

When Bushy is first speaking to the queen, before Green enters with the news about the rebels, he also uses language which prepares us for several later scenes in the play when Richard will become more of a central focus. In a later scene, Richard has an important moment in which he asks for a mirror and then, gazing at his image, he meditates publicly on his situation as king and as an ordinary mortal. Here, Bushy uses a metaphor which obliquely prepares us for that important dramatic moment:

> Each substance of a grief hath twenty shadows,
> Which shows like grief itself, but is not so;
> For sorrow's eye, glazed with blinding tears,
> Divides one thing entire to many objects,
> Like perspectives, which rightly gazed upon
> Show nothing but confusion. . . .
>
> (14-19)

Again, the key idea is that there is a difference between what you *think* you perceive and what is *actually* there, and beyond that, there is the natural distortion which a confused emotional state will bring to one's perceptions. Here the idea is graphically expressed in the image of an eye filled with tears through which one's experience is refracted. As this might be true of the queen in this scene, it is also true to a certain extent of Richard in a later scene. There it will be Bolingbroke who comments sarcastically about the difference between true emotion and "shadows." (This idea is one which fascinated Shakespeare throughout his life, perhaps because he was so closely associated with the stage where it is the business of a good actor to convey the *substance* of true emotions through mere *shadows* (acting) of those emotions.) As a concluding note on this idea, consider the following two brief passages:

> Howe'er it be, I cannot but be sad —
> As, though on thinking on no thought I think,
> Makes me with heavy nothing faint and shrink.
>
> (30-32)

This is spoken by Richard's queen in the scene we are discussing. And this is spoken by another of Shakespeare's mentally tortured heroes, Prince Hamlet, speaking of Denmark.

> . . . for there is nothing either good
> Or bad but thinking makes it so. To me it is a prison.
>
> (II.ii. 255-56)

With the announcement of the arrival of the rebel forces and the death of the Duchess of Gloucester, all talk of imaginary worries ceases. It would be foolhardy to ignore the signs of things to come. An important figure in this scene is the Duke of York, for he has lost a sister-in-law and is dissatisfied with the king, yet he has been appointed to be the guardian of the realm in the king's absence. His feelings are divided:

> Both are my kinsmen.
> Th' one is my sovereign, whom both my oath
> And duty bids defend; t' other again
> Is my kinsman, whom the king hath wronged,
> Whom conscience and my kindred bids to right.
>
> (111-15)

His last words of confusion make it absolutely clear that there is no hope of any real resistance to Bolingbroke, but because he is duty-bound, the Duke of York will, for now, fight for the king.

The last moments of the scene are given over to the three representatives of Richard's court still remaining — Bushy, Bagot, and Green. They present a picture of expedience and cowardice, Bagot being the only one who will go to join the king in Ireland. There is no question concerning whether or not they will join the Duke of York in his battle against Bolingbroke's army. These men are like rats, leaving a sinking ship; here, the ship is England, the ship of state.

ACT II – SCENE 3

Summary

Somewhere in Gloucestershire, once more in England, Bolingbroke questions Northumberland about the way to Berkeley. These "high wild hills and rough uneven ways" have exhausted them both. Northumberland replies that Bolingbroke's "fair discourse" and his good conversation have made the journey seem light and easy. Bolingbroke replies graciously that his companion's words have special value for him.

Northumberland's son, Henry Percy, comes onto the scene and pledges his services to Bolingbroke for life. Northumberland and Bolingbroke then discuss the military situation and are soon joined by the forces of Willoughby and Ross, and both men reaffirm their pledge to right the wrongs done to Bolingbroke in his absence. The Lord of Berkeley enters then, bearing a message from the Duke of York. Berkeley addresses Bolingbroke as "My Lord of Hereford," and Berkeley is rebuffed by the rebel leader, who tells Berkeley to address him by his proper title – Lancaster – if he wants an answer.

The Duke of York, unattended, enters next and is greeted formally and respectfully by Bolingbroke, who kneels to him. York, however, will have none of this formality and tells his nephew to

> Grace me no grace, nor uncle me no uncle;
> I am no traitor's uncle, and that word "grace"
> In an ungracious mouth is but profane.
>
> (86-88)

York reminds Henry and his rebels that "in my loyal bosom lies his [King Richard's] power," but Bolingbroke stands firm in his claim that he has every right to be doing what he is doing. He was banished as Hereford, but now that his father is dead, he returns as Lancaster to claim what is his and "to rouse [Richard's] wrongs." He further entreats old York to think of him as a son (". . . methinks in you/ I see old Gaunt alive"). He continues the kinship argument, trying to persuade York that if the situation had been reversed and it was *York* (instead of Gloucester) who had been killed by Richard, that it is certain that old Gaunt would have backed *Aumerle* (York's son).

Northumberland reiterates the point that *all* of them are concerned primarily with righting the wrongs that have been done to Bolingbroke, and Bolingbroke asks York to join them in attacking Bristol Castle, where the "caterpillars of the commonwealth," Bushy, Bagot, and their accomplices, are hiding. York finds the argument to be strong, and he says, "It may be I will go with you. . . . Things past redress are now with me past care."

Commentary

Bushy, Bagot, and Green had the last words in Scene 2, as they prepared to escape to Ireland, in Bagot's case, or to ensconce themselves in Bristol Castle, as Green and Bushy decided to do. By the end of this scene, the forces of Bolingbroke will be preparing to go to Bristol themselves to clear the land of these "caterpillars of the commonwealth." The scene itself is almost melodramatically opposed to the one which precedes it, setting off the forces of good against their evil opponents.

The way in which Bushy, Bagot, and Green disport themselves is in striking contrast to the behavior of the Bolingbroke faction. Even their lines are overdressed, somewhat genteel and effete, in comparison with the speeches of Bolingbroke and his men. For example, the soldiers have been on their feet for some time. They speak of the hard road they have traveled, and the distance they have yet to go, but as befits their heroic status, they do not complain too loudly. Of particular importance here is the implied reason for their forbearance in these hard times. Notice the way, for example, in which Northumberland speaks to Bolingbroke. It is as though Shakespeare wants to prepare us in advance for Bolingbroke's ascent to the throne. Explaining his renewed energy despite the physical hardships, Northumberland claims that the "noble company" of Bolingbroke has been its chief source. This way of speaking about someone is usually closely associated with a *royal* personage; the impression given is that the very presence of royalty – in this case, Bolingbroke – emanates some lifegiving source. When Henry Percy comes onto the scene and tenders his service to Bolingbroke, one almost imagines him bending his knee and pledging himself as one would to a king. With the arrival of Willoughby and Ross, the effect is redoubled: Shakespeare has these various entrances strung out in this way to give the dramatic illusion of great numbers of people supporting the king-to-be. It is as though Bolingbroke will almost *have* to become the new ruler by popular acclaim. Though no admirer of democracy himself, Shakespeare's idea here is that there is a will of the people (albeit the nobility) which might, in some cases, supercede the divine right of kingship.

When Bolingbroke, in mid-sentence, decides to use his new title of Lancaster, we get the feeling that the popular support *might* have had some effect on this leader of men. But at this point, Bolingbroke still feels uneasy about his position, and he is never too actively in pursuit of power, as, for example, Richard III is, in Shakespeare's play of that name. There is a feeling in this scene that circumstances are mounting which are likely to force certain kinds of commitments from the nobility and, specifically, from Bolingbroke. One should be alert to various shades of indecisiveness and commitment in this scene. This element is used as dramatic material throughout the play.

With all of these "royal indications" in mind, imagine the dramatic effect when Bolingbroke kneels to the Duke of York and calls him "my gracious uncle." It is clear that the duke is the king's representative, but it would be unlikely that Bolingbroke would at this point be thereby showing obeisance to the *king*. Bolingbroke is testing both himself and his uncle with the irony and the seriousness of their situation, and the ensuing conversation between the duke and Bolingbroke is quite serious. Treating issues of importance to the country, Bolingbroke argues soundly that he has been wronged, and in so arguing, he uses language that strikes the central theme of rights of inheritance:

> Will you permit that I shall stand condemned,
> A wandering vagabond, my rights and royalties
> Plucked from my arms perforce, and given away
> To upstart unthrifts? . . . I lay my claim
> To my inheritance of free descent.
>
> (119-36)

The last lines of the scene voice the central dilemma in the words of Bolingbroke and York: Bolingbroke speaks of "weeding" the country of what is choking it, and York grapples with his own conscience over what this weeding entails:

> It may be I will go with you, but yet I'll pause,
> For I am loath to break our country's laws.
> Nor friends, nor foes, to me welcome you are.
> Things past redress are now with me past care.
>
> (168-71)

ACT II – SCENE 4

Summary

A short scene closes this act. In a camp in Wales, the Lord of Salisbury is speaking with a Welsh captain and is worried that he has heard "no tidings from the king." The captain is ready to disperse his troops, but is urged by Salisbury to maintain his forces one more day. The captain, however, refuses; he believes the rumor that "the king is dead." Unnatural omens and portents seem to prove the supposition and "our countrymen are gone and fled." Salisbury, likewise, laments Richard's dying glory – "like a shooting star." Symbolically, Salisbury sees the sun set "weeping in the lowly west."

Commentary

This scene serves in place of a stage battle to tell us that Richard's cause has been lost. The language used by Richard's allies is conventional in its reference to the natural elements being somehow in harmony with the momentousness of the occasion. When great men fall, so goes the popular belief, the echoes of that fall are heard in the earth's crust itself. The tradition can be traced back at least to the time of the crucifixion of Christ, at which time earthquakes and natural calamities were witness to the event. Shakespeare, along with his contemporaries, uses this idea fairly frequently; it is an important motif in all of his history plays. Salisbury's comment on the fall of Richard being "like a shooting star" makes reference to the particular image of Richard in the play as someone who does possess, however one may judge it, a kind of style or romantic glory. This is how he is known and how he knows himself. It is also a conventional metaphor for the "tragic" fall from greatness by a heroic or noble figure.

ACT III – SCENE 1

Summary

Here, Bolingbroke makes his first public, political act. Standing before the castle of Bristol, he passes sentence on Bushy and Green. (Bagot went to Ireland.) He gives a long account of the men's wrongs, including the charges that they "misled a prince, a royal king . . . [and] made a divorce between his queen and him." Furthermore, they seized Bolingbroke's lands, ruined his parks, and removed the coat of arms from his property and, finally, they unjustly urged Bolingbroke's exile. Bolingbroke has had to live in a land not his own, where he "sighed [his] English breath in foreign clouds,/ Eating the bitter bread of banishment." Bolingbroke has not proclaimed himself king, but his actions are very much like those of a king, and the lords present all recognize his authority. He orders the execution of Bushy and Green forthwith. But before the two men allow themselves to be led proudly away, believing their cause to be just, Bushy defiantly proclaims that "more welcome is the stroke of death to me/ Than Bolingbroke to England." Green adds that he is confidant that "heaven will take our souls."

Bolingbroke then turns to the Duke of York and asks him to see that the queen is looked after and kindly commended. York assures him that he has already dispatched a messenger to her. Bolingbroke then announces that he will set out for Wales, where the king has joined Glendower.

Commentary

In order for Bolingbroke's character to assume sufficient dramatic stature, he must be seen to grow into the role of king. Although the entire play is not devoted to the "education of a king," as it is in Shakespeare's *Henry IV, Part I*, it is an important element here for the proper sympathies must be aroused. Two simple things, therefore, take place in this scene, both involving Bolingbroke in something of a public role. We first see him as a dispenser of justice, and it is right that we discern some righteous indignation in his manner of dispatching Bushy and Green. He has good cause to be angered by these corrupters of the king. Note that this is where the emphasis is – on the *tempters* and not on the *tempted*. In *Henry IV, Part I.*, Shakespeare returns to this idea in much more complex form. The play involves some of the same characters as this one. Bolingbroke is there the aging King Henry IV, and it is his son, Prince Hal, who must learn to be the next king. The great worry of King Henry is that his son is being led astray by the low company he is keeping, chief among them being Jack Falstaff.

As benefits the good ruler, the last item which Bolingbroke attends to shows him to be a compassionate man: "For God's sake, fairly let her be entreated," he instructs his companions regarding the queen. He can dispense harsh justice when necessary, but he also has an expansive heart. Compare Bolingbroke's behavior here with the cunning of Richard's public dealings earlier in the play. Shakespeare is writing some rather effective propaganda for Henry Bolingbroke and his successors.

ACT III – SCENE 2

Summary

Bolingbroke was right; Richard has indeed landed back in Wales and is now at Carlisle with his army. He is joyous to be back in his native country again, especially after a difficult crossing of the Irish Sea. He weeps for joy and is convinced that his presence will be enough to deter the rebel forces. In a highly emotional soliloquy, he declares,

> Dear earth, I do salute thee with my hand,
> Though rebels wound thee with their horses' hoofs.
> As a long-parted mother with her child
> Plays fondly with her tears and smiles in meeting,
> So, weeping, smiling, greet I thee, my earth,
> And do thee favours with my royal hands.
>
> (6-11)

He bids the land itself rear up and attack Bolingbroke and his men, but the Bishop of Carlisle wisely suggests that they do something more practical than prattle. "The Power that made you king," he says, will "keep you king in spite of all"; he admonishes that "the *means* that heavens yield must be embraced/ And not neglected" (emphasis mine). Aumerle, York's son, agrees "that we are too remiss/ Whilst Bolingbroke, through our security/ Grows strong and great in substance and in power." Richard does not catch their meaning, however, and reiterates his faith that "The breath of worldly men cannot depose/ The deputy elected by the Lord."

Salisbury enters with the bad news that the Welsh army, believing that the king was slain, disbanded. He says that Richard stayed too long in Ireland; had he returned only a day earlier, Salisbury could have brought him an army of twelve thousand Welshmen. Hearing this, the king falls into despair. "Time hath set a blot upon my pride," he moans; Aumerle turns and reminds him that he should carry himself like a king. Recovering his poise, Richard proclaims confidence in York: the crown *will* be preserved.

Scroop, a loyal follower of Richard, comes on the scene with yet worse news. He announces that the entire British nation, including women, old men, beardless boys, and clergymen have risen up in arms against the king. He also tells the king that Bushy and Green have made their peace with Bolingbroke, but before he can explain what he means, Richard launches into an attack on his fickle friends. (Of course, what actually happened was that those who were captured were executed, but Scroop is unable to reveal this to the king until Richard's tirade is over.)

Aumerle asks a very practical question: "Where is the Duke my father?" York, remember, had been left in charge of the kingdom. The king ignores Aumerle, however, and launches into an extended monologue about the sad fate of kings in this transitory world.

> For God's sake, let us sit upon the ground
> And tell sad stories of the death of kings. . . .
> (155-56)

Carlisle then begs Richard not to be so morbidly self-absorbed, but to put his fear of the foe to good use in opposing him. Richard accepts this chiding and says that he has already taken control of himself: "This ague fit of fear is over-blown/ An easy task it is to win our own." Richard's mood, however, is reversed when Scroop continues his report with the information that the Duke of York has joined the rebels who are backing Bolingbroke. Richard plunges once again into despair, and Aumerle is unsuccessful in coaxing him out of it. As the scene ends, Richard says darkly that he will go to "Flint Castle; there I'll pine away." He orders his officers to send their troops home.

Commentary

Richard has been absent from the stage for quite some time by the beginning of this scene so it is necessary for Shakespeare to use bold strokes in re-establishing the character of the king. The number of times which Richard vacillates in his mood and apparently changes his mind in this scene is a clear indication that he is *not* what one would conventionally think of as a solid and inspiring leader. Throughout, he is cajoled and rather babied by his companions. There is sorely lacking in him a sense of manly resolve and rightness.

His first long speech seems promising, however; it is patriotic and rather cock-sure, but too often Richard is fond of "poeticizing." There is something slightly absurd in his entreaty to the *elements* to do his fighting for him. "But let thy spiders," he tells his England, "that suck up thy venom,/ And heavy-gaited toads lie in their way,/ Doing annoyance to the treacherous feet/ Which with usurping steps do trample thee;/ Yield stinging nettles to mine enemies. . . ." The king is supposed to be divine, according to conventional wisdom, but he is also meant to be a natural warrior and a leader. The problem with this theory is that the mortal king who fills the role isn't always up to the standard of the idea, and here, Shakespeare does seem to be indicating the weakness of this theory.

The other men around Richard are good, strong soldiers and are ill at ease when their sovereign indulges in his romantic ecstasies. This is especially clear as the scene progresses, and they must repeatedly insist that he stop acting the weakling.

This would be very simple characterization indeed if it weren't for the fact that Shakespeare gives to Richard, here and elsewhere, such grand lines of poetry that it is difficult to dismiss him as "just" a whining incompetent. This man, who is also a king, deeply feels his *inadequacy*, and perhaps the *absurdity* of his situation, but, more importantly, he seems to observe himself perform. This, at times, renders him virtually immobile. He seems childishly subject to the passing change in fortunes, exchanging phrases like "Have I not reason to look pale and sad?" for "Awake, thou coward majesty! . . ./ Is not the king's name twenty thousand names?" It is true that he indulges himself and cries his woes aloud, and often the tone seems self-indulgent, but on many occasions, he does reach majestic poetic stature:

> Let's talk of graves, of worms, and epitaphs;
> Make dust our paper and with rainy eyes
> Write sorrow on the bosom of the earth. . . .
> For God's sake, let us sit upon the ground
> And tell sad stories of the death of kings:
> How some have been deposed, some slain in war;
> Some haunted by the ghosts they have deposed,
> Some poisoned by their wives; some sleeping killed;
> All murdered: for within the hollow crown
> That rounds the mortal temples of a king
> Keeps Death his court, and there the antic sits,
> Scoffing at his state and grinning at his pomp,
> Allowing him a breath, a little scene,
> To monarchize. . . .
>
> (145-65)

Richard is guilty of "monarchizing," but, one might say, with *style*. Richard is quick, however, to attack the friends he thinks have turned on him—"O, villains, vipers, damned without redemption"—although when he learns that he has misjudged them and that they have been executed as his allies, he doesn't show the remotest sign of remorse. This leaves a strong impression on us, and most likely such actions do not pass unnoticed by his present associates. Richard's fickleness, they would note, can have dangerous consequences for themselves. This, combined with the almost-certain victory of the armies of Bolingbroke, who have the entire nation in their sympathy, leaves the king a pitiful figure by the end of the scene.

ACT III – SCENE 3

Summary

Bolingbroke's forces have marched the hundred miles from Bristol to Flint Castle on the northeastern coast of Wales when this scene opens. Now Bolingbroke stands before the castle with York,

Northumberland, and their attendants. He has sent Northumberland's son Henry Percy into the castle. When Percy returns, he announces that Richard is inside, along with Aumerle, Lord Salisbury, Scroop, and the Bishop of Carlisle. Bolingbroke instructs his lords to deliver a message to Richard that Henry wishes to speak to him. "On both his knees," he instructs them to tell Richard, he will lay his "arms and power,/ Provided that [his] banishment [be] repealed,/ And lands restored again be freely granted."

First Bolingbroke, and then York, notices Richard on the castle wall, and both of them describe his majesty. Bolingbroke sees "the blushing discontented sun" peeking out from "envious clouds"; York urges Bolingbroke to notice Richard closely. To York, Richard still "looks . . . like a king! Behold his eye,/ As bright as is the eagle's. . . ."

Richard speaks first to Northumberland and upbraids him for not showing the requisite courtesy of bending his knee to the king. He wonders if some act of God has dismissed him from his "stewardship." He further instructs Northumberland to tell Bolingbroke that his very presence on English soil is in defiance of the king's express command, and that it is, therefore, treasonous. He accuses Bolingbroke of instigating "the purple testament" of civil war, and he warns him that "ere the crown he looks for live in peace/ Ten thousand bloody crowns of mothers' sons/ Shall ill become the flower of England's face." Northumberland tries to soothe Richard's ire, and he tells him that it is *not* Bolingbroke's intention to use force in any way: "His coming hither hath no further scope/ Than for his lineal royalties. . . ." Richard answers that "all the number of his fair demands/ Shall be accomplished without contradiction." He then turns to Aumerle in shame and wonders aloud if he should send back a defiant answer to Bolingbroke instead. Aumerle advises him to remain calm, that they would do better to give themselves time to find allies before attempting a fight. Richard then cries out in agony, "O that I were as great/ As is my grief, or lesser than my name!" When he hears that he has a message from Bolingbroke, he begins an extended, self-mocking monologue, stripping himself in words of all the accouterments of his royal household and position of power:

> I'll give my jewels for a set of beads,
> My gorgeous palace for a hermitage,
> My gay apparel for an almsman's gown. . . .
>
> (147-49)

At the end of this heavily ironic speech, he refers to his adversary as "King Bolingbroke," asking "Will his Majesty/ Give Richard leave to live till Richard die?"

Bolingbroke shows deference to the office of king by kneeling before Richard and addressing him as "My gracious Lord." Richard refuses to accept Bolingbroke on bended knee with an offer of obeisiance, however, and he bids him rise; he says that he will give him what he wants, adding "Your own is yours, and I am yours, and all." Richard then says that he will ride to London; the kingship, it is understood, will be decided on there.

Commentary

The most striking detail in this scene is the appearance of Richard on the castle walls. There must be something majestic about Richard's entrance for the scene to have any power. That Shakespeare wanted it that way can be seen in the reactions which he ascribes to the first two people who see the king. They both see him in a *glorious* aspect, perhaps seemingly more glorious because he is seen from above and from afar. His position above, high above the others, on the castle wall, says as much as the words he speaks. Notice that he presents a strong position to those below him when he speaks to them as the king, but that he weakens visibly in his indecisive aside to Aumerle towards the end of the scene.

After the strong buildup of Bolingbroke as a natural leader, it comes as somewhat of a reversal to see the king back in a position of power, even if it is largely a symbolic position. But the emphasis here is on the fact that Bolingbroke, unlike Richard, is *not* an ambitious man, and he is still rather awed by the idea of majesty and its present physical manifestation. He remains apart throughout most of this scene, as if to emphasize the fact that he does not feel entirely legitimate in his present role. Remember, it is to be characteristic of Bolingbroke that he feels uneasy about his stewardship of the nation. Thus, it is a stroke of dramatic genius to have him appear hesitant about confronting the king, who has just appeared high on a castle wall. Richard's strong warning that the crown will not rest easily on a usurper's head is not lost on Bolingbroke. This theme of ill-fitting royal garments is one which Shakespeare will use again and again in the great tragedies, especially in *Macbeth*.

In this regard, it is important to note that before Richard makes his appearance, we witness a conversation between the Duke of York and Bolingbroke in which the duke reminds him of the importance of what is about to transpire, and that there was a time when had Bolingbroke dared to act as he now is, the king would have wasted no time in having him executed. Bolingbroke's answer, tellingly, is rather ambiguous:

> *York*: Take not, good cousin, further than you should,
>   Lest you mis-take: the heavens are over our heads.
> *Bolingbroke*: I know it, uncle, and oppose not myself
>   Against their will.
>
> (16-19)

"Oppose not myself/ Against their will" is the key phrase here. If Bolingbroke emphasizes "oppose not myself," the meaning would be that he is acting in his own self-interest, as he perhaps has the right to do. But there are other shades of meaning apparent if one pauses between "myself," and "Against their will." In that case, his reply could be taken to mean that the heavens themselves would favor Bolingbroke's cause; all it needs is an emphasis on the "against."

When Richard does appear above, Bolingbroke's confidence obviously seems to weaken. His words express a certain awe before the majesty of the king:

> See, see King Richard doth himself appear,
> As doth the blushing discontented sun
> From out the fiery portal of the east,
> When he perceives the envious clouds are bent
> To dim his glory, and to stain the track
> Of his bright passage to the occident.
>
> (62-67)

The phrase "envious clouds" could, of course, refer to Bolingbroke himself, intentionally on his part or not, but that doesn't remove from the passage itself the feeling that we are in the presence of some glorious being, far above us. Earlier, Gaunt made a similar reference to Richard in a negative sense – as one who would expend himself in a "fierce blaze of riot." Here, coming out of "the fiery portal of the east," the context makes him seem heroic.

In Richard's two long speeches, one finds reason for the awed responses of the spectators. There is an authority and dignity with which he speaks to them at first, upbraiding them for their failure to show proper respect for the office of king. When Richard continues, however, his characteristic self-pity begins to take over. What prevents it from descending into mawkishness is a sarcasm in his tone of voice. When Bolingbroke bends his knee to the king, Richard greets him with the words:

> Fair cousin, you debase your princely knee
> To make the bare earth proud with kissing it.
> Me rather had my heart might feel your love,
> Than my unpleased eye see your courtesy.
> Up, cousin, up; your heart is up, I know,
> Thus high at least, although your knee be low.
>
> (190-95)

Here, stage directions are inserted after "Thus high at least." The actor playing Richard is instructed to point to the crown on his head. Bolingbroke, reminded of who addresses him, is rather tight-lipped during this scene, as he usually is in the presence of the king. Thus his awkwardness in the situation leaves him no option but to allow the king to do the speaking. The king, at the very end of the scene, plays on Bolingbroke's reticence, and more or less *forces* him to give an order:

> *Richard*: . . . Set on towards London, cousin, is it so?
> *Bolingbroke*: Yea, my good Lord.
> *Richard*: Then I must not say no.

ACT III – SCENE 4

Summary

Back in the Duke of York's garden, the queen is waiting for news of her husband, and her two lady attendants are trying to distract her gloom. No matter what they suggest as diversion, though, the queen sighs that it would only remind her that the world is cruel and that her sorrow is too heavy to be lifted. While they are walking and she is weeping, they notice a gardener and his men. The queen decides to spy on them in the hope that they might have something to say about the nation and its problems ("They will talk of state; for everyone doth so. . . .").

The gardener gives elaborate instructions to his apprentices about how to prune and trim the plants which they are working on in order to ensure the proper growth and governance of their garden, to prevent its being choked by weeds, and to save it from being in a state of chaos. The servants speak up and make explicit reference to England being like a garden, and they compare Richard and his followers to weeds which once threatened its health. Bolingbroke is named as the one who has "plucked up" those weeds, "root and all." Bolingbroke, they say,

> Hath seized the wasteful King. O, what pity is it
> That he hath not so trimmed and dressed his land
> As we this garden!
>
> (55-57)

The queen holds her silence as long as she can; then she comes forward and accuses the gardener of being beyond his station in talking of the deposition of a king:

> Dar'st thou, thou little better thing than earth,
> Divine his downfall? . . .
>   Speak, thou wretch.
>
> (77-80)

The gardener defends himself by telling the queen that what he has just said is nothing more than common knowledge; all she needs to do is go to London and she will find things exactly as he has described them. The queen decides to do this and she departs. After she has left, the gardener tells his servants that, "in the remembrance of a weeping queen," he will plant a "bank of rue" where the queen's tears have fallen to the earth.

Commentary

This type of scene in Shakespeare's plays has a very special function: there is something contemplative about it, as if Shakespeare wants the audience to have sufficient time to consider some of the issues – political and individually human – which are at stake. That is not to say that there is no emotion in the scene, for we witness the queen's distraught state of mind and her forced silence while the representatives of the common people discuss the demise of Richard; there is clearly an emotional strain in her bearing and in the delivery of her lines in this scene. Also, it is not to be assumed that the gardeners are without feeling, either to the queen or to the nation's desperate condition. The core of the scene, nevertheless, is the long discourse on the sort of care needed to keep a garden at its most productive, a clear and very common metaphor for the kind of governance necessary to keep the nation functioning at its most productive. There is a definite solemnity with which the gardener gives the instructions:

> Go thou, and like an executioner,
> Cut off the heads of too fast growing sprays,
> That look too lofty in our commonwealth;
> All must be even in our government.
> You thus employed, I will go root away
> The noisome weeds, which without profit suck
> The soil's fertility from wholesome flowers.
>
> (33-39)

The gardener is by no means advocating democracy in any form when he says "all must be even in our government"; he is referring to those members of the nobility who have gained excessive favor with the king and who therefore have too much power. To bring things back to "normal," with the proper hierarchy assuming its natural function, these excessive "weeds" and "caterpillars" (an image already referred to) must be removed. Richard is accused only in that he was wasteful and because he did not aid nature in this political pruning operation. The common people, or at least the artisan class as here represented, are perfectly orthodox in their beliefs, recommendations, and wishes.

> Superfluous branches
> We lop away, that bearing boughs may live;
> Had he done so, himself had borne the crown,
> Which waste of idle hours hath quite thrown down.
>
> (63-66)

This scene began, remember, with the queen's attending ladies trying to divert her with various trifling games and songs, but these delights are ineffectual in her present state. It is interesting that one feature of Richard's reign was his delight in courtly entertainments and glamorous display. Starting this scene with oblique reference to "entertainments," inappropriate entertainments at that, it is a subtle variation on one of the themes of this play. The gardener refers to "some few vanities" that will be the only things to weigh in the balance with Richard against Bolingbroke. The vanities are also references to his frivolous entertainment-filled lifestyle.

When the queen speaks of "old Adam's likeness" in referring to the gardener and later asks "What Eve, what serpent, hath suggested thee/ To make a second fall of cursed man?" she is continuing the religious thread that runs throughout the play. As well as describing England as a garden, Shakespeare has her invoke the idea of the Garden of Eden to make it clear that more is at stake than just the *ordinary* affairs of an *ordinary* man. The very act of pruning the garden, if it involves also pruning the king of his power, is an act against God's divine will. The queen reminds us of this point. The gardener would probably agree, but he is really just a powerless man reporting what has happened. Yet the gardener remains a sympathetic character. Even though he is from a lower order of society, he responds to events very much like old Gaunt and perhaps York in his better moments. At the very end of this scene, it is significant that Shakespeare has the queen curse the gardener – "Pray God the plants thou graft'st may never grow" – but the gardener feels no spite; rather, he feels pity for her. This pity which Shakespeare evokes for the queen acts as a prelude and a cue to our response to her husband when we see him in his fallen state later in the play. The gardener's last words understandably evoke sympathy from us:

> Poor queen! so that thy state might be no worse,
> I would my skill were subject to thy curse.
> Here did she fall a tear; here in this place
> I'll set a bank of rue, sour herb of grace.
> Rue, even for ruth, here shortly shall be seen,
> In the remembrace of a weeping queen.
>
> (103-8)

ACT IV – SCENE 1

Summary

This act has only one scene, and it takes place in London, in Westminster Hall, about forty days after the king's surrender at Flint Castle. It focuses on a meeting in Parliament, held to decide the matter of kingship and also to discuss Bolingbroke's actions, as well as those of Richard and his accomplices. Among those present for the council are Bolingbroke, Aumerle, Northumberland, Percy, the Earls of Fitzwater and Surrey, the Bishop of Carlisle, and the Abbot of Westminster. Bagot, who escaped earlier to Ireland and thereby escaped execution at Bristol, has now been captured and is now being questioned about Richard's actions.

Bolingbroke wants to know, first of all, who is responsible for Gloucester's death. Bagot's answer is immediate; he points to Aumerle, the son of York. Aumerle, he says, once boasted that he could dispose of his uncle Gloucester and, moreover, that not even one hundred thousand crowns would be enough to bribe him to help return Bolingbroke to England; England, indeed, would be "blest" if Bolingbroke were killed. Aumerle, of course, denies the charge, but the Earl of Fitzwater, Henry Percy, and another lord substantiate Bagot's accusations. Aumerle is defended by the Earl of Surrey, but Fitzwater charges Surrey with lying and swears that he heard the banished Mowbray say that it was Aumerle who arranged for Gloucester's assassination.

Mowbray, as it turns out, cannot affirm or deny the charges. The Duke of Carlisle informs the group that Mowbray was killed during a crusade to the Holy Land. The Duke of York enters then and announces that Richard, "with willing soul," has yielded up his "high sceptre" to Bolingbroke. To Bolingbroke, he says, "Long live Henry, fourth of that name." Hardly has Bolingbroke accepted the throne, however, than the Bishop of Carlisle objects: no one but God, he says, can judge Richard. He objects to Richard being tried for "apparent guilt" without even being present. Bolingbroke's "trial" of the king, he says, is a "black, obscene" deed, and he prophesies that if Bolingbroke is crowned king, "the blood of English shall manure the ground,/ And future ages groan for this foul act." The civil wars that follow, he vows, will be worse than the Crucifixion itself. Northumberland interrupts the bishop's tirade and orders him arrested and charged with treason.

When Bolingbroke speaks, he calls for Richard to be brought before them so that he himself can surrender "in common view." When Richard is brought in, he remarks on the many once-friendly faces which are now ready to condemn him; Christ had only one Judas. Yet he tempers his emotion when he hands his crown to Henry. He reminds him of the many "cares" that go with the crown; he then renounces his claim to the throne and wishes Bolingbroke "many years of sunshine days."

Northumberland, not swayed by Richard's poignant words of fatalism and resignation, demands that Richard read aloud the charges against him – "Committed by your person and your followers . . . [so that] men/ May deem that you are worthily deposed." Richard, however, says that his tears prevent him from seeing the list of charges. He sobs that he is nothing – a king of snow, melting before "the sun of Bolingbroke." He asks only to "be gone and trouble you no more." Bolingbroke, therefore, orders him to be taken to the Tower of London; the coronation will be performed on the coming Wednesday, he says as he exits.

Alone with the clergymen, Aumerle proposes a plot to do away with Bolingbroke, and the Abbot of Westminster invites Aumerle to his home for further talk. Together, they will conceive such a plot that will "show us all a merry day."

Commentary

Shakespeare sets up a parallel here with the opening scenes of the play. This simple scene, you should note, comprises the entire fourth act. You will recall that the first words of the play were Richard's: he asked Gaunt to bring forth his son, Bolingbroke, to explain charges of treason that he leveled against Mowbray. The situation has virtually reversed itself by Act IV. Here it is Bolingbroke who is doing the ordering and the judging of the cases. He asks Bagot what he knows about the death of Gloucester, significantly the same issue which preoccupied Richard and the nobles in the first scene of the play. The fact is, Richard was conducting something of a sham inquiry in the earlier scene – that is, he was only trying to keep the facts of the matter under cover while not allowing his nobility to become embroiled in too open a dispute. Bolingbroke accused Mowbray – and justifiably so – of treason, and later we find out that it was indeed Mowbray who had a hand in the assassination of Gloucester. Yet the upshot of that first dispute was the exiling of Bolingbroke and Mowbray – on Richard's orders. Years have passed since then, and it is only after suffering the loss of his father, old Gaunt, and the humiliation of having his property unlawfully seized, that Bolingbroke now finds himself in the position of one who can see the full truth revealed concerning what Richard has done and what kind of a man and a king he truly is. Bolingbroke is a victim of grave injustice. Politically it is important for Bolingbroke to raise this issue of Gloucester again so that it be publicly known that *he* has been wronged – he did not deserve banishment – and that the king and his henchmen have been involved in shady actions which run counter to (Act I, Scene 1, and Act IV, Scene 1) have their the best interests of the nation. Thus, the parallel scenes places in the dramaturgical geometry of the play; the revelations and outcome are significantly different because of the political reality which has changed during the course of the play.

The main accusation in this scene is against Aumerle, York's son, who allegedly had involved himself in the plot against Gloucester. Shakespeare constructs the scene in such a way as to emphasize the heated feelings and potentially anarchic situation of the nobles. Aumerle defends himself against first one, Bagot, and then another, Fitzwater, and then yet another, a nameless lord. The repeated attacks on Aumerle and his challenge to fight all of them for his honor are a graphic representation in miniature of the chaos that has been predicted in the event that the anointed king might be deposed. Surrey and Aumerle are pitted against Fitzwater, Bagot, and a nameless lord.

Bolingbroke is silent through much of this bickering, waiting for the opportunity to quell the stormy atmosphere. This he does by seizing on a detail of Fitzwater's report – "I heard the banished Norfolk [Mowbray] say/ That thou, Aumerle, did'st send two of thy men/ To execute the noble Duke" – and announcing that all previous disputes and challenges are now concealed until the noble Mowbray returns from abroad. Bolingbroke's cleverness as an arbitrator is obvious here. One way of forcing all those present to cease their arguments is to make the outcome of the argument hinge on the words of someone who is absent and who won't be able to return for some time.

The Bishop of Carlisle's report that Mowbray died in Italy after spending some time abroad fighting the "black pagans, Turks, and Saracens" changes the tone yet again. All in the company are made to consider the fact that he is buried on foreign soil; this should bring them back to an awareness of the wrongs done to many nobles like him who were forced into exile by King Richard. With the question of Gloucester's assassin conveniently put aside for the moment, Bolingbroke utters a prayer-like commendation of the late Duke of Norfolk: he also ends the dispute for the time being:

> Sweet Peace conduct his sweet soul to the bosom
> Of good old Abraham! Lords appellants,
> Your differences shall all rest under gage,
> Till we assign you to your days of trial.
>
> (103-6)

The next lines in the text announce Bolingbroke as the new king, Henry IV, but before he can gracefully accept York's bid to ascend the throne, the Bishop of Carlisle delivers a long speech warning of the consequences. Remember, here, that it was York in the earlier scenes who delivered this sort of warning. Here it is someone else, a clergyman, warning Bolingbroke and the rest that what they are doing goes against God's will:

> O, if you raise this house against this house,
> It will the woefullest division prove
> That ever fell upon this cursed earth!
> Prevent it, resist it, let it not be so,
> Lest child, child's children, cry against you "woe!"
>
> (145-49)

The heated exchanges and challenges to armed combat which opened this scene are almost a case in point, proving the credibility of the bishop's prophecy.

This speech is an important one because of where Shakespeare positions it in the play. At this point, we have to wonder how Bolingbroke will respond to it. He is aware of the gravity of consequences, and he is not wholly convinced of the rightness of what he is doing. Remember, he is not characterized as an overly ambitious man. He remains quiet throughout Carlisle's speech, and it is Northumberland who orders the Bishop arrested for treason. Bolingbroke doesn't respond in words to the speech, but his first words after it are firm:

> Fetch hither Richard, that in common view
> He may surrender. . . .

(156-7)

Foremost here, we should note Bolingbroke's attentiveness to the bishop's words.

The second part of this act belongs to Richard, with Bolingbroke staying largely in the background. Now one should profitably think of Richard in three ways: first, as a king, one who is aware of the behavior appropriate to the office; next, as a man who is suffering the humiliation of defeat; and, finally, as an actor, as a performer with an awareness of situations and specific audiences. It is exactly where these three "roles," as it were, overlap, that Shakespeare is at his finest as a dramatist. During Richard's speeches in this act, we should always consider where the "performing" and the "reality" become interchangeable. Since we know that Richard is intensely introspective, we need to be aware of clues in his speeches which suggest that we are hearing the "real" Richard, as well as the one who is "putting on a show" and, finally, the Richard who is aware of himself as such. This is a complicated matter, but one which deserves attention.

When thinking of Richard as an "actor," we should recall the two central props which Richard uses in this scene: the crown itself and a mirror which he asks to have brought on especially for him. These are the props of a practiced performer, and he uses them well.

After the first fifteen lines, in which Richard describes himself as a Christ who has more treacherous "apostles" than Jesus did, he asks to hold the crown. During these fifteen lines, he pointedly reminds everyone present that they have, not too long ago, all responded to him as *king*. In former times, the gathered multitude would utter an "Amen" or a "God save the king" after Richard declared his "God save the king." Here, however, there is no response, and Richard has made his point dramatically: "Will no man say 'Amen,' " he asks sarcastically of the silent nobles.

He takes the crown in his hands and bids Bolingbroke take it from him. They hold the crown on either side, while Richard teases his successor with the moment:

> Give me the crown.
> Here, cousin, seize the crown. Here, cousin,
> On this side my hand, and on that side yours.
> Now is this golden crown like a deep well
> That owes two buckets, filling one another,
> The emptier ever dancing in the air,
> The other down, unseen, and full of water.
> That bucket down and full of tears am I,
> Drinking my griefs, whilst you mount up on high.
>
> (181-90)

Here, Richard holds the crown on one side, with both hands, and Bolingbroke on the other, also with both hands. These two possessors of the crown look at each other in all of their manifestations: one on the way up, the other on the way down; one virtually a king, one virtually an ex-king. Here, one might profitably jot down the ways in which they are alike, the ways in which they are dissimilar, and the ways in which this crown (used in this way) is like a mirror into which each looks into his soul and into the soul of his counterpart.

In cataloguing the process of his deposition, Richard is no doubt forcing his audience of nobles to be clearly aware of what they are doing, and he also seems to be working his way up to an emotional outburst. The formality of the repetition makes the speech seem less spontaneous than some of his outbursts, but it prepares the way for something else in the next speech.

> With mine own tears I wash away my balm,
> With mine own hands I give away my crown,
> With mine own tongue deny my sacred state,
> With mine own breath release all duteous oaths.
> All pomp and majesty I do forswear;
> My manors, rents, revenues I forgo;
> My acts, decrees, and statues I deny.
>
> (207-13)

Here Richard is the king stripping himself of all the trappings of his office. In the next speech, he is an ordinary man who is embarrassed that he is to be forced to read an account of his transgressions in public:

> Must I do so? and must I ravel out
> My weaved-up follies? Gentle Northumberland,
> If thy offences were upon record,
> Would it not shame thee, in so fair a troop
> To read a lecture of them?
>
> (228-32)

When Carlisle was defending the king's divine right of rule in the first part of this scene, he used a word which is associated with the pattern of natural imagery running throughout the play. One thinks of the gardener's speech when Carlisle describes the king as God's "captain, steward, deputy elect,/ Anointed, crowned, *planted* many years" (italics mine). Now that Richard is being forced to step down, he describes himself in relation to Bolingbroke in natural imagery which was conventionally associated with royalty:

> O, that I were a mockery king of snow,
> Standing before the sun of Bolingbroke,
> To melt myself away in water drops!
>
> (260-62)

The command to see his own face in a mirror that he may better contemplate himself is perhaps Richard's greatest historical posture. His language is highly poetical, even at one point reminiscent of the famous "face that launched a thousand ships" speech from Marlowe's popular tragedy *Dr. Faustus*. Richard says:

> Was this face the face
> That every day under his household roof
> Did keep ten thousand men? Was this the face
> That, like the sun, did make beholders wink?
> Is this the face which faced so many follies,
> That was at last outfaced by Bolingbroke?
> A brittle glory shineth in this face;
> As brittle as the glory is the face,
> For there it is, cracked in a hundred shivers.
>
> (281-89)

Just before the last line, stage instructions indicate that the actor playing Richard should fling the mirror to the floor. Clearly, Richard is suffering here, but one wonders if he doesn't relish this opportunity for his self-pitying display. Note Bolingbroke's response to the display and Richard's response to that response: "The shadow of your sorrow hath destroyed/ The shadow of your face," says Bolingbroke, after remaining silent through all of Richard's soliloquy. This is a biting remark, for it accuses Richard of play-acting, dealing with "shadows" and pretence instead of showing real emotion. This remark is the more effective because of Bolingbroke's previous long silence. Notice the clipped few words with which Richard responds to this accusation. He is obviously caught off guard:

> Say that again.
> The shadow of my sorrow! Ha! let's see.
> 'Tis very true, my grief lies all within;
> And these external manners of laments
> Are merely shadows to the unseen grief
> That swells with silence in the tortured soul.
>
> (291-96)

This witty answer comes only after Richard has bought himself time to recover with "Ha! let's see."

The last exchanges between Richard and Bolingbroke are in the form of short sentences. Richard's rhetorical flourishes are at an end; he wants to bring the whole sordid business to a conclusion. His lines are the last ironic gasps of a defeated, once-lordly sovereign:

> *Richard*: Being so great, I have no need to beg.
> *Bolingbroke*: Yet ask.
> *Richard*: And shall I have?
> *Bolingbroke*: You shall.
> *Richard*: Then give me leave to go.
> *Bolingbroke*: Whither?
> *Richard*: Whither you will, so I were from your sights.
>
> (309-15)

Richard puns on the word "conveyors" in his exit line, calling them all thieves who "rise thus nimbly by a true king's fall."

The scene and the act do not end, however, with the exit of the deposed Richard and the man who has just announced his own coronation date. Shakespeare presses the point that civil strife is in the air after the deposition by having the last people on stage act and sound like conspirators. The Abbot of Westminster, the Bishop of Carlisle, and Aumerle remain behind. The Abbot's last line is: "I'll lay/ A plot shall show us all a merry day." The play is not yet over. Richard's spirit of greed and power has infected even a man of the church.

ACT V – SCENE 1

Summary

The last act opens with Richard on his way to the Tower. The queen is onstage, waiting for her husband to pass by so that she may tell him goodbye. When she sees him, she likens him to a "beauteous inn" that houses Grief; she likens Bolingbroke to a "common alehouse." She urges her husband to stand tall; it pains her to see him not only deposed, but physically bowed. She wonders if Bolingbroke has also usurped Richard's intellect, for he seems, truly, a ruined man. Richard begs her not to grieve and urges her to leave England and to enter a convent in France.

Northumberland enters and tells Richard that Bolingbroke has changed his mind: Richard is to go to Pomfret and not to the Tower. The queen, he says, has been ordered to France. Richard turns to Northumberland and compares him to a ladder that Bolingbroke used to ascend to Richard's throne. He warns Northumberland that fear and hate will soon separate him and Bolingbroke. But Northumberland refuses to argue with Richard, and he also refuses to allow the queen to follow her husband to Pomfret or him to follow her to France. With deep sorrow, Richard turns to his wife and pleads that their goodbyes be brief, for they make "woe wanton with this fond delay." They part, then, for the last time.

Commentary

In this scene we see Richard in a close-up portrait with his wife, and the emotional quality of the scene balances that of the one which preceded it. Then, he was a man of display before his former subjects; here he is a private man saying goodbye to his wife. The queen's lines, in which she describes him at the beginning of the scene set the tone. Richard is a man to be pitied, a shadow of his former self, a "withering rose." When she compares him to Bolingbroke, she uses a metaphor which characterizes Richard as something elegant and special, while Bolingbroke is common. There is an irony here, of course, as it is Bolingbroke's very "commonness" which accounts in part for his transition to the throne. Earlier in the play, Richard commented on Bolingbroke's popularity with the common people. This will be picked up again in the *Henry* plays, in which Bolingbroke's son, Hal, is noted for having "the common touch," in the best meaning of the phrase.

A curious thing happens in this scene. Not only does the queen's pity set the tone in general for this scene, but the fact that her pity finally becomes annoyance is also significant. She becomes angered by what seems to her to be Richard's too-easy compliance with his fate. Although it is a piteous sight to gaze on greatness fallen low, to her it is also loathsome to see that former greatness going to its slaughter like a lamb. She uses the conventional symbol of the proud lion to make her point: Richard should act like the king of beasts and continue to struggle to the end. This is not the first time that Shakespeare presents Richard within the framework of this metaphor, but one should resist the temptation to label him too quickly; the author's characterization of Richard is a complex one, and Shakespeare doesn't allow a simple progression of responses to the king.

While we can sympathize with Richard in his private suffering, it is a fact that this private suffering occasionally degenerates into self-pity. It seems as though Richard almost *enjoys* the fantasy of imagining weeping, aged women sitting around a fire during a deep winter's night and telling the woeful and lamentable story of poor King Richard.

With relief, we finally see Richard seem to spring to life during his verbal attack on Northumberland in the next part of the scene. His first two lines, calling Northumberland a mere "ladder" which Bolingbroke used to climb to the throne, opens an attack upon Northumberland and expresses a warning to him and those like him: treason and distrust will breed more of the same, and none of those involved will see a happy end to this business. This is really the first time in the play where Shakespeare has Richard sound this theme so forcefully and explicitly, and Northumberland's easy dismissal of the advice — "My guilt be on my head, and there an end" — betrays a suspiciously cocky and over-confident attitude.

An important point about the conclusion to the scene is the physical action which Shakespeare adds to it. Where it may be difficult to sympathize unqualifiedly with Richard, especially when he is dramatizing his own situation, it is easy to imagine him kissing his wife farewell, then kissing her farewell again, as if to delay the inevitable parting. The farewell is poignant, the tone much like that when Gaunt parted for the last time from Bolingbroke.

> One kiss shall stop our mouths, and dumbly part;
> Thus give I mine, and thus take I thy heart.
>
> (95-96)

ACT V – SCENE 2

Summary

In this scene, two or three months have elapsed since Richard was taken to Pomfret. The Duke of York is telling his wife what has happened – how Richard and Bolingbroke arrived in London, how the crowd "threw dust and rubbish" on Richard's head, and how Bolingbroke was hailed with many welcomes and blessings. He thinks that "Heaven hath a hand in these events," and he says that he has sworn allegiance to Bolingbroke.

York sees his son, Aumerle, approaching and says that not only has Aumerle been reduced in rank but that he himself has made a pledge in Parliament for Aumerle's loyalty to Bolingbroke. When York and his wife speak to their son, Aumerle is clearly out of sorts: he does *not* know who the favorites are at court ("the violets now/ That strew the green lap of the new come spring"), nor does he care, and, furthermore, he tells his father that he does *not* know who's jousting at Oxford. His spirit pales, however, when his father mentions to him a sealed paper which he has spied in Aumerle's pocket. A quarrel ensues, and York seizes the paper and reads it. He loudly denounces his son for being a traitor, and he calls for his boots. Despite his wife's pleas and protestations, he means to reveal what he has learned to Bolingbroke. He and his wife quarrel bitterly over Aumerle's treason. York's wife calls her husband unnatural for disclaiming their son, and he calls her a fool for her blind love. After York leaves, his wife pleads with Aumerle to get to the king before York does. Meanwhile, she herself will saddle up and try to delay

York: "Never will I rise up from the ground/ Till Bolingbroke have pardon'd thee."

Commentary

There is something oddly farcical about this scene in an otherwise humorless play: we get a glimpse into the household of one of the minors actors in the political drama where the strife of the outside arena is seen in miniature.

Earlier, York was a defender of Richard and the divine right of kingship. When the situation became intolerable, he switched his allegiance to Bolingbroke. This was an important switch because it was not done capriciously. York had difficulty in coming to his decision, and although one might be tempted to see York as a political time-server, it doesn't seem that Shakespeare wanted him to be judged too harshly. York's heart seems to be in the right place, and the interests of the nation at large seem to have motivated him to do what he did. In this scene, we see that his son, Aumerle, has remained faithful to the previous ruler. Why not? His father's sympathies had been there too at one time. Aumerle's personal loyalty supercedes his questionable duty to the new king. Questionable, in fact, is the only word we can use concerning loyalty in this case, because one must remember the new king's legitimacy as a monarch is in doubt.

The struggle between the father and son seems serious enough, because finally Aumerle's mother has to break in and try to make her husband leave the matter alone and put all thoughts of their turning their only child over to the authorities completely out of his head. They struggle over his boots, most likely (this is not completely clear from the text); she tries to keep them from him, and he tries to put them on so that he can ride to inform Bolingbroke of the plot against his life. Her lines are those of a distracted mother: "Strike him, Aumerle. Poor boy, thou art amazed." His are those of a perhaps over-zealous patriot: ". . . were he twenty times my son,/ I would appeach him."

The purpose of this scene is twofold: first, it shows the results of the political uncertainty and impending chaos at the local level, where most ordinary humans would experience it. (A family spat is a civil war in miniature.) And second, it presents the odd games which fortune plays with political loyalties and political necessities. Who is correct in his loyalty? The father's loyalty to the newly crowned king, or the son's loyalty to the man whom he has served? Shakespeare raises the question without answering it. Aumerle's part in the plot and the outcome of his mother's appeal will feature importantly in the next scene.

One final note on this scene should be made concerning the description of Richard, again the performer. This is important as a prelude to Richard's final scene and his now-famous soliloquy. York describes him thus:

> As in a theatre, the eyes of men,
> After a well-graced actor leaves the stage,
> Are idly bent on him that enters next,
> Thinking his prattle to be tedious;
> Even so, or with much more contempt, men's eyes
> Did scowl on gentle Richard.
>
> (23-28)

One thing this speech does is identify Bolingbroke as the next "actor" in the role of king. The two men gazed into each other's faces through the hollow crown in an earlier scene; we shall see that in more ways than one they will prove to be "mirror images" of one another.

ACT V – SCENE 3

Summary

Bolingbroke, now Henry IV, laments to Henry Percy that Prince Hal, the heir to the throne, is wasting his life with dissolute companions, and that it has been "full three months since I did see him last."

Aumerle suddenly rushes on stage and asks for a private audience with the king, and when it is granted, he proceeds to beg forgiveness for his involvement in an assassination plot against the crown. With the door locked, Aumerle is prepared to confess, but before he does so, the Duke of York comes to the door and demands that the king should beware of the traitor in his midst. The door is opened, and York dashes in and loudly accuses his son.

"O heinous, strong and bold conspiracy!" shouts Bolingbroke, "O loyal father of a treacherous son." Before any action can be taken, however, the Duchess of York arrives and begs forgiveness of the king in behalf of her son. The king throws up his arms and responds to the turn of events by saying that

> Our scene is altered from a serious thing,
> And now changed to "The Beggar and the King"
>
> (79-80)

The duke and duchess then revive the family squabble of the previous scene and fall on each other in front of the king; they all kneel, making their various pleas, until the king silences them with his decisive judgment: "I pardon him, as God shall pardon me." Bolingbroke then declares that he will execute all of the other conspirators. Quietly, the duchess takes her son in hand and they leave the stage. She vows to Aumerle that she will pray until "God make thee new."

Commentary

Bolingbroke is now the leader of the nation. What does that mean? For one thing, as Richard predicted, he will never be fully secure for the rest of his days. There is a conspiracy afoot, the first of many, one supposes. And, to make matters worse, as is brought out in the first part of the scene, the king has an unregenerate son, Prince Hal, who whiles away his time with Jack Falstaff (particularly in the *Henry IV* plays of the tetralogy).

Another errant son, York's, breaks onto the scene as the agent of the conspiracy. One must imagine Bolingbroke taking the threat when it is revealed to him by York, quite seriously. There is a real danger to the throne. But when the duchess enters the scene, a bit of the farce of the previous scene spills over into this one. Bolingbroke is now involved in a petty domestic dispute, or what seems like such. There is a pronounced difference between the glamour associated with rulers and ruling and between the tedious reality of this sort of administration and arbitration on a daily basis. This does seem to be Shakespeare's point, or at least one of them, because this scene is in such marked contrast with the rather philosophical heaviness of the entire play up until now. Our last view of Richard was a philosophical one; Shakespeare focused primarily on the idea of kingship and what it was. Here, the reality is exposed, with all its boring, melodramatic features. Richard was aloof. That was one reason for his downfall. Henry is *not* aloof; for that reason, one can easily imagine (from this scene) the price which he will pay for keeping himself caught up in petty embroilments.

The vehemence with which York denounces his son seems odd, as if Shakespeare wanted to discredit an over-zealous patriotism. York's words, echoing the theme of civil strife, are harsh:

> If thou do pardon, whosoever pray,
> More sins for this forgiveness prosper may.
> This festered joint cut off, the rest rest sound;
> This let alone will all the rest confound.
>
> (83-86)

The wisdom is politically sound perhaps, but in reference to his own son, it is certainly extreme. Bolingbroke pardons the son as an act of mercy, showing himself the good ruler in this, but he also despatches the other conspirators without hesitation: "Destruction straight shall dog them at the heels." He seems to believe firmly in justice and mercy—as a good ruler must—and Shakespeare *did* want to show him as a good ruler.

ACT V – SCENE 4

Summary

This short scene, consisting of only eleven lines, takes place a few months later. In Windsor Castle, Sir Pierce of Exton is speaking to his servant; he interprets Bolingbroke's words "Have I no friend will rid me of this living fear" to mean that Bolingbroke wants someone to kill Richard and put an end to all thoughts of a counter-coup in the country. He explains to his servant that Bolingbroke uttered these words twice—and looked at Exton "as [if he would] say, 'I would thou wert the man. . . .'" Exton's servant confirms Bolingbroke's words and his actions. Exton says finally, "Come, let's go./ I am the King's friend, and will rid his foe."

Commentary

This scene's action is short and straightforward: Sir Pierce Exton interprets Bolingbroke's words "Have I no friend will rid me of this living fear" to mean that he wants someone to kill Richard and put an end to all thoughts of a counter-coup in the country. He explains this to another man and they go to kill Richard. Because of this information, our reception of Richard's final soliloquy will be that much more acute.

ACT V – SCENE 5

Summary

The scene opens as Richard is sitting alone in his cell at Pomfret Castle. His only companions, he says, are his thoughts. Thus he speaks aloud. He "peoples" the world with his thoughts and "plays in one person many people" in his imagination. When he hears music from outside his prison cell, it disturbs him: "How sour sweet music is/ When time is broke, and no proportion kept." The music maddens him, for the giving of this music to him is a sign of love in the giver, and, to Richard, love "is a strange brooch in this all-hating world."

His soliloquy – in which he compares himself with a clock measuring time, his thoughts being the minutes, his eyes being the dials, and his groans being the striking of the hours – is interrupted when a groom, one of his former servants, enters. The groom remembers having tended to Richard's horse during happier days, and he would like to talk to his former king, but Richard becomes irritated when he hears that Bolingbroke now rides proudly on Richard's "roan Barbary." Richard curses his horse, then speaks words of forgiveness.

A keeper breaks off their conversation and offers Richard his meal. Richard, however, says that he won't eat until the food is first tasted by the guard; he is afraid of being poisoned. The keeper says that Sir Pierce of Exton "commands the contrary."

Exton enters with henchmen and a fight breaks out. After killing one of the would-be assassins, Richard is killed by Exton, but before he dies, he curses his killer:

> That hand shall burn in never-quenching fire
> That staggers thus my person.
>
> (109-10)

Richard's dying words affect Exton; "O would the deed were good!" he says. Clearly he fears the consequences of what he has done.

Commentary

Here we see Richard at his most naked and honest. His thoughts, he says, could fill this little world in place of people. During his reign, he needed people as audiences and companions; this explains the flatterers in his court, those who contributed to his downfall. But even the world of thoughts, like the world of people, has a falling out with itself: there is not one *single* thought that enters his head that cannot be immediately countered with its contrary. Even the Bible is not immune to this fact of contradiction. "Come, little ones," says the word of God, but the same book also says that it is as hard to "come," as it is for a camel to pass through the eye of a needle. The association between contrary thoughts, opposing ideas, and the topsy-turvy turn of events in England and in Richard's life is apparent here:

> Thoughts tending to content flatter themselves
> That they are not the first of fortune's slaves,
> Nor shall not be the last; like silly beggars
> Who, sitting in the stocks, refuge their shame,
> That many have and others must sit there;
> And in this thought they find a kind of ease,
> Bearing their own misfortunes on the back
> Of such as have before endured the like.
>
> (23-30)

Optimistic or rationalizing thoughts, then, are false flatterers to themselves and serve no useful purpose in the end. Richard recapitulates his experiences succinctly: "Thus play I in one person many people." He has played many people and many roles throughout the course of this play, and now in his imagination, he re-runs the gamut of the types. He has played the king, and he quakes from fear of treason; he has played the beggar, and he feels crushed by penury into thinking he was better off as king. The end result of this "logic" is that he *would* be better off dead:

> But whate'er I be,
> Nor I, nor any man that but man is,

> With nothing shall be pleased, till he be eased
> With being nothing.
>
> (38-41)

The chords of music heard from outside the cell have a marked effect on Richard. This scene is the most contemplative in the play, and its "philosophy" speaks of a different kind of concern to Shakespeare in this part of the play from what has gone before. Compare the tone of this scene with the "petty squabbling" found in the two preceding ones. In evoking this difference, the music serves the function of being a mood setter. As an art form, music seems able to "articulate" things which cannot be expressed in any other way. Richard's melancholy is thus underscored. Also, the perfect measure and construction of the phrases of music jar on Richard's ear because it unhappily reminds him of his own discordant state of mind:

> And here have I the daintiness of ear
> To check time broke in a disordered string;
> But for the concord of my state and time
> Had not an ear to hear my true time broke.
> I wasted time, and now doth Time waste me.
>
> (45-49)

The play on words—"time" in music, in the sense of measured duration, and "Father Time"—leads to Richard's observation on his own demise:

> So sighs, and tears, and groans
> Show minutes, times, and hours. . . .
>
> (57-58)

At the end of the speech, Richard seems to grow energetic in his anger, shouting, "This music mads me." As he is not so predisposed, music cannot exercise its calming effect on him.

Shakespeare presents the interlude with the groom as a way of reminding Richard of former, better times, and therefore redoubling the pain of his present state. The groom also serves to show that among some of the common people, there is still respect and feeling for Richard. In addition, the groom has secret thoughts which are perhaps rebellious in nature: "What my tongue dares not, that my heart shall say."

To impress us with the villainy of murdering the king, Shakespeare has Exton recoil in horror from his own accomplishment:

> As full of valor as of royal blood!
> Both have I spilled. O, would the deed were good!
> For now the devil that told me I did well
> Says that his deed is chronicled in hell.
>
> (114-17)

The tradition that regicide originates in hell is here repeated.

ACT V – SCENE 6

Summary

Some days after Richard has been killed, Bolingbroke is talking with York, and he tells him that rebel forces "have consumed with fire" a town in Gloucestershire, and it cannot be ascertained whether or not the rebels themselves have been killed or captured. But there is good news, for Northumberland announces that "the heads of Salisbury, Spencer, Blunt, and Kent" have been sent to London. It is next Fitzwater's turn to speak: "The heads of Brocas and Sir Bennet Seely," men who were involved in the Oxford plot to kill Bolingbroke, have also been sent to London. Henry Percy enters then and tells them that the "grand conspirator," the Abbot of Westminster, "hath yielded up his body to the grave," and that Carlisle is being brought as a captive before them. The king sentences Carlisle to life imprisonment; he spares his life because of the "high sparks of honor in thee have I seen."

Exton enters then and presents Richard, lying in his coffin, to Bolingbroke and is rebuked by the king. Exton declares that he killed Richard because of Bolingbroke's own words, but Bolingbroke is deaf to these excuses. He banishes Exton and vows to "make a voyage to the Holy Land" to expiate the guilt which he has accrued to himself.

Commentary

This last scene of the play swells with details of civil horror: a razed town, six beheadings, one life imprisonment, one banishment, and the corpse of a murdered king. The prophecies of doom seem to be fulfilling themselves. Bolingbroke thanks "gentle Percy" for his part in fighting the rebels. (In *Henry IV, Part I,* Shakespeare shows Henry Bolingbroke's armies in pitched battle against this same Percy.) The mercy which Bolingbroke shows Carlisle, in sparing his life, attests to the general misery of the scene momentarily, but no sooner is the sentence of life imprisonment offered, than Exton arrives with Richard's coffin. The note of damnation and possible regeneration through penance which Bolingbroke's last speech contains concludes the play in the religious imagery which has been threaded throughout.

SIXTEENTH-CENTURY POLITICAL THEORY

Since *Richard II* and the *Henry IV* plays are basically political ones, it is necessary to understand the political doctrine behind them if one is to do justice to Shakespeare's intentions. Elizabeth I, the fifth Tudor to rule England, had come to a throne which was in many ways insecure because of rival claims. Henry VIII, her father, had found it especially necessary to inculcate the doctrine of absolute obedience to the Crown after the break with Rome in 1536. During his reign he had experienced the Pilgrimage of Grace, a rebellion in northern England, and, later, the Exeter Conspiracy, an alleged attempt to depose Henry and place a Yorkist on the throne of England. After Henry VIII's death, England endured the Western Rebellion of 1549; during Elizabeth's reign there occurred the Rebellion of 1569, as well as plots against the queen's life, notably the Babington Plot, which led to the trial, conviction, and execution of Mary, Queen of Scots. Throughout the century and beyond, England had reason to fear an invasion and the uprising of native Catholics. The danger was by no means restricted to the year 1588, when Philip II of Spain sent his Armada to subdue England.

In view of such challenges to Tudor supremacy, there was a need for a political philosophy which would prevent challenges to royal authority and prevent devastating civil war. The basic arguments were developed during the reign of Henry VIII and augmented as new crises arose during the reigns of Edward VI and Elizabeth I. It found expression in officially approved pamphlets and tracts, and also in drama and non-dramatic poetry. Especially it was emphasized in official sermons, the first group of which was introduced in the year

1549. These included strongly worded instructions on the subject of obedience. They were augmented in 1570, following the Rebellion of 1569 and the papal decree of excommunication of Queen Elizabeth I. Every Englishman was required to hear the sermons on obedience three times during the year. The gist of the doctrine was this: the ruler was God's lieutenant on earth; no subject, however exalted, had the right to actively oppose him. To do so was a sin against religion, punishable by suffering here and now and by eternal damnation after death. Even if the ruler were a tyrant, the subject had no right to oppose him; for the head of state ruled with God's sufferance. In support of this doctrine, appeals were made primarily to biblical authority. Texts such as Romans 13 and Proverbs 8, as well as ones in Matthew, were cited repeatedly. John of Gaunt, Duke of Lancaster, summed up the doctrine accurately and concisely in his response to his sister-in-law, the Duchess of Gloucester, who reminded him that the reigning king, Richard II, had been responsible for the death of her husband and Gaunt's brother:

> God's is the quarrel, for God's substitute,
> His deputy anointed in His sight,
> Hath caus'd his death; the which if wrongfully,
> Let Heaven revenge; for I may never lift
> An angry arm against His minister.
>
> (I.ii.37-41)

That Henry IV should so suffer is to be explained by the fact that he, son of John of Gaunt, did "lift an angry arm against [God's] minister." He endures rebellion; he sees the apparent waywardness of Prince Hal as part of his punishment; he is not permitted to lead a crusade against the foes of Christianity and do penance for his grievous sins. But, according to Tudor political theory, he wore the crown by God's authority; no subject had the right to oppose him. All this should make understandable the Percys' position and make unacceptable the view that Henry IV is a hypocrite.

CHARACTER SUMMATIONS

Richard II

As a king, Richard is supposedly divine and all powerful; as a man, he is an ordinary mortal and prey to his own weaknesses. The private tragedy of the play, for Richard, is in his being forced to face this duality. Shakespeare demonstrates that Richard is perhaps temperamentally not fit for the role which history would have him play. His decisions as a monarch seem irrational and arbitrary; he won't listen to the sane advice of old Gaunt, and he insensitively seizes wealth belonging to his noblemen.

It is only during his deposition and his imprisonment that Richard shows his greatest strength as a dramatic figure. Although occasionally he seems to demonstrate self-pity (Bolingbroke accuses him of this), he also reveals himself to have an acute awareness of the ironies and absurdities in the structure of power in his kingdom. Although he keeps reminding those present of his God-given mandate to rule, he seems also to take pleasure in passing on the trials of kingship to his successor.

Richard's last speeches are among the most beautiful in the play. It is as though Shakespeare were allowing the man himself, stripped of political power, a chance to achieve a human power which surpasses suffering and becomes self-knowledge.

Henry Bolingbroke

Bolingbroke contrasts with Richard in many ways. He seems practical minded, honest, and sensitive — in many ways, the "natural" king. It is also important to realize that in the early stages of the play Bolingbroke is, at best, a reluctant rebel. The insult to himself and his father and the urging which he receives from his peers are the determining factors in his effort to depose Richard. He is keenly aware of the magnitude of the crime which he is embarking on, and he quickly learns the tediousness of being a ruler, as is particularly evident in the scene which precedes Richard's prison cell monologue. Whereas Richard's tragic situation catapults his speech into a kind of poetry, Henry's newly placed crown lowers him down into the center of a domestic squabble. His last decision, to make a pilgrimage to the Holy Land, underscores his uneasiness with his new role as king.

John of Gaunt

Bolingbroke's father serves as a kind of spiritual touchstone for the play. Near death, he is impatient with the prevarications of the king and his courtiers; he accuses them of undermining the solid state of England. His rousing patriotic speeches put the political theme of the play directly before the audience. When Richard insults old Gaunt, it is tantamount to sacrilege and treason. When Richard, in effect, steals Gaunt's wealth after his death, it gives Henry Bolingbroke more than enough personal reason for rebelling against the king.

The Duke of York and Aumerle

York and Gaunt should be thought of together. Both seem to represent solid qualities in the English character. It is significant that York struggles with his own sense of what is orthodox and right before throwing in his lot with the rebels. Like old Gaunt, York has a son, but whereas Bolingbroke is the one to depose the king, York's son Aumerle remains loyal to Richard. The father and son are at each other's throats before the end of the play over the question of loyalty to the present ruler. Bolingbroke forgives Aumerle of his possible treachery, but the point is made that the political struggle has repercussions — even down to the ordinary family level.

QUESTIONS FOR REVIEW

1. How do the political themes and private themes in the play interconnect?

2. In what ways can Richard be considered a tragic figure?

3. Discuss the imagery of gardens and gardening in the play.

4. Contrast Richard and Henry as rulers.

5. Is this play humorless?

6. How do the minor characters such as Mowbray, Aumerle, Bushy, Bagot, and Green function in the play?

7. What is the particular function of the women in this play?

8. To what extent does the death of Gloucester affect Richard's deposition?

76

9. Defend York's change of allegiance to Bolingbroke.

10. Richard is often said to be an "unkingly" ruler. Discuss.

SELECTED BIBLIOGRAPHY

ADAMS, J. Q. *A Life of William Shakespeare*. Boston: Houghton Mifflin Co., 1923.

ALEXANDER, PETER. *Shakespeare*. Oxford: Oxford University Press, 1964.

BEVINGTON, DAVID. *Shakespeare*. Arlington Heights, Ill.: A.H.M. Publications, 1978.

BLOOM, EDWARD A., ed. *Shakespeare 1564-1964*. Providence: Brown University Press, 1964.

BRADLEY, A. C. *Shakespearean Tragedy*. London: The Macmillan Co., 1904.

CHARLTON, H. B. *Shakespearean Tragedy*. Cambridge, England: Cambridge University Press, 1948.

CRAIG, HARDIN. "The Great Trio," *An Interpretation of Shakespeare*. Columbia, Missouri: Lucas Brothers, 1966.

FARNHAM, WILLARD. *The Medieval Heritage of Elizabethan Tragedy*. Berkeley, California: University of California Press, 1936.

GIBSON, H. N. *The Shakespeare Claimants*. New York: Barnes & Noble, Inc., 1962.

HEILMAN, ROBERT B. *Magic in the Web*. Lexington, Kentucky: University of Kentucky Press, 1956.

KNIGHT, G. WILSON. *The Wheel of Fire*. London: Oxford University Press, 1930.

LEAVIS, F. R. *The Common Pursuit.* Hardmonsworth, Middlesex: Penguin Books, Ltd., 1963.

RIBNER, IRVING. *Patterns in Shakespearean Tragedy.* New York: Barnes & Noble, Inc., 1960.

SEWELL, ARTHUR. *Character and Society in Shakespeare.* Oxford: Clarendon Press, 1951.

SPIVACK, BERNARD. *Shakespeare and the Allegory of Evil.* New York: Columbia University Press, 1958.

STIRLING, BRENTS. *Unity in Shakespearean Tragedy: The Interplay of Theme and Character.* New York: Columbia University Press, 1956.

NOTES

NOTES

NOTES

RICHARD III

NOTES

including
- *Historical Background*
- *Critical Introduction*
- *Brief Synopsis*
- *Scene-by-Scene Summaries
        and Commentaries*
- *Notes on Characters*
- *Review Questions*
- *Selected Bibliography*

by
James K. Lowers, Ph.D.
Department of English
University of Hawaii

NEW EDITION

INCORPORATED

LINCOLN, NEBRASKA   68501

Editor	Consulting Editor
Gary Carey, M.A. *University of Colorado*	*James L. Roberts, Ph.D.* *Department of English* *University of Nebraska*

Cliffs Notes, Inc.   Lincoln, Nebraska

CONTENTS

NOTES ON CHARACTERS

REVIEW QUESTIONS

SELECTED BIBLIOGRAPHY

RICHARD III

ON USING THE *NOTES*

Cliff's Notes are intended as an aid to the student in arriving at a mature understanding and appreciation of Shakespeare's *Richard III*. At no time should they be used as a substitute for the close reading—and rereading—of the play itself.

It is true that any literary piece must be considered as an independent work of art. But it is no less true that quite often some background material must be acquired if the student is really to understand the work and to do justice to the author's intentions. Indeed, anyone who ignores what has been called the "Elizabethanness" of Shakespeare cannot hope to understand him.

As regards *Richard III,* all this means that the student should have sufficient knowledge of the historical events upon which the play is based and of how the dramatist made use of the records of those events. Further, he should have some knowledge of the Tudor attitude toward history and of the political, ethical, and religious doctrines which inform the work, since in *Richard III* history and tragedy meet. Finally, it is useful to know that Shakespeare followed certain literary traditions as relate to characterization of the protagonist, ingredients of tragedy, and style. To ignore such matters indicates that one is content to remain solely at the story level, which in this instance particularly, requires little effort and presents no challenge.

The student should read the play first at his normal rate in order to get the "story" and characters in mind. Then he should go back and read act by act critically, noting development of character, emergence of theme or themes, style, movement of the action to the climax and its fall to the catastrophe. It is here that the *Notes* should prove most helpful, providing as they do a summary of the action, critical commentary, and discussion of characters.

THE HISTORICAL BACKGROUND

Shakespeare's *Richard III* covers events in the latter years of the Wars of the Roses, that is, from the attainder and execution of George, Duke of Clarence, in 1478 to the defeat of Richard III at Bosworth Field in 1485. That war, a prolonged, intermittent conflict between the two noble houses of Lancaster and York which began in 1455, was closer to Shakespeare and

6

THE HOUSES OF YORK AND LANCASTER[1]

Edward III (1327-77)

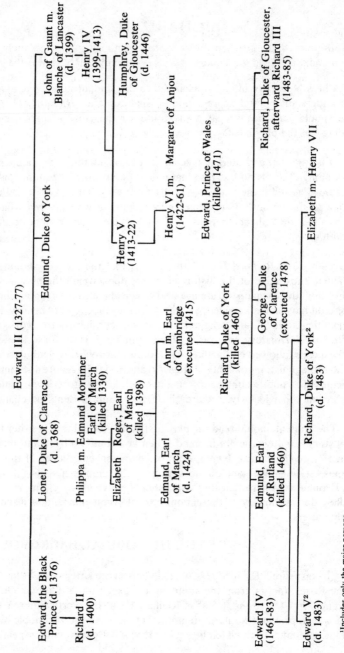

his generation than are the Napoleonic wars to the present generation. On the throne of England when the dramatist wrote sat the granddaughter of Richmond, the first of the Tudors, who, it was firmly believed, was the godly savior of an England long torn by dissension and civil war. Particularly because throughout the sixteenth century England had reason to fear civil strife as well as foreign invasion, Elizabethans continued to manifest a keen interest in the historical events of the preceding century. As has been now well established, Shakespeare's generation viewed history as a mirror in which could be read lessons important to ruler and subject alike. Moreover, the chronicle histories which provided materials for Shakespeare's play were written with a Tudor bias, presenting and interpreting character and event from the point of view accepted as orthodox in sixteenth-century England.

Since constant reference to earlier events in the conflict are found in *Richard III*, it is desirable briefly to review the story of the Wars of the Roses, which lasted for thirty years and in which some eighty princes of the blood, many members of the nobility, and at least 100,000 commoners were slain. This was the dynastic struggle between the house of York and the house of Lancaster. Actually, the Lancastrians never adopted the Red Rose as their symbol, it having been used first by Henry Tudor (Richmond) in 1485.

Head of the White Rose party was Richard Plantagenet, third Duke of York, whose claim to the throne was an impressive one. On his mother's side of the family, he was descended from Lionel, Duke of Clarence, elder brother of John of Gaunt, from whom the Lancastrians were descended. Unfortunately for Richard, however, parliament had declared for the younger line, which had the advantage of straight descent through the males.

Richard of York was able to capitalize upon Henry VI's notorious weakness as a ruler and his misfortunes. Following Jack Cade's Rebellion (1450) he was hailed as a popular champion, particularly because of his opposition to the Duke of Somerset, who conducted affairs for the king. There was even a proposal that he be recognized as heir to the throne, the first suggestion of the devastating quarrel which became known as the Wars of the Roses. Taking some liberty with history, Shakespeare dramatized the origin of these two hostile parties in *Henry VI, Part Two*, and continued the story of events in the third part, wherein the Yorkists emerged triumphant.

By the year 1453, when Henry VI became quite ill, the Duke of York succeeded in getting control of the government and was appointed "Protector and Defender of the Realm" by parliament. But the king recovered late in the next year, and York was replaced by his rival Somerset. He did not remain quiet for long. When a council was summoned to make provisions "for the safety of the King against his enemies," the duke led a force of his supporters in a march on London. Somerset, joined by the king and a host of nobles, led an army from London to meet the threat, and the two forces met at St. Albans. The Wars of the Roses had begun. Somerset was killed, and Margaret of Anjou, Henry's energetic queen, emerged as head of the Lancastrian party. During the next four years, England experienced a period of restiveness before warfare broke out again. Although York was supported by the powerful Earl of Warwick, head of the house of Neville, the Yorkists were defeated and the duke himself fled to Ireland.

But King Henry's government, now controlled by Margaret and her council, proved anything but efficient. Faced by poverty and disaster, the average Englishman yearned for the return of Richard of York. In June, 1460, Warwick and Edward, Earl of March, the duke's eldest son, moved on London and were joined by York, who again claimed the crown. This time parliament ruled that the head of the house of York should be heir to the hapless Henry VI. But Margaret was not to be repressed. She succeeded in mustering a strong force in the north and met the Yorkists at Wakefield. In this battle, the duke lost his life. And, since Edward was just a youth of eighteen, Warwick became the head of the White Rose party. In the next year the new leader was overwhelmingly defeated in the second Battle of St. Albans. Nevertheless, Warwick managed to join forces with Edward and to occupy London. Thus Margaret lost the fruits of her victory. Young Edward was declared king by the citizens and lords of Yorkshire and did not hesitate to take the throne, although this did not constitute a legal election.

Subsequent events worked in Edward's favor. Margaret's Lancastrian forces were defeated near Towton in York on March 29, 1461. Henry and his son fled to Scotland. By 1464, Edward was full master of England. Nevertheless, his position was jeopardized by his marriage to Elizabeth, a widowed daughter of Richard Woodville. Warwick, his chief supporter, was enraged, not only because the Woodvilles were of Lancastrian connection but because Warwick himself had all but completed a plan for the English monarch to marry the sister of Louis XI of France. Edward IV aggravated matters by favoring his wife's relatives at the expense of the Nevilles. Henry had returned to England in 1465 and had been placed in the Tower of London. Not long thereafter, however, the former king was released, and Edward was forced to flee to Holland. Thanks to the support of Charles of Burgundy, Edward was able to muster a force and to return to England. Once more the unfortunate Henry was imprisoned, and Warwick's army was defeated, the earl himself being slain. To cap all this, the Lancastrians suffered a devastating defeat at Tewkesbury on May 4, 1471. Margaret was taken prisoner and the young prince was put to death. Henry VI was reported to have died "of pure displeasure and melancholy," but in all probability Edward IV ordered that he be put to death.

For *The Tragedy of Richard III*, Shakespeare picked up the story with the attainder of the Duke of Clarence, who had married a daughter of Warwick and had served his father-in-law from 1469 to 1471, and who had been involved constantly in quarrels with the king and with his other brother, Richard of Gloucester. Inevitably, there are frequent references to earlier events in the play.

A CRITICAL INTRODUCTION

The history of this period dating from the reign of Richard II to the defeat of Richard III at Bosworth Field in 1485 was dramatized in two tetralogies. The first includes *Richard II* (1595), the two *Henry IV* plays (1597-98), and *Henry V* (1599).[1] In these plays Shakespeare presented the tragic fortunes of Richard II which culminated in his deposition and murder: the rebellions which harassed the reign of the usurper and regicide, Henry IV; and the triumph of Henry V, who escaped punishment in this world for the sins of his father because he engaged English forces in a war against a foreign enemy, France, winning his famous victories. The second tetralogy includes the three *Henry VI* plays (1590-92)[2] and *Richard III* (1593). Obviously, the latter plays predate those comprising the first tetralogy, but there is sufficient evidence, external and internal, that Shakespeare, like his contemporaries, saw in the deposition of Richard II, a lawful anointed ruler, the source of England's troubles during the entire period. This is a point worth keeping in mind because it makes understandable why the descendants of Lancastrian Henry IV as well as the members of the Yorkist party should be made to suffer grievously.

The first Quarto of *Richard III* (1597) provides the only external evidence for dating the play, but internal evidence is sufficiently great to point to the earlier date of composition cited above. Certainly the close relation to *Henry VI, Part Three*, wherein the character of Richard of Gloucester is

---

[1]Here and elsewhere the generally accepted dates of composition are given.

[2]Whether Shakespeare was actually the sole author of the *Henry VI* plays is still disputed, but there is little doubt that they are substantially his works.

fully established, indicates that the play was written soon after that chronicle history reached an appreciative public. The style is unmistakably that of early Shakespeare — the poet-dramatist who was still under the influence of his predecessors. As Sir Edmund K. Chambers pointed out (*William Shakespeare,* Vol. I. 1930, p. 302), it is a highly mannered, rhetorical style marked by frequent exclamations, violent and vituperative speeches, cumulative passages of parallel lines with parisonic endings and beginnings, as in these lines spoken by Queen Margaret:

> I had an Edward, till a Richard kill'd him;
> I had a husband, till a Richard kill'd him:
> Thou hadst an Edward, till a Richard kill'd him;
> Thou hadst a Richard, till a Richard kill'd him.

> (IV.iv.40-43)

The elaborate imagery, repetitions, quibbles, and conceits in the wooing scene (I.ii) provide good examples of the early playwright who is rather pleased with his cleverness rather than wholly concerned with character portrayal. All of these stylistic devices may be found in later Shakespeare, to be sure, but never in such abundance. Significant also is the fact that the blank verse in this play is largely end-stopped — that is, there is a grammatical or rhetorical pause at the end of most lines rather than an overrunning of sense from one line to another, which gives a more naturalness to the discourse. The student will find it useful to read aloud and to compare Richard's opening soliloquy with any of those in the late tragedies to appreciate the stylistic difference.

Certain elements of style in *Richard III* are to be traced to the Roman dramatist Seneca, and these merit notice here. The ten tragedies attributed to Seneca were available in translation by 1581; indeed the first dates from 1559. These had great influence upon many of Shakespeare's predecessors and contemporaries. The tone and temper of the Roman's works, his sensationalism and moralizing, his stress on the tragedy of the individual had wide appeal. Comparatively ignorant of the Greek tragic writers, Shakespeare's generation found in Seneca inspiration and, to an appreciable extent, the model for their own tragedies. As for style, the self-revealing soliloquy, the long speeches characterized by full-blown rhetoric, the often epigrammatic alternating lines of speech and reply called *stichomythia* (as in the dialogue between Richard and Anne beginning "I would I knew thy heart," I.ii.193 ff.) all found a place in Elizabethan tragedy, including *Richard III.* Likewise with reference to the sensationalism in developing the theme of murder and revenge. Indeed Elizabethans went beyond Seneca, in whose plays violence is reported or described, not presented onstage.

More often than not, such violence was depicted before the eyes of Elizabethan audiences. Among the Senecan trappings of tragedy are ghosts, foreboding dreams, signs and omens of impending catastrophe – all of which appear in *Richard III*.

With the stress on the individual, Seneca pointed the way to the one-man play, the drama in which the protagonist almost completely dominates the action. Because Shakespeare followed this lead he achieved a unity theretofore unknown in chronicle history plays. The *Henry VI* plays, for example, are notably epic in structure. The shifted emphasis to the titular hero makes justifiable the title *The Tragedy of Richard III*. This brings us to the hero-villain and the second line of influence, a knowledge of which adds appreciably to an understanding of the play. The reference is to the stage Machiavel. It has been argued that Machiavelli, author of *The Prince* (1513), was actually an early political idealist seeking to unify Italy by appealing to the ambitions of the Renaissance princes. But for most Elizabethans the Machiavellian was practically equated with the Devil. Political cunning, overreaching by diplomacy and intrigue came to be known as Machiavellianism, the philosophy of which seems to have been that the end justified the means, however cruel they may be. Christopher Marlowe brought the Machiavellian villain to the stage in his *The Jew of Malta* and *The Massacre of Paris*. In Shakespeare's *Henry VI, Part Three* (III.iii. 124-95), Richard of Gloucester soliloquizes, identifying himself as one whose criminal ambitions will lead him to "set the murderous Machiavel to school." He thus early emerged as the complete Machiavellian villain-hero. The specific characteristics of this type must await our comments on Richard himself.

The dramatized story of Richard had wide appeal, and Shakespeare's play was not the only one based upon his career. Other versions were performed in the public theaters and at Cambridge University. As late as 1602 Ben Jonson started to write a play entitled *Richard Crookback*. It is not only the fact that the evil character of Richard was bound to be fascinating for so many and that the accompanying sensationalism had quite as great an appeal; English history had its special attraction for the Elizabethans. And was not the queen's grandfather the man who defeated Richard and established the Tudor dynasty? Most Englishmen were deeply interested in plays which dealt with the dynastic question, for Elizabeth I never had named her successor. Dissension and civil war, it was feared, might well follow the death of the aging queen.

Richard Burbage, distinguished tragedian in Shakespeare's company, won wide acclaim for his creation of the title role, and the king's exclamation "A horse! A horse! My kingdom for a horse!" was much admired and was imitated by Shakespeare's fellow dramatists. Further evidence popularity is the fact that no less than six Quarto editions of the play were published between 1597 and 1622. Throughout the years it has remained a favorite among the history plays. If it must relinquish first place to *Henry IV* (thanks especially to the presence of the incomparable Falstaff), *Richard III* has held its own very well. During the nineteenth and well into the twentieth centuries it was often the choice of leading actors because the titular hero dominates the action and because the rhetorical school of acting still flourished. There are other reasons, of course. Bernard Shaw, reviewing Sir Henry Irving's production for the *Saturday Review* in 1896, wrote as follows:

> The world being yet little better than a mischievous school-boy, I am afraid it cannot be denied that Punch and Judy holds the field still as the most popular of dramatic entertainments. And of all its versions...Shakespear's Richard III is the prince of Punches: he delights Man by provoking God, and dies unrepentant and game to the last...

This is sound criticism. Especially, Shaw's remarks stress the fact that the spectacle of the unconscionable, dedicated sinner, one possessed with inordinate ability and endowed with a fine wit, is irresistibly fascinating.

Quite accurately the blank verse of *Richard III* has been described as "simple." As has been stated above it is early Shakespearean blank verse. But already the distinctive Shakespearean accents are noticeable. It would do the playwright an injustice to underestimate the effects he attains or to dismiss the style as predominantly one of rant, bombast, fustian. In the first place, the standards of realism, as we understand the term today, are no more applicable to the style of the play than they are to much of the action and the portrayal of character. Surely no one would step forth and, voicing his thoughts aloud, declare that he is determined to be a villain. Nor would it be possible for the most gifted individual to effect the complete *volte-face* which we witness when Richard, first excoriated by the grief-stricken widow of Edward, Prince of Wales, succeeds in winning the hand of that lady even as she follows the hearse of the murdered Henry VI. Shakespeare did not offer all this as a slice of life. His audiences were familiar with the story of Richard conceived as the arch-villain whose nemesis was the first of the Tudors. It had been told by Sir Thomas More, whose vividly written tragical history in prose was printed complete in 1557; and More's work had been used by the chronicle historians, Richard Grafton, Edward Hall, and Raphael Holinshed, the latter being Shakespeare's chief source.

In *Richard III* one does not have any great difficulty in finding lines which manifest the sure touch of a superior poet. Consider, for example,

the fourth one of the opening scene: "In the deep bosom of the ocean buried."
Or take the following memorable lines spoken by Queen Elizabeth, whose
daughter Richard wishes to marry:

> Send to her by the man that slew her brothers
> A pair of bleeding hearts; thereon engrave
> Edward and York: then haply will she weep.
> Therefore present to her, — as sometimes Margaret
> Did thy father, steep'd in Rutland's blood, —
> A handkerchief; which, say to her did drain
> The purple sap from her sweet brother's body;
> And bid her wipe her weeping eyes withal.
>
> (IV.iv.271-78)

Finally, listen to Gloucester's reply when he is warned to beware of falling:

> Our aery buildeth in the cedar's top
> And dallies with the wind and scorns the sun. (I.iii.264-65)

These are as attractive as poetry as they are dramatically effective.

All this is not to deny that the formal verbal patterning seems to be
excessive and to pose a special problem for modern readers and members
of the audience. Yet such a style is consistent with the basic pattern of
retributive justice which provides the major theme of this historical tragedy
— God's inexorable punishment visited upon those guilty of the heinous
crimes of murder and perjury. The first example is found in Act I, scene ii,
when the distraught Lady Anne laments the death of Henry VI, the "holy
king":

> O cursed be the hand that made these holes!
> Cursed be the heart that had the heart to do it!
> Cursed the blood that let his blood from hence. (14-16)

The device is especially prominent in the speeches of Queen Margaret, one
example of which has been quoted above.

In keeping with the major theme, Richard of Gloucester functions as
the Scourge of God before he himself is scourged for his heinous crimes.
If Shakespeare remained faithful to the received interpretation of Gloucester's character, he nevertheless manifested his originality and ability as a
dramatist throughout the play. Most of the best known speeches are his
creations. These include the opening soliloquy, Clarence's impassioned
outbursts, and the long tirades of Queen Margaret. Similarly with reference

to much of the action and shorter dialogue. The wooing scene between Richard and Anne, for example, is original with Shakespeare, as is the ironic exchange between the titular hero and the young Duke of York. If Holinshed gave him the lead for depicting the villain's hypocritical display of religiosity when the mayor appeared and when the well-schooled Buckingham offered Richard the crown (III.vii), it remained for Shakespeare to make the most of the hint; for the chronicle historian reported no more than that Richard appeared "with a bishop on every hand of him."

In order to concentrate our interest, the poet-dramatist crowds into the space of a few days the funeral of Henry VI (1471), the murder of Clarence (1478), and the death of Edward IV (1483). The historic time from the burial of Henry VI to the Battle of Bosworth Field (1485) was more than fourteen years. The *dramatic* time was some eleven or twelve days with four intervals—between I.ii and I.iii; II.iii and II.iv; IV.v and V.i; and V.ii. Shakespeare thus achieved a degree of unity unknown to the episodic *Henry VI* plays and helped to justify the title *The Tragedy of Richard III.*

LEADING CHARACTERS IN *RICHARD III*

Richard, Duke of Gloucester, Afterward Richard III

Richard was the youngest son of the third Duke of York who was killed at Wakefield in 1460. In *Henry VI, Part Two,* and more particularly in *Henry VI, Part Three,* he first appeared as a vigorous Yorkist and warrior. But then he emerged in the latter play as "hard-favored Richard," "a ragged fatal rock," and "an undigested lump"—each phrase suggesting that his deformity was the reflection of his profoundly evil character. As has been stated above, he identified himself as one who would outdo Machiavel, that is, as a super-Machiavel, in his efforts to win the crown of England. The basic characteristics of the stage Machiavel of Elizabethan drama are indeed his: boundless ambition, egotistical action, masterly dissembling, defiance of God, great if misguided intellectuality. Yet it has been well observed by C. H. Tawney that "Richard would be intolerable from an aesthetic point of view if he did not excel all the characters that surround him in prudence, energy..., consistent courage, quite as much as he surpasses them in ruthless cruelty and selfishness." Moreover, Richard, denounced as "hell's black intelligencer," "that foul defacer of God's handiwork," and "that black bottl'd spider, that foul bunch-back'd toad," possesses a sardonic wit and a fine sense of irony.

King Edward IV

Edward IV, the eldest son of the Duke of York, ruled England from 1461 to 1483. Anything but a weak ruler, he nevertheless had his difficulties

First, his marriage to Elizabeth Woodville, which had led to the disaffection of the Earl of Warwick, the chief support of the Yorkists, was a continuing source of trouble, for he tended to favor her relatives at the expense of the Nevilles and other families the members of which had favored the Yorkist cause. Second, his reputation as a loose gallant, and particularly his relationship with the beautiful Jane Shore, daughter of a London goldsmith, made possible charges that his mistress adversely influenced his conduct of public affairs. Finally, a well-known clergyman, one Dr. Ralph Shaw, referred to in Act III, scene v, 104, publicly charged that, in the words of the chronicler Robert Fabyan (*The Concordance of Histories*, 1516), "the children of King Edward IV were not legitimate, nor rightful heirs of the crown." This charge was based upon the widely circulated story that Edward had been secretly married before his union to Lady Elizabeth Grey and that his first wife was still alive. Richard of Gloucester of the play capitalized upon all three of these sources of difficulty. Edward appears in *Richard III* as the ailing ruler, one actually on his deathbed. His great concern is to quiet dissension and to insure the orderly succession of the crown.

George, Duke of Clarence

The third son of the Duke of York and brother to Edward IV and Richard of Gloucester first appeared in *Henry VI, Part Three*. In that play he is described as a "quicksand of deceit" and for good reason. Clarence had been elevated to a dukedom by his newly crowned brother after the defeat of Queen Margaret's forces near Towton. But he joined the disgruntled Warwick and was betrothed to the earl's second daughter. It was to Clarence as well as to Warwick that the liberated Henry VI resigned his government, while Edward IV was forced to find haven on the Continent. But once more Clarence changed loyalties, removing the red rose from his helmet and proclaiming himself to be the "mortal foe" of Warwick, who denounced him as "perjur'd and unjust." In *Henry VI, Part Three,* Clarence also is made to join Edward and Richard in stabbing Prince Edward, son of Henry VI and Margaret of Anjou. History records that he was constantly involved in quarrels with his older brother.

Henry, Duke of Buckingham

Buckingham inherited his title from Humphrey Stafford, one of the commanders of the royal forces at the first Battle of St. Albans. Understandably Queen Margaret first praises him as blameless. Holinshed described him as "easie to handle," and for a time so the Richard of this play found him to be. To Richard he was the "deep-revolving, witty [i.e., cunning]

Buckingham" who functioned as the villain-hero's Warwick, or king-maker. But unlike Warwick, Buckingham is depicted as, to use another of Richard's phrases, one "of many simple gulls," susceptible to gross flattery and convinced that his fortunes will be advanced if he serves the ambitious Richard. Too late he learns that he has judged falsely.

Henry Tudor, Earl of Richmond, Afterward King Henry VII

Richmond was the nearest male representative of the Lancastrians. He was the son of Owen Tudor and Katherine, the widow of Henry V. He was also the lineal descendant, by Katherine Swynford, of John of Gaunt. Henry thus inherited the Lancastrian line, although he was debarred by parliament from the throne. Nevertheless, he had many English supporters, and when he escaped to France after the Battle of Tewkesbury, he bided his time for a while and then issued a manifesto calling upon Englishmen to join him in crushing Richard, "the unnatural tyrant who bore rule over them." Thanks to his marriage to Elizabeth, daughter of Edward IV, he was able to unite the dynastic claims of both parties. Shakespeare followed his sources in depicting Henry as the God-sent savior of England.

Queen Margaret, widow of Henry VI

She appeared with increasing prominence in each of the *Henry VI* plays. Daughter of the Duke of Anjou, titular King of Naples, and niece of Charles VII, she was a determined, strong-minded woman who offered a complete contrast to her pious, well-meaning, weak husband. When the Duke of Somerset was slain in the first Battle of St. Albans (1455) Margaret came forward as head of the royal party prosecuting the civil war against the Yorkists. After her defeat at Tewkesbury, she was imprisoned, but was then released on payment of a ransom by France. Actually she died in 1482 but survived in Shakespeare's play, where she functions as a terrifying chorus, a symbolic figure standing for the doom of the house of York.

Elizabeth, Queen to Edward IV

Elizabeth was the widowed daughter of Sir Richard Woodville and patron of the Woodville faction, who were of Lancastrian connection. In the play, this faction is represented by her brother, Earl Rivers, and her two sons by her first husband, the Marquis of Dorset and Lord Grey. In *Richard III* she appears to yield to Richard's blandishments; but since she survived to see her daughter become Queen of England, it may be questioned that she was the "relenting fool and shallow changing woman" described by Richard.

Lady Anne

The widow of Edward, Prince of Wales, son of Henry VI, was the daughter of the Earl of Warwick and thus a Neville. The fact that she possessed much property is not the sole reason why Richard of Gloucester should have turned ardent wooer. The Neville connection fitted in with his ambitions to gain the crown.

The Duchess of York

The mother of King Edward IV, Clarence, and Richard was the daughter of Ralph Neville, first Earl of Northumberland. Since her husband first made his bid for the crown, she had endured "accursed and wrangling days," surviving not only the Duke of York's death, but also the deaths of her sons. She also endured the agonizing realization that Richard was one who was "damned," one who had come "on earth to make [her] earth a hell" and who deserved his mother's "most grievous curse."

William, Lord Hastings

Hastings, an adherent to the Yorkist cause, was described as "a noble man" by Holinshed. He served as lord chamberlain to Edward IV, but was opposed by Queen Elizabeth because the king favored him. Like Buckingham, then, he was at odds with the Woodvilles. Holinshed links him with Buckingham as one whom Richard first considered as "easie to handle." It is difficult to avoid the conclusion that Hastings was obtuse. When Richard arrested members of the queen's faction, he decided that the action was necessary to the safety of the realm, and he was confident that his own position was secure. Obtuse or not, he emerged as one representing loyal nobility, faithful to the throne rather than to one faction or another. Inevitably, Richard denounced him as a traitor and saw to it that he was put to death without a trial, as Shakespeare's sources reported.

BRIEF SYNOPSIS

The wars being over, Richard of Gloucester determines to gain the throne occupied by his brother, Edward IV. He first manages to turn Edward against the Duke of Clarence, who is imprisoned in the Tower on the charge of treason. Next, he wins the hand of Lady Anne, even as she follows the hearse bearing the body of the murdered Henry VI. As part of his plan, Richard succeeds in convincing Hastings and Buckingham that the queen and her faction are to blame for Clarence's imprisonment. Hired murderers carry out his instructions to put Clarence to death.

Richard joins the other members of the hostile factions in solemnly vowing in the presence of the dying Edward to hold the peace. The remorseful king learns that Clarence has been put to death before he himself dies. When the young Prince Edward is sent for from Ludlow to be crowned,

Richard moves quickly to meet this turn of events. Buckingham, now Richard's "second self," promises to separate the prince from the queen's kindred. Lord Rivers, Lord Grey, and Sir Thomas Vaughan are imprisoned by Richard and are executed. The frightened queen seeks sanctuary for her son.

With a great display of courtesy and devotion, Richard has Prince Edward and his brother lodged in the Tower. Finding that Hastings remains loyal to the prince, the villain-hero denounces him as a traitor and orders his execution. Soon thereafter Rivers, Grey, and Vaughan meet like fates. Next, Richard convinces the Lord Mayor of London that he has acted only for the security of the realm. He has Buckingham slander the dead Edward, implying that the late king's children are illegitimate and that Edward himself was basely born. When citizens of London, headed by the lord mayor, offer him the crown, Richard accepts it with pretended reluctance. Arrangements are made for his coronation.

The despairing queen-mother fails in an attempt to visit her sons in the Tower just before Richard is crowned. To secure his position, the new king suggests to Buckingham that the young princes be put to death. But the duke falters at the thought of such a monstrous deed. Dorset, it is learned, has fled to Britanny to join Henry, Earl of Richmond. This turn of events does not deter King Richard. He has rumors spread that his wife is mortally ill; he arranges a lowly match for Margaret, Clarence's daughter; he imprisons Clarence's son; he engages Sir James Tyrrel to undertake the murder of the little princes. Buckingham, now treated disdainfully and denied the promised earldom of Hereford, resolves to join Richmond. Anne dies, and Richard offers himself as husband for his niece, Elizabeth of York. Richmond lands at Milford at the head of a mighty army. Joined by many nobles, he marches inland to claim the throne. Buckingham is captured and slain.

The two armies meet at Bosworth Field, and the two leaders are encamped on either side. That night the ghosts of Richard's victims appear, indicting him and prophesying his defeat. In contrast, Richmond has "fair-boding dreams" and is assured that "God and good angels" stand ready to assist him. Both Richard and Richmond address their troops before the battle begins. Richard fights courageously but is overcome and slain in personal combat with Richmond, who accepts the crown and proposes to marry Elizabeth of York, thus ending the dissension between the two great factions.

SUMMARIES AND COMMENTARIES
ACT I – SCENE 1

Summary

Appearing on a London street, Richard, Duke of Gloucester, soliloquizes, providing much exposition and revealing a great deal about himself. The long years of the Lancastrian supremacy are over, and the house of York, like the rising sun, is now in the ascendant. Those who have distinguished themselves in the grim arts of war are relaxing in the pleasure of love. Richard refers particularly to his brother Edward IV.

The thought of his handsome brother reminds Richard of his own deformity. He has one withered arm and a hunched back and so concludes that he is unfit for love. Therefore he will play the villain. The first of his wicked plots is already under way: he has told Edward about a prophecy which says that someone with a name beginning with "G" will murder Edward's heirs. The king has taken this to mean his other brother, George, Duke of Clarence.

Richard's thoughts are interrupted by the entrance of Clarence, who is guarded by Brackenbury, Lieutenant of the Tower, much to the apparent surprise and concern of Richard. Clarence explains that he is being sent to the Tower because Edward has listened to the prophecy about the letter "G." Richard is quick to attribute the king's action to the fact that he is ruled by his wife, Elizabeth Woodville, who with her brother had had Lord Hastings imprisoned. He declares that the king's blood relatives and supporters are no longer safe.

Richard and Clarence then talk disparagingly of the queen and of the king's mistress, Jane Shore, whom they accuse of ruling the kingdom by gossip. Brackenbury intervenes, not wishing to overhear such dangerous talk. Insisting that there is no question of treasonable discourse, Richard then demonstrates his wit and sense of irony as he slyly speaks of the "noble Queen" and catalogues the attractions of Jane Shore. With resignation, Clarence agrees to accompany Brackenbury, and his brother assures him that he will either deliver him from prison or take his place as a prisoner. Alone, however, Richard restates his determination to have his brother's soul sent to heaven.

Hastings, newly released from prison, enters. He vows that he will avenge himself upon those responsible for his imprisonment, and brings news that the king is ill. Richard blames this illness on Edward's self-indulgence and promises to follow Hastings to his bedside. The scene ends with another soliloquy in which Richard elaborates his evil plans. Clarence must be disposed of at once, before King Edward's death. Then Richard will marry Warwick's daughter Anne, though he had killed her husband, Edward, Prince of Wales, and her father-in-law, Henry VI. He explains that the marriage will further his ends. Aware that his plans are barely started, he goes off to take definite action.

Commentary

In having the titular hero appear first onstage and soliloquize at length, Shakespeare was following a convention that he later outgrew. In the more mature plays, the way is prepared by means of expository dialogue before the tragic hero's entrance. This opening soliloquy accomplishes all that a prologue would, and subtlety is the last thing to look for here. Gloucester paints himself as an unnatural monster. He is lame, ugly, "rudely stamped." A common belief of the time was that the warped moral being of the individual was often reflected in his physical appearance.

In the first two lines is found a typical Shakespearean play upon a word — the word *sun* in this instance. Edward IV was the son of the Duke of York and bore a sun on his armorial crest. Metaphorically, he was the bright sun of the Yorkist party, now in the ascendant. And, of course, the sun is a well-known symbol of royalty. Notice how skillfully Shakespeare sustains the sun metaphor:

> Why, I, in this weak piping time of peace
> Have no delight to pass away the time,
> Unless to see *my shadow in the sun,*
> And descant on mine own deformity.   (24-27)

As a dedicated Machiavellian, he takes pride in his deviousness and treachery, and emerges as one filled with envy (a Deadly Sin) and motivated by criminal ambition. The adjective "piping" and the verb "descant" relate to the shepherd's life, the shepherd being a familiar symbol of the tranquility which Richard scorns.

Already the action has begun to rise. We know about Gloucester's ambition; we know what is the first step he has taken to realize that ambition. When he protests to Clarence, "Alack, my lord, that fault is none of yours," we witness the first display of Machiavellian dissembling. His exchange with the apprehensive Brackenbury provides a good example of his wit and gift for irony. These two qualities are further illustrated by his use of "abjects" for "subjects" and by his expression of deep concern for his brother:

> Meantime, this deep disgrace in brotherhood
> Touches me deeper than you can imagine.   (111-12)

"Disgrace in brotherhood" has three levels of meaning: the unnatural action of a brother (Edward IV); my own underhanded behavior; disgrace to a brother (Clarence). Similarly, the word "lie" in the final words to Clarence means, on the surface, that Gloucester will take Clarence's place in prison; but it also means that the villain-hero will tell more lies about his brother.

With the arrival of Lord Hastings, two circumstances which may work to Richard's advantage are revealed. First, Hastings is determined to avenge himself upon those who were responsible for his imprisonment; therefore, Richard may find him a useful ally. Second, King Edward is "sickly, weak, and melancholy." The reader will not miss the irony of Gloucester's voiced reaction: "Now, by Saint Paul, this is bad indeed." He will make use of such sacred oaths frequently and thus provide further evidence of his hypocrisy. Despite his outward show of loyalty and fraternal love, he does not fail to indict Edward as one whose "evil diet" has "overmuch consumed his royal person." What with the Woodville faction alienating powerful nobles like Hastings, and with the ruler incapacitated as the supposed result of a dissolute life, a way may be found for Richard to seize power. His plan to marry Lady Anne, if carried out successfully, will work to his advantage. But immediately all depends upon what happens to Clarence and to Edward.

A recapitulation of what has been accomplished in this first scene should be useful. Richard is presented as by far the most important character in the play. The present situation in the kingdom is made clear: Edward IV, the ailing ruler, appears to be dominated by his wife, and the older nobles are resentful. The relation between the three sons of the Duke of York is set forth: Edward is a dying king; Clarence a traitor and perjurer; Richard the destroyer of his brother. The scene also provides the motives for Richard's villainy and shows that by his lying words he will be able to stir up more dissension. Finally, the scene prepares for the courtship of Lady Anne.

ACT I – SCENE 2

Summary

Lady Anne, second daughter of the Earl of Warwick, appears onstage, following the funeral cortege of the slain Henry VI, whom she identifies as her father-in-law. She is escorting the body of this "holy King," last great member of the house of Lancaster, to Chertsey in Surrey for burial. Making reference also to herself as the wife of Edward, the "slaughtered son" of the dead ruler, she calls upon the ghost of Henry to hear her lamentations. Heaping curses on the murderer she implores God to punish him: Let any child of his be born prematurely and prove to be monstrous; if he marry, let his wife endure the misery of his death, even as Anne herself now suffers.

At this point Richard enters and violently stops the procession in order to speak to Anne. She denounces him vehemently and utters the prophetic cry, "Thou hast made the happy earth thy hell." She points out that King Henry's wounds have started to bleed again as a result of Richard's presence. Gloucester appeals to her charity. In a dialogue of quick and studied repartee, she heaps more curses upon him, while he parries with flattering words and begs for the chance to explain himself. Though she scorns him and even spits upon him, he is not to be deterred. He presses his suit, declaring that if he was guilty of Henry's and Edward's death, he had been motivated solely by his desire to possess her beauty. When she denounces him as a "foul toad" which infects her eyes, Richard insists that the beauty of her eyes makes him weep — he, who remained dry-eyed when his brother Rutland and his father had been slain. This recital merely excites her scorn; so he bares his bosom, gives her his sword, and — admitting that he indeed killed Henry and Prince Edward — invites her to kill him. When Anne refuses to be his executioner, he urges her to tell him to kill himself, but to do so not in rage. At last Anne is in some doubt and she says: "I would I knew thy heart." Richard is quick to press his advantage and prevails on her to accept a ring. When she takes it, she states that she promises nothing in return. Nevertheless, when he asks her to repair to Crosby Place, his London residence, and there to wait for him while he buries King Henry with his "repentant tears," she promptly agrees to do so.

Alone, Richard gloats over this conquest of Lady Anne made when the odds were so great against him — the fact that she changed from a mood of venemous hate to one of ready acquiescence and found him "to be a marvelous proper man," particularly in contrast to her dead husband, whom he had killed at Tewkesbury some three months earlier. He reveals his plan to "have her...but not keep her long." In view of his success so far, he finds that his deformity pleases him.

Commentary

There has been some dispute as regards the question of whether or not Lady Anne Neville actually had been married to Prince Edward, although there is no question as to the betrothal of the two. Margaret of Anjou did object at first to the proposed marriage of her son to Warwick's second daughter; but, perhaps under pressure of Louis XI, she finally gave her consent. Edward and Anne were married on December 13, 1470, by the

Grand Vicar of Bayeux. The queen, however, left herself as free as possible to disavow or annul the marriage later. It is doubtful that the young couple ever lived together as man and wife. (Cf. Paul M. Kendall, *Richard the Third,* New York, 1956, p. 123).

When the dramatist has Anne point out that the wounds of the dead King Henry have started to bleed again, he makes effective use of the popular belief that the wounds of a murdered man bleed in the presence of the murderer.

It will be noticed that Anne repeatedly addresses Richard as "thou" and "thee," whereas the villain-hero addresses her as "you." Anne shifts to the latter form when she tacitly indicates her willingness to favor Richard's suit: "Well, well, put up your sword." The familiar "thou" and "thee" are a way in which Anne makes clear how she looks down on Gloucester with contempt. Thus, in *Othello* (I.i.118-19), Brabantio, aroused in the night to be told that his daughter has eloped, denounced Iago in these words: "Thou art a villain." To which Iago replies: "You are — a Senator."

In this contrived scene Richard's heartless cruelty and extreme egotism receive sufficient emphasis early and late. It is not stoicism primarily that explains his failure to shed a tear when Rutland and the Duke of York were slain, for he was already dedicated solely to the advancement of his own fortunes to the exclusion of any concern even for blood relatives. Near the end of the scene he callously refers to the corpse of Henry VI: "But first I'll turn yon fellow in his grave" — that is, he will toss or tip the body of his royal victim into the grave. He then tells the sun to shine so that he may see his shadow as it passes. Richard is saying that his physical deformity, symbol of his evil nature, is most pleasing to him, since it makes possible his advancement.

If the stress were placed solely upon Richard's monstrosity, upon the extreme violence of his actions, the villain-hero would not be the fascinating character that he is. Playing the role of a lover with consummate skill, he exhibits the daring, the superior wit, the profound sense of irony, the sheer intellectuality which mark him as one who indeed can outdo Machiavel. He is apparently unperturbed when Anne denounces him as a "dreadful minister of Hell" and as a "foul devil"; he seems to turn the other cheek and addresses her as a "Sweet saint" and gently reproves her for knowing "no rules of charity." Would even a ferocious beast know "some touch of pity" as Anne declares? Then, concludes the villain, he is not a beast! Once having conceded that he did kill Henry VI, Richard claims a kind of credit: he has helped the king to reach heaven. Essaying, for the nonce, the role of the Petrarchan lover, that swain whose avowals of undying love for his lady were recorded in the sonnet cycles already so popular in Shakespeare's England, Richard uses a typical conceit, or fanciful metaphor: he has been wounded to the quick by a glance of Anne's beautiful eyes.

But, like most of Shakespeare's villains, Richard can be completely honest with himself, as we learn from his soliloquies. That Anne, whose murdered husband is represented as having been a paragon of physical attractiveness and virtue, should have permitted this misshapen villain to win her so easily is, to Richard, most comically ironical. One other point, not to be ignored, is the irony in Anne's words when she exclaims: "I'll rest betide the chamber where thou liest" (112). In view of what we learn later, after Anne has been married to Richard for some time, this line is prophetic.

Finally, this scene reveals Richard's boundless energy. He has wasted no time in arranging the match with Lady Anne, as, at the end of the previous scene, we learned he planned to do.

ACT I – SCENE 3

Summary

At the palace, Queen Elizabeth is discussing with Lord Rivers, her brother, and Lord Grey, her son, the king's illness. Elizabeth is especially concerned with what her fate will be if her husband should die. As she points out to Lord Grey, her young son, the Prince of Wales, is "put unto the trust of Richard Gloucester," whom she knows to be her enemy and that of all the Woodville faction. The Duke of Buckingham and the Earl of Derby (also called Lord Stanley) enter and courteously greet the queen. To Derby she remarks that the Countess Richmond, his wife, would not say amen to his prayer for her happiness, for she is a woman of "proud arrogance" who does not cherish the queen. Derby insists that his wife is the victim of "false accusers" — either that or her attitude toward Elizabeth stems from perverse sickness, not malice. In response to a question, Buckingham reports that King Edward seems to have improved in health: he "speaks cheerfully" and is especially desirous of ending the quarrel between the queen's brothers and the offended Buckingham and Hastings. Elizabeth can only voice her fervent wish that all were well and to express the fear that her fortunes will not improve.

Richard, Hastings, and Lord Dorset (son to Elizabeth by her first marriage) enter. "They do me wrong, and I will not endure it." These are the first words of Richard, who presents himself as injured innocence, enraged because the queen's relatives have misrepresented him to the king. He offers himself as a simple, plain man, wronged by the insinuations of sly flatterers whom he cannot match because deception is no part of his character. When Rivers protests, Richard accuses him and all his family for troubling the king with vulgar complaints against him. Elizabeth explains that the king, seeing the hatred of the two families, merely wishes to find the cause of their ill will by having them meet with each other. Richard retorts surlily that he can no longer understand matters, now that the world is upside down, with every common fellow made a gentleman and every gentleman rudely treated like a common fellow.

The queen brings the quarrel into the open, saying that Gloucester envies the advancement of her family. Richard counters with the charge that the queen is responsible for Clarence's imprisonment. She protests. When Lord Rivers breaks in to defend her, Richard taunts her with having married a "handsome bachelor stripling," implying that she, an older widow, was not fit for one so young. The queen is stung by this and threatens to tell the king of all the insults she has borne from Richard.

Old Queen Margaret, widow of Henry VI, enters and stands apart, listening to the wrangling of her enemies, and now and then interjecting scathing comments on the words of successive speakers. To her it is a source of satisfaction that Elizabeth has small happiness in being Queen of England. Richard continues to speak to Elizabeth in his defense. Margaret interrupts him, calling him a devil and blaming him for the death of her husband and her son. Richard continues to address Elizabeth, ignoring the withering remarks of the aged Margaret. He states that, while Elizabeth and members of her family were on the side of the Lancastrians, he was the loyal Yorkist who helped Edward to the throne. Clarence, he continues, forsook his father-in-law Warwick, committing perjury in order to fight on Edward's side; for this offense he is now imprisoned. Interspersed between each of his statements are Margaret's denunciations, but Richard continues to ignore her. Lord Rivers argues that he and members of his family have been loyal always to their lawful king, as they would be to Richard, were he the ruler. Richard is quick to protest that he would rather be a beggar: "Far be it from my heart, the thought of it!" When this causes Elizabeth to bemoan her joyless lot once more, Margaret insists on being heard.

"Hear me, you wrangling pirates," she exclaims, and describes them as rebels who now are quarreling over that which they took from her. All who hear her join in reviling her for the indignity done to the Duke of York, whose severed head was fitted with a mock crown, and for the murder of his son Rutland. Margaret retaliates by asking whether all her sorrows and wrongs are not enough to justify that act of hers. Edward IV, Elizabeth, Rivers, Dorset, Hastings—all are the recipients of her curses as she calls upon God to punish her adversaries. Especially she curses Gloucester: may the "worm of conscience" afflict him; may only "deep traitors" be his friends; may he be deprived of restful sleep. She concludes by making much of his deformity as a sign that hell and the evil forces of nature have marked him for their own. Richard tries to turn the curses back on her. And when Elizabeth states that Margaret has indeed cursed herself, this "Poor painted [imitation] Queen," as she bitterly calls herself, concentrates her attack upon her royal successor and the Woodville faction in general, whom she identifies as upstarts. Ironically, Gloucester interposes an endorsement of her denunciation of Dorset and boasts that his own exalted status will prevent his fall. When Buckingham tries to restrain Margaret, she voices words of praise for him: since he had not fought against the Lancastrians, her curses do not apply to him. But Buckingham rejects her offer of "league and amity." It is then that Margaret warns him to beware of Richard upon whom "Sin, death, and Hell have set their marks." Finally she leaves.

Gloucester now sanctimoniously voices sympathy for Margaret and expresses regret for his part in having opposed her. When Elizabeth says that she is blameless, he points out that she has benefited by Margaret's downfall, whereas Richard himself had merely sought to help others. Again he makes reference to his brother Clarence, saying that Clarence suffers for the same reason and asking God to pardon those who are responsible for his brother's imprisonment. Lord Rivers sarcastically remarks on this "virtuous and Christianlike conclusion," but Richard remains unperturbed. His aside, however, makes it clear that, in praying for the forgiveness of any responsible for Clarence's fate, he avoided cursing himself.

Catesby enters and summons the group to the king's chambers. All except Richard leave, and in the final soliloquy he gloats over his villainy. He has furthered his ends by fooling Hastings, Derby, and Buckingham into believing that the queen's family is behind Clarence's ruin. When they try to persuade him to seek revenge, he puts on a saintly air and talks of returning good for evil. A fitting conclusion to this villainous speech is the entry of the two murderers whom he has hired to get rid of Clarence. They have come for the warrant which will provide for their admission to the Tower. He instructs them to feel no pity and not to be swayed by Clarence's eloquence. The first murderer assures Richard that they are doers, not talkers, and will carry out his instructions. They are instructed to go to Richard's home at Crosby Place after the deed is done.

Commentary

In the first scene, reference was made to the bitter quarrel between the members of the Woodville faction, headed by Queen Elizabeth, and high-ranking Yorkists, as well as such aristocrats as Lord Hastings, lord chamberlain to King Edward IV. Now the quarrel itself is dramatized, recrimination following recrimination. The extent of the dissension is indicated by the fact that the Countess Richmond, wife of Lord Stanley, Earl of Derby, detests Elizabeth as an upstart. It may be noted here that the countess is the mother of the Earl of Richmond, who will prove to be Richard's nemesis. But it is the Duke of Buckingham, in a sense an outsider as regards this quarrel, who clearly leans toward Gloucester, despite Queen Margaret's ominous warning. We may expect Richard to make the most of this turn of events.

A kind of suspense is achieved when Buckingham reports that the king's health seems to have improved and that Edward has moved to establish peace within his realm. Nothing is farther from Richard's wishes, to be sure; and he is relentless in his attack upon those who stand in his way. As the accomplished dissembler, he is no less effective than he was in the previous scene. Now he presents himself as the loyal, selfless subject of Edward IV opposed to those who are criminally ambitious—those whom he describes as "wrens" (the smallest of English birds) who "make prey where eagles dare not perch." The eagle, of course, is a symbol of royalty. Richard thus makes tacit reference to himself; and so when he confidently states that he is not one headed for catastrophe, since he was "born so high" (in contrast to the others present in this scene). Were not the Yorkists descended from Edward III? Once more Richard's feigned religiosity is apparent, as when he swears "By holy Paul" and "By God's holy mother." It is a good touch also to have him voice sympathy and Christian forgiveness for Queen Margaret, who has scathingly denounced him.

Especially important is the role of Queen Margaret, who makes her first appearance in this scene. As has been pointed out in the discussion of her character above, actually she had died in 1482. Even if she had survived, the appearance of this one-time champion of the house of Lancaster among her enemies is quite fantastic. Nevertheless, her role is a key one. Margaret immediately establishes herself as a terrifying chorus whose violent curses directed first to her successor, Queen Elizabeth, then repeatedly to Richard, and finally to Elizabeth's relatives, reveal her as a symbolic figure, "the doom of the House of York." At one point she denounces Richard as an "abortive, rooting hog." The reference is to his premature birth—evidence of his unnaturalness and perhaps the cause of his deformity —and to Richard's armorial crest, upon which was depicted a boar. The adjective "rooting" is meant to describe his destructive activities.

In this play, which has been called the most religious that Shakespeare ever wrote, it is Margaret who repeatedly emphasizes the major theme: God's inexorable justice visited upon those guilty of the heinous sins of murder and perjury. Richard is first to be charged with unforgivable crime —the murder of Henry VI and Edward, Prince of Wales. And when Gloucester, recalling that his brother Clarence had foresworn himself by deserting Warwick, hypocritically implores that Christ forgive the sinner, Margaret bitterly calls for God's vengeance upon Clarence. Once more it is a mathematical kind of justice—the logic of which so appealed to Elizabethans—that she emphasizes when she summarizes her indictment of those responsible for the fall of the house of Lancaster. Her speech begins with these words addressed to Elizabeth:

> For Edward thy son, which now is Prince of Wales
> For Edward my son, which was Prince of Wales.
>
> (200-201)

It ends with her fervent prayer:

> That none of you may live your natural age.
> But by some unlooked accident cut off!
>
> (213-14)

In the course of the subsequent action, vengeance will indeed be visited upon each of those whom Margaret indicts.

But what of this aged former queen who has suffered and is suffering so much? Richard reminds her of her own offenses—how she had deserved the Duke of York's curses and how the young Duke of Rutland had been killed by the Lancastrians. Familiar as they were with the history of these times, members of Shakespeare's audiences would not fail to recall that Henry VI, although widely praised for his piety, was the grandson of a regicide and usurper, one who had seized the throne from the lawful, anointed King Richard II, from which deed all these troubles had stemmed. Did not the Bible say that the crimes of the father would be visited upon the children even unto the third generation?

ACT I – SCENE 4

Summary

The action now takes place in the Tower of London, toward which, as we learned at the end of scene iii, the murderers repair. The imprisoned Clarence tells Brakenbury, the Lieutenant of the Tower and therefore his jailer, about the miserable night he has endured. He explains that he thought that he was on a ship bound for Burgundy when his brother Gloucester induced him to come and walk the deck. As they talked of their adventures during the recent wars, Richard stumbled and, when Clarence tried to help him, Clarence himself was struck by his brother and fell overboard. The royal prisoner then gives a most vivid description of his dream of drowning, which was continued to the point where his soul was being ferried over the "melancholy flood" of the River Styx by the ferryman Charon. There he met Warwick, whom he had betrayed, followed by the ghost of Prince Edward, whom he had stabbed at Tewkesbury. Clarence hears himself described as "false, fleeting, perjured Clarence." Convinced that he was in hell, Clarence remembers all the deeds which might have sent him there. He prays God to punish him if He must, but to spare his wife and children.

As Clarence sleeps, Brakenbury, moved by the recital, reflects on the sorrow of princes who, despite their high rank, often feel "a world of restless care," as do lesser folk. He is interrupted by the two murderers. They show their warrants and are left in charge of the sleeping prince, while the lieutenant goes back to the king to resign his commission.

The murderers discuss killing Clarence while he sleeps, but the mention of "judgment" arouses the conscience of the second murderer. It is the fear that he will face damnation despite the warrant to perform the deed received from Richard. In contrast, the first murderer is obviously one who will dare damnation to earn the promised monetary reward. At the mention of that reward, the second murderer finds that his conscience no longer is an impediment. As the two are talking about the inconveniences of conscience and holding a kind of dialogue between conscience and the devil, they finally decide to strike Clarence over the head and then drop him into a butt of malmsey wine. Clarence awakes and calls for a cup of wine. Grimly ironical, the first murderer replies: "You shall have wine enough, my lord, anon"—that is, immediately.

In the colloquy that follows, Clarence learns that these are his executioners, and is first led to believe that they have been sent on the orders of King Edward to put to death one guilty of treason. He is eloquent in his own defense and attempts to dissuade the murderers, but they remain adamant. They remind him of his heinous crimes of perjury and murder, for (we now learn) he had joined his brother Richard in killing Prince Edward. Clarence declares that he had acted solely on behalf of his brother Edward, who therefore is quite as deep in sin as is Clarence himself. In this exchange, the royal prisoner refers repeatedly to his brother, meaning Edward, but soon learns, to his utter dismay, that the determined first murderer uses the term to refer to Gloucester. Again Clarence invokes God's name, urging his adversaries to relent. And again the second murderer wavers, even warning Clarence that the first murderer is about to strike him. But it is too late. Clarence is stabbed several times, and his murderer leaves with the duke's body, which he will throw into the "malmsey butt within." Now the second murderer is indeed conscience-stricken. The scene ends with the actual murderer accusing the accessory of cowardice and threatening to denounce him to Richard.

Commentary

This is a highly dramatic scene which contains much that is doctrinally and thematically important. Clarence's long speeches addressed to Brakenbury follow the tradition established by that popular collection of tragical histories in verse entitled *Mirror for Magistrates*, a work of accretion, the first edition of which appeared in 1559. Other editions followed in 1571, 1574, 1575, 1578, and 1587. (Cf. Lily B. Campbell, *Shakespeare's Histories: Mirrors of Elizabethan Policy*, San Marino, California, 1947, Chap. XVI.) Significant is the fact that the *Mirror* dealt primarily with English history from the reign of Richard II to the fall of Richard III at Bosworth's Field in 1485. It mirrors the instability of fortune and the punishment of vice, and, as we are told in one of the prose introductions, seeks "by example of other's miseries to dissuade all men from sins and vices." Successively the ghosts of fallen great persons tell their stories in long monologues, announcing their own guilt and usually stressing the theme of divine vengeance. In the development of this theme in Shakespeare's play, the supernatural, including portentous dreams, has an important place. In Clarence's terrifying dream appears the ghost of Warwick to denounce him as "false, fleeting, perjured Clarence."

Clarence's first long speech (9-33) is, of its kind, quite superior as poetry. If indeed Shakespeare still writes a predominantly Marlovian type of verse, the lines of which are usually end-stopped, he incorporates specific details in a way hardly characteristic of Marlowe, so that every line evokes a picture. Notable is the way in which the poet builds up to climaxes: "All scattered in the bottom of the sea" (28) and "And mocked the dead bones that lay scattered by" (33). Following each the rhythm of Clarence's lines changes appropriately.

The second long speech (43-63) contains Clarence's outburst of self-incrimination, leaving no doubt of his particular guilt. But he remains a human being and invites our sympathy. Unselfishly he thinks of his family and courageously he meets his violent death. Nevertheless, one must not lose sight of the fact that he is a grievous sinner who must endure the inevitable punishment of a just God in accordance with the orthodox doctrine which informs this play.

The two murderers are exceptionally well individualized. Their prose dialogue is most realistic and packed with grim humor. Note, for example, the second murderer's speech in which he indicts conscience on the grounds that "it makes a man a coward" (137-48). When asked scornfully if he is afraid, he replies: "Not to kill him, having a warrant for it, but to be damned for killing him, from which no warrant can defend us" (112-14).

The question is one regarding vengeance in general. The proper authority, functioning as God's minister on earth, as he is called in Romans 13, can and must execute public justice; but no one, however exalted his position, can rightfully execute private revenge. This is the import of Clarence's argument as he seeks to dissuade the murderer:

> Erroneous vassal! The great King of Kings
> Hath in his tables of His law commanded
> That thou shalt do no murder. And wilt thou then
> Spurn His edict, and fulfill a man's?
> Take heed, for He holds vengeance in His hands,
> To hurl upon the heads that break his law.
>
> (200-205)

The second murderer, to whom these lines were addressed, has an answer:

> And that same vengeance doth He hurl on thee,
> For false swearing, and for murder too.
>
> (206-07)

Clarence argues that these crimes were committed for Edward's sake, and that the king is therefore quite as deep in sin as is Clarence himself. He goes on:

> If God will be revenged for this deed,
> Oh, know you yet, He doth it publicly.   (221-22)

— that is, the king will observe the due process of law.

And then the doomed Clarence learns that these murderers serve his brother Gloucester, whose motive is criminal ambition, not revenge, public or private. What conclusions are to be drawn from all this? There is no doubt that Clarence deserved extreme punishment. But how to account for the fact that two murderers hired by an arch-villain perform the deed? Is this an example of God's inexorable justice? According to Tudor theory it was exactly that. Just as God may permit the rebel to rage in order to punish a sinful ruler, so may He use even such sinners as Richard and, at a different level, the hired assassins, to execute his justice against Clarence. They function as the Scourge of God. But, still in keeping with the larger concept of justice, they will be scourged in turn ultimately. In the previous scene Margaret had implored God to punish Clarence: her prayer has been answered. At the end of this scene, the second murderer acknowledges the fact that the two have "most grievous murder done," and he will have no share in the promised reward, the thought of which earlier had led him to spurn the urgings of conscience. There is, then, no contradiction, no inconsistency, here in the sustaining of the play's major theme.

ACT II – SCENE 1

Summary

The scene shifts to the palace. King Edward, whom we meet for the first time, has called the queen and members of the family and court to his bedside. He commands them to be reconciled to one another and to swear to refrain from enmity in the future. Successively Rivers, Hastings, the queen herself, Dorset, Buckingham solemnly take the sacred vow. Only Gloucester is absent "To make the perfect period of this peace," to use the king's words. But Richard makes his appearance immediately, wishing all present "a happy time of day." When he is told that all differences have been settled and that hate has now given place to "fair love," he pronounces the king's action to be "a blessed labor" and, insisting that he desires "all good men's love," declares himself to be devoted to all present. He concludes by piously thanking God for his humility.

When Queen Elizabeth, anxious that the new-found amity be extended to all members of the court group, urges the king to pardon Clarence,

Richard delivers the shocking news that Clarence is dead: Edward's reprieve had arrived too late. Almost at once Derby enters and begs that his servent's life, declared forfeit for murder, be spared. This request fills Edward with remorse as he contrasts the zeal of a master for a servant with the neglect of Clarence. Especially he remembers all that Clarence had done for him, and he blames not only himself but all others present, none of whom had interceded in Clarence's behalf. Edward concludes that he and the rest have rendered themselves subject to God's punishment. Calling Hastings, the lord chamberlain, to accompany him, he leaves with the queen and some members of the court.

Gloucester promptly takes advantage of the occasion to draw Buckingham's attention to what he describes as the guilty looks of the queen's relatives. He charges that they had urged the king to put Clarence to death, and he predicts that "God will avenge it." He then asks Buckingham to join him in comforting Edward.

Commentary

Conflict is, of course, the essence of drama. In Act I Richard emerged ahead in his conflict with a society, indeed with the state itself. Now events occur which suggest that the odds have shifted. The ailing king appears to have quieted the quarreling factions, as the first two lines of the scene make clear. This is a solemn occasion for all concerned, for England's king is on his deathbed. As Tudor political philosophy had it, the subject, whatever his rank, is to the ruler as is the child to his parent. Vows made to a king are especially sacred, thus the import of Edward's admonition beginning "Take heed you dally not before your King" (13-15). Note that both Rivers and Hastings are vehement in their avowals, and so the rest. But most eloquent is Buckingham, who had been held blameless by the rapacious Queen Margaret. Each has committed himself irrevocably, inviting God's punishment if the oath is violated.

The ethical significance of Clarence's death is now made crystal clear: inexorable justice is operating once more. Practically all of the characters in this scene deserve or will deserve divine punishment. And in this connection, note that the last two lines of King Edward's long reply to Derby are portentous:

> O God, I fear Thy justice will take hold
> On me and you, and mine and yours for this!

How ironical are Richard's words addressed to Buckingham, spoken as they are by the one who is directly responsible for Clarence's death: "God will revenge it" (138).

Score another point for the villain-hero, that master dissembler who had intercepted the orders countermanding the execution of Clarence. So far from amity flourishing, the split is greater than before. The immediate point is that God's justice continues to be administered and Richard continues to function as His scourge. Significantly, it is Buckingham who has the final line. If we had any doubts heretofore, we now know that he has committed himself to serve Richard for his own purposes.

ACT II – SCENE 2

Summary

In a mood consistent with Edward's remorse and sorrow, this scene introduces the young son and daughter of Clarence, who suspect that their father is dead. They are talking to their grandmother, the Duchess of York, who is weeping not, as they think, for Clarence but for the mortally sick king. Richard has succeeded in convincing these children that Edward, influenced by Queen Elizabeth, is responsible for their father's death. He has assured them of his devotion to them and has told them to rely on him. Richard's mother, fully aware of her son's intent, laments that she has given birth to so foul a monster. But Clarence's young son finds it impossible to believe that his uncle could be such a villain.

Queen Elizabeth, grief-stricken and all disheveled, enters. All now learn that King Edward is dead, and a general chorus of grief ensues. The duchess weeps for her husband and two sons, the queen for her husband, and the children for their father. Dorset and Rivers try to comfort the queen, Rivers immediately introducing the comforting thought of her son, who should be summoned from Ludlow immediately to be crowned.

Gloucester comes in with Buckingham, Derby, Hastings, and Ratcliff. He is in good form as usual, offering words of comfort to Queen Elizabeth and asking his mother's blessing. Buckingham suggests that the Prince of Wales be brought from Ludlow with a small group of followers and succeeds in convincing Rivers that a larger group might lead to a new outbreak of trouble. All the while, Richard presents himself as one only too ready to cooperate in carrying out the will of the others. All except Buckingham and Gloucester retire to discuss the proposal. The exchange between the two makes clear the fact that Richard has been letting Buckingham play the man of action and do the talking and that there is an arrangement for them "to part the Queen's proud kindred from the king." They set forth for Ludlow.

Commentary

The first part of this scene serves to point up the tragedy that has befallen the house of York. There is much that is formally ritualistic here, and the pronounced religious tone is evident enough. Thus one of Clarence's children, having been led to believe that King Edward was directly responsible for his father's death, says:

> God will avenge it, Whom I will importune
> With daily prayer to that effect.   (14-15)

And Dorset, seeking to comfort his bereaved mother, Elizabeth, voices the orthodox views on Christian forbearance in the passage beginning "God is displeased That you take with unthankfulness His doing" (89-95). In this way, the major theme is kept to the fore.

To some it may seem that the Duchess of York takes a rather heartless attitude toward the death of Clarence when she explains that she laments "the sickness of the King," not the loss of her other son: "It were lost sorrow to wail one that's lost" (11). But this is consistent with Christian teaching, certainly with that which flourished in Shakespeare's England. Elsewhere in Shakespeare, one finds expression of the idea that life is a loan from God to be repaid when He demands it, and Dorset's speech addressed to Elizabeth repeats this idea. Undue grief for the dead was thought to imply a question of God's dealings with mortals. Moreover, Edward is not only the duchess's son; he is the king, and she is one of his subjects. What happens to Edward is a matter of public concern; the welfare of the state is involved. And, of course, all this adds to the religious tone.

Queen Elizabeth, "with her hair about her ears," is the very symbol of tormented grief. Her first speech provides a good example of the highly mannered, rhetorical style to which reference was made in the critical introduction above. This is typical of early Shakespeare, reflecting the influence of Seneca—at least the Seneca of the popular stage. In this connection, note the sententious elements in her speech, as when she exclaims:

> Why grow the branches now the root is withered?
> Why wither not the leaves, the sap being gone?   (41-42)

Senecan also is the exchange between the children and the two queen-mothers beginning "Oh, for our father, for our dear lord Clarence!" (72-79) These lines provide an example of *stichomythia*, which has been defined in the introduction.

Edward did not die a violent death, as did Clarence. Nevertheless, his death is part of the larger pattern: the grievous sinner cannot escape God's justice.

While tracing the dominant theme in *Richard III*, we must not ignore the skill with which Shakespeare delineates the character of Gloucester, who early and late holds the interest of all readers and members of an audience, whether or not they be interested in or concerned about the major theme of the play. Consistently this Machiavellian villain who rejects God gives us a good example of his cynical humor in his aside after his mother complies with his expressed wish that she give him her blessing.

The action continues to rise and an element of suspense is introduced in this scene. Rivers urges Queen Elizabeth to see to it that her son be crowned as soon as possible. Obviously, the coronation would be a great setback for the ambitious Richard, and might make it impossible for him to advance his evil fortunes. But Richard is never to be underestimated. He has taken steps to forestall the coronation and to remove the prince from the protection and influence of the queen's family. And Gloucester, who more than once has made reference to his simplicity and humility, grossly flatters his dupe, Buckingham, speaking of himself as a child willingly guided by this "oracle" and "prophet." At his level, let it be remembered, Buckingham is no less selfishly ambitious than Richard.

ACT II — SCENE 3

Summary

Three London citizens meet in a street and discuss the news of the king's death. Each has a clearly marked character. The first citizen is optimistic, almost buoyantly so. The second citizen is not so confident as he voices the traditional fear that change, particularly in matters relating to the state, are not usually for the better. He places his hope in the conviction that Edward IV's young son will be guided wisely by his counselors. The third citizen, however, is a thoroughgoing pessimist. He predicts "a troublesome world," especially because the new king is "in his nonage," that is, his boyhood. When Henry VI, then a mere child, came to the throne, virtuous uncles were at hand to give him prudent counsel. Not so now, for "full of danger is the Duke of Gloucester," and "the Queen's kindred [are] haughty and proud." In a series of sententious lines, he concludes that it is wise to fear the worst. All three, instructed to appear before the justices, depart together.

Commentary

This short scene allows for the necessary passage of time for the arrests of which we learn in the next scene. But its chief importance is to emphasize the fact that (as in all Shakespeare's chronicle history plays) the state is the real protagonist in the larger sense; for it is the welfare of England, the well-being of all subjects, that is of first importance. When the sententious third citizen exclaims "Woe to that land that's governed by a child," he is para-phrasing Ecclesiastes 10:16 ("Woe to thee, O land, when thy king is a child..."). The text is voiced twice by Buckingham in Edward Hall's chroni-cle history of these events (1548) and had long since become proverbial. Note that the third citizen expresses the conviction that, if England is to suffer as a result of Edward IV's death, it deserves to suffer, since all things are in God's hands (36-37). This constant reference to God is a tacit re-minder that His justice always is operative, whatever the conditions may be, and particularly so with reference to the state. The "virtuous uncles" of Henry VI (21) were the Dukes of Bedford and Gloucester, who prosecuted the war against France. The commoners of England, it is clear, are aware of the bitter rivalries at court, rivalries which may lead to violence and de-struction at this time of the succession. And they can only voice their hopes and fears and remain passively obedient.

ACT II – SCENE 4

Summary

The archbishop announces that the party bringing the young prince will arrive within a day or so. This begins a conversation about the appearance of the prince, whom the mother, grandmother, and younger brother are anx-ious to see. The queen hopes that he has grown; his grandmother has heard, however, that the nine-year-old duke has almost overtaken him. The boy hopes this is not so, for his uncle Gloucester has told him that "small herbs have grace, great weeds grow apace." The old duchess retorts that, since Richard grew slowly, if this were so he should be full of grace, about which she ironically expresses her doubts. The precocious boy remembers a story he has heard that Richard was born with all his teeth, and must have grown fast, since he could "gnaw a crust at two hours old." A biting jest indeed for a boy of nine! Since getting teeth early was also believed to be a sign of villainous disposition, the two women recognize the boy's shrewd-ness, and his mother rebukes him for being mischievous.

Dorset enters with the upsetting news that Lord Rivers, Lord Grey, and Sir Thomas Vaughan have all been sent to Pomfret Castle, imprisoned by the "mighty dukes," Gloucester and Buckingham. Dorset does not know what accusation had been brought against them. The queen, rightly seeing the downfall of her house, bemoans the tyranny that preys on the young king's innocence. The Duchess of York cries out against yet another indication of the dreadful war of blood against blood and self against self for the crown. The queen takes the boy to sanctuary, led by the Archbishop of York, who gives the Great Seal into her keeping.

Commentary

The young Duke of York's instinctive dislike and distrust of his uncle is a prelude to the news that Gloucester has struck his first blow against the princes. Having seen to it that the queen's son and brother, as well as Sir Thomas Vaughan, constant and faithful attendant on young Edward from the new king's infancy, are imprisoned in Pomfret Castle, Richard now has all active power in his hands. That Pomfret should be the place of imprisonment is in itself especially ominous, for there Richard II and many others had met their deaths.

This scene derives, at least ultimately, from More's account, in which it is stated that the archbishop had been roused "not long after midnight" by a messenger from Lord Hastings, who had reported that Gloucester and Buckingham had taken young Edward V, then on his way to London, from Stony Stratford back twelve miles to Northampton. It has been argued that "if the Archbishop knew that the young king had been carried back to Northampton, he must also have known that the lords who accompanied him were sent to prison." Long since it has been pointed out, however, that "Shakespeare deviates a little from historical truth in order to attain dramatic effect: he makes the messenger arrive *during* the archbishop's interview with the queen, whereas, actually, it was the news that the messenger brought that led to the interview" (*Variorum*, p. 184). As Shakespeare dramatizes the event, one must assume that the news of the return to Northampton made the archbishop so apprehensive that he hurried to the queen bearing the Great Seal, without which the highest acts of state could not be ratified formally.

ACT III – SCENE 1

Summary

A flourish of trumpets announces the arrival of the young prince, followed by Gloucester and Buckingham, Cardinal Bourchier, Catesby, and others. From the first the prince is melancholy. He wants (that is, lacks) "more uncles" to welcome him and is not convinced when Richard implies that they were false friends from whom he is better protected. The lord mayor, appropriately attended, enters and greets the uncrowned king. The youth responds courteously and then again complains about not seeing his mother and brother.

As the prince further complains about the absence of Hastings, that lord enters with the news that the queen has taken the young Duke of York into sanctuary, he knows not why. Buckingham tells Cardinal Bourchier to fetch the boy by force if necessary, but that dignitary objects to violating the "holy privilege." Buckingham overcomes the objections by reasoning that the law of sanctuary is not valid in such a "gross" age and that the boy is too young and innocent to need or ask for sanctuary in any case. The cardinal is easily convinced, and he sets out, accompanied by Hastings.

The prince asks his uncle where he will stay until the coronation. Richard advises him to resort to the Tower, the thought of which does not appeal to the prince. Since Julius Caesar was then credited with having built the Tower of London, the prince and Gloucester engage in a dialogue concerning Julius Caesar and the nature of reputation and fame.

Hastings and the cardinal return, bringing with them the young Duke of York, who, after greeting his brother and referring to his father's death, quickly takes the opportunity to flout his uncle. He refers to his own growth, trying to make Richard repeat the compromising speech about the young king's idleness referred to in the previous scene. He next begs a dagger from his uncle and jests about the possibility of Richard's giving him his sword. This sharp speech culminates in the boy's joking allusion to his uncle's crooked shoulders. Buckingham expresses admiration for the young duke's precosity, but Richard apparently ignores it. He urges Edward and his brother to leave for the Tower. Meanwhile, he will entreat Elizabeth, the queen-mother, to join them there. The duke demurs, saying that he will not sleep quiet in the place where his uncle Clarence had been murdered. Edward, however, says that he fears no uncles dead. And to Gloucester's "nor none that live, I hope," he retorts "and if they live, I hope I need not fear." His thoughts, obviously, are about Lord Rivers. The children go unhappily to the Tower.

Buckingham again comments on the wit of the young duke, suggesting that he may have been incited by his mother to taunt Richard. Richard's reply, "No doubt...he is all his mother's," brings out at once the contrast between the two children and Gloucester's deep hatred of the queen-mother and her faction. Buckingham calls Catesby over and takes the initiative in sounding him out as to the possibilities of winning Hastings over to their side. Catesby suggests that Hasting's great loyalty to Edward IV will keep him from doing anything against the prince, and that Stanley will do whatever Hastings does. Buckingham sends him off to sound out Hastings and summon him to the Tower to join the counsel in discussing the coronation. It is Richard who gives Catesby the final order: "Shall we hear from you, Catesby, ere we sleep?"

After Catesby has left, Buckingham wonders what will be done with Hastings if he proves unwilling to go along with their plots. As if there were no possible question, Richard says, "Chop off his head," and reminds Buckingham to ask for the earldom of Hereford and related properties when Richard becomes king. Buckingham replies that he will indeed claim the promised reward, and the two retire to sup and arrange their plans.

Commentary

In this scene we witness the always energetic Gloucester preparing for the removal of obstacles in his quest for the crown. The chief obstacles are, of course, the uncrowned boy, King Edward, and his brother, the Duke of York. But there are also Lords Stanley and Hastings to be considered, and they must be dealt with. Richard is nothing if not the capable executive. He leaves to the well-schooled Buckingham the task of making suggestions and arguments so that Richard himself usually appears as one seeking to be helpful and cooperative. Buckingham provides an interesting contrast to Catesby, who also serves Richard. Catesby awaits only instruction to carry out an order without question; he requires no special handling. But Buckingham is vain of his talents and responds readily to Gloucester's flattery, as when he is called "my thought's sovereignty" — i.e., king of my thoughts (2). He possesses considerable political ability and the powers of subtle contrivance. Sophistry characterizes his words to young Edward beginning "Sweet Prince, the untainted virtue of your years/ Hath not yet dived into the world's deceit" (7-15) and his reply to the cardinal, whom he finds to be "too senseless obstinate,/ Too ceremonial and traditional" (44-56). In pursuit of his own goal, he is not troubled much by conscience. When Richard informs him that, if Hastings does not prove pliable his head must be chopped off, Buckingham thinks only of the promised reward: the earldom of Hereford, together with all "movables" (goods) which had been confiscated by King Edward IV.

Of interest also are the contrasting characters of the two royal brothers. Edward is grave, thoughtful, conscious already of his responsibilities; thus his rebuke to the Duke of York: "A beggar, brother?" (112) The ironic dialogue about Julius Caesar and the nature of fame leads him to express his own ambition to win renown: "I'll win our ancient right in France again ..." (92). The implication is that, if he be permitted to survive and to rule England, internecine conflict would no longer occur; rather, the ruler would win fame in fighting a foreign enemy. In the polemical literature of the age, the horrors of civil war were frequently contrasted with the glory to be won in a conflict legitimately waged against the country's foe. Tacitly suggested also is that Edward's villainous uncle will achieve not fame but infamy in the annals of history.

The Duke of York is a "parlous boy" (154), that is, dangerously cunning from the points of view of Buckingham and Richard. He is "bold, quick, ingenious, forward, capable [intelligent]." Like his royal brother he is deeply suspicious of his uncle Gloucester. Indeed, his instinctive dislike and distrust, established in the previous scene, is emphasized here. When he asks for his uncle's dagger, he means much more than that involved in a natural request made by a pert, forward lad; he intimates that Gloucester should be rendered harmless by being disarmed. Farther along in the dialogue he wittily alludes to Richard's deformity and tacitly calls him a fool. This is introduced with the play upon the word *bear* (127). "Because I am little, like an ape/ He thinks that you should bear me on your shoulders" (130-31). In Buckingham's words, "With what sharp-provided wit he reasons!"

In this scene, Shakespeare arouses the tragic emotions of pity and fear for the boy king and his brother. He does so particularly by means of the double meanings typically found in Richard's discourse, as when he says "A greater gift I'll give my cousin" (115), and in his ominous asides: "So wise so young, they say, do not live long" (79) and "Short summers lightly have a forward spring" (94). Furthermore, established here are the probable positions of Hastings and Stanley.

The doctrinal element is not absent from this scene. That Buckingham, actually the voice of Richard, should reject the concept of sanctuary as a "holy privilege" and that Edward V is not to Richard a "dread sovereign" underscores the fact that the sins involved are sins against religion, against God—sins which invite His inexorable justice. For in accordance with politico-religious thinking in the Age of Elizabeth, the sovereign was indeed to be dreaded—to be held in awe or "feared" in the Biblical sense. Again let it be remembered that the ruler was accepted as God's lieutenant on earth by the orthodox.

42

ACT III — SCENE 2

Summary

The scene begins with the arrival of a messenger at Lord Hasting's house at four o'clock in the morning. The messenger comes from Lord Stanley, who has had a premonitory dream about "the boar" which destroyed his helmet. Stanley is so disturbed that he wishes Hastings to flee with him to the north. Hastings scorns the advice and sends the messenger back. He knows of the two councils which are to be held; but since he will be in one and his servant Catesby in the other, there can be nothing to fear. Moreover,

> To fly the boar before the boar pursues
> Were to incense the boar to follow us,
> And make pursuit where he did mean no chase. (28-30)

Stanley is instead to rise and go with him to the Tower. As the messenger leaves, Catesby enters and cunningly tests Hastings' loyalty by saying that things will never be right in the kingdom until Richard wears the crown. Hastings remains loyal to the young prince and does not waver in his devotion even when told that his enemies, members of the queen's family, have been put to death at Pomfret. Not even if his life were at stake would Hastings move to prevent the "true descent" of Edward IV's heirs. The wary Catesby, his mission accomplished, sanctimoniously approves Hastings' declaration of loyalty: "God keep your lordship in that gracious mind!" (56)

The confident Hastings now begins to boast of those he will get rid of within a fortnight, relying as he does on the favor of Richard and Buckingham. Catesby encourages this opinion, but his aside makes clear that Hastings has, as it were, pronounced sentence upon himself and that Richard and Buckingham will see to it that Hastings is put to death as a traitor.

Stanley appears, still uneasy, and Hastings reasserts his buoyant confidence. Stanley reminds him that the lords imprisoned at Pomfret had been no less sure of themselves. When he is told that those lords are to be beheaded, he again voices his fears, suggesting that those who are to die may be better men than some who have brought charges against them. When Catesby and Stanley leave, Hastings continues to express his complete confidence in an exchange with a pursuivant whom he had met earlier when on his way to be imprisoned in the Tower. A priest enters and greets him. Hastings thanks him, acknowledges indebtedness for the priest's service, and promises to reward him on the next Sabbath. Buckingham enters and remarks that, unlike his friends at Pomfret, Hastings has no need for a priest

—that is, no urgent need for confession and absolution. Hastings replies that the thoughts of Rivers, Vaughan, and Grey had indeed come to his mind as he talked with the priest. He then asks whether Buckingham is going to the Tower. The latter's reply is sinister enough, although Hastings is unaware of the fact:

> I do, my lord, but long I shall not stay.
> I shall return before your lordship thence.   (120-21)

Commentary

In *Romeo and Juliet,* the romantic tragedy which dates some two years later than *Richard III,* Shakespeare assigns these lines to Romeo near the end of the play:

> How oft when men are at the point of death
> Have they been merry! Which their keepers call
> A lightening before death.   (V.iii.88-90)

"A lightening before death"—that is the theme of this scene in which Hastings is the chief character. He remains merry and confident, unperturbed by the report of Stanley's ominous dream of the boar that razed the helmet. Since Gloucester's crest is the boar, the interpretation of this dream poses no problem: those who stand in Richard's way invite death.

Shakespeare follows Holinshed in identifying Catesby as one of Hastings' servingmen. But already we have learned that Catesby had become dedicated to Richard, whose most recent orders he is now carrying out. As far as Hastings is concerned, the concept of tragedy in this scene is medieval. He is at the top of Fortune's Wheel, supremely confident of his own well-being and future. Stanley's dream, the ironical comments and the aside of Catesby, the appearance of the priest, and Buckingham's sinister remarks—all are either ignored or misunderstood by Hastings. But they indicate that Fortune's Wheel is about to turn once more. He seems to invite disaster when he gloats over the thought of the impending executions of Rivers, Vaughan, and Grey, as well as to predict the downfall of others. Nevertheless, in his unshakable loyalty to Edward IV and to Edward's heir, he appears to be an exemplum of righteousness. By implication, at least, Catesby acknowledges as much when he says: "God keep your lordship in that gracious [holy] mind." Catesby, who is in the process of violating his trust to his master, is not moved by such graciousness. Then why, one may ask, should Hastings be marked for death? The answer is that, as an active adherent to the Yorkist cause he also is guilty. Recall that Queen Margaret had identified him as one of the "standers-by" when her son had been "stabbed with bloody daggers" (I.iii.210-12). All this, therefore, is part of the fulfillment of the curse upon the house of York.

ACT III – SCENE 3

Summary

This scene at Pomfret Castle concludes the story of the queen's relatives. Ratcliff, one of Richard's henchmen, enters leading Rivers, Grey, and Vaughan to death. Rivers protests that he is dying "For truth, for duty, and for loyalty." Grey thinks of the prince and prays that he may be kept safe from this pack of bloodsuckers. As Ratcliff hurries them Rivers speaks again, remembering that Pomfret was the scene of Richard II's murder. Grey thinks of Margaret's curse, and Rivers recalls that she cursed Hastings, Buckingham, and Richard also. He prays in one breath that those curses will be fulfilled, and in the next asks God to consider the blood about to be shed enough to save Elizabeth and the prince. Again enjoined by Ratcliff to hurry, they embrace each other and leave to meet their doom.

Commentary

The careful reader may be surprised to find Ratcliff at Pomfret, which is in Yorkshire, since he appears at the Tower of London in the next scene. Obviously Shakespeare trusted to the imagination of his audience rather than to their geographical knowledge. This, to be sure, is a minor point. There are two major ones to be made. First, it is again made clear that the dethronement and murder of Richard II, a lawful, anointed king, started all these bloody events; for that was the prime action which invited vengeance upon the guilty members of the houses of Lancaster and York. Second, Gloucester, arch-villain though he is, continues to be the immediate instrument of divine justice. Grey acknowledges his own guilt and that of Rivers and Vaughan: all three had been accessories to the murder of Queen Margaret's son.

ACT III – SCENE 4

Summary

This is the meeting at the Tower to which Hastings and Stanley have been summoned to discuss the date of the coronation. The Bishop of Ely suggests the following day, but as Richard is not yet present they hesitate to decide without him. Cunningly, Buckingham asks who is most intimate with Richard. To the bishop's reply that he himself is, Buckingham answers ironically that, unlike faces, hearts remain unrevealed. He then calls upon Hastings, who, confident that he stands high in Gloucester's affections, offers to speak for him. At that very moment Gloucester enters, and Buckingham is careful to let him know what Hastings had said.

For no apparent reason other than unusually high spirits, Richard begs the bishop to send for some fine strawberries Richard had seen in his garden. When the bishop leaves, Richard calls Buckingham aside to report that Hastings will never consent to oppose the coronation of the prince. The two leave the stage. Lord Stanley (called Derby in this scene) expresses the opinion that the coronation should be postponed until the next day. The bishop returns, looking about for Richard, and Hastings remarks that Gloucester "looks most cheerfully and smooth"; he is sure that Richard's face reveals the heart of a man who is offended with no one. As Stanley, still uneasy, prays that this is true, Gloucester and Buckingham return.

Richard's mood has changed completely. He demands to know what should be done with those who have planned his death by means of witchcraft. Hastings has the answer: they should be put to death. Drawing back his sleeve to show his withered arm, Richard blames the queen and Mistress Shore. "If they have done this, my gracious Lord—." So Hastings begins. He is not allowed to finish. Gloucester seized upon the conditional *If* and denounces him as the "protector of this damned strumpet," Jane Shore. Hastings further hears himself declared to be a traitor and sentenced to death. Lovel and Ratcliff are ordered to carry out the sentence.

Only Hastings and his executioners remain onstage. In his dying speech Hastings laments the fate of England and regrets his own foolish confidence, his ignoring of ominous portents. Even his horse, clad in ceremonial dress and proceeding at a walking pace, had stumbled three times on its way to the Tower, as if unwilling to carry its master to his death. He remembers the priest, whom he now needs for himself, and the pursuivant who had listened to him gloat over the impending deaths of Rivers, Vaughan, and Grey. He remembers also Queen Margaret's curse.

Catesby abruptly orders him to hurry in order not to delay Gloucester's dinner. Lovel rudely interrupts his final musings on the vanity of man and the shortness of life. Prophesying "the fearfulls't time" for England and the same fate as his for those who smile at him today, Hastings is led off to the block.

Commentary

Buckingham's reply to the Bishop of Ely's questions ("Who knows the Lord Protector's mind herein? Who is most inward with the noble Duke?") sums up the whole extent of Buckingham's deception of others and of Richard's deception of him. It is, then, a prime example of irony in a scene packed with irony.

Richard's superior cunning, no less than his heartlessness, again is dramatized here. With what skill he first presents himself plausibly as the man of good will. "I have been a sleeper," he explains to the "noble lords and cousins" assembled in the Tower (24). Richard a sleeper—he who continues to reveal himself as the most energetic character in the play! The apparently irrelevant bit relating to the strawberries in the bishop's garden, the details of which appear in More's account and in Holinshed, serves Shakespeare's purpose in this connection, for it shows Richard displaying affability and good humor, a careless ease in the midst of his crimes. Little wonder that Lord Hastings should be deceived completely. Hazlitt (*Characters of Shakespeare's Plays*, 1817-18, p. 153) found Hastings' belief that "with no man here he [Richard] is offended" (58) to be one of the "finest strokes in the play," showing as it does "the deep, plausible manners of Richard." One conclusion to be drawn is that Hastings is not to be dismissed as incredibly naive, even if he is not wary as is Stanley. He is one of those individuals who, to borrow a line from another Shakespearean play, "believe men honest who but seem so." In no circumstance must one underestimate Gloucester's skill as a dissembler.

After Edward IV's death, Jane Shore had become Hastings' mistress. It will be recalled that Richard had told Catesby to inform Hastings that his "dangerous adversaries" were to be executed and to bid him "give Mistress Shore one gentle kiss the more" (III.i.185). The attractive daughter of a London goldsmith had indeed been accused of witchcraft, and Hastings' relations with her therefore worked to Richard's advantage. Shakespeare's audiences would not have considered the accusation to be absurd. Although skepticism was widespread, most Elizabethans firmly believed that witches existed and practiced their evil craft.

It need hardly be pointed out again that Richard functions as God's Scourge, for Hastings also was guilty of heinous crime: he was among those who "stood by" when young Edward of Lancaster was stabbed at Tewkesbury. But Richard remains the most grievous sinner. In this instance he takes vengeance into his own hands. Despite his title of lord protector he has no right to act without due process of law; he makes use of a trumped-up charge.

Sir Richard Ratcliff and Lord William Lovel, whom we meet in this scene, survived to join Catesby as Richard's most confidential ministers during the usurper's short reign. The following lines were affixed to the door of St. Paul's Cathedral on July 18, 1484, at the instigation of William Colyngburne:

> The Cat, the Rat, and Lord our dog
> Ruleth all England under a Hog.

Lovel became the king's chamberlain; Catesby speaker in parliament in

1484; Ratcliff sheriff of Westmorland. The last named was probably closest to Richard, as his role in this play suggests.

In his next-to-last speech (98-103), Hastings moralizes in a completely medieval manner. He pictures himself as one among the many who thoughtlessly sought the "momentary grace of mortal men" rather than "the grace of God." Such reflections are typical of those expressed by the tragic figures in Boccaccio's *De Casibus Virorum Illustrium* and its progeny, including the Elizabethan *Mirror for Magistrates,* which is recognized as one of the sources for Shakespeare's *Richard III.*

ACT III – SCENE 5

Summary

Outside the Tower, Richard and Buckingham come in wearing battered, rusty armor. They are engaged in further deception, namely to pretend that they are in terror of an attack on their lives. Richard instructs Buckingham to speak breathlessly and turn pale, and Buckingham replies that he can counterfeit like an experienced actor. Then the lord mayor enters, brought by Catesby. It is now apparent that the act is put on for his benefit. And it is a good act. The mayor witnesses an excited Richard rushing about as he gives incisive orders for defense against enemies who apparently are about to enter. Buckingham plays his role well enough as he exclaims: "God and innocency defend and guard us!" (20) And then Ratcliff and Lovel – "friends" – enter with Hastings' head.

Richard protests his unsuspecting love for Hastings and talks of having confided in him and of being convinced of his innocence in other things, since he frankly acknowledged his relations with Jane Shore. Richard and Buckingham convince the lord mayor that Hastings had plotted to murder the two of them that day, and that only this extreme peril forced them to execute him before the lord mayor arrived. Gloucester is careful to point out that the "peace of England" as well as their own lives was involved. Even after the mayor wholly agrees that Hastings fully deserved death, Richard protests that Lovel and Ratcliff had carried out his intentions too hastily, for he would have liked the lord mayor to hear the traitor's confession so that he, in turn, could reassure the citizens who might misinterpret Richard's action. After further assurances on both sides, the mayor leaves and Gloucester instructs Buckingham to follow and talk to the citizens at an advantageous moment. He is to imply that Edward IV's children are illegitimate, making the most of the late king's alleged notoriety in matters relating to sex. Further, Buckingham is to suggest that Edward himself was illegitimate. But the latter charge is to be handled skillfully, since Edward's mother survives. Buckingham promises to do his work as well as if he were to gain the crown for himself. Thus having taken the necessary steps to prepare the populace to look on himself as the only true heir to the throne, Richard dispatches Lovel to a priest, Doctor Shaw, and Catesby to Friar Penker; both churchmen are to meet him at Baynard's Castle within the hour. Then he leaves to put Clarence's children out of sight so that no one will have access to them.

Commentary

Here Shakespeare prepares for the scene in which Gloucester is offered the crown. Not without significance is the fact that it reveals a wary Richard who does not take into his confidence Buckingham, the man whom he had called his "other self," his "oracle" and "prophet," his "thought's sovereign."

The stage direction, "Enter Gloucester and Buckingham, in rotten armor, marvellously ill-favored" derives from the First Folio (1623). It follows More's account: "And at their coming, himself [Richard] with the Duke of Buckingham stood harnessed in old ill faring briganders [body armor for foot soldiers], such as no man should when that they would vouchsafe to put on their backs except that some sudden necessity had constrained them." Obviously the two have dressed themselves appropriately for the roles they are about to play for the benefit of the Lord Mayor of London—that is, to make him believe that their concern is for the safety of the state.

At the beginning of this scene we find Gloucester schooling Buckingham in the devices and methods of the Machiavellian villain. And Buckingham proves to be an apt pupil. His first speech (5-11) incorporates an interesting bit of dramatic criticism, a commentary on "ham" acting. This play is sufficiently melodramatic, one which lends itself to the rhetorical school of acting with all its excesses. But Shakespeare tells us thus early in his career that he recognizes such acting for what it is. It should be recalled that he himself was an actor as well as a playwright. The student will find relevant a more famous expression of dramatic criticism written by the mature Shakespeare in *Hamlet,* III.ii.1-40.

The lord mayor was Sir Edmund Shaw (or Shaa), who had been elected in 1482. History reports that he indeed took an active part in influencing the succession of the crown on the death of Edward IV. The grateful Richard later made him a privy councilor. Doctor Shaw, whom Gloucester sends for at the end of the scene, was the lord mayor's brother. He was chosen by Richard to preach a sermon at St. Paul's Cross on June 22, 1483, wherein he impugned the validity of Edward IV's marriage to Elizabeth Woodville and even asserted that Edward and Clarence were bastards. More states that both Shaw and Friar Penker were great preachers, but adds that both were "of more learning than virtue, of more fame than learning." He further states that the brothers Shaw were taken into the confidence of Richard and Buckingham after Hastings' death.

ACT III – SCENE 6

Summary

In this very brief scene a scrivener reads the indictment of Hastings which he has just copied so that it may be given a public reading at St. Paul's Cathedral without delay. It had taken him eleven hours to copy the original draft, which must have taken quite as long to prepare. Yet Hastings was executed only five hours ago. Obviously the whole proceeding is unjust. But the scribe departs, commenting that anyone with sense enough to see what is going on must also have sense enough to keep quiet about it.

Commentary

Although the audience already is fully aware of why Hastings has been rushed to his death, Shakespeare chose to emphasize the complete illegality of Richard's action. He does so here by introducing the professional writer of legal documents with his undramatic but pointed speech. Like the lengthy exchange between Clarence and his murderers (I.iv), the scene underscores the fact that the Shakespeare of *Richard III* was especially interested in the theme of revenge and develops it from more than one point of view (cf. Lily B. Campbell, *Shakespeare's "Histories,"* 1947, pp. 312-13). Further, the scrivener gives expression to what has been called "the smothered feeling of indignation that boils in men's minds under a tyrannical dynasty" (C. C. Clarke, *Shakespeare's Characters,* 1863, p. 470). Recall how Shakespeare had used the three London citizens for a comparable purpose in Act II, scene iii.

ACT III – SCENE 7

Summary

Buckingham, returned from haranguing the mob, meets Richard at Baynard's Castle, as had been arranged. Richard asks at once about the reactions of the London citizens. Buckingham reports that they were silent, and goes on to describe his own recital of Edward's engagements to

Lady Lucy and the sister-in-law of the King of France before his marriage. He contrasted Edward's dissimilarity to their father and Richard's likeness, and went on to dwell upon Richard's 'discipline in war, wisdom in peace;... bounty, virtue, fair humility." When they said nothing, he asked the mayor the cause of their silence. The mayor explained that they were used to be spoken to on public matters only by the recorder, the chief legal authority of the City of London. At Buckingham's insistence, the recorder did report Buckingham's argument, but took care to indicate that he was not speaking for himself. When he had finished, ten of Buckingham's paid followers cried, "God save King Richard!" Taking advantage of this, the duke thanked the multitude for their applause, complimented them on their wisdom, and came away. Buckingham explains that the mayor is coming and advises Richard to pretend to be afraid and to answer only after much urging. Richard is to retreat with two churchmen, while Buckingham makes out a case for his holiness. Above all, Richard is to appear most reluctant when he is requested to accept the crown. As a knock at the door is heard, Gloucester goes up the "leads" (the flat roof top) to prepare himself for his latest and perhaps most challenging role.

The mayor and the citizens enter, followed by Catesby, who tells them that Richard, "divinely bent to meditation," is in the company of "two right reverend Fathers," and begs them to return tomorrow or the next day thereafter. Buckingham then directs Catesby to plead with Richard to come and talk with them. While Catesby is gone, the duke takes the opportunity to point up the contrast of Richard's holy occupation with the late king's self-indulgence. He concludes with apparent fear that Richard will not accept the kingship. "Marry, God forbid His Grace should say us nay!" exclaims the mayor. Catesby comes back with the timely message that Richard is apprehensive as to the reason for the delegation which waits upon him. Again Catesby departs to convey Buckingham's reassurance. Just as the duke finishes a comment on the religiosity of men like Richard, the lord protector himself appears above, standing between two clergyman — "Two props of virtue for a Christian Prince," as Buckingham is quick to point out. The duke implores Richard to pardon them for interrupting him in his holy devotions and to listen to their request. The soul of humility, Richard protests that it is he who is at fault for neglecting his friends. Or, he continues, he may have been guilty unwittingly of greater offense. Buckingham follows this cue: Richard's fault is his failure to rescue the country by becoming king at this time of crisis.

In a nicely contrived refusal, Gloucester protests that he would turn away in reproof, except that they might misinterpret his action as "Tongue-tied ambition." He argues that, even though he were to receive the crown as his due, he does not consider himself to be worthy of such greatness; fortunately the young prince, who merits the crown, will receive it in due course. According to Buckingham this nicety of conscience shows his integrity. But, he points out, the prince cannot be the real heir, since Edward married his mother when she was a widow and Edward himself betrothed successively to Lady Lucy and to Bona, sister of the King of France. Thus, only by courtesy is young Edward called the prince; it is Richard's duty to save the kingship from an impure line. The mayor, Buckingham once more, Catesby — all plead with him, but again Richard refuses. Buckingham lauds him for the compassion and nobility that cause him to refuse, but points out that they will not accept the prince in any case, so that Richard's refusal would mean the downfall of the house of York. "Come, citizens," he concludes. "'Zounds! I'll entreat no more." Gloucester greets this with a pious injunction against swearing. When Catesby and one of the citizens urge him to call them back and accept, he does so sorrowfully.

Richard is at pains to make clear that he is accepting the burden on their entreaty, though to do so goes against his conscience. All have returned to the stage now, and Richard tells them that they must shoulder the blame if he does not fulfill his office well, since they urged him to it. Buckingham salutes him with the title of king and promptly suggests that the coronation take place the very next day. "Even when you please," says Richard, "since you will have it so." The arrangements having been concluded, they depart. And Richard returns to his "holy meditations."

Commentary

It may be argued that this final scene of Act III is quite as contrived as is the scene in which Richard woos and wins Lady Anne (I.ii), but in its way it is no less entertaining and theatrically effective. The element of suspense is first introduced. We learn that Buckingham has followed his directions to the letter, but that there is little evidence of popular support for Richard, who inveighs against the citizens, calling them "tongueless blockheads." Yet this apparent setback is really a challenge which, ably assisted by Buckingham and Catesby, he meets successfully. He succeeds in making the mayor and his group believe that the office seeks the man, not the man the office; and that they must assume responsibility accordingly. The arrival of the mayor, *et al.*, and the dramatic appearance of Richard aloft, standing between two bishops, provide first-rate spectacle.

Much already has been said about Richard's superior intellect and cunning; his entire performance in this scene substantiates all that. But Buckingham's accomplishments must not be ignored. As a matter of fact, they add to those of Gloucester, who picked and schooled him in the art of dissembling. Here Buckingham proves himself capable enough to coach his master on how to present himself to the lord mayor and the citizens. The duke has even picked up Richard's trick of using pious oaths, as when he swears "by the holy Mother of Our Lord" (2) which, in context, is deeply ironical.

Once more much is made of the allegation that Edward IV's heirs are not legitimate. Lady Elizabeth Lucy had been one of the king's mistresses, but there is no record of a betrothal, despite Buckingham's assertion that the Duchess of York had been a witness to such a ceremony (180). But all chroniclers agree that Edward was secretly married to Elizabeth Woodville when the Earl of Warwick had already succeeded in obtaining King Louis of France's consent to the marriage of the Lady Bona. These events are dramatized in *Henry VI, Part Three,* III.iii. In accordance with canon law which prevailed before the Reformation, Edward could not have married Elizabeth Woodville legally. But, of course, Edward remained in England and may not have had news of Warwick's action. More telling is the accusation of "loathed bigamy" (189). Bigamy, defined as either marrying two virgins successively, or once marrying a widow, had been declared unlawful and infamous by canon law in the thirteenth century. The reader will recall, however, that Lady Anne was a widow when Richard wooed her. The essential point is that Buckingham marshals every possible argument in an attempt to prove that Richard is the rightful heir to the throne.

It should be understood that when he salutes Richard as "England's royal king" (240), he is using the term *royal* in a very special sense well understood by Shakespeare's generation. It meant that Richard was not merely royal in rank, having been chosen king, but royal in descent. Essential to Richard's purpose is that he be accepted as a lawful king, not as a usurper.

ACT IV – SCENE 1

Summary

This scene opens with a gathering of those whom Richard has wronged and who will suffer far more acutely in the future. Queen Elizabeth, the old Duchess of York, and Dorset enter from one side. They are on their way to visit the princes in the Tower. At the same moment Richard's wife, Anne, Duchess of Gloucester, comes in leading Clarence's young daughter, Lady Margaret Plantagenet. They are also on their way to the Tower.

As they exchange greetings and make their errands known to one another, Brakenbury enters. Queen Elizabeth immediately asks how the princes are. He replies that they are well, but that the king has ordered that they are to have no visitors. The reference to "the King" appalls Elizabeth, and she demands an explanation. Brakenbury begs her pardon and says that he means the lord protector. The women are now thoroughly alarmed, and each protests that she has special right to see the children. But Brakenbury insists that he cannot violate his oath.

The Earl of Derby (Stanley) enters and greets the Duchess of York as "the looker-on of two fair queens," meaning, of course, Elizabeth and Anne. He has come to escort Anne to Westminster for the coronation. Both women express utter horror at the news. When Dorset tries to comfort his mother, she immediately thinks of his danger and commands him to join Richmond in Brittany. Stanley, stepfather to Richmond (to whom he refers as his son), strongly approves of her counsel. The old duchess curses the womb that brought forth Richard.

Stanley urges Lady Anne to hurry. She replies that she would rather be tortured by the ancient method of encircling her brow with red hot steel than be crowned queen. Elizabeth, so far from being offended at Anne, voices words of commiseration. Anne recalls how she had denounced Richard for making her a widow and had uttered a curse on the woman who married him. Now she realizes that she is the victim of her own curse, for she has not known a moment's rest since her marriage because of Richard's "timorous" dreams. She fears that Richard will do away with her. With grief and foreboding the women part, the old duchess wishing for the grave and Queen Elizabeth remaining behind to look back at the rough outline of the Tower. She prays that it will use her young children well, knowing perhaps too well that her entreaty to the stones is useless.

Commentary

This scene is important chiefly because we get the first hint of a possible turn of events which could lead to Gloucester's downfall. Queen Elizabeth says to Dorset, her son:

> If thou wilt outslip death, go cross the seas,
> And live with Richmond, from the reach of Hell. (42-43)

This is the first mention of Henry Tudor, Earl of Richmond. Since Shakespeare was dramatizing history, his audiences knew that Richmond would emerge as Richard's nemesis.

It is not without interest that Stanley, who had married the widow of Owen Tudor and is thus Richmond's stepfather, should endorse Elizabeth's advice so emphatically, although it is he who came to escort Anne to Westminster, where Richard is to be crowned King of England. His behavior here is quite consistent with what history tells us about the Stanleys. They had flourished during the entire period of the Wars of the Roses by shifting loyalties when events seemed so to dictate to their advantage and, in the words of Mr. Paul M. Kendall, "by developing an ambiguity of attitude which enabled them to join the winning side, by exploiting the relative facility with which treason in this age might be lived down, provided it were neither too passionate, too overt, nor too damaging" (*op. cit.*, p. 404).

A turning point in the action is indicated also by the report of Richard's "timorous dreams." Here Shakespeare remained quite faithful to his sources. More reported that Gloucester was "sore wearied with care and watch, rather slumbered than slept, troubled with fearful dreams," and that he would sometimes leap out of bed and run about the chamber. Now, since Richard has been established as a Machiavellian villain devoid of conscience, some explanation is called for. It may be argued that conscience does not bother Richard at all, but rather fear for his own life as he wades through blood on his journey to the crown. Or perhaps Stopford Brooke had the right answer: "Shakespeare, with his belief that in the far background of an evil nature the soul lives, but unknown, unbelieved in by its possessor, shows how it awakens at night when the will sleeps, and does its work on the unconscious man. Then, and only then, conscience stirs Richard. Then, and then only, fear besets him" (*On Ten Plays in Shakespeare*, 1905, p. 115). What is most important is that Richard is suffering the unquiet mind. God's justice now is reaching out to him; his doom has begun even before he wears the coveted crown.

Never does Shakespeare let us forget the dominant theme of the play. Anne, who recalls how she had implored God that Richard's wife be made to suffer, again invites divine vengeance on herself when she exclaims

> Anointed let me be with deadly venom,
> And die ere men can say God save the Queen. (62-63)

Certain other points of lesser significance require comment. Note the ritualistic quality of the duchess' farewell addressed successively to Dorset, Anne, and Elizabeth (92-94)—further evidence that the language is highly rhetorical throughout this play. Queen Elizabeth's outburst beginning "Oh, cut my lace in sunder" (34-36) has been cited as an example of sheer rant. But in Tudor England the busks or corsets worn by fashionable women so tightly controlled their figures that one can understand the queen's need for drastic relief in this moment of great emotion.

When Anne refers to herself as having been made "so young, so old a widow" (73), she means that she had been made old in sorrow. The Duchess of York, indeed an elderly lady, makes reference to her "eighty odd years" (97). Had her husband lived he would have been just seventy-three; the duchess actually was sixty-eight. Shakespeare purposely exaggerated her age as one means of showing how utterly devoid of virtue Richard was. Reverence for age, particularly for an aged parent, was an essential part of the Elizabethan Order picture. At the family level, as at the political level, Gloucester destroys order.

ACT IV – SCENE 2

Summary

With this scene, the climax of the play has been reached. Richard now wears the coveted crown. He enters the palace in pomp, acknowledges Buckingham, his right-hand man, and tries the duke's loyalty to the utmost by inciting him to arrange for the immediate murder of the little princes. The wary Buckingham does not pick up Richard's indirect suggestion, and the newly crowned king is forced to speak openly: he wishes the "bastards" dead. Now Buckingham's reply is circumspect, and when Richard taunts him, he asks leave to consider. Angry, Richard rails against Buckingham, saying he will speak only to unfeeling and thoughtless boys hereafter. He calls a page over to ask if he knows of anyone who would do murder for money. The page suggests one Tyrrell for whom "gold were as good as orators to tempt." While the page goes to get Tyrrell, the king resolves to confide no more in Buckingham.

Stanley enters with the news that Dorset has fled to Richmond. Without appearing to have heard, Richard orders Catesby to spread the rumor abroad that his wife Anne is ill and likely to die. He will make certain that she sees no one. Meanwhile he must find some commoner to marry and dispose of Clarence's daughter; Clarence's son poses no problem, since he is weak-minded. Richard knows that to murder the princes and then to marry their sister Elizabeth, as he hopes to do, involves great risks:

> Uncertain way of gain! But I am in
> So far in blood that sin will pluck on sin.   (64-65)

Stanley, who had moved to one side, did not hear a word of this heartless speech.

Tyrrel enters and arrangements are made to dispose of the princes, whom Richard describes as foes to his rest and his "sweet sleep's disturbers." Buckingham, having considered the king's suggestion about murdering the children, returns. Richard ignores him and talks to Stanley, warning him to take care, since Richmond is his stepson. The duke interrupts with a request for the rewards he has been promised, especially the earldom of Hereford. The king continues to ignore him. He recalls a prophecy of Henry VI that Richmond would be king, and another made by an Irish bard that Richard himself would not live long after he saw Richmond. As Buckingham again interrupts, Richard asks the time and sarcastically compares the duke to the "Jack" on a clock, a mechanical figure that appears to strike the hour—in just such a way does Buckingham keep begging and interrupting Richard's thoughts. Left alone on the stage, the duke now fully understands his position. Recalling the fate of Hastings, he resolves to flee to his manor at Brecknock, without his rewards but at least with his head.

Commentary

In this climactic scene, wherein Richard enters in state amid the sounding of trumpets, preparation is made for the murder of the little princes, the death of Anne, and the plan for Richard to marry his niece, Elizabeth of York. Even more important is the fact that the newly crowned Richard definitely begins his descent on Fortune's Wheel. Crediting Buckingham for making possible this advancement to the throne, the king asks:

> But shall we wear these honors for a day?
> Or shall they last, and we rejoice in them? (5-6)

Anne's account of his "timorous dreams" told us that now Richard was a man beset with fears. Like Macbeth he has murdered sleep. And as he explains to Tyrrel, the princes are foes to his rest and his "sweet sleep's disturbers" (74). His words concerning how "sin will pluck on sin," quoted in the summary, anticipate those of Macbeth, the later Shakespearean tragic hero who also willfully embraced evil, driven first by inordinate ambition and then by fear:

> I am in blood
> Stepped in so far that I should wade no more,
> Returning were as tedious as go o'er.
> (*Macbeth*, III.iv. 136-38)

But Buckingham—the "deep-revolving [artful, cunning] witty Buckingham," who had been so pliant heretofore—can not bring himself to be the agent in the murder of the princes. Such utter heartlessness belongs only to Richard, the self-avowed villain who would outdo Machiavel. But surely this is not the sole answer. Buckingham knows quite as well as does Richard that here indeed is "uncertain way to gain."

For Richard the disaffection of Buckingham is the first serious check in his fortunes. Shakespeare develops this part of the scene with consummate skill. When the king says "Edward lives" (10), he expects the duke to reply that Edward will not survive for long. Instead, Buckingham merely says, "True, noble Prince." And Richard's vehement exclamation,

> Oh, bitter consequence,
> That Edward should live true noble Prince!

implies that, in his opinion, the duke is acknowledging the prince's right to the throne.

The news of Dorset's flight to Richmond is additional evidence that Richard has begun his fall. That he should appear to ignore Stanley, who brought him this latest intelligence, and to proceed to instruct Catesby to spread the rumor that Anne "is sick, and like to die," and then to question and instruct the newly arrived Tyrrel as regards the little princes – all this is only new proof of his capacity for prompt action, for dealing with first things first. Earlier commentators suggested that, in view of Richard's words with Catesby, the king himself planned to poison his wife. However, it has been established that Anne was suffering from tuberculosis and that she had been crushed in spirit by the recent death of her son.

Henry VI's prophecy, recalled by Richard in this scene (98-104), is to be found in *Henry VI, Part III*, IV.iv.68-74. The last of the Lancastrian rulers addressed young Richmond as "England's hope" and spoke of him as one "Likely in time to bless a royal throne." It is irrelevant that Richard himself was not present when the words were spoken, although he speaks of himself as "being by." The main thing is that Richmond is becoming an increasingly important figure, the very mention of whose name is ominous to Richard.

ACT IV – SCENE 3

Summary

In soliloquy Tyrrel describes the murder of the children, which has taken place offstage. He is shaken with horror at the very thought of the bloody deed; even the underlings he had hired to do the actual killing melted with compassion. As he retells the story Dighton and Forrest had told him, he describes for the audience the children, sleeping in each other's arms, a prayer book lying on their pillow. For a moment Forrest became conscience-stricken, but recovered himself to join Dighton in smothering the innocent children. Now the latter is conscience-stricken and filled with remorse as he brings his report to the "bloody King."

Richard is pleased to learn that the princes are dead and buried. He instructs Tyrrel to see him after supper and give him all the details and receive the promised reward. As Tyrrel goes out, Richard summarizes his accomplishments. Clarence's son is in prison, his daughter "meanly... matched" in marriage, the princes are dead, Anne has "bid the world goodnight." And now, since Richmond wants to marry young Elizabeth, daughter of Edward IV, Richard must carry out his plan to marry her first. He is about to leave and to present himself to her as a "jolly thriving wooer," when Catesby enters.

Now the mood changes for Richard. Catesby brings the disquieting news that Ely has fled to Richmond and that Buckingham is gathering forces in Wales. The king is more distressed to hear of Ely's withdrawal. The news, however, instead of crushing him, fills him with a zest for battle. Urging speed, he goes off to muster men for the fight.

Commentary

Authentic classical drama never included scenes of violence on the stage but depended upon reports usually made by a messenger. In Elizabethan drama, notably the Seneca of the popular stage, such scenes were presented in full sight of the audience. But Shakespeare was not influenced by classical tradition here. Surely a matter of good taste was involved. The actual scene of the two children being put to death would have been intolerable even for audiences nurtured on scenes of violence. Actually, Tyrrel's recital is far more effective as a means of arousing the emotions of pity and horror. The utter bestiality of the crime is first emphasized by identifying Dighton and Forrest as "two fleshed villains, bloody dogs"—that is, they are like vicious animals which have been allowed to taste human blood. The description of the victims, "those tender babes," more than suffices for Shakespeare's purpose. Now we are fully ready emotionally to witness the bloody king's downfall. Richard's hurried questions—"...am I happy in thy news?"..."But didst thou see them dead?"..."And buried...?"— and his concern to hear all the details of the murders reveal the state of his anxiety.

In the summary of his accomplishments which precedes the bad news he is to receive, we learn that Anne has died and the king is free to marry Elizabeth of York. Holinshed wrote that she died "either by inward thought and pensiveness, or by infection of poison, which is affirmed most likely." Richard's public reputation, made clear by the discourse of the two London citizens (II.iii) is such that, whatever the true facts may be, he is suspect.

Richard, whose intellectuality is never to be underestimated, is perceptive enough to realize that, in seeking to marry Elizabeth, Richmond aspires to wrest the crown from him. Characteristically, he will not delay wooing her for himself.

John Morton, Bishop of Ely, who was among those present in the Tower of London to make arrangements for the coronation of Edward V (III.iv), fled to join Richmond after plotting with Buckingham, according to Holinshed. News of his flight especially oppresses Richard. But once more the villain-hero proves himself to be a man of action above all else. "My counsel is my shield," he exclaims (56); that is, he will waste no time in deliberation; he will fight.

ACT IV – SCENE 4

Summary

The first part of this scene, a long lament, opens appropriately with old Queen Margaret saying that she has lurked about and watched the waning of her adversaries. She is going to withdraw to France, confident that everything will continue as badly as it has begun. Queen Elizabeth enters with the Duchess of York, weeping for her children. Margaret declares that the loss is a deserved one, since Edward IV, the children's father, had been a principal in the murder of Margaret's son Edward. When Elizabeth asks her when she could sleep when the little princes had been put to death, Margaret replies bitterly: "When holy Harry died, and my sweet son." The duchess, overcome with her own woes, sits down on the ground that has been "made drunk with innocents' blood." Elizabeth wishes that the earth would open up and offer her a grave as easily as it offers her a seat.

Queen Margaret joins them, insisting that her sorrows have precedence, since they are the oldest. She begins a long recital of their joint woes, identifying Richard III as the author. The Duchess of York interrupts to accuse Margaret of being responsible for the deaths of her husband (Richard, Duke of York) and Rutland, one of her sons. Margaret continues, insisting that the deaths of Edward IV, the young princes, and Clarence were debts paid for crimes committed against the house of Lancaster. So died the "beholders of this tragic play," Hastings, Rivers, Vaughan, and Grey – yet Richard, "Hell's black intelligencer," still lives. She utters a prayer that she may yet survive to say "The dog is dead."

Elizabeth recalls Margaret's prophecy that the time would come when she would ask for Margaret's help in cursing Richard, "That bottled spider, that foul-backed toad!" Margaret reminds her of what she had said at greater length about Elizabeth. She compares Elizabeth to a flag borne by a standard-bearer which attracts all shots:

> Where is thy husband now? Where be thy brothers?
> Where are thy children? Wherein dost thou joy?
> Who sues to thee, and cries "God save the Queen"?
>
> (92-94)

Just as Elizabeth once usurped her place as queen, so now she usurps a just share of Margaret's sorrow. When she is about to leave after this tirade, Elizabeth asks her to stay and teach her how to curse. Margaret gives her a grim recipe, and, on further urging, points out that woe will teach Elizabeth what she wants to know. Finally she leaves. The duchess asks why calamity should be so full of words. Elizabeth describes them as "Windy attorneys to their clients woes" which "Help not at all, yet do they ease the heart." The duchess urges Elizabeth to accompany her and smother Richard in the breath of bitter words, since he had smothered Elizabeth's children. At this point the king himself enters, marching, with drums and trumpets.

Richard asks who intercepts his march, whereupon the duchess and Elizabeth attack him for his wrongs. He threatens to drown his mother's words in a flourish of trumpets unless she speaks fair of him. When he shows his impatience, she states that she can think of no single hour, from his birth onward, when he has not been a source of trouble to her. She warns him that, though this is their last meeting, she leaves him with a "heavy curse": may his adversaries crush him: "Bloody thou art, bloody will be thine end." Elizabeth voices her amen to all that the duchess has said, but Richard nevertheless detains her.

When Elizabeth states that she has no more sons for Richard to murder and that her daughters will be "praying nuns, not weeping queens," the king begins his suit for the hand of her daughter Elizabeth, whom he praises as "Virtuous and fair, royal and gracious." Understandably, the queen-mother wonders what new torture Richard has in store for her, and she is provoked into a violent harangue against him. He protests that he means to do her good—he will marry her daughter if she will only forget past grievances and give her consent. Elizabeth is horrified. When he asks how to go about winning the young lady, she bitterly suggests that he has done everything calculated to win a girl's heart—murdered her brothers, her aunt (Anne), her uncles (Clarence and Rivers). Making use of all of his persuasive powers, the king claims that what is done cannot be undone; that he will make up for the loss of the princes, her children, by making her daughter the mother of kings and herself the happy grandmother. Elizabeth obviously is moved by the proposal and agrees to let him know her daughter's mind shortly. This jolly, thriving wooer asks her to bear to the girl his "true love's kiss." Once she has left, however, he refers to Elizabeth with amusement: "Relenting fool, and shallow, changing woman!"

Ratcliff and Catesby come with the news that Richmond, with a powerful navy, is off the coast of Wales waiting for Buckingham's support. Richard orders Catesby to go immediately to the Duke of Norfolk, and Ratcliff to leave for Salisbury. Not until he has upbraided Catesby for delaying does he become aware of the fact that he had neglected to give instructions. Norfolk is to be told to raise the greatest possible "strength and power" and to meet Richard at Salisbury.

Lord Stanley (Derby) enters with the news that Richmond, aroused by Dorset, Buckingham, and Ely, "makes for England, there to claim the crown." Richard asks why should this be, since the royal throne is occupied and no other heir of York survives. He accuses Stanley of planning to rebel against him and fly to his enemies. Stanley protests that he is loyal to Richard and promises to bring his forces down from the north. But the king still does not trust him; he insists that Stanley leave his son George as assurance of his loyalty.

As Stanley leaves, messengers enter successively with news of the revolt of Courtney and the Bishop of Exeter in Devonshire, and of the Guilfords in Kent—that is, risings in the southeast and southwest parts of the kingdom. Furious, Richard strikes the third messenger before he has a chance to speak, and then learns that this time the news is good: Buckingham's forces have been dispersed by flood. Still another messenger reports that Sir Thomas Lovel and Dorset head a force in Yorkshire to the north. But this bad news for Richard is offset by the report that Richmond, his fleet broken up by a tempest and mistrusting those on shore who said they came from Buckingham, has hoisted sail and made for Brittany.

Catesby comes in to say that Buckingham has been captured, but that Richmond had landed with a "mighty power" at Milford. "Away for Salisbury!" exclaims Richard. There is no time to reason: "A royal battle might be won and lost." His final order is that Buckingham be brought to Salisbury.

62

Commentary

In this scene Queen Margaret makes her last appearance and once more, in a completely ritualistic manner, "tells o'er [the Yorkist] woes again" by viewing her own. Her grim forebodings are now being fully realized, and she stresses that mathematical kind of justice which is involved — an eye for an eye, a tooth for a tooth. Probably most would agree with the Duchess of York. Queen Margaret *does* represent "Blind sight, dead life" (26); but she is also the "Brief abstract and record of tedious days" (28), the grim commentator upon bloody deeds who never tires of pointing out the inevitability of God's punishment for grievous sins. As we follow her long discourse, which is briefly interrupted twice, we might well ask as does the Duchess of York: "Why should calamity be full of words?" (126) But Shakespeare forestalls criticism of Margaret's extreme volubility by providing Queen Elizabeth's explanation. In *Henry VI, Part Three,* this same Margaret, having just witnessed the slaughter of her princely son, had said:

> No, no, my heart will burst an if I speak;
> And I will speak that so my heart will burst.
>
> (V.v.58-59)

So in *Titus Andronicus,* the titular hero, who had sought to ransom his captive sons by cutting off his hand as directed and sending it to the emperor, voiced similar thoughts:

> Then give me leave, for losses will have leave
> To ease their stomachs with their bitter tongues.
>
> (III.i.233-34)

And in *Macbeth,* written late in Shakespeare's career, Malcolm counsels the distraught Macduff, who has just learned that his wife and children have been killed:

> Give sorrow words. The grief that does not speak
> Whispers the o'er-fraught heart and bids it break.
>
> (IV.iii.208-09)

The main thing, however, is that in her recital Margaret brings focus upon Richard as the arch-criminal:

> I had an Edward — till a Richard killed him.
> I had a Harry — till a Richard killed him.
> Thou hadst an Edward — till a Richard killed him.
> Thou hadst a Richard — till a Richard killed him.
>
> (40-43)

Granted that later she indicts Edward IV and Clarence, along with Hastings, Rivers, Vaughan, and Grey. But the emphasis remains on the villain-hero who "yet lives" (71), the recipient of Margaret's most vehement curses. Once she leaves the stage, the Duchess of York and Queen Elizabeth read the catalogue of Richard's crimes in ritualistic manner, now addressing the king himself. The force of the Duchess' words

> Bloody thou art, bloody will be thy end.
> Shame serves thy life and doth thy death attend.
>
> (194-95)

strikes home when one recalls her blessing of her son early in the play. Whether present or absent, then, Richard remains the center of interest.

As the king urges the queen-mother to let him marry her daughter, he argues that he will advance her "to the dignity and height of honor, the high imperial type of this earth's glory" (243-44). Here indeed is the key to Richard's own ambition which drove him to extreme cruelty and bloodshed. He was beset with the same "thirst and sweetness of a Crown" which motivated Marlowe's Tamberlaine and which made Macbeth willing "to jump the life to come."

There are similarities between this wooing scene and the earlier one. For example, at one point the king says: "Say I did all this for love of her," when Elizabeth denounces him for the murders of Clarence and Lord Rivers (281-88). Moreover, the same kind of one-line speeches (*stichomythia*) serves to link the two wooing scenes. Finally, Richard's last words (431) are somewhat reminiscent of those he spoke just after Anne had left him. How do the scenes differ? Chiefly in that sardonic humor finds no place in this later scene: tragic gloom now pervades the action.

This has been called an "outrageous courtship." And so it is. In the chronicle histories, both Hall and Holinshed are appalled at the queen's inconstancy. They record that the queen-mother had already promised the princess to Richmond and later was persuaded by Richard to grant his suit. It may be added that in these prose histories Elizabeth even sends orders for Dorset to desert Richmond and return to England. But not until the next scene does Shakespeare let us know that the queen has "heartily consented to the match with Richmond." Mr. J. Dover Wilson is quite right in saying that "it is rather strange that Shakespeare should leave his audience in doubt for over a hundred and twenty lines whether or no the ancestress of his own Queen Elizabeth had sold her daughter to a man whose hands were red with blood of her sons..."(*Richard III*, Cambridge, 1954, p. xliv).

Judged solely by the action in this scene, Queen Elizabeth may indeed be a "shallow, changing woman" who is moved by selfish ambition. Or one may argue that she saw in such a match the only chance to bring an end to the bloody strife. Did not Richard argue:

> Without her, follows to this land and me,
> To thee, herself, and many a Christian soul,
> Death, desolation, ruin and decay.
>
> (407-09)

If the villain refers to "this land" first, he makes reference to himself before he mentions others who will suffer. But perhaps Elizabeth is no less concerned about her own fate than is the egotistical Richard.

Again one must anticipate Elizabeth's action in scene V. Mr. J. Dover Wilson himself joins the many other critics in concluding that Shakespeare intended us to believe that Richard is tricked in this, his second courtship. That this interpretation would seem to be the correct one is consistent with what we learn in Richard's talk with Catesby, Ratcliff, Stanley, and the messengers. Clearly he is losing his grip on himself. Note how he fails to instruct Catesby and how he changes his mind about Ratcliff's mission. Most of the news is bad now. As Richard hears the tidings, he cries: "Out on you, owls..." (509). The owl, of course, is a symbol and portent of death.

There is one piece of good news for Richard. Buckingham's army has been dispersed and scattered by sudden floods. A bit later we learn that the duke himself has been captured. How does this fit into the scheme of things? Buckingham is a perjurer and an accessory to murder; it would not do to have him survive and fight on the side of righteousness. Again we recall Margaret's dire prophecy when Buckingham ignored her counsel and allied himself with one upon whom "Sin, death, and Hell have set their marks" (I.iii.297-301). No Tudor loyalist would have failed to see divine intervention evident in the sudden floods which were the immediate cause of Buckingham's downfall.

The latter part of this scene provides a good illustration of how Shakespeare telescoped historical events for his purpose. Richard did lead a force toward Salisbury to meet Buckingham in October, 1483. Cut off from his Welsh levies, Buckingham was captured and put to death on October 31. Shortly thereafter, Richmond embarked from Brittany with an invading army; but his ships were dispersed by a storm. He did appear in one vessel off Poole. Richard, endeavoring to lure him ashore, sent false information to the effect that the troops ashore were led by Buckingham.

But Richmond did not fall into the trap; instead he returned to France. Not until two years later did he invade England. To help him repel this invasion, Richard sent for the Duke of Norfolk.

ACT IV – SCENE 5

Summary

Derby (Lord Stanley) sends Sir Christopher Urswick to his stepson Richmond with the message that his son George is held captive. For fear of causing his son's death, Derby cannot send aid to Richmond immediately. He learns that Richmond now is in Wales. Supporting the claimant to the throne are many "of noble fame and worth." They are headed for London. Derby finally instructs Sir Christopher to tell Richmond that the Queen-Mother Elizabeth heartily has given her consent to the marriage of Richmond and her daughter.

Commentary

The powerful forces mustered to oppose Richard are identified. Those who will join Richmond are led by such nobles as Sir Walter Herbert, son of the Earl of Pembroke, who had been a staunch Yorkist; Sir Gilbert Talbot, uncle to the Earl of Shrewsbury; and Sir William Stanley, Derby's brother. Derby's real feelings toward Richard are finally made clear, although he dares not openly oppose the king. Thus, by the end of this act, Richard is supported only by Ratcliff, Catesby, and Lovel. That Richard's last stratagem has failed is also revealed: Elizabeth of York will marry Richmond.

Derby's reference to Richard as "this most bloody boar" emphasizes the king's heartless cruelty which has led him to the brink of ruin. The student will recall that, in Act I, scene iii, Anne had denounced him as a "hedgehog," the first insulting reference to Richard's crest of the wild boar. In Act I, scene iv, the villain-hero had referred to Clarence as being "franked up to fattening for his pains." A frank is a sty for fattening hogs. But it is Richard himself, of course, who is bestial. Here, in the lines assigned to Derby, Shakespeare sustains the metaphor.

ACT V – SCENE 1

Summary

As Buckingham is led to his execution at Salisbury, he is told that Richard will not grant him an audience. He thinks of Henry VI, Henry's son Edward, Hastings, Rivers, Grey, Vaughan, and others who had died "By underhand corrupted foul justice." If from the other world they view his plight, he continues, let them mock his fate. It is All Souls' Day, and he recalls that on another such sacred day he had given Edward IV his pledge to remain at peace with the dying king's children and the queen's allies, inviting God's punishment if he broke that pledge. He then recalls Margaret's curse when he had scoffed at her warning. "Wrong hath but wrong, and blame the due of blame," he concludes. He is saying that this unjust death is only retribution for the unjust deaths he has been responsible for.

Commentary

According to Holinshed (who follows Hall closely here), Buckingham made a full confession in the hope that Richard would agree to see him. He "sore desired" the meeting whether "to sue for pardon...or whether he being brought to his presence would have sticked him with a dagger." The execution actually took place in Shrewsbury.

This scene again makes apparent that throughout the play Shakespeare never lets one lose sight of the major theme: the execution of God's judgment on those guilty of perjury and murder. To Buckingham's credit, let it be said, he acknowledges his own guilt, and his words add up to a justification of God's ways to man.

ACT V – SCENE 2

Summary

The scene shifts to Richmond's camp near Tamworth. Richmond, entering with drums and trumpets, addresses his "Fellows in arms" and "most loving friends," inciting them against Richard, "that wretched, bloody, and usurping boar," who has placed upon them the "yoke of tyranny" and has despoiled their "summer fields and fruitful vines." He acknowledges the receipt of good news from Lord Stanley and reports that Richard is at Leicester, only one day away. In God's name, he urges them on. Oxford and Herbert predict that all Richard's friends will desert him, since they are only friends through fear. "All for our vantage," exclaims Richmond, and again invoking God's name he commands them to march onward.

Commentary

This is a scene that could easily be cut out. Shakespeare included it as essential to the theme he develops throughout the play and to point up Richmond's virtures. From a political point of view, never to be ignored in the chronicle history plays, Shakespeare now teaches the orthodox lesson: Richmond is the rightful heir to the throne, moving against a usurper and murderer. He fights in God's name to save England from the ravages of one who, for a time, had been permitted to function as the Scourge of God.

ACT V – SCENE 3

Summary

On Bosworth Field, Richard, fully armed, enters with Norfolk, the Earl of Surrey, and others. He orders that their tents be pitched. When Richard chides Surrey for looking sad, the earl assures him that his heart is light. Then the king rallies Norfolk, who agrees that they must take blows as well as receive them. Richard states that he will rest here for the night; where he will rest tomorrow, he knows not. Philosophically he adds: "Well, all's one for that." He has reason to be confident, for he learns that his forces outnumber Richmond's three to one. With characteristic vigor, he gives commands preparatory to the battle and calls for men of competent leadership.

On the other side of the field Richmond enters, accompanied by several distinguished nobles. While some soldiers are pitching his tent, Richmond takes note of the sunset, which gives promise of a fair day tomorrow. Calling for ink and paper, he plans the deposition of his forces for the battle. Before parting from the rest, he sends Captain Blount off with an important message to Stanley, whose forces lie about half a mile south of the king's. As they withdraw into the tent to finish the battle plans, Richard, with Norfolk, Ratcliff, Catesby, and others, claim our attention.

It is now nine o'clock, and time for the evening's repast; but Richard decides not to sup. His thoughts are solely on the fight with Richmond. He calls for ink and paper; he asks if his armor is in readiness; he orders Norfolk to check the sentinels. Next, the king instructs Catesby to send a herald's officer to Stanley, ordering that lord to bring his regiment before morning unless he wants his son's head to be forfeit. He asks about the "melancholy Lord Northumberland" and is somewhat cheered to hear that the earl and Surrey have gone among the soldiers encouraging them. But Richard concedes that his own spirits lack alacrity and his mind its wonted cheerfulness. Therefore, he calls for a bowl of wine. Having instructed Ratcliff to come about the middle of the night to arm him, the king asks to be left alone.

Now attention is attracted to Richmond, who is in his tent with various lords and attendants. Derby (Lord Stanley) enters, and the two exchange greetings. Derby brings blessings from Richmond's mother, who prays constantly for her son's welfare. He counsels Richmond to put his fortunes to the test in tomorrow's battle, but explains that in view of his son's plight, he cannot openly join the claimant's forces. Regretting that the encroaching battle prevents them from more time together, Stanley leaves. Richmond prepares himself for sleep, aware that he must be rested before he fights the good fight. Alone, he solemnly prays for God's good will, and to Him he commends his "watchful soul."

As both Richard and Richmond sleep, they are visited by a procession of ghosts of those the king had killed. They come in order of their deaths —Prince Edward, Henry VI, Clarence, Rivers, Grey, Vaughan, the little princes, Hastings, Lady Anne, and Buckingham. Each ghost appears to Richard as an image of retribution, indicting him for his crime and telling him to "despair and die." In the words of Anne, each fills his sleep with perturbations. In contrast, each ghost offers praise and words of comfort to the sleeping Richmond: let him "live and flourish," for good angels guard him and fight on his side. The ghost of Hastings especially urges him to "Arm, fight, and conquer, for fair England's sake!" And the two princes urge him to "Live, and beget a happy race of kings!"

As the ghosts vanish, Richard starts out of his sleep. He has been dreaming of "bloody deeds and death." He cries out for a horse and for someone to bind his wounds. Realizing that he has been dreaming and that he is a victim of "coward conscience," he goes through a self-examination that ends in bitter condemnation of isolated and unpitied guilt. Ratcliff enters to rouse him for battle. Still unnerved, he tells Ratcliff his dream. Ratcliff tries to rally him, and Richard turns his mind to the question of his followers' loyalty. He leaves with Ratcliff to eavesdrop at their tent and see if any mean to shrink from him.

Attention is now directed to Richmond's tent, where nobles enter to greet their leader. He has rested well, having enjoyed the "sweetest sleep and fairest-boding dreams." He tells the lords how the souls of Richard's victims had come to his tent and "cried in victory." Told that it is now four o'clock in the morning, Richmond replies that it is "time to arm and give direction." There follows his formal address to his soldiers.

"God and our good cause fight on our side, he assures the troops, and adds that the "prayers of holy saints and wronged souls" stand before their faces. Even Richard's followers, he continues, want him to be defeated.

Denouncing the king as "A bloody tyrant and homicide," Richmond urges his men to fight against God's enemies and their country's foes. Then may they expect to thrive in a prospering land, their wives and children free from danger. Richmond declares that he himself will fight unto death if necessary. If he wins, all will share in the gain. He calls for drums and trumpets to sound "boldly and cheerfully." And with the stirring cry, "God and Saint George! Richmond and victory!" he leads the way offstage.

It is Richard's turn now to receive full attention. He asks what Northumberland has said of Richmond and is pleased to hear Ratcliff tell him that the earl thinks very little of Richmond's capacity as a soldier and that Surrey was no less pleased with Northumberland's opinion. Richard then asks the time of day. He takes notice of the weather and remarks that the sun should have risen an hour ago. At first Richard is dashed by the thought that the skies are lowering down on him, but he realizes that the sun is not shining on Richmond either. Aroused from these thoughts by Norfolk, Richard tells that noble his plan of battle. A vanguard of horse and foot is to be spread out in front, with archers in the midst. Norfolk and Surrey are to command the foot and horse. Richard will follow in the main battle, his power on each side well-winged with foot and horse. Norfolk approves all this, but passes Richard a taunting note he has found on his tent that morning. Richard dismisses it from his mind and sends his captains to their commands. He is determined not to let "babbling dreams" disturb his soul nor his conscience to bother him. Strong arms will be his conscience and swords his law:

> March on, join bravely, let us to't pell-mell —
> If not to Heaven, then hand in hand to Hell.   (312-13)

In his oration, to the troops, Richard denounces the enemy as a pack of foreign vagabonds and robbers who threaten to devastate the land and attack wives and daughters. He makes much of their being French, reminding his soldiers that their fathers had beaten the French on French soil. He concludes with a stirring call to arms. At this moment, a messenger comes, saying that Stanley refuses to bring his forces in. Richard wants to have young George's head cut off at once, but is persuaded to wait until after the battle, since the enemy are already past the marsh. Crying "A thousand hearts are great within my bosom" and invoking the name of Saint George, the king charges into action.

Commentary

Here Shakespeare especially remained quite faithful to Hall and Holinshed in his account of Richard and Richmond just before the Battle of

Bosworth Field. Now, so near to the end of the play, the conflict has become completely centralized. Early there is evidence that Richard's downfall may be imminent. Surrey looks sad, and his insistence that he is really light of heart is not convincing. A bit later the king inquires about the "melancholy Northumberland." He has reason to be doubtful about that noble. Holinshed reported that Richard suspected him, and later wrote that, when it came to fighting, Northumberland stood aside "with a great company and intermitted not in the battle." And Lord Stanley still poses a problem for the king. Nevertheless, Richard's soldierly courage is apparent, as when he says,

> Here will I lie tonight.
> But where tomorrow? Well, all's one for that.   (7-8)

More to the point is Norfolk's report that Richmond's forces are far outnumbered by Richard's.

Richmond, having risen from "sweetest sleep," is in his tent carefully drawing up his plan of battle. He makes reference to his "small strength," but says nothing that suggests doubt or fear. In fact, his opening lines reflect confidence and peace of mind:

> The weary sun hath made a golden set,
> And by the bright track of his fiery car
> Gives signal of a goodly day tomorrow.   (19-21)

Richmond's prayer, voiced in formal, impressive language, is anything but humble in tone. To understand its full import, one must take the historical point of view. The most obvious point to make is that Shakespeare was writing about Elizabeth I's grandfather, the first of the Tudors, whose claim to the throne had never been wholly secure. Richmond is moving against the man who wears the crown. Throughout the sixteenth century and beyond, the doctrine of absolute obedience to the ruler was inculcated. Even if, like Richard of this play, he was a usurper and murderer, no subject legitimately could rebel against him. In *Richard II*, written two years later, the wise old John of Gaunt, uncle to the king and a voice of orthodoxy, replies to the Duchess of Gloucester, who has implored him to avenge the murder of her husband, Gaunt's brother, a crime attributed to Richard II:

God's is the quarrel, for God's substitute,
His deputy anointed in His sight,
Hath caused his death. The which if wrongfully,
Let Heaven avenge, for I may never lift
An angry arm agains His minister   (I.ii.37-41)

Granted that Richard II was not an arch-criminal as is Richard III. But, according to the accepted doctrine, it was through God's sufferance that Richard III wore the crown; he functioned, for a time, as has been stated earlier, as the Scourge of God. Now his time to be scourged approaches. Richmond presents himself as God's captain and prays that he and his followers may be "Thy ministers of chastisement." In other words, he now becomes the instrument of God's justice. Thus heralded, the ghosts appear, bringing blessings to Richmond ("Live and flourish!") and curses on Richard ("Despair and die!").

Admittedly the verse in this "ghost" part of the scene is mediocre; in such pageant-like scenes Shakespeare never achieved his best poetry. His aim was to make the most telling use of the supernatural as a way of keeping his major theme to the fore. Since the ghosts appear in the order of their deaths, Shakespeare recapitulates, crime by crime, the whole catalogue. Richard's sleep indeed is filled "with perturbations," to use Anne's phrase. And as the last ghost vanishes, the king wakes in terror and calls for another horse. He has dreamed prophetically that "white Surrey" has been killed under him. His waking thoughts relate directly to the last words spoken by the ghost of Buckingham.

Things have come full circle now. Richard is a deeply troubled soul in contrast to Richmond, God's captain. When he first appeared in the play, the villain-hero revealed his over-powering egotism; he gloated that he was "subtle, false, and treacherous"; he had expressed his determination "to prove a villain." He spoke these words with an insolence that showed him to be utterly devoid of conscience. Now his words appear as overwhelming reproof as he makes his first — and last — homage to moral law. Especially the horror of his isolation from humanity oppresses him: "There is no creature loves me,   And if I die no soul shall pity me" (200-201).

"Cowardice conscience" afflicts him. Only when he slept and will was dormant could conscience stir. In that sense it was cowardly. But so vivid had been his dream that he cannot immediately escape conscience even when he wakes: "O Ratcliff, I fear, I fear—," he exclaims. The fact that he feels impelled to eavesdrop on his troops illustrates his faltering confidence.

Richmond's oration to his soldiers requires only brief comment. If there has been any doubt up to this point, now that doubt is resolved: Richmond emerges unmistakably as the divinely appointed champion of justice opposing one who "hath ever been God's enemy." The action now assumes the character of a holy crusade, not against an anointed ruler, but against a bloody tyrant who has enslaved trueborn Englishmen.

When Richard re-enters, he has completely recovered himself. For one thing, it would not do to have the tragic hero collapse before the battle and prove himself to be a straw man. Like Macbeth, that other great criminal, he is the soul of courage, a worthy adversary. Does the sun "disdain to shine" on his army? It does not shine for Richmond either. Richard is his Machiavellian self again: "Conscience is but a word that cowards use," he now exclaims (309).

In the chronicle histories of Hall and Holinshed, Richard was made to confess the murders of the little princes and to express sorrow for the deed when he addressed his army. Not so in Shakespeare's play. In the king's oration there is no place for regrets, despondencies, or sense of violated honor. We have here what has rightly been called "a masterpiece of bold mockery of the foe" (Brooke, *op. cit.,* p. 122). Northumberland had reported that Richmond was "never trained in arms" (272); now Richard refers to his adversary as a "milksop, one that never in his life/ Felt so much cold as over shoes in snow" (325-26). The epithet derives from Holinshed, and Shakespeare makes the most of it. Similarly, Richmond's followers are described in the most contemptuous terms—"overweening rags of France," "famished beggars," "poor rats," "bastard Bretons." No leader could have done more to instill confidence in his troops, to convince them that "Victory sits on our helms." If Richmond is to defeat Richard, God indeed must be on his side.

ACT V—SCENE 4

Summary

The battle is in progress. Catesby is crying to Norfolk to rescue the king, whose horse is slain and who continues to fight on foot. Richard enters, crying out for a horse. Catesby urges him to retire. He refuses, for he is determined to risk all. He leaves this part of the field, still crying for a horse and seeking Richmond.

Commentary

Of chief importance in this scene is evidence of King Richard's unsurpassed courage and martial skill. He is depicted as one "enacting more wonders than a man." From one point of view, this goes far to enhance his stature as the tragic hero; from another point of view, it redounds to Richmond's credit, for the claimant is opposed by one who seems to be superhuman in courage and determination.

Richard's cry ("A horse! A horse! My kingdom for a horse!"), so stirring in context, is the best-known line in the play. It was much admired, quoted, and imitated by his contemporaries. The line does not appear in either Hall or Holinshed. One close to it ("A horse, a horse, a fresh horse") is found in *The True Tragedy of Richard the Third,* a quite inferior version of the villain-hero's rise and downfall which, according to critical consensus, predates Shakespeare's historical tragedy. As Mr. J. Dover Wilson notes, "A stage-entry on horseback being impractical, such a cry was an effective one for a general entering on foot in a battle scene" (*op. cit.,* p. 256).

As regards the "six Richards in the field," Shakespeare employed the same device in *Henry IV, Part One,* wherein several of Henry's knights were dressed like him in the Battle of Shrewsbury. Obviously it was a precaution, since the leader's death often meant defeat.

ACT V – SCENE 5

Summary

As prepared for in the previous scene, Richard and Richmond fight, and Richard is slain. Richmond retreats and returns, receiving the congratulation of his friends for the victory, which is now assured. Derby (Lord Stanley) is carrying the crown, which he has taken from Richard. He places it on the head of Richmond. To the new king's question about young George Stanley (Richmond's half-brother), Derby replies that the youth is safe in Leicester. Richmond asks the names of nobles on both sides who have been slain and orders that they be buried "as becomes their births." In accordance with his wishes, all soldiers who have fled are to be pardoned if they return in submission to him. After taking the sacrament, he will marry Elizabeth of York, Edward IV's daughter, thus uniting the Yorkist and the Lancastrians. The harsh wars which have caused so much grief and injury, even among members of the same family, are now over. God willing, England will enter a reign of peace and prosperity. His concluding words are

74

a prayer that traitors may perish and peace reign, now that civil wounds are healed.

Commentary

Appropriately in the final scene there is a clearing of the moral atmosphere. The "bloody dog" is dead; order is restored. In hand-to-hand combat Richmond slays the adversary who had performed apparently superhuman deeds on the battlefield. Everywhere the new king's moral superiority is emphasized: his concern for George Stanley, his chivalry in ordering that all nobles slain, enemies included, be given proper burial; his proclamation of an amnesty; his profound religiosity. Shakespeare lived and wrote in an England beset with repeated threats to peace: the Northern Rebellion (1569); the Ridolphi Plot (1572); the Babington Plot (1586); attempted foreign invasion and fear of a rising against a queen who had been declared excommunicate and deposed by the Papal Bull of 1570. In official sermon and numerous polemical tracts and ballads the horrors of civil war and the heinous crime of treason were dominant themes. In the latter part of this scene, Shakespeare finds occasion to offer the same doctrine. To Elizabethans especially, Richmond's fervent prayer was most apposite and inspiring.

NOTES ON CHARACTERS

RICHARD, DUKE OF GLOUCESTER, AFTERWARD RICHARD III

Richard is Shakespeare's first villain-hero. Self-acclaimed as one who will "outdo Machiavel," he possesses all of the traits of that Elizabethan stage villain. Primarily he is motivated by boundless ambition to gain and hold the crown, and by his pronounced egotism. Utterly heartless, he does not hesitate to move against his own brothers, arranging for the murder of Clarence, misleading and later slandering Edward IV, and putting to death his own nephews. It is implied in the text that he also poisoned his wife Anne so that the way would be clear for his political marriage to his niece, Elizabeth of York. A master of dissembling and a man obviously not without charm, despite his physical deformity, he deludes Edward IV, for a time convinces Queen Elizabeth and her family that he has no further quarrel with them, and manages to gain the support of the Lord Mayor of London, among others. Add to all this the energy with which he initiates and carries out every action necessary to his gaining the crown and, for a time, retaining it, and one can understand why he dominates the play to an extent to which no other Shakespearean tragic hero does. His soliloquies and asides reveal a Richard who is honest at least with himself. Courage and soldierly prowess also belong to him. Finally, he possesses an unexcelled sense of irony and a sardonic wit which go far to explain his special attraction to audiences and readers.

HENRY, EARL OF RICHMOND, AFTERWARD HENRY VII

Richmond is not heard of until Act IV, scene, i, when Queen Elizabeth urges her son Dorset to save himself by joining Richmond in Brittany. It is true that, in Act I, scene ii, we find a reference to his mother, the Countess Richmond, who is married to Lord Stanley, Earl of Derby; and we learn that the countess has not been friendly to Edward IV's queen. But by the end of Act IV, we learn that "Richmond is on the seas," and he then definitely emerges as Richard III's nemesis. Inevitably, Richmond provides the strongest contrast to Richard. If the latter is "hell's black intelligencer" and "that foul defacer of God's handiwork," Richmond is "God's Captain," the agent of divine justice to be imposed upon Richard. It will not do to criticize him adversely as one who is intolerably stuffy in his proclaimed religiosity and conviction of righteousness. In the words of Mr. J. Dover Wilson, Shakespeare "could hardly have done other than represent Henry of Richmond as a kind of St. George and the king he slays as much like a dragon as a human may be" (*op. cit.*, p. xix).

EDWARD IV

Edward IV appears only briefly in this play. The eldest son of the Duke of York is depicted as one who already is paying for his sins and those of the house of York in general. His reign has been characterized by strife including the Woodville faction and those who bitterly oppose the queen and her family. Edward dies believing that amity has been restored and that the succession of the crown to his son has been assured. He is, then, prominent among those who are deluded by Richard, as the death of Clarence illustrates. The fact that his personal life had been a notorious one, particularly as relates to Jane Shore, worked to Richard's advantage after Edward's death.

GEORGE, DUKE OF CLARENCE

The third son of the Duke of York is Richard's first victim. He is the unhappy, "false, fleeting, perjured Clarence," who learns only just before his violent death that it is his own brother Richard who has plotted against him. His account of his terrifying dream (I.iv) is one of the most memorable parts of the drama. Clarence invites sympathy, not only because we know that he is opposed by an evil monster, but because he acknowledges his guilt, expresses greatest concern for his wife and children, and dies courageously.

HENRY, DUKE OF BUCKINGHAM

Buckingham is ambitious to become the Earl of Hereford and to gain the "movables" of the earldom, brashly ignores Queen Margaret's warning and aligns himself with Richard of Gloucester. He becomes convinced that he is indeed Richard's "second self," his "counsel's consistory," his "oracle" and "prophet." He is at his zenith when he sets the stage and gives the directions for the reception of the lord mayor and the urging of Richard to accept the crown. He sees himself as a second Warwick, a king-maker, and is confident of prompt reward. Not until Richard sounds him out regarding the plan to murder the little princes does Buckingham waver in his unquestioning obedience to the new king. Although he escapes to Wales and raises forces to oppose his former master, he is not allowed to survive, so deep in sin has he fallen.

QUEEN MARGARET OF ANJOU

The widow of Henry VI, one-time vigorous prosecutor of the Lancas-trian cause, has survived into old age as a kind of Fury voicing curses and horrible prophecies. In her speeches, so highly rhetorical and formalistic, the major theme of the play receives repeated emphasis. She lives to see, and practically to gloat over, the fulfillment of one curse, one prophecy, after another. It is she who makes understandable why—in accordance with that mathematical scheme of justice which she constantly dwells upon —Queen Elizabeth, the Duchess of York, and even the little princes should suffer.

WILLIAM, LORD HASTINGS

The chamberlain to Edward IV and loyal adherent of the Yorkist cause is also among those deluded by Richard. Because he was a victim of the machinations of the Woodvilles, he understandably first sided with Gloucester, whose protestations of innocence he accepted readily. Hastings long remains supremely confident, blithely ignoring portents of catastrophe. No one could have been more surprised than he when Richard ordered that he be seized and put to death. The one debit in his account is that he exults when he learns that members of the queen's faction have been executed. To that extent, he invites his own downfall. But as a devoted Yorkist, he also shares in the doom of that noble house.

LORD STANLEY, EARL OF DERBY

The stepfather of Richmond moves through a good part of this play cautiously endeavoring to avoid offense to Richard without really commit-ting himself. He offers marked contrast to Hastings, whose sense of well-being he never shares so long as Richard lives. Unlike Dorset and others, he does not cross the seas to join Richmond; he waits to see the ultimate turn of events. Placed in a position where he dares not lead his troops in support of the claimant, he nevertheless survives to witness the fall of Richard II and the crowning of his stepson.

QUEEN ELIZABETH

The wife of Edward IV is from the first a woman who finds no peace. Only briefly does she find a degree of comfort when her dying husband requires members of the quarreling factions to take the vow of amity. But no sooner does she become a widow than her troubles multiply—the news of the executions of her "proud kindred"; the necessity of urging Dorset to flee; the cruel murder of her two young sons. And then there is Queen Margaret to inform her that all this is the working out of divine justice. Aware that the author of her chief woes is Richard III, she still appears to be won over by his facile argument and to agree to the marriage of her daughter to the king. But the subsequent action, wherein it is revealed that the young lady will marry the virtuous Richmond, exonerates her from the charge that she is a "relenting fool, and shallow changing woman."

LADY ANNE

The widow of Edward, Prince of Wales, son of Henry VI, became the wretched wife of Richard of Gloucester. Prior to her appearance in Act I, scene ii, it was from Richard himself that we learned of his villainy. Anne's first function, then, is to provide chapter and verse for Richard's villainy by excoriating him as the heartless murderer of her husband and her father. Yet she is rather easily swayed by Richard's blandishments and agrees to marry him. In a sense, she willfully embraces evil when she accepts Richard as her husband—the man she had just denounced as a "foul devil," "a dreadful minister of Hell." It is not Queen Margaret who is called upon to bring down curses on Anne's head; she does so for herself. And each curse is realized: she does not find rest as Richard's wife; she does not survive long as Richard's queen. Thus, in a way, she expiates her own initial sin.

THE DUCHESS OF YORK

The mother of Edward IV, Clarence, and Richard invites nothing but the deepest sympathy in this play. She has survived the violent deaths of her husband and of her son Clarence; she has seen another son, King Edward IV, languish and die, leaving his realm split with dissension. But the greatest cross she bears is the knowledge that she is the mother of the monstrous Richard: "He is my son—yea, and therein my shame—." Yet when mother and son first exchange words, she cannot deny him the blessing he hypocritically asks for. There is supreme irony and pathos in her words:

> God bless thee, and put meekness in thy mind,
> Love, charity, obedience, and true duty.   (II.ii.107-08)

Nor is this blessing to lead one to assume that the duchess becomes one who is deceived by the arch-villain. It is a heartfelt plea to God that Richard may reform. Old in years and sorrow, she can find sympathy even for that terrifying figure, Queen Margaret, doom of the house of York.

REVIEW QUESTIONS

1. What characteristics peculiar to the Machiavellian villain-hero are revealed in Gloucester's first soliloquy, Act I, scene i?

2. Richard is early referred to as a "hedgehog" and later repeatedly as the "boar." What is the significance of this appellation?

3. In the introduction, reference is made to Senecan elements in this play. What is one example each as regards (a) style, (b) character, (c) theme, (d) tragic elements?

4. In what way are the two wooing scenes (I.ii and IV.iv) similar to each other? How do they differ?

5. What dramatic purpose is served by such minor characters as the three London citizens and the scrivener?

6. Keeping in mind the major theme of this play, how can you account for the fact that the villain-hero flourishes for such a relatively long time?

7. Why is Queen Margaret's appearance in this play unexpected? How do you account for it?

8. What is the first indication that Richard's fortunes, which have been in the ascendant, have reached a turning point? What do you consider to be the climax of the play?

9. George Bernard Shaw insisted that Richard was a splendid comedian. What can be said in support or in refutation of this opinion?

10. According to a long-lived theory, tragedy evokes the tragic emotions of pity as well as fear. What scenes are especially notable for arousing our sense of pity?

11. "In Buckingham we have an admirable foil to Richard." How may one defend this statement?

12. What is meant by dramatic irony? Illustrate your definition by three examples from this play, each differing with regard to the person or persons concerned.

13. Especially since this play is based upon chronicle history, considerable knowledge of antecedent action is needed. Shakespeare does not choose to use a prologue to provide such information. Exactly how, and by whom, is it provided?

14. Since the major theme of this play is God's vengeance visited upon those guilty of heinous crimes, how can one explain the deaths of the queen's kinsmen, Hastings, and the little princes?

15. When the Duchess of York and Queen Elizabeth berate King Richard in Act IV, scene iv, he exclaims:

> Let not the Heavens hear these telltale women
> Rail on the Lord's anointed.

Is this another example of Richard's hypocrisy? Or can he properly call himself the Lord's anointed?

16. Both Richard and Richmond use the name St. George as a battle cry. Why is this appropriate in both instances? Why is it nevertheless ironic that Richard should use the name of St. George?

17. What justification does Richmond have for identifying himself as "God's Captain?"

18. Aside from his "timorous dreams" reported by Anne, what evidence do you find that Richard has begun his descent on Fortune's Wheel?

19. Why is it appropriate that Buckingham should not survive to aid Richmond?

20. In what ways do Lord Stanley (Derby) and Lord Hastings provide an interesting contrast?

21. How does Shakespeare succeed in centralizing the conflict in this play and thus achieve a superior chronicle history play which is also a tragedy?

22. Shakespeare develops the major theme of *Richard III* with unstinted use of the supernatural. What are four examples? Which do you find to be most effective?

23. With reference to the proposal of marriage of her daughter, how may the Queen-Mother Elizabeth's apparent changeableness and double-dealing be explained?

80

24. More than one reference is made to Jane Shote in this play, although she does not make her appearance. Who was she? In absentia, what does she contribute to the action?

25. On his way to his death, Lord Rivers exclaims against Pomfret, calling it a "bloody prison." Is this to be explained only by reference to his own impending fate? Exactly why is Pomfret truly a "bloody prison"?

SELECTED BIBLIOGRAPHY

Allen, J. W. *A History of Political Thought in the Sixteenth Century,* 1928. Basic to the understanding of Tudor political theories which inform Shakespeare's chronicle history plays.

Berman, Ronald. *A Reader's Guide to Shakespeare's Plays,* 1965. "A discoursive bibliography" which properly includes scholarly articles as well as books relating to *Richard III.*

Boyer, C. V. *The Villain as Hero in Elizabethan Tragedy,* 1914. Contains studies of the Machiavellian "lion and the fox" which anticipates later ones; includes a good presentation of possible influences from Seneca.

Campbell, Lily B. *Shakespeare's "Histories": Mirrors of Elizabethan Policy,* 1947. Penetrating analysis of the religious, ethical, and political ideas in *Richard III:* topical meanings of the play.

Clemen, Wolfgang. *The Development of Shakespeare's Imagery,* 1951. Valuable study of the "formal and artificial" manner modified by a firm architecture of style.

Chambers, E. K. *William Shakespeare: A Study of Facts and Problems,* 2 vols., 1930. Indispensable for bibliographical and historical approach to the play.

Cunliffe, John. *The Influence of Seneca on Elizabethan Tragedy,* 1893. First of the notable studies of this subject; a work which has not become dated.

Furness, H. H., Jr. *Richard the Third.* New Variorum edition, 1908. A storehouse of information including textual criticism, varied interpretations of character and action, stage history.

Kendall, Paul M. *Richard the Third,* 1955. Eminently scholarly and read-able biography of Richard which provides the essential details relating to this turbulent period in English history.

Lewis, Wyndham. *The Lion and the Fox,* 1927. Analysis of Richard as the dedicated Machiavellian.

Marriott, J. *English History in Shakespeare,* 1918. One of the basic studies of this subject so necessary to an understanding of the chronicle history plays.

Palmer, J. *Political Characters in Shakespeare,* 1954. Stimulating analysis of Richard as "brave, witty, resourceful, gay, swift, disarmingly candid, engagingly sly with his enemies."

Reese, M. M. *The Cease of Majesty,* 1961. Useful discussion of the structure and the language of the play, and of the action in which each successive blow of fate is a fulfillment of a curse until the appearance of the foreordained savior of England.

Spivack, B. *Shakespeare and the Allegory of Evil,* 1958. Detailed examination of the morality element in *Richard III.*

Tillyard, E. M. W. *Shakespeare's History Plays,* 1944. Finds *Richard III* to be an undervalued play; defends the credibility of the play in which is found a great combination of evil, humor, and artistry in crime.

NOTES

LET CLIFFS NOTES HELP YOU GET BETTER ACQUAINTED WITH THESE AUTHORS

■ ISAAC ASIMOV ■ TENNESSEE WILLIAMS ■ PLATO ■ F. SCOTT FITZGERALD ■ SHAKESPEARE ■ CHARLES DICKENS ■ GEORGE ELIOT ■ JANE AUSTEN ■ WILLA CATHER ■ WALT WHITMAN ■ ARTHUR MILLER ■ SALINGER ■ MACHIAVELLI ■ FRANZ KAFKA ■ EDGAR ALLEN POE ■ EDITH WHARTON ■ THOMAS SINCLAIR ■ PERCY SHELLEY JONATHON SWIFT ■ EMILY BRONTE ■ KATE CHOPIN ■ DANIEL DEFOE ■ DANTE ■ HENRY JAMES ■ WILLIAM FAULKNER ■ JAMES FENIMORE COOPER ■ MARK TWAIN ■ CHARLOTTE BRONTE ■ EDWARD ALBEE ■ ERNEST HEMINGWAY ■ JOHN STEINBECK ■ STEPHEN CRANE ■ GEORGE BERNARD SHAW ■ THOMAS HARDY ■ NATHANIEL HAWTHORNE ■ JAMES JOYCE ■ DOSTOEVSKY

GET CLIFFS NOTES

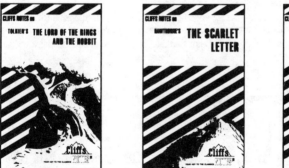

Cliffs Notes are America's most widely used study aids for literature. More than 200 titles are available covering well-known poems, plays and novels. Each provides expert analysis and background of plot, characters and author, in a way which can make the most difficult assignments easier to understand.

Available at your bookseller or order from Cliffs Notes.

See back cover for complete title listing.

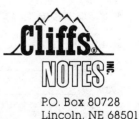

P.O. Box 80728
Lincoln, NE 68501

Your Guides to Successful Test Preparation.

Cliffs Test Preparation Guides

Efficient preparation means better test scores. Go with the experts and use **Cliffs Test Preparation Guides**. They'll help you reach your goals because they're: • Complete • Concise • Functional • In-depth. They are focused on helping you know what to expect from each test. The test-taking techniques have been proven in classroom programs nationwide.

Recommended for individual use or as a part of formal test preparation programs.

SHAKESPEARE'S SONNETS

NOTES

including
- *Brief Survey of Sixteenth-century Sonnets*
- *Critical Comments on Shakespeare's Sonnets,*
  with essays on The Fair Young Man,
  The Dark Lady, *and* The Rival Poet.
- *Critical Analyses of Individual Sonnets*
- *Questions for Review*
- *Select Bibliography*

by
James K. Lowers, Ph.D.
University of Hawaii

Cliffs Notes
INCORPORATED
LINCOLN, NEBRASKA 68501

Editor

Gary Carey, M.A.
University of Colorado

Consulting Editor

James L. Roberts, Ph.D.
Department of English
University of Nebraska

Cliffs Notes, Inc.   Lincoln, Nebraska

CONTENTS

THE SONNET IN THE SIXTEENTH CENTURY: A BRIEF SURVEY

English poetry owes much to the Italian, especially for one of its best known lyric forms, which, often modified, has been employed by many of the greatest poets, including William Shakespeare. The reference, of course, is to the sonnet. The greatest Italian sonneteers were Petrarch, Dante, Tasso, Ariosto, Michelangelo, and Vittoria Colonna. It was particularly Petrarch to whom the English poets turned. The first requirement of the strict Italian, or Petrarchan sonnet was that it be limited to fourteen lines organically divided into an octave rhyming *abba abba,* and a sestet in which several rhyme schemes were permitted. At the end of the octave there was a *volte,* or turn, so that structurally speaking the first eight lines provided the subject and sufficiently amplified it, and the sestet provided the resolution. Almost from the beginning the English poets felt free to modify the strict Italian form, typically by eliminating the *volte* and varying the rhyme scheme.

It has been correctly said that the love sonnet, in its origin, developing as it did from the love songs of the Troubadours, was "the literary equivalent of that chivalry which led the knight of the Middle Ages to show his devotion to his lady by fighting in field or tournament for her protection and honor." In the hands of Petrarch's imitators, Italian, French and English, the sonnet became chiefly a literary exercise, providing the poet, sometimes a gifted amateur, the opportunity to display his ingenuity in the expression of love which was entirely fictitious or directed to an imaginary person. Certain conventions were usually followed. The male lover is the speaker; he is deeply in love with a fair young lady whom he describes in superlatives. But the lady is as cold as she is chaste and beautiful, and the man's love remains unrequited, although he cannot choose but to continue in a state of adoration and misery.

SIR THOMAS WYATT AND THE EARL OF SURREY

To Sir Thomas Wyatt (1503-1542) belongs the credit of introducing the Petrarchan love poetry into England. Although much of his poetry, including certain sonnets, is notable for its fine energy, he was also a persistent imitator of the foreign models. Many of his sonnets are quite literal translations of the Italian originals. But Wyatt wrote others in which justice in love is dominant and in which the male lover is depicted as being in love involuntarily and expressing his fervent desire to escape from his bondage. He thus introduced what may be called the anti-Petrarchan theme, which later writers were to make use of also. On occasion the speaker adopts anything but the hopelessly adoring pose of the abject Petrarchan lover and asserts a manly independence.

Henry Howard, Earl of Surrey, born in 1517 and beheaded in 1547, is the second of the English sonneteers. In both form and content he broadened the scope of the sonnet, although most of his are imitations of the Italian amorous poets and develop the same characterizations and themes. As to form, it is he who introduced a new structural scheme. Many of his poems are divided into three quatrains and a concluding couplet. Sometimes called the Surreyan or English sonnet, the form is best known as Shakespearean, since England's premier poet-dramatist adopted it and used it with greatest effectiveness. The usual rhyme scheme is *abab cdcd efef gg.* The resulting effect is different from that of the Petrarchan sonnet in two ways: the rhyme scheme is more obvious and more easily followed by the ear; the structure is more directly progressive since the rhyme scheme is developed climactically and is terminated with an epigrammatic, summarizing couplet. There is one danger, however—one from which Shakespeare did not always escape: occasionally the poet has said all that needs to be said at the end of the third quatrain, and the couplet embodies a redundancy. These virtues and limitations will be illustrated in the discussion of Shakespeare's sonnets.

To some extent Surrey also broadened the scope of the sonnet as regards themes. Instead of limiting his subject to the celebration of love, he developed the theme of friendship, notably in the sonnets to Clere and to Wyatt.

The poems of Wyatt and Surrey circulated in manuscript during their lifetime and were included in *Songs and Sonnets* (1557), the first printed collection of English verse, better known as *Tottel's Miscellany,* which became a source of inspiration to later poets.

SIR PHILIP SIDNEY

During the quarter of a century following the publication of the poems by Wyatt and Surrey, the sonnet was ignored by poets. In 1582, it is true, Thomas Watson published his *Hekatompathia, or Passionate Century of Love,* a series of quite unoriginal love poems written not as quatorzains but as eighteen-line sonnets. And after his death in 1593, his *Tears of Fancy or Love Disdained,* a short sequence of regular sonnets, appeared. These have the interest of bearing the closest relationship to Shakespeare's sonnets of all those written at the end of the century, although Watson lacked Shakespeare's golden touch and originality.

But it was Sir Philip Sidney (1554-1586) who must be credited with starting the great vogue of sonnet writing in which so many poets participated during the last decade of the century. Years before its publication in 1590, his sonnet sequence, *Astrophel and Stella,* circulated in manuscript. It may be argued that without these poems Shakespeare's sonnets would not have been written. Sidney's poems (which include some lyric pieces or songs in various measures) are unified in that, following the now established tradition, the speaker expresses some phase of his feeling in relation to his mistress. Sidney borrowed freely from the French Petrarchans, Ronsard and Desportes, recording a passion first thwarted and then suppressed. Although not infrequently the poet achieved complete originality and first-rate poetry, he usually introduced the conventional conceits in lines admittedly of lyric beauty. To quote Seccombe and Allen *(The Age of Shakespeare,*London, 1903, p. 13):

> Love lurks in dark bush, which is Stella's eyes, and from thence shoots the poor poet unawares: he calls his friends to fly the dangerous spot. Venus, angry with Cupid for not having sufficiently stimulated Mars, breaks his bow and arrows; but grandam nature takes pity on the crying boy and makes him two nice bows out of Stella's eyebrows, and finds any number of arrows for him in her eyes.

We shall see that Shakespeare was to improve immeasurably on this sort of poetry.

DANIEL, DRAYTON, AND OTHERS

Many of the most important poets, as well as minor ones, followed the fashion during the years 1591-1597, publishing sonnet series constructed more or less closely on the model of *Astrophel and Stella.* In points of style, the sonnet books of Samuel Daniel, Henry Constable, Thomas Lodge, Barnaby Barnes, Michael Drayton, and Edmund Spenser have close affinities, and each book bears a title:

Lodge called his sequence *Phillis;* Spenser used the Italian *Amoretti* for his. All are made up of a series of short poems ostensibly concerned with some fair lady, although none is intended to tell a story despite the inclusion of some narrative elements. Spenser's comes closest to sustained narrative in that it does record the progress of his courtship with Elizabeth Boyle, the woman he married. Usually the lady, be she Lodge's Phillis or Daniels' Delia, is no more than a name, if not an absolute fiction. We shall see that several of the sonnets in Shakespeare's sequence, which bears no title, are very close to those of his contemporaries in theme and style. But others lack the richness and the range of subjects found in Shakespeare's sonnets.

SHAKESPEARE'S SONNETS

DATE OF COMPOSITION

Early and late attempts have been made to determine when Shakespeare's untitled sequence of 154 sonnets were written. The chief external evidence is found in Francis Meres' *Palladis Tamia* (1598), a little thesaurus of contemporary wits in which Shakespeare is placed at the head of the dramatists and high among the non-dramatic poets. Meres made reference to Shakespeare's "sugred sonnets" which circulated among his friends. This clearly indicates that at least some of the poems had become well known. In support of this conclusion, it may be added that Sonnets 138 and 144 were printed in *The Passionate Pilgrim,* which was published in 1599. And, since Shakespeare himself called his *Venus and Adonis* the "first heir" of his invention, one may argue that the sonnets were written after 1592-1593, the accepted date of composition of the narrative poem. The line "Lilies that fester smell far worse than weeds" appears in Sonnet 94 and in the play *Edward III* to which the date 1594 has been assigned. But it is a matter of dispute whether the sonnet quoted the play, or the play the sonnet.

The sonnets appear to extend from 1593 or 1594 until within a few years of their actual publication in 1609. The consensus is that most of them belong to the earlier period when the sonnet vogue was at its height, for Shakespeare usually responded promptly to popular taste, as his plays indicate. Many commentators have stressed the parallels of imagery, theme, and mood found in *Two*

Gentlemen of Verona, Love's Labour's Lost, A Midsummer Night's Dream, Richard II, and *Romeo and Juliet,* plays written between the years 1592 and 1595. *Love's Labour's Lost* especially reveals the poet's keen interest in the sonnet, for it includes seven quatorzains and many significant parallels of thought, imagery, and phraseology. Moreover, in the play Rosaline is the Dark Lady who wins Biron's heart. She is described in terms quite like those found in the second division (127-154) of Shakespeare's poems. Indeed, the relationship between the sonnets and the play is indicated by several thematic resemblances, especially the repeated reference to eyes and the stress upon Rosaline's dark beauty. Consider the following passage from *Love's Labour's Lost:*

> *Biron.* Of all complexions the cull'd sovereignty
> Do meet, as at a fair, in her
>   fair cheek,
> Where several worthies make one dignity,
>   Where nothing wants that want itself doth seek.
>
> *King.* By heaven, thy love is black as ebony.
>
> *Biron.* Is ebony like her? O wood divine!
> A wife of such wood were felicity.
>   O who can give an oath? Where is a book
> That I may swear beauty doth beauty lack
>   If that she learn not of her eye to look?
> No face is fair that is not full so black.
>
> (IV.iii.234-253)

These lines bear comparison with sonnets 127 and 130 in particular. It should be pointed out, however, that in the poems the Dark Lady is a *femme fatale*—almost an evil spirit that has enslaved the male lover.

Although the general opinion is that most of the sonnets should be assigned to the years 1592-1595, there is nothing to prevent the conclusion that the poet added to their number in subsequent years. In mood and language, certainly Sonnets 107 and 152 could very well belong to the *Hamlet* period. And in Sonnet 146 can be heard what Neilson and Thorndyke (*Facts About Shakespeare,* 1913, p. 87) call "a note of emotion more profound than can be heard before the date of *Hamlet.*"

Notice should be paid also to the so-called "dating" of Sonnet 107. Lines seven and eight read:

> Incertainties now crown themselves assur'd
> And peace proclaims olives of endless age.

It has been argued that the great public event referred to was either the defeat of the Armada in 1588 or (in view of the line "The mortal moon hath her eclipse endur'd") to the death of Queen Elizabeth in 1603. Much depends upon the meaning of the word endur'd. If one concludes that the "mortal moon" was Elizabeth, who was often addressed as Cynthia, Goddess of the Moon, the word must indicate, not that she had died, but that she had triumphantly passed through some crisis. Mr. Peter Quennell, (Shakespeare, 1963, p. 137) points out that 1596 was the year of the Queen's "grand climateric," when she had reached the age of sixty-three. Elizabethans believed that a dangerous crisis occurred in one's lifetime every seven years. And since the number sixty-three is seven times the portentous number nine, the Queen's loyal subjects had reason to be gravely concerned and alarmed. It so happened that the English won the great victory over the Spaniards at Cadiz in 1596, and with Spain suffering such a defeat, the period of national crisis seemed to be drawing to a close. Those who so interpret Sonnet 107 are convinced that it and most of the other poems belong to the period 1594-1596.

The sonnets are filled with what appears to be allusions or references to persons, events, or specific years or seasons; and these have been used by critics in an attempt to date them from the late 1580's to 1609. For example, those who believe that the young man addressed in the first 126 sonnets is either the Earl of Southampton or the Earl of Pembroke are past masters at unearthing internal evidence for dating given sonnets. Since in the first seventeen sonnets the poet urges the youth to marry and beget heirs in order to defeat Time the Destroyer, the Southamptonites are convinced that reference is to their candidate, who, as royal ward, was urged to marry in the early 1590's, but refused to do so. Similarly, the Pembrokites believe that all this applies to their candidate, who, in 1595, refused to marry the daughter of Sir George Carey, and two years later violently objected to the plans for him to marry Lady Bridget Vere.

Some critics use the Rival Poet sonnets in their attempt to date the poems. Those who favor Marlowe insist on an early date of composition since Marlowe died in 1593; those favoring George Chapman, in contrast, argue for the later date. The best that can be said is the sonnets could have been written anytime from 1585 to 1609. In all probability 1593-1594 and 1598-1601 were the periods of most productivity.

THE DEDICATION TO MR. W. H.

Thomas Thorpe (1580-1614), described as "a publishing under-strapper of piratical habits" who, in the absence of any regular copyright protection for authors, "hung about scriveners' shops and from time to time, collusively, 'picked up' a manuscript in which he could 'deal'," and brought out the first edition of Shakespeare's sonnets in 1609. His dedication read as follows:

TO. THE. ONLIE. BEGETTER. OF.
THESE. INSVING. SONNETS.
MR. W. H. ALL. HAPPINESSE.
AND. THAT. ETERNITIE.
PROMISED.
BY.
OUR. EVERY-LIVING. POET
WISHETH.
THE. WELL-WISHING.
ADVENTURER. IN.
SETTING.
FORTH.
T.T.

And this has led to a series of conjectures as to the identity of Mr. (i.e., Master) W. H. Many critics interpret *begetter* to mean the one who procured the manuscript of the sonnets for Thorpe. But others identify him as the Fair Young Man addressed in the first division, Sonnets 1 through 126. The question, then, is who was Mr. W. H.? Perhaps it will be well to dispose of the minor conjectures before discussing the favorite ones.

In his *Life of William Shakespeare*, 1898, p. 391, Sir Sidney Lee called attention to the fact that an edition of the *Four-Fold Meditations* of Father Robert Southwell, the Jesuit martyr, printed in 1609, was dedicated "to the Right Worshipful Gentleman, Matthew Saunders, Esquire" by one W. H., who wished him "long life, a prosperous achievement of his good desire." Lee identified this W. H. with William Hall, a printer, who, he argued, was the "onlie begetter" referred to by Thorpe. Another guess is William Hervey (or Harvey), who married the mother of the young Earl of Southampton in 1598. It is argued that if Southampton was the beautiful youth then this guess is a reasonable one. Moreover, Harvey was a likely person to have access to the original manuscript; and he has a sound claim to be the "W. H." of Father Southwell's *Meditations,* since the Southampton family were staunch Catholics. W. Hall, the printer, published anti-Catholic books.

A third candidate is one William Hughes. Some commentators are sure that there is a pun on his name in Sonnet 20, line 7: "A man in hew all *Hews* in his controlling." Oscar Wilde revived an old theory that this W. H. was a boy actor. The difficulty, however, is that in the rather complete records of the acting companies his name does not appear.

This brings us to the two leading candidates, Henry Wriothesley, third Earl of Southampton, who must be given first position, and William Herbert, third Earl of Pembroke. The Southampton identification, first made by Nathan Drake *(Shakespeare and His Times,* 1817, II, 62-71) was inevitable in view of Shakespeare's dedication of *Venus and Adonis* to him and the circumstances relating to efforts to get him to marry which have been discussed in the earlier section. The young earl loved poetry and drama and may well have sought out Shakespeare and offered himself as the poet's patron. So goes the argument. A chief objection to this theory, however, is that the youthful aristocrat would not have been addressed as "Master," nor would Thorpe have reversed the initials of his name. Moreover Sonnets 127-154 are not addressed to the Fair Young Man. It has been argued further that the earl, as his portraits testify, did not possess that surpassing beauty attributed to the youth addressed in the first long division of the sonnets, and that Southampton, who was twenty-one in 1594, could not be the "lovely boy" of the poems.

The claim for William Herbert, third Earl of Pembroke, first was made by James Boaden in 1832 *(Gentlemen's Magazine,* CII, ii, 217 ff.). Boaden was in search of a young man "who, from his youth and station, called for no other topics than the Sonnets afford; who was beautiful enough that the Poet should wish his *straying youth* removed from temptation; great enough to be courted, as willing and able to patronize a condition that could not exist without it, and who actually became the patron of Shakespeare; one moreover whom as the Sonnets tell us, rival poets were courting, with all the arts, and more than the *charms* of verse." There is indeed much to be said in Pembroke's favor. With his brother Philip, he was dedicatee of the First Folio of Shakespeare's works, published in 1623. He was wealthy, notorious for sensuality but averse to marriage, and a bountiful patron of literary men. As to the title "Mr.", the Pembrokites argue that the use of it was not improper or presumptuous, since at that time there was not any grander title of courtesy. Those who believe that Mary Fitton, one of Queen Elizabeth's Maids of Honor, was the Dark Lady of Sonnets 127-154 are particularly convinced that Pembroke is the right choice, for he had an affair with the lady, who bore him a child out of wedlock. Little wonder that the earl remains a favorite candidate.

These are the essential facts relating to the identity of "Mr. W. H." The evidence is not too much stronger for one candidate than for another, and the question of identity really remains unsolvable like that relating to the dating of the sonnets.

ORDER AND ARRANGEMENT

Since the publication of the second edition of the sonnets in 1640, there has been much discussion regarding the order and arrangement of Shakespeare's poems. John Benson, the publisher, pirated Thorpe's 1609 Quarto and, perhaps in an attempt to conceal that fact, rearranged the sonnets in so-called "poems" varying from one to five sonnets in length and supplying a title for each. In the words of the late Hyder Rollins *(New Variorum,* 1941, II, 74), Benson "is largely responsible for the obsession for uprooting and resetting the sonnets in the nineteenth and twentieth centuries that overmastered many amateur as well as professional scholars." If one assumes, as most critics do, that Shakespeare did not authorize the Quarto of 1609, then there is no certitude that the Quarto arrangement is his. Further, some critics, including Clara Longworth de Chambrun *(The Sonnets of William Shakespeare,* 1938, p. vi) and H. D. Gray ("The Arrangement and Date of Shakespeare's Sonnets," *PMLA,* 1915, XXX, 630 f.) insist that it is the modern reader's privilege and even duty to rearrange the order of the sonnets if such rearrangement will aid his understanding and appreciation of them.

Malone and Stevens, in their 1780 edition of Shakespeare's works, initiated in England the still widely held belief that the first 126 sonnets were addressed to a man, and that the rest of the poems were addressed to a woman. By and large, this remains what may be called the orthodox view. The majority of the critics remain sufficiently well satisfied with Thorpe's ordering of the first group, but entertain serious doubts as regards the second, in which they find no particular logic. George Lyman Kittredge, the distinguished American Shakespearean, was representative of the dissenters. In his edition of the poet's works (1936), he pointed out that it is customary to describe Sonnets 1-126 "as a continuous series and to assume that they are all addressed to the same person. . . . This idea takes it for granted that Thorpe's arrangement is Shakespeare's." That, however, is pure assumption, Kittredge continues, pointing out that, if one compares 108 with 70, he will see that the theory of a continuous and orderly series is not a sound one. Sonnet 108 "calls the recipient 'sweet boy', while 70 is addressed to some one who has 'pass'd by the ambush of young days'." Kittredge is prominent among those who insist that Sonnets 127-154 do not make an orderly sequence. He further points out that if the Dark Lady "is to be identified with the stolen mistress of 40-42, that is further disproof of the continuity and completeness of the supposed cycle 1-126." He could well have added that 129 and 146, which have a general ethical content, seem out of place in the second series, 127-154.

Yet there remain many who accept the order in which Thorpe printed the sonnets, although conceding that occasionally that order is disturbed or reversed. Gottlob Regis (*Shakespeare-Almanack,* Berlin, 1836) was the first to identify what he described as the logical, cohesive groups. He was followed two years later in England by C. A. Brown (*Shakespeare's Autobiographical Poems,* London, 1838). Since Brown's theory has been so widely favored, particularly among those who accept an autobiographical interpretation of the sonnets, it may be summarized here. For Brown, the sonnets are really six "poems" — five addressed to Shakespeare's friend, each ending with an *Envoy*; the sixth addressed to the poet's mistress. Brown's analysis is as follows:

1. To his friend, persuading him to marry, 1-27.
2. To his friend, who has robbed the poet of his mistress, forgiving him, 27-55.
3. To his friend, complaining of his coldness, and warning him of life's decay, 56-77.
4. To his friend, complaining that he prefers another poet's

praises, and reproving him for faults that may injure his character, 78-101.

5. To his friend, excusing himself for having been sometimes silent, and disclaiming the charge of inconstancy, 102-106.

6. To his mistress, chiefly on her infidelity, 127-152. Brown found no place for Sonnets 145 and 146 in his sixth "poem." Nor did he believe that Sonnets 153 and 154 belonged to the sequence.

The cautious Sir Edmund K. Chambers (*William Shakespeare,* 1930, I, 560 f.) remained his skeptical self as regards theories relating to the order of the sonnets. He wrote: "The unity of the sonnets is one of atmosphere. The thread of incident is a frail one. Each sonnet is generally self-contained. A few are linked. On the other hand, there is occasionally a jar in the continuity, which may suggest misplacement." He concluded by pointing out that "subjectivity has had full swing" in the revisers of the order of the sonnets as they appeared in the 1609 Quarto.

It may well be argued that the sonnet sequence is not a way of telling a story. Nevertheless, many found narrative elements in Shakespeare's sonnets in the order in which Thorpe printed them. Gollancz, one of the more distinguished nineteenth century editors of Shakespeare's works, made the following analysis of the sequence, which, with some modifications, has recommended itself to many:

A. "The Better Angel": Sonnets 1-126

1. Love's Adoration: Sonnets 1-26 (26 is an envoy, followed by an "Interval").

2. Love's Trials: Sonnets 27-99 (32, 42, 55, 75, 96, and 99 are envoys, each followed by an "Interval," the one after 99 lasting a year or two).

3. Love's Triumph: Sonnets 100-126 (126 is the envoy).

B. "The Worser Spirit": Sonnets 127-152

C. "Love's Fire": Sonnets 153 and 154

Particularly in Sonnets 1-126 he found a continuous story conducted through various stages to its termination.

In contrast to Gollancz, Mr. G. B. Harrison (*Shakespeare: the Complete Works*, 1952, pp. 1592-1593) finds no continuous story in the sonnets, but he does provide a useful grouping illustrating narrative elements:

Sonnets 1-17: The poet calls upon the Fair Young Man to marry and thus "preserve" his beauty.

Sonnets 18-128: The poet speaks on various topics and occasions and in several moods. The sense of intimacy increases from sonnet to sonnet, and admiration is changed into love.

1. At the beginning the poet is shy and finds it difficult to speak in the presence of his friend. He finds himself able to express himself only in writing (Sonnet 23).

2. The poet, separated from the youth by the necessities of travel, keeps him constantly in mind (Sonnet 27).

3. The poet is an outcast, but the thought of his love comforts him (Sonnet 29).

4. The poet cautions his friend not to honor him publicly if he is to avoid scandal (Sonnet 36).

5. The friend steals the poet's mistress, but is forgiven (Sonnets 40-42).

6. The poet wears the youth's picture at his breast as he goes on a journey (Sonnets 47-49).

7. The poet is advanced in age (Sonnet 73).

8. Because others seek the patronage of the youth, especially a poet whose verse bears "proud, full sail," the poet becomes jealous (Sonnets 78-86).

9. The poet rebukes the youth for wantonness (Sonnet 96).

10. Away for a spring and a summer, the poet returns to the Fair Young Man (Sonnets 97-98).

11. The poet congratulates the youth on his release from a "confined doom" (Sonnet 107).

12. The poet again is reconciled with the youth after absence (Sonnet 109).

13. The poet is disgusted with his profession (Sonnets 110-111).

14. The poet offers a defense against the charge of ingratitude (Sonnet 117).

15. The poet expresses his regrets at having given away the "tables" the youth had given to him (Sonnet 126).

The next twenty-six sonnets are addressed to the Dark Lady, who has become an obsession with the poet.

1. She is described as being a skilled player of virginals.

2. She is untrue to him.

3. She is of loose moral character.

4. She is physically unattractive.

5. She is false to her own husband.

6. But the poet cannot help loving her.

The collection ends with two conventional love sonnets on Cupid.

THE QUESTION OF AUTOBIOGRAPHY

Before the first quarter of the nineteenth century, the question of autobiography in the sonnets received very little attention. It is true that in 1780, Steevens voiced his disgust with the tone and diction in Sonnets 1-126, the large group supposedly addressed to the Fair Young Man. He and Malone, his fellow editor, did make some effort to find out who might possibly fit the roles of friends and rivals. As Mr. G. B. Harrison has pointed out (*op. cit.*, p. 1592), most critics have tended to join one of two parties, whose respective views have been expressed by William Wordsworth and Matthew Arnold. Wordsworth wrote as follows:

> Scorn not the Sonnet; Critic, you have frowned,
> Mindless of its just honor; with this key
> Shakespeare unlocked his heart.

But according to Arnold, Shakespeare did no such thing; rather he remained impersonal when he recorded human passions:

> Others abide the question. Thou art free.
> We ask and ask—Thou smilest and art still,
> Out-topping knowledge.

Browning also rejected Wordsworth's view. "Did Shakespeare unlock his heart?" he asked. "Then so much less the Shakespeare he."

In the New Variorum edition of the sonnets (Vol. II, pp. 133-165) Hyder Rollins summed up or quoted verbatim the views of some 185 critics on the question of autobiographical interpretation of the poems. Of this number 110 reject the theory that Shakespeare indeed laid bare his heart, as opposed to 66 who are sure that he did so. Only 9 take the middle position, arguing that some of the sonnets are dramatic or literary exercises, and that others are distinctly autobiographical.

Sir Sidney Lee was a leader among those who refused to read autobiography into the sonnets, although he did go so far as to admit that a very few might possibly be autobiographical. "Autobiographical confessions," he insisted, "were very rarely the stuff of which the Elizabethan sonnet was made." He further pointed out that "adapted or imitated conceits are scattered over the whole of Shakespeare's collection," and that imitation and sincerity can never go hand in hand. George Saintsbury (*Cambridge History of*

English Literature, 1910, V, 259) agreed with Lee, declaring that to attempt to find the poet's life story in the poems is to follow a will-o'-the-wisp, and that we may never identify the friend, the mistress, and the Rival Poet. One other distinguished scholar may be quoted in support of this position. Writing judiciously as usual, George Lyman Kittredge (S.A.B., 1936, XI, 172 f.) had this to say:

> Baffled in their attempts to discover the undiscoverable . . . inquisitive spirits have retired from their assault upon the dramas of Shakespeare, and fallen furiously, in unabashed discomfiture, upon the defenceless sonnets.

Kittredge points out that a good sonnet necessarily appears to be a confession. "In a word, a sonnet must be either patently artificial, and then it is *bad*—or *good*, and then it sounds like autobiography." He concludes by asserting that "nothing can prove them [the sonnets] autobiographical except the discovery of outside evidence that they accord with facts of the poet's life; and no such evidence is forthcoming."

A number of distinguished Shakespearean critics, however, are no less sure that Shakespeare did reveal himself in the poems. F. J. Furnivall (ed. *Shakespeare*, 1877, pp. lxiii, lxvi) was an early leader of this group. "No one," he wrote, "can understand Shakespere who does not hold that his Sonnets are autobiographical, and that they explain the depths of the soul of the Shakespere who wrote the plays." Edward Dowden (ed. *Shakespeare*, 1888, p. 16 f.) rushed to Furnivall's support, flatly stating that he believed that "Shakespeare's sonnets express his own feeling in his own person." A. C. Bradley (*Oxford Lectures*, 1909, pp. 330-332), Sir Walter Raleigh (*Shakespeare*, 1907, pp. 87 f.), and W. M. A. Creizenach (*English Drama*, 1916, p. 92) also believed that the sonnets disclose the poet's most intimate feelings.

Three persons, be they fictitious or not, are either addressed or referred to in the poems: the Fair Young Man, the Dark Lady, and the Rival Poet. It is with these three that we are next concerned.

THE FAIR YOUNG MAN

As has been stated above, the Earl of Southampton and the Earl of Pembroke respectively have most often been identified as the beautiful youth addressed in Sonnets 1-126. There are many, however, who deny that Shakespeare intended more than flattery in his expression of deep regard for the young man, following a long established tradition both in England and abroad. This was the position taken by Sir Sidney Lee, who believed that the Poet sought no more than to attain and retain the patronage of a young nobleman, and who emphasized the fact that so many of the poems are thoroughly conventional, embodying purely derivative and traditional elements. But if all this be true, it is odd that Shakespeare should on occasion, as in Sonnets 69, 95, and 96, rebuke his friend, however mildly. As Mr. Peter Quennell has written (*op. cit.*, p. 143), "Either the whole collection is a stupendous literary fraud composed with the deliberate intention of flattering a vain, attractive youth . . . or the Poet means what he says." More recently Mr. J. Dover Wilson (*Shakespeare's Sonnets*, 1963, p. 41) expressed his conviction on the matter: "One cannot read the Sonnets attentively without realizing that the friendship between player and nobleman was . . . very real, came indeed to be intimate." It is indeed hard to avoid the conclusion that the poems were addressed to a real young man who is portrayed with all the emphasis of passionate personal feeling conveyed in the language of romantic adoration.

What does one learn about this youth from the sonnets? First that he is surpassingly beautiful. The word *handsome* will not do to describe the young man. The Poet speaks of his "love's fair brow" and describes him as being more lovely than a summer's day. To him the youth is his "sovereign" and his "Lord of love." Sonnet 20 tells us that the young man's beauty was of feminine cast. But the Poet does not neglect to speak of the "beauty of his mind" of which his physical beauty is a reflection. We learn also that the youth belongs to the upper class of society. That should be apparent from the Poet's imploring him to perpetuate his family line by begetting an heir—something that would be especially important to those who bear proud names. The adjective *gracious* used to describe the young man's bearing is most appropriate to a nobleman, and so with reference to the noun *presence*, which has aristocratic connotations. Sonnet 55 clearly indicates that he is indeed a young aristocrat. It may further be noted that, from time to time, the Poet gives expression to a sense of inferiority in relation to his friend, as in Sonnets 36 and 37.

If the youth can be gracious and kind, he is not without his faults. Much to the Poet's regret, he is on occasion given to wantonness, as we learn from Sonnets 35, 40, 42, and 89. He even wins the favors of the Poet's mistress.

And what exactly is the nature of this love of a man of mature years for a youth of perhaps seventeen or eighteen years of age? Understandably, to many it has appeared strange or even repellent, for Shakespeare uses words of affection normally employed by the male lover addressing his fair lady. To him the youth is his "Rose," his "Sweet Boy," and "the world's fresh ornament." The Poet's emotion, which originally is that of admiration, develops until it becomes adoration. But before one jumps to any conclusion regarding the propriety of the Poet's attitude toward the Fair Young Man, he should recall Edmund Malone's remarks to his fellow editor, Steevens, on the subject of Sonnet 20, which Steevens found to be quite offensive:

> Such addresses to men, however indelicate, were customary in our author's time and neither imparted criminality, nor were esteemed indecorous. To regulate our judgement of Shakespeare's poem by the modes of modern times, is sure as unreasonable as to try his plays by the rules of Aristotle.

As a matter of fact Sonnet 20, wherein the youth is described as having "a woman's face" and is called the Poet's "master mistress" provides complete refutation of the idea that the first 126 sonnets celebrate a homosexual love affair. The last six lines read as follows:

> And for a woman wert thou first created,
> Till Nature as she wrought thee fell a-doting,
> And by addition me of thee defeated,
> By adding one thing to my purpose nothing.
> But since she pricked thee out for woman's pleasure,
> Mine be thy love, and thy love's use their treasure.

Not to be ignored also is the fact that, on occasion, the youth becomes the Poet's rival for the affections of the older man's mistress, and that the affair with the Dark Lady is the chief theme of Sonnets 127-154.

THE DARK LADY

Attempts to identify the Dark Lady, who is prominent especially in Sonnets 127-152, have been quite as numerous as have the efforts to identify the Fair Young Man. Among the candidates are

Shakespeare's wife, Anne Hathaway; Lady Penelope Rich, the Stella of Sir Philip Sidney's *Astrophel and Stella*; either Anne or Jane Davenant, first and second wives of an Oxford innkeeper; Mary Fitton, Maid of Honor to Queen Elizabeth I; and one Lucy,a Negro prostitute. The Pembrokites particularly have favored Mary Fitton, since the Earl of Pembroke had an affair with her, and she gave birth to his son. But there survive three portraits of the lady, who turned out to have had gray eyes and a fair complexion.

Since, as Hyder Rollins has pointed out (*Variorum*, Vol. II, p. 242) the Dark Lady is inextricably bound with the problem of auto-biography, date, arrangement, the identity of the friend, and (some insist) the Rival Poet, efforts to identify her will no doubt be multi-plied. But perhaps Sir Sidney Lee was correct: she may be no more than a conventional literary figure, by means of which Shakespeare carried forward the anti-Petrarchan theme. The Italian sonneteers began early to mock the traditional attributes of female beauty as Shakespeare does, notably in Sonnet 130. Woman, who embodies *amor sensuale*, was depicted as inferior to man. All Shakespeare's reproaches and curses, all his attempts to justify the lady's mis-deeds by admitting himself to be at fault are commonplace among the Petrarchans like Bembo and Tasso. The Dark Lady may well be an ingeniously constructed counterpoise to the Petrarchan ideal.

Real or fictitious, the Dark Lady is a fascinating creature. She fascinates by some nameless spell; she can turn the heart hot and cold. Assuming that just one lady is referred to, one first finds reference to her in Sonnet 40, in which, along with the next two sonnets, the Poet laments the fact that his friend has sought out the lady, who is tempted by his beauty and "straying youth." The Poet expresses his grief, but forgives the Fair Young Man. She reappears in Sonnet 127 and thereafter is the dominant figure in the poems. The Poet praises her dark beauty and especially her eyes of "raven black." In Sonnet 128, we learn that she is an accomplished mu-sician. Then immediately we are told that she represents evil; and the Poet, in a moment of deep remorse, bewails the fact that he cannot "shun the heaven that leads men to this hell." The love de-picted here is actually lust; it is wholly physical.

In Sonnet 130, the mood changes. In the wittiest, most satirical poem in the sequence, Shakespeare achieves high comedy as he again praises the dark beauty of the lady. Here he is the complete anti-Petrarchan, poking fun as he does at the dedicated Petrarchan. The fact of the matter is that he is satirizing the Petrarchanism of a fellow poet, Thomas Watson. Practically every line of the Shakespearean sonnet provides amusing satirical comment on the seventh poem of Watson's *Passionate Century of Love* (1582). On the left are Watson's lines; on the right, Shakespeare's comment:

Her yellow locks exceed the beaten gold	If hairs be wires, black wires grow on her head.
Her sparkling eyes in heav'n a place deserve	My Mistress' eyes are nothing like the sun
Her words are music all of silver sound	I love to hear her speak, yet well I know That music hath a far more pleasant sound.
On either cheek a rose and lily lie	I have seen roses damasked, red and white, But no such roses see I in her cheeks.
Her breath is sweet perfume, or holy flame	And in some perfume is there more delight Than in the breath that from my mistress reeks.
Her lips more red than any coral stone Her neck more white than aged swans that moan	Coral is far more red than her lips red If snow be white, why then her breasts are dun.

Next the Poet charges the lady with cruelty, but nevertheless refers to her as "the fairest and most precious jewel" and adds that "In nothing art thou black save in thy deeds" (Sonnet 131). After lauding once more her dark beauty, the Poet then speaks of her "cruel eyes" and revives the charge that she has enslaved the Fair Young Man as well as himself. As he writes in Sonnet 134, "Thou hast both him and me." There follow two of the "Will" sonnets in which occur the erotic pun on the Poet's own name, emphasizing the lecherous nature of this ardent love affair. In Sonnets 137 and

138, the Poet accuses the lady of falsehood, referring to her "eyes of falsehood" and her "false-speaking tongue." He concludes Sonnet 138 with a line incorporating another erotic pun, once more underscoring the physical aspect of his love: "Therefore I lie with her, and she with me."

Subsequently, the Poet dwells upon her cruelty again, her "proud heart." In Sonnet 141 he states that, although he cannot help loving her, he discerns "a thousand errors" in her. He then speaks of his "sinful loving," the "false bonds of love," and her infidelity. The Dark Lady appears as his "worser spirit" in contrast to his "better angel," the Fair Young Man, whom she tempts from his side in Sonnet 144. He describes his love as a fever in Sonnet 147 and identifies Reason as the physician whose ministrations he ignores. The Poet concludes vehemently:

> For I have sworn thee fair, and thought thee bright,
> Who art as black as hell, as dark as night.

The Poet goes on to denounce the lady for her "foul faults," her continued cruelty, her cheating. And in Sonnet 151 he again underscores the fleshly aspect of his love with an erotic pun:

> ... flesh stays no further reason,
> But, rising at thy name, doth point out thee
> As his triumphant prize.

Finally in Sonnet 152, he charges the Dark Lady with being "twice foresworn," one who has broken her bed-vows:

> For I have sworn thee fair; more perjured eye,
> To swear against the truth so foul a lie.

It is apparent that love as it is revealed in the sonnets was a stormy one, marked by deep passion and often violent emotion.

THE RIVAL POET

The Rival Poet, referred to in Sonnets 76-86, is the third mysterious person in Shakespeare's poems. The Poet may refer tacitly to him also in Sonnets 100-103. Whoever he was, Shakespeare speaks of him as "a worthier pen" (79.6), "a better spirit" (80.2) to whom he was "inferior far" (80.7), and makes reference to "the proud full sail of his great verse" (86.1) and to the fact that he had been taught by spirits "to write above a mortal pitch" (86.5 f.). For generations commentators have sought his identity, and many names have been suggested. Recently M. A. L. Rowse, a Southamptonite who dates the sonnets rather early, revived the nomination of Christopher Marlowe, arguing that the phrase "the proud full sail of his great verse" must surely be applicable to him. Mr. Rowse further argues that "that affable familiar ghost/Which nightly gull him with intelligence [i.e., news or information]" is a reference to Mephistopheles, the devil who for a twenty-four year period served Dr. Faustus, the protagonist in Marlowe's well-known tragedy. In contrast, there are those who claim that Marlowe was the author of many of the sonnets, including the Rival Poet ones, and that the Rival Poet therefore was Shakespeare himself!

There is actually no reason why a single rival should be preferred to plural rival poets, since in Sonnet 85 Shakespeare refers to "others" who wrote admirable verse. But most commentators insist on one person. In addition to Marlowe, Michael Drayton, Samuel Daniel, George Peele, Thomas Nash, Thomas Lodge, Richard Barnfield, Barnaby Rich, Robert Greene, Edmund Spenser, George Chapman, and Ben Johnson have their champions.

Ben Jonson's name was presented rather early by one J. G. R. (*Notes and Queries*, February 12, 1859, p. 122), but has not been accepted widely. It was argued that Sonnets 78 and 80 especially refer to him, and that the figures of ships ("proudest sail" and "saucy bark") are exactly like those Thomas Fuller later used in describing the wit-combats of Jonson and Shakespeare at the Mermaid in which the two were compared to a Spanish great galleon and an English man-of-war.

William Minto (*Characteristics of English Poets from Chaucer to Shirley*, 1874, pp. 290-292) was first to suggest Chapman, who has remained a favorite choice for many. Minto argued that Chapman's *Shadow of the Night*, 1594, goes far to establish his identity with Shakespeare's rival, especially since the purpose of the work is to extol the wonderful power of Night in imparting knowledge to her votaries. F. J. Furnival (*Shakespeare*, 1877, p. lxv n.) joined Minto, insisting that the first line of Sonnet 86 was an unmistakable reference to the swelling hexameters of Chapman's Englishing of Homer.

One of the unique and far-fetched theories propounded was that Dante was the Rival Poet. This was advanced by an anonymous writer in *Blackwood's Magazine*, 1884-1886. He reasoned as follows. Shakespeare calls his rival "a spirit," thus showing that he was not a living contemporary. Also the "compeers by night" (86.7) are Homer, Virgil, Horace, and others. The "affable familiar ghost" (86.9) is Beatrice.

Old theories will be revived; new ones advanced—tomorrow, tomorrow, and tomorrow. But like the Fair Young Man and the Dark Lady, the identity of the Rival Poet will probably remain a mystery.

DOMINANT THEMES

IMMORTALITY THROUGH OFFSPRING

In the first large division of the Sonnets, Time is the great enemy of youth and beauty. The Poet, like so many of his contemporaries, viewed with pain and sorrow the corrosive effects of Time and sought answers to the question of how it could be defeated and youth and beauty preserved. In Shakespeare's sequence three answers are propounded. The first of these, along with the extolling of the young man's unmatched beauty, is the theme of the first seventeen sonnets. These constitute a group in which the youth is urged to defeat the "bloody tyrant" Time by marrying and begetting an heir, thus achieving a kind of immortality through offspring. Characteristically, Shakespeare develops the theme in three quatrains, wherein he generalizes; then, in the final couplet, he particularizes, addressing the young man directly. His initial argument is that the youth owes it to himself and to the world to conquer "wasteful Time" by continuing his life and beauty through his children.

In the very first sonnet the theme is introduced. It should be noted that the poem includes praise of the youth's beauty and blame for his failure to try to preserve it. In lines 5-8, he is accused of harboring self-love, thus making "a famine where abundance lies" and "waste in niggarding"—that is, in hoarding his beauty. The Poet then implores the young man to "pity the world" and give it its due—the propagation of species. The argument and plea are continued in the second sonnet, wherein Shakespeare finds another metaphor, a martial one, to make his case:

When forty winters shall besiege thy brow,
And dig deep trenches in thy beauty's field,

Thy youth's proud livery, so gazed on now,
Will be a tattered weed [garment] of small
worth held. . . .

The argument is carried forward in the third sonnet by means of a metaphor from husbandry:

For where is she so fair whose uneared [untilled] womb
Disdains the tillage of thy husbandry?

(5-6)

The Poet insists that the youth is the image of his mother, and that in him she "Calls back the lovely April of his prime." The poem ends with the dire prophecy: "Die single and thine image dies with thee."

Sonnet 4 provides a kind of explication of all the Poet has been saying so far. In a series of questions and statements, he drives home the lesson of the right use of one's endowments. It is clear that Shakespeare had in mind the Parable of the Talents: the wise use of God's gifts and Nature's gifts is imperative. Lines 3 and 4 contain the key idea:

Nature's bequest gives nothing but doth lend,
And being frank she lends to those are free.

Being generous and liberal, Nature lends her gifts to those who possess these same qualities, not to "niggards," that is, not to misers. The contrast between the youth's alleged miserliness and Nature's munificence is repeated in lines 7 and 8, this time in terms of usury:

Profitless usurer, why dost thou use
So great a sum of sums yet canst not live?

The term *use* here means both "invest" and "use up." Similarly, *live* means both "make a living" and "endure." The inevitable conclusion is that if the youth does not make use of his beauty properly and unselfishly by seeking to perpetuate it, he is doomed to oblivion, since he will die childless.

Sonnets 5 and 6 are a set of closely related poems in which the individual's mortal partaking of immortality finds expression in the erotic image of distillation, the use of which does not make for an obtrusion of its physical nature.

A second set, sonnets 9 and 10, deserves some special attention. In these poems, the Poet develops the argument that

> beauty's waste hath in the world an end,
> And kept unused, the user so destroys it. . . .
>
> (11-12)

Sonnets 12, 15, and 16 constitute a final set of closely related poems. Here especially the Poet inveighs against devouring Time, making reference to "Time's scythe" and to "this bloody tyrant Time." So the major theme is clearly set forth and developed from more than one point of view: the youth owes it to himself and the world to conquer Time, to continue his life and beauty by fathering children.

It may be pointed out that Sonnets 12 and 15, so notable for their musical quality, thanks largely to the effective use of alliteration and attractive vowel runs, are of unusual merit. They are almost always included in anthologies of lyric poetry. Note the beauty of the opening lines of Sonnet 12:

> When I do count the clock that tells the time,
> And see brave day sunk in hideous night;
> When I behold the violet past prime,
> And sable curls are silvered o'er with white. . . .

These indeed convey the sense of sorrow, of poignancy, at the thought that youth and beauty must be cut down by Time's scythe. The contrast of "brave day" (i.e., splendid day) with "hideous night" is particularly good. And as Mr. Edward Hubler has pointed out (*The Sense of Shakespeare's Sonnets*, 1952, p. 25): "No sonnet beginning with 'When' is an undistinguished poem." The reason is that the structure of such sonnets, and there are several in the sequence, is periodic, making for tightness of organization, logical progression, and avoidance of the tacked-on couplet.

IMMORTALITY THROUGH VERSE

It is not without interest to find that the word *time* is used seventy-eight times in Sonnets 1-126 and not once in the remaining sonnets. Of this first large group, nine develop the theme of poetry's power to conquer Time, which is variously described as "swift-footed" and "devouring," reference also being made to "Time's fell hand" and to "Time's injurious hand."

Sonnet 18 introduces this new theme, along with those related to the young man's beauty and to his temperate, unspoiled nature. This sonnet, one of the best known in the sequence, is memorable for the skillful and varied presentation of subject matter. Initially, the Poet poses a question—"Shall I compare thee to a summer's day?"—and then corrects it. The imagery is the very essence of simplicity. In the second quatrain, legal terminology is introduced ("summer's lease") in rather daring contrast to the commonplace images in the first quatrain. The Poet returns to the opening image in lines of comparable simplicity but marked by a fuller tone and deeper feeling. Then follows the concluding couplet:

> So long as men can breathe or eyes can see,
> So long lives this, and this gives life to thee.

There are many classical and medieval antecedents for such a self-claim of immortality. They may be found, for example, in Ovid, *Amores*, I.xv. 41 f.; in Horace, *Odes*, III, 30; in Propertius I.vii. 21-24; in Dante, *Inferno*, IV, 97 ff., and elsewhere. It may be added this sense of Time's hostility is fundamental, not only to the sonnets, but to the plays of the years 1592-1595. Indeed, the theme was a commonplace one at this time. Usually, it was associated with the Platonizing philosophy of the court poets such as Sidney, or with the "otherworld" attitude inherited from the medieval period. In Shakespeare's sonnets it is the first attitude which prevails. Natural fear of the action of Time is not offset by the religious view in his sequence.

In Sonnet 19, the Poet assures the young man that his "love shall in [his] verse ever live long"; in Sonnet 38, he addresses the youth, urging him to be the tenth Muse and "let him bring forth/ Eternal numbers to outlive long date." Again, in Sonnet 54, he insists that the beauteous and lovely youth will not really fade or perish because the Poet "distills" his "truth." And so from several points of view the theme is presented: in Sonnets 60, 63, 65 (wherein the young man is described as "Time's best jewel"), 81, and 100. In that last sonnet, the Poet berates his "forgetful muse":

> Give my love fame faster than Time wastes life;
> So thou prevent's his scythe and crooked knife.

All in all, this group comprises a most interesting and successful set of poems.

IMMORTALITY THROUGH LOVE

The theme of immortality through love is developed implicitly and explicitly in several of the first one hundred and twenty-six poems. Not only is the youth granted immortality through verse, but since the Poet's enduring love is repeatedly stressed, the Poet himself gains a kind of immortality. "O, let me true in love but truly write," exclaims the Poet (21.9). And in Sonnet 22 he argues that, so long as he holds the affection of the youth, he can defy Time:

> My glass shall not persuade me I am old,
> So long as youth and thou are of one date. . . .
>
> (1-2)

The same idea is expressed in other words in Sonnet 25:

> The painful warrior famouséd for fight,
> After a thousand victories once foiled,
> Is from the book of honor razéd quite,
> And all the rest forgot for which he toiled.
>   Then happy I that love and am beloved
>   Where I may not remove, nor be removed.
>
> (9-14)

The concept of Time defeated by love also finds expression in Sonnet 62:

> 'Tis thee, myself, that for myself I praise,
> Painting my age with beauty of thy days.
>
> (13-14)

In Sonnet 100, the Poet asks:

> Give my love fame faster than Time wastes life;
> So thou prevent'st his scythe and crooked knife.
>
> (13-14)

Especially in Sonnet 116, one of the finest in the sequence, the theme is presented: Love is not love, the Poet argues:

> Which alters when it alteration finds,
> Or bends with the remover to remove.
>
> (4-6)

It is "an ever-fixéd mark/ That looks on tempests and is never shaken . . ." (5-6). Finally, in Sonnet 123, the Poet insists that Time will never be able to boast that he does undergo a change of heart: "I will be true despite thy scythe and thee" (14).

THE THEME OF COMPENSATION

In at least three sonnets, often referred to as the "despair" sonnets, Shakespeare states that the Fair Young Man provides compensation for all the failures and disappointments in his life. The first is Sonnet 25, in which he writes:

> Let those who are in favor with their stars
> Of public honour and proud titles boast,
> Whilst I, who fortune of such triumph bars,
> Unlook'd for joy in that I honour most.
>
> (1-4)

The youth's love more than compensates for his adverse fortune. Better known is Sonnet 29, with its magnificent simile in the third quatrain. This deserves quotation in full:

> When in disgrace with Fortune and men's eyes,
> I all alone beweep my outcast state,
> And trouble deaf heaven with my bootless cries,
> And look upon myself and curse my fate,
> Wishing me like to one more rich in hope,
> Featured like him, like him with friends possessed,
> Desiring this man's art, and that man's scope,
> With what I most enjoy contented least;
> Yet in these thoughts myself almost despising,
> Haply I think on thee, and then my state,
> Like to the lark at break of day arising
> From sullen earth, sings hymns at heaven's gate;
> For thy sweet love rememb'red such wealth brings,
> That then I scorn to change my state with kings.

In Sonnet 37 there is an even more explicit treatment of this same theme: The Poet's awareness of his friend's love more than makes up for all his own deficiencies. The Poet speaks of himself as one who has been "made lame by fortune's dearest spite" but goes on to say, "I in thy abundance am suffic'd" (11). Again in the beautiful Sonnet 30 he repeats that the youth is a priceless compensation, not only for many disappointments and unrealized hopes, but also for the loss of earlier friends:

> But if the while I think on thee, dear friend,
> All losses are restor'd and sorrows end.
>
> (13-14)

This subject of lost friends and loves is the main subject of Sonnet 31, which ends with these lines:

> Their images I lov'd I view in thee,
> And thou, all they, has all the all of me.

Finally in Sonnet 66, Shakespeare declares that the youth provides compensation for his own deficiencies, disappointments, and losses. Moreover, he compensates for all that "sea of trouble," those "whips and scorns of Time" of which Hamlet speaks in his second soliloquy; and, like Hamlet, the Poet gives expression to the death wish: "for restful death I cry" (1). But in the final couplet he reverses his attitude:

> Tir'd with all these, from these would I be gone,
> Save that, to die, I leave my love alone.

As Mr. J. B. Leishman has stated (*Themes and Variations in Shakespeare's Sonnets*, 1961, p. 209) there is "no real precedent in previous love-poetry either for Shakespeare's topic or for Shakespeare's treatment of it."

LOVE IN ABSENCE

A total of twenty-three sonnets develop the theme of absence. Although none of these may be counted among the poems of distinction in the sequence, all are interesting for what they glance at and for what they give us of the Poet's mind. Certain ones, notably 36, 49, 57, derive their power from the Poet's fears for the dissolution of the friendship as a result of the separation. The concept of identity — the idea of one soul in two bodies — was commonplace in Shakespeare's time; and this finds a place in the absence sonnets.

In Sonnet 27, the Poet describes himself as being weary with toil and vainly trying to sleep. He continues his travels mentally:

> Lo, thus, by day my limbs, by night my mind,
> For thee, and for myself, no quiet find
>
> (13-14)

And in the next sonnet he again speaks of himself as one "debarred the benefit of rest," so much does he suffer in absence from his dear friend. In Sonnet 39 he speaks of the youth as being the better part of himself. "O, absence," he continues, "what a torment wouldst thou prove," were it not for thoughts of love.

It is again the sleepless poet who speaks in Sonnet 43:

> All days are nights to see till I see thee,
> And nights bright days when dreams do show thee me.
>
> (13-14)

In the next sonnet he complains against "injurious distance" which has separated him from the young man, but expresses satisfaction in the fact that "nimble thought can jump both sea and land" so that mentally he is united with his friend. Here and in Sonnet 45, the Poet wishes that he were entirely made of the lighter elements, "slight air and purging fire," so that he could actually leap the distance to his friend, as his thoughts and wishes, being incorporeal and therefore free of earth and water, were able to do.

In Sonnet 47, the Poet finds solace in a picture of the young man which he carries with him:

> So, either by thy picture or my love,
> Thyself away are present still with me. . . .
>
> (9-10)

In Sonnet 49 he especially is concerned that the separation may lead to the dissolution of the prized friendship. In Sonnet 50, he complains that his "grief lies onward and [his] joy behind," as he wearily rides farther away from the one he loves. He continues the same subject in Sonnet 51, concluding:

Since from thee going he [the horse] went willful slow,
Towards thee I'll run and give him leave to go.

(13-14)

Later, in Sonnet 97, the Poet, aware that it is summer, nevertheless compares the youth's absence, or his own, to a bleak winter:

What freezings have I felt, what dark days seen,
What old December's bareness everywhere!

(3-4)

"Summer and his pleasure" wait on the youth, he continues: And, "thou away, the very birds are mute" (12). And so in Sonnet 98, wherein the Poet, with his sure eye for nature, describes the beauties of spring, all of which serve only to remind him of the young man:

Yet seemed it winter still, and, you away,
As with your shadow I with these did play.

(13-14)

In Sonnet 99, the nature theme once more prevails:

More flowers I noted, yet I none could see,
But sweet or color it had stolen from thee.

(13-14)

Yet again, in Sonnet 113, all things remind him of youth — the birds, flowers, the day, the night:

Incapable of more, replete with you,
My most true mind thus maketh mine eye untrue.

(13-14)

THE FAREWELL SONNETS

In addition to the "Absence" sonnets, there is an interesting group, nos. 87-93, in which the Poet says his farewell to the beautiful young man from whom he is to be, for some reason not made clear, permanently separated. In the first he writes:

> Farewell, thou art too dear for my possessing,
> And like enough thou know'st thy estimate [value].
>
> (1-2)

With quiet resignation he admits that his claims on the youth have expired. "For how do I hold thee but by thy granting?" he asks, adding that the great gift of close friendship had been granted by some mistake which must now be corrected:

> Thus have I had thee as a dream doth flatter,
> In sleep a king, but waking no such matter.
>
> (13-14)

In the next sonnet, the Poet generously states that when the youth is disposed to value him slightly he will not protest but will fight against himself and for the youth, since he is aware of his own limitations:

> Such is my love, to thee I so belong,
> That for thy right myself will bear all wrong.
>
> (13-14)

In Sonnet 89, he again speaks in behalf of the friend he is about to lose:

> Thou canst not, love, disgrace me half so ill,
> To set a form upon desirèd change,
> As I'll myself disgrace, knowing thy will.
>
> (5-7)

"Then hate me when thou wilt," he exclaims in Sonnet 90, and the youth must not delay in breaking the relationship; such delay would only prolong the Poet's suffering:

> But in the onset come; so shall I taste
> At first the very worst of fortune's might. . . .
>
> (11-12)

In the next sonnet the Poet measures the value he places upon the young man's friendship:

Thy love is better than high birth to me,
Richer than wealth, prouder than garments' cost. . . .
(9-10)

And he understandably concedes that, with the loss of such love, he can expect only wretchedness. In the last two sonnets in the group, the Poet finds some solace in the thought that, although he is to be separated from the young man, he has no reason to believe that the youth has been unfaithful to him. The separation, it would seem, will result from the force of circumstances.

DARK BEAUTY: THE ANTI-PETRARCHAN THEME

In the discussion of the Dark Lady, it has been pointed out that Shakespeare departed radically from the strict Petrarchan tradition, according to which the lady was invariably of fair complexion. In Sonnet 127 he insists that black is now "beauty's successive [legitimate] heir" and that blond has become illegitimate, since "every tongue says beauty" should be black. Sonnet 130, which has been quoted and discussed above, carries forward this anti-Petrarchan theme amusingly. It will be recalled that the Poet practically boasts that "black wires," not golden strands, grow on his lady's head, and that he sees no "roses damasked red and white" in her cheeks. Again in Sonnet 132 he praises the dark beauty of his lady love, concluding wittily:

Then will I swear beauty herself is black,
And all they foul that thy complexion lack.

LOVE TURNED TO LUST

A group of nine sonnets have as their theme "Love turned to lust," again illustrating the range of topics in the sequence. The Poet depicts himself as being sensually enslaved by the fascinating Dark Lady. The theme is introduced in Sonnet 129, early in the second large division of the poems. Lust, he writes, is "Enjoyed no sooner but despised straight":

Past reason hunted, and no sooner had,
Past reason hated as a swallowed bait
On purpose laid to make the taker mad. . . .
(6-8)

"All this the world well knows," concludes the Poet. "Yet none knows well,/ To shun the heaven [sensation] that leads men to hell." The "Will" sonnets—135, 136, 143—place the same emphasis on the torments of lust, the term *will* meaning carnal desire. And also in Sonnet 138, with its erotic pun on the verb *lies,* the Poet speaks of the lady's "false-speaking tongue" and, making use of an erotic pun, goes on to say:

> Therefore I lie with her, and she with me
> And in our faults by lies we flattered be.
>
> (13-14)

It is of a "sensual feast" that he speaks in Sonnet 141, and in Sonnet 142 he frankly admits that such love is his sin. He accuses the lady of being promiscuous and robbing "other's beds' revenue of their rents," i.e., robbing wives of what their husbands owed them. Next, in Sonnet 144, he describes the lady as his "worser spirit" in contrast to the Fair Young Man, his "better angel," whom she seeks to corrupt. Finally, he describes his love as a fever, and states that he errs in not following the advice of Reason, his physician. "Past cure am I," he admits, in Sonnet 147, adding that "Desire is death" and that he has become "frantic-mad."

RELIGION

A religious theme is, perhaps, the last one to look for in an Elizabethan sonnet sequence, wherein love is the chief subject. But in Sonnet 146 Shakespeare developed that theme with unusual intensity. This is the one strictly religious poem in the group. In the words of Mr. Edward Hubler (*op. cit.,* p. 62), "Shakespeare presents Christianity without apology." He speaks vehemently of the inherent willfulness of the flesh and insists that only when sin is defeated will death be conquered. And sin will go down to defeat only when man has learned to emphasize the spiritual as opposed to the physical, to concern himself with his soul, the center of his "sinful earth."

> So shalt thou feed on Death, that feeds on men,
> And Death once dead, there's no more dying then.

The thought in this final couplet makes one recall the words of St.

Paul: "O death, where is thy sting? O grave, where is thy victory? The sting of death is sin..."—words hailing the triumph of the spirit.

OTHER FACETS OF INTEREST

NATURE IMAGERY

One of the many interesting elements in Shakespeare's sonnets is the nature imagery. To quote Mr. Edward Hubler once more (p. 30):

He saw nature precisely and was always able to find the right words for her loveliness....It is to the exercise of this talent that the absence sonnets of widest fame owe their renown. Two of them ("How like a winter" and "From you I have been absent") are remembered for passages of unobtrusive melody and lines of easy grace.

Particularly, Shakespeare always wrote well on nature's morning loveliness and her plenitude. References to the beauty of early morning are many:

Sonnet 7

Lo, in the orient when the gracious light
Lifts up his burning head. . . .

(1-2)

Sonnet 29

Like to the lark at break of day arising
From sullen earth. . . .

(11-12)

Sonnet 33

Full many a glorious morning have I seen
Flatter the mountain tops with sovereign eye,
Kissing with golden face the meadows green,
Gilding pale streams with heavenly alchemy. . . .

(1-4)

Nor does the Poet neglect "swart-complexioned night" (Sonnet 28).

The seasons, to be sure, receive full attention—especially spring. Although he admits that "Rough winds do shake the darling buds of May" (18), he notes more often "April's first-born flowers" and writes with enthusiasm of "proud-pied April, dressed in all his trim" and of the "lily's white" and the "deep vermilion of the rose"(98). Elsewhere he notices "summer's green, all girded up in sheaves" (12), and he speaks of "sweet-seasoned showers" (75). Fall and winter also receive attention. With reference to fall, best known are the following opening lines from Sonnet 73:

> That time of year thou mayst in me behold
> When yellow leaves, or none, or few, do hang
> Upon those boughs which shake against the cold,
> Bare ruined choirs where late the sweet birds sang.

But fall is not always a season of sadness; it can be "teeming autumn, big with rich increase" (97). The Poet recalls the "stormy gusts of winter's day" (13) and "old December's bareness everywhere"(97). One cannot help being impressed with this seemingly effortless poetry of nature.

ASTROLOGY

Inherited from the medieval period was the idea that fate was often due to the influences of heavenly bodies, which in their eternal movements in the sky turned up good or bad fortune for mankind. Since the moon was nearest to the earth, it was deemed to have the strongest influences working for mundane variability and mutability, and particularly at times of eclipse showing its powers most obviously in such matters of essential mortality as generation and corruption. The prime importance of the moon in relation to earthly events was recognized by the Middle Ages in countless treatises on astrology and in constant application of astrological doctrine to daily life. The moon was, then, the ruling queen of variability, not only for professional astrologists, but for the unlearned and the practical man of affairs. Available was the *lunarium,* a sort of almanac listing under all the days of the month the chances, lucky or unlucky, which the moon conferred upon common undertakings. Comparable guide books relating to the influence of the stars were available. Such books continued to be popular throughout the sixteenth century. Astrological language, therefore, is common in Shakespeare and in all Elizabethan writings.

"The fault which lies in the stars," which had become an obsession in the later classical world as well as in the Middle Ages, no less interested Shakespeare and his generation. The stars, it was believed, could work for good or ill. The seven chief ones were dominating and often terrifying forces operating upon mankind. It was a brave man indeed who, like Romeo, dared to defy the stars.

In view of all this, it is not surprising that astrology (sometimes called astronomy) should find a place in Shakespeare's poems. In Sonnet 14 the first reference occurs. The Poet denies that he depends upon the stars to determine his fate:

> Not from the stars do I my judgment pluck,
> And yet me thinks I have astronomy;
> But not to tell of good or evil luck,
> Of plagues, of dearths, or seasons quality. . . .
>
> (1-4)

What he is leading up to is a familiar conceit: the Fair Young Man's beautiful eyes are the stars that guide him. In Sonnet 25 Shakespeare refers to "those who are in favor with their stars," implying that he is not numbered among them—or would not be, were it not for his love for the youth. And in Sonnet 26, he speaks of "whatever star that guides" him. Later, in Sonnet 60, he makes the first mention of "crooked eclipses" which fight against his glory. Finally, in Sonnet 107 he states that "The mortal moon hath her eclipse endured..." This line has been variously interpreted. It has been argued that Shakespeare may refer to 1588, when the Spanish Armada, thought to have assumed a crescent formation, was destroyed; to 1595, when the moon actually underwent a total eclipse; to the same year, when Queen Elizabeth I survived a critical period in her horoscope; or to 1599, when the Queen survived a dangerous illness.

THE ACTING PROFESSION

In two of the sonnets Shakespeare makes reference to the acting profession in a most interesting way. It will be recalled that he was not only a poet-dramatist but also an actor in the Lord Chamberlain's Men, which became the King's Men when James I came to the throne in 1603. There is evidence that he acted the role of the

Ghost in *Hamlet* and, in all probability, that of Prospero in *The Tempest.* He was also listed among the Dramatis Personae for Ben Jonson's *Everyman in His Humour,* which was performed at the Curtain Theatre in 1598 and was, indeed, the theatrical success of that year. There is little reason to doubt that Shakespeare played many other roles. It is inevitable, then, that reference to the acting profession should find a place in the sequence.

The first occurs in Sonnet 23, wherein the Poet compares himself to "an imperfect actor on the stage,/Who with his fear is put beside himself." Most interesting, however, is Sonnet 110. In a mood of despair, Shakespeare writes:

> Alas, 'tis true I have gone here and there
> And made myself a motley to the view....
>
> (1-2)

Motley, of course, was a garment of various colors formerly worn by court jesters. It also meant a jester or a fool. It is not to be assumed that Shakespeare played the role of a clown or a fool at the Globe or elsewhere, as, for example, when his company toured the provinces. Rather, he seems to be referring to the low social status accorded actors at that time. They were officially classified with "sturdy rogues and beggars." It was for this reason that actors became the so-called "servants" of some noble or even of the Crown. Under such an arrangement they were protected from harassment by the law.

STYLE

As has been made clear, most of the sixteenth century writers of love poetry vied with each other in the use of fanciful, far-fetched metaphors and extravagant terms of praise in describing the lady who was the supposed object of their affections. Sir Philip Sidney, the most distinguished formal critic of the Elizabethan age, objected strenuously to this practice, setting forth his views in *The Defense of Poetry* (1595). Ironically, he was, on occasion, an offender himself in his sonnet sequence, *Astrophel and Stella.* In the critical work he had the following to say:

> But truly many of such writings as come under the banner
> of irresistible love; if I were a mistress, would never per-
> suade me they were in love; so coldly they apply fiery

speeches, as men that had rather read lovers' writings, and so caught up certain swelling phrases (which hang together like a man that once told me the wind was at northwest, and by south, because he would be sure to name winds enough), then that in truth they feel those passions which easily (as I think) may be revealed by that same forcibleness or *energia* (as the Greeks call it) of the writer. But let this be sufficient though short note, that all miss the right use of the material point of poesy.

Now for the outside of it, which is words, or (as I may term it) diction, it is even well worse. So is it that Honey-flowing matron Eloquence appareled, or rather disguised, in a courtesan-like painted affection: one time with so far-fetched words that many seem monster, but seem strangers, to any poor Englishman; another time, with coursing the letter, as if they were bound to follow the method of a dictionary; another time, with figures and flowers extremely winter-starved.

Judging by his practice in his sonnet sequence, Shakespeare endorsed Sidney's views. Like him he rejected "taffeta phrases, silken terms precise, thrice-piled hyperboles." In *Love's Labour's Lost,* a feast of language in which various aberrations of language are illustrated and satirized, these are a source of good comedy: Byron, the most gifted practitioner of such extravagant, affected language, is brought to the point where he vows never again to so offend against truth and reality.

Like Sidney, in his sonnets, Shakespeare rejects all such affectation, making a plea for honesty in the expression of his passion. On occasion he modestly insists that he writes only "rude lines" which are "outstripped by every pen," for he will not employ fanciful conceits and other extravagances of expression (Sonnet 32). Thus, in Sonnet 76 he writes:

Why is my verse so barren of new pride [adornment],
So far from variation or quick change?
Why with the time do I not glance aside
To new-found methods and to compounds strange?
Why write I still all one, ever the same,
And keep invention in a noted weed,
That every word doth almost tell my name,
Showing its birth, and where they did proceed?

(1-8)

And in Sonnet 83 he declares that he never saw that the Fair Young Man "did painting need." Again in Sonnet 85 he states that his Muse is "tongue-tied" and in Sonnet 103 he complains: "Alack, what poverty my Muse brings forth." It is, of course, in Sonnet 130 that he satirizes most wittily the typical conceits of Petrarchanism.

Just as he will avoid affected language and high astounding terms as he applies in the sonnets noted above, so Shakespeare will not be guilty of coursing the letter—the over-use of alliteration, a practice upon which Sidney also frowned. When he does use alliteration, he does so with complete effectiveness, creating a beautiful, haunting melody. The most notable example is found in the opening lines to Sonnet 30:

> When to the sessions of sweet silent thought
> I summon up remembrance of things past. . . .

Many more lines could be cited; but the essential point is that the Poet used alliteration judiciously.

In a century fascinated by language and seeking to bring English to a state of perfection so that it could be used as effectively as any other language, ancient or modern, some writers, Spenser chief among them, revived obsolete words and introduced many archaisms into their works in an effort to enrich the language. Shakespeare would have none of this, as is made clear in Sonnet 106: he will not use an "antique pen" to praise the beauty of the youth.

It is notable that most of Shakespeare's verses are marked by what was called "monosyllabic strength." When he does use the polysyllabic term, one usually derived from the Latin, he does so because he seeks to obtain dignity and solemnity, as in Sonnet 116 (the Latin loan words are italicized):

> Let me not to the *marriage* of true minds
> *Admit impediments:* love is not love
> Which *alters* when it *alteration* finds
> Or bends with the *remover* to *remove.*

> (1-4)

Each of these terms, ultimately from the Latin, long since had been naturalized and posed no difficulty for the reader.

Nor does Shakespeare make excessive use of compounds, a practice also frowned upon by Sidney. Indeed, his use of the compound is quite a judicious one, as may be illustrated by these lines from Sonnet 30:

44

Then can I grieve at grievances foregone,
And heavily from woe to woe tell o'er
The sad account of *fore-bemoaned* moan,
Which I new pay as if not paid before.

(9-12)

USE OF COLOR IN THE SONNETS

The late Miss Carolyn Spurgeon pointed out the "many lovely colour groups . . . in the sonnets." The first notable example is found in Sonnet 12: violet, sable, silver, white, green. In the entire sequence color, as an element of beauty, is used no less than forty-two times. Shakespeare is particularly effective in Sonnets 73 (yellow, sunset, fire, ashen, black) and 99 (violet, purple, lily, roses, red and white). A close study of the poems reveals the fact that there are thirteen colors employed, with the great preponderance of gold, red, and green.

SELECTED CRITICISM: GENERAL

The criticism of Shakespeare's sonnets over the years has been quite favorable in general, although there have been those who found serious limitations in them, particularly in view of the fact that so many are addressed to the Fair Young Man in terms of adoration. Following are some of the representative views.

In his *Supplemental Apology,* 1797, p. 82 f., George Chalmers established himself as the first to criticize the Shakespeare of the sonnets adversely. He found them to be obscure and tedious. He did credit Shakespeare with "many happy phrases and elegant lines," but added that these are "generally darkened by conceit and marred by affectation."

More than a century later, George Gilfillan went to the opposite extreme, lauding the Poet's works *(Poetical Works of William Shakespeare and the Earl of Surrey, 1856, p. xxvi)*:

Let . . . [readers] admire the Sonnets for the exquisite beauty of their imagery, which appears in more lavish abundance than even in the dramas—for the melody of their versification, a melody unparalleled for its compass, variety, and richness . . . for the blended power and sweetness of its language.

Moving up to the present century, we find many critics expressing their appreciation of the sonnets and pointing out their particular virtues. Mr. J. W. Mackail (*Approach to Shakespeare,* 1930, pp. 118f.) insisted that the sonnets, early and late, should be read and studied as poetry for their own sake. He thus rejects the historical approach and especially is distrustful of autobiographical interpretation of the poems. He placed Shakespeare above such great sonneteers as Wordsworth and Rossetti, and he concludes: "But just as Shakespeare's dramatic work eclipses that of all his contemporaries . . . so beside Shakespeare's sonnets the whole mass of other Elizabethan sonnet-literature pales and thins."

In the same year apeared *The Age of Shakespeare,* Vol. I., wherein Thomas Seccombe and J. W. Allen write interestingly and informatively about Shakespeare, the non-dramatic poet (pp. 28-29). They find the sonnets to be among "the most splendid legacies left by Elizabethan England," but argue that they remain unequal and, to some degree, conventional. No one can dispute them when they cite Sonnets 153 and 154 as "poor examples of the thoroughly conventional style." These critics also point out that Shakespeare's addressing so many of the sonnets to a man is "itself remarkable, and widely differentiates his series from those of Daniel, Lodge, Drayton, and Spenser." They state also that Shakespeare further demonstrated his originality in the Dark Lady sonnets. Unlike the Petrarchans with whom practically all of the other Elizabethan sonneteers may be classed, he does not plead or despair or rage (except against himself on occasion). "His passion is tragic with the tragedy of youthful experience." Seccombe and Allen conclude: "Two poets—and only two—of the Elizabethan Age produced love poetry in which the true note of absolute passion is struck—Shakespeare and Donne." In comparison to Donne, who "seems sometimes to set down his impressions hot and crude, in Shakespeare the passion is always mastered by the artist."

Mr. L. C. Knights ("Shakespeare's Sonnets," *Scrutiny,* 1934, III, p. 152) finds that two interests predominate in the sequence: "One is the exploration, discrimination, and judgment of modes of being —attention consciously directed towards the kind of integration of personality that is implied by the development of technique. The second is an overwhelming concern with Time."

Thomas Marc Parrott (*William Shakespeare,* 1934, p. 193) is among those who remind us that the sonnets indeed gain by selection. "All the sonnets are [not] of great and equal value. . . . Many of them are slight things, occasional verses, too often marred by the Elizabethan fondness for strained conceits. But when the poet is ·

strongly moved he rises to very lofty heights of thought and to such perfection of expression as is matched, if matched at all, only in the plays." Mr. Parrott points out that Shakespeare is especially moved by the theme of Beauty—"beauty revealed in the person of his friend, beauty that irresistibly evokes love, beauty warred upon by Time, love triumphing over the wreckage of Time and conferring immortality on the beautiful beloved in enduring verse." The critic concludes:

> In the great sonnets . . . we may hear the voice of the supreme master of English poetry opening his heart, revealing his profoundest thoughts and most poignant emotions in accents surer of immortality than the eternity promised to the beloved friend.

The judicious views of Mr. C. S. Lewis (*English Literature in the Sixteenth Century*, 1954, pp. 498-509) must not be ignored. He proclaims the sonnets to be not only unique in a period of the Renaissance but as the supreme love-poetry of the world. And he wisely points out the difficulty one encounters if he tries to read the sequence like a novel, for "the precise mode of love which the poet declares for the man remains obscure." He concedes that the "language is too lover-like for that of ordinary male friendship," and finds "no real parallel to such language between friends in sixteenth century literature." But Mr. Lewis denies that the sonnets seem to be "the poetry of full-blown pederasty." He cites, for example, the incessant demand that the man should marry and found a family. "What man in the whole world, except a father or a potential father-in-law, cares whether any other man gets married?" he asks, and he concludes: "Thus the emotion expressed by the sonnets refuses to fit into any pigeon-holes."

Finally, we may listen to Mr. W. H. Auden and learn the view of a successful contemporary poet (Introduction to *The Sonnets*, Signet Classics, 1964, p. xvii f.): "Probably more nonsense has been talked and written, more intellectual and emotional energy expended in vain, on the sonnets of Shakespeare than on any other literary work in the world." Auden finds that they have become "the best touchstone for separating the sheep from the goats"—that is, those who love and understand poetry, and those who "only value poems either as historical documents or because they express feelings or beliefs of which the reader happens to approve."

Mr. Auden goes on to point out that the Shakespearean sonnet, with its seven different rhymes, "almost inevitably becomes a lyric of three symmetrical quatrains finished off with an epigrammatic couplet. As a rule Shakespeare shapes his rhetorical argument in conformity with this. . . ." Major pauses occur after the fourth, eighth, and twelfth lines as a rule, although there are occasional exceptions. "It is the concluding couplet in particular which, in the Shakespearean form, can be a snare. The poet is tempted to use it, either to make a summary of the preceding twelve lines which is unnecessary, or to draw a moral which is too glib and trite." But Mr. Auden feels that Shakespeare was wise to choose the English sonnet form: English is relatively poor in rhymes in comparison with the Italian. Moreover, with the English form, the poet can accomplish certain things which are impossible for the Petrarchan form, with its sharp division between octave and sestet. For example, in Sonnets 66 and 129, Shakespeare is able "to give twelve single-line exempla of the wretchedness of this world and the horrors of lust, with accumulative effect of great power."

CRITICISM OF INDIVIDUAL SONNETS
IMAGERY IN THE EARLY SONNETS

In the early sonnets, the main and unifying image is the wealth of love. Indeed, in Sonnets 1-17, we find Shakespeare's most sustained and explicit statement of ideal love. It is interesting to see how he draws his imagery from everyday life in the world about him. In Sonnet 1, for example, he writes of love in terms of commercial gain and merchandise. He begins: "From fairest creatures we desire *increase*. . . ." The underlined term means not only Nature's increase through generation, but also commercial gain. The word looks forward to "contracted" in line 5—another obvious trade term. The sonnet ends:

Pity the world, or else this *glutton* be,
To eat the world's due, by the grave and thee.

The youth is thus told that, instead of honoring the contract with another person and so giving the world that which he owes to it, he "mak'st waste in niggarding [hoarding]." In this way Shakespeare introduces and develops the important idea of plentitude.

The same theme is repeated in Sonnet 2, but here the Poet does not call the act of loving "increase" but "use," a word not infrequently meaning "usury" and thereby linked with "niggarding" of the previous sonnet. The term "treasure" also is used in line 6, the reference being to the youth's matchless beauty. In line 8, Shakespeare speaks of "thriftless praise"—unprofitable praise. But the term "thrift" in Shakespeare's England had various meanings: (1) careful garnering of resources; (2) profit; (3) increase, or what was derived from thriving or breeding, and so "usury." This leads the Poet to lines 9-11 beginning, "How much more praise deserved thy beauty's use." So beauty is conceived as a treasure which decays unless, through love, its natural increase is made possible.

The theme is most fully developed in Sonnet 4. One should note the use of the terms *unthrifty, legacy, bequest,* and *free.* One important sense of free in this passage is "to be generous, liberal." The implication is that Nature's generosity should be matched. Shakespeare, calling the young man a "beauteous niggard" (miser), claims that he abuses the "bounteous largesse" Nature has given him and thus is a "Profitless usurer," having "traffic with [himself]" alone. Then, asks the Poet, what acceptable audit can the young man leave? The sonnet concludes:

> Thy unused beauty must be tombed with thee.
> Which used, lives th' executor to be.

In Sonnet 6, Shakespeare picks up this final couplet, or the idea imbedded therein, and again makes clear and effective use of the image of love's usury. This sonnet is notable for the ingenious multiplying of conceits and especially for the concluding pun on a legal will:

> Be not self-willed, for thou art much too fair
> To be death's conquest and make worms thine heir.

It will be noticed that the idea of "willing love" helps to expand the definition of the contract of love, and that "willing" is used not only in the legal sense but in the sense of desiring. Again the Poet insists that, once the wealth of beauty has been recognized through love for another person, it must be used if it is to increase and not decay.

Sonnet 9 is no less interesting for its imagery. Here the concept of love is not entirely distinguished from commercial wealth. Shakespeare relates the "traffickers" in love to the world at large.

The idea once more is that, when an unthrifty person makes ill use of his inherited wealth, only those among whom he squanders it benefit:

> Look what an unthrift in the world doth spend,
> Shifts but his place, for still [always] the
>   world enjoys it. . . .

(9-10)

The paradox lies in the fact that the hoarding of love's beauty is the surest way of squandering it:

> . . . beauty's waste hath in the world an end
> But kept unus'd, the user so destroys it.

(11-12)

And in the final couplet, the Poet argues that such waste must be felt by all.

These are not the only images used in the early sonnets, to be sure. In Sonnet 8 Shakespeare derived his imagery from music. The first twelve lines elaborate a comparison between music and the Fair Young Man, who is — or should be — the very embodiment of harmony. But music, "the true concord of well tunèd sounds," scolds him because he remains single — a single note, not a chord. And here we have a two-fold meaning of the key term *note:* (1) unmarried; (2) a single note. The idea is that the youth destroys the harmony he should make as part of an ensemble. The strings of a lute, for example, struck simultaneously, produce one sound, but one that is actually made up of many sounds. In this it is like a family, which is the union of father, mother, and child. The sonnet concludes:

> Whose speechless song, being many, seeming one,
> Sings this to thee, "Thou single wilt prove none."

Most critics agree with Dowden that, in the last line, Shakespeare is making reference to the proverbial saying that one is no number. Here the Poet brings to culmination the musical image, saying that a chord, being really many blended sounds, although it seems to be only one should prove to the youth that, if he remains single, he will "prove no true music."

SONNET 30: POETRY AS SOUND

Attention has already been called to the fact that this sonnet is memorable, among other things, for the effective use of alliteration. But alliteration is just one way in which a poet may enhance the melody of his work. Rhyme, of course, is another device for so doing. A third is assonance, the identity of vowel sounds in accented syllables. Sonnet 30 is no less notable for the Poet's use of this device. Note the short *e* sounds in the first two lines: Wh*e*n, s*e*ssions, rem*e*mbered — and so elsewhere in the poem. Still another device is the attractive vowel runs, long and short. For example, consider the long sounds in line one: sw*ee*t, s*i*lent, th*ou*ght; and in line 7: w*ee*p, l*o*ng, s*i*nce, c*a*nceled w*o*es. It will be noted that the nasal consonants in *long since* and *cancelled* prolong the short vowels preceding. Related to this device, and contributing to the distinctive rhythm of the lines, is the variation of accents in the normally iambic pentameter lines, a way which any good poet succeeds in avoiding sing-song monotony. In line seven, one finds an example. Here there is no obvious alternation of alternating short and long syllables. Following is the pattern: __ /__ ///__ /__ /. And so in line 6: __ /__ //__ //__ /. One can well understand why the Shakespeare of the sonnets has been held to be without rival in achieving attractive rhythm, melody, and sound.

SONNET 55: THE TEXTURE OF A POEM

Sonnet 55 might very well have been used to illustrate the poem as sound, so attractive is the phrasing; but it is especially interesting as an example of superior texture, that is, the characteristic disposition of elements. As such it is one of the deservedly famous sonnets in the sequence, what with its treatment of Time in a tone of solemn dignity. One of the very best discussions of this poem is that of Mr. Hallet Smith (*Elizabethan Poetry,* 1952, pp. 178-180). It actually reads like a sonnet prefatory to a volume of love poetry. In the first four lines, the Poet dwells upon the contrast between the brightness of physical things, specifically monuments, and the memory of the youth addressed in the poem. Brightness and color are indicated by the use of the adjective *brightness*, which at no time suggests a meretricious quality as regards a prince's memorials. But in line four the Poet expresses a kind of scorn of such monuments and of gravestones in general as a means of insuring immortality.

Once bright stones may become "unswept...besmear'd with sluttish time." As Mr. Smith explains, the adjective *sluttish* suggests the lazy, careless housemaid who does not perform her duties well. Thus the aristocratic associations of the first lines are demolished and the surviving brightness of poetry is emphasized.

No less interesting is the second quatrain in which the Poet's technical virtuosity is quite impressively illustrated. Rhythm and sound combine to provide an onomatopoetic effect appropriate to the violence and disorder of war and civil strife:

> When wasteful war shall statues overturn,
> And broils [civil strife] root out the work of
> masonry. . . .
>
> (5-6)

In the next line, "Nor Mars his sword nor war's quick fire" rhetorically conveys the idea of speed and violence. "Mars his sword," by the way, is the older genitive form, which Shakespeare uses elsewhere. The rhythmical violence of the seventh line is completely eliminated by the simplicity and quiet of the eighth line: "The living record of your memory."

The conflict between Time and forgetfulness is emphasized in the third quatrain with its impressive epithet "all oblivious enmity." The Poet speaks of the youth as "pacing forth" as if he were entering the Court, and implies that he has become the cynosure of all eyes and will inevitably "find room/Even in the eyes of all posterity." His nobility and superiority are thus insisted upon, as well as is the power of the verse to insure him immortality.

But despite this praise, so well deserved, Sonnet 55 has one limitation. It ends in a couplet of diminished force, for the Poet has said all that he needed to say in the twelve preceding lines, which had used up his emotion, leaving no need for any repetition. For the record, it may be noted that Sonnets 19, 30, 34, 42, 60, 84, 86, 91, 92, 131, 133, [139], and 141 suffer accordingly.

SONNET 60: SHIFTING IMAGERY

This is another sonnet on the subject of Time the Destroyer which has been justly praised for its imagery and superb melody. Miss Elizabeth Holmes (*Aspects of Elizabethan Imagery*, 1929, p. 42), for example, has this to say:

> [Here] the growth of one figure out of another to shape a
> continuous body of thought can be seen in its perfection,
> where the fifth line. . . .is the link between the image of the
> sea in flood, and that of a growing then declining light,
> since it includes suggestions of both.

It has been suggested (Anon., *Blackwood's*, 1880, CXXVIII, 164)
that Robert Browning imitates the thought in this sonnet in *The
Ring and the Book,* XI, 2348-2366, where Count Guido reflects
"that all men are like waves hastening to break on the shore of
death." He thus paid tacit tribute to Shakespeare's poetic power.

A full understanding of this poem depends upon careful explication. In line 4, Shakespeare refers to the "sequent toil" of the
waves making "toward the pebbled shore." He refers to the successive waves, one following another endlessly. Beginning with the second quatrain, the Poet changes the image from the sea to the
heavens, and "nativity," or birth, is compared to the sun crawling
up the sky, called "the main [great body] of light" to distinguish it
from the "main of waters." This has been explained (Beeching, ed.,
1904) as follows:

> Life beginning at a point in time within the shining sphere
> of the Heavens, whose aspect is charged with fate, crawls to
> maturity only to be thwarted by their fateful powers, and
> time despoils the worth of his gift.

In the third quatrain the image is changed once more. Time appears in person with his conventional dart and scythe, and also
with a spade, perhaps as a gravedigger: "And nothing stands but
for his scythe to mow." And then, as in earlier sonnets, Shakespeare
declares that his verse will conquer Time itself:

> And yet to times in hope, my verse shall stand
> Praising thy worth, despite his cruel hand.

SONNET 64: SHAKESPEARE'S DICTION

Sonnet 64, a poem of remarkable insight and beauty, lends itself to a useful consideration of Shakespeare's diction. It is one of
the sonnets in which is found an intense consciousness of the problem of mutability. Both the object of the poet's passion and his experience of love itself are felt to be fatally exposed to the ravages of
Time: "Time will come take my love away."

In the first line the Poet speaks of Time's *fell* hand, that is, "cruel hand." In the next line he refers to "the rich proud *cost* of outworn buried *age*." The italicized terms, respectively, meaning "splendor or pomp" of "past time." *Sometime* lofty towers" of line three means "once lofty towers." And "brass *eternal*" of line 4 is "everlasting brass." In the same line "mortal rage" signifies the "rage of mortality"—of death. *Advantage* in line 6 means "inroads." In line 8 the Poet refers to "Increasing store," which means that now one increases in abundance (store) with the other's loss; no one repairs its loss with abundance taken from the other. The "interchange of *state* in line 9 stands for "interchange of condition." But *state* as used in the next line means "greatness," which is *confounded*, or destroyed. The final line may be paraphrased as follows: "But weep because it has that which it fears to lose."

SONNET 73: STRUCTURE

This well-known sonnet especially illustrates the virtues of the English form at its best. In the first quatrain the Poet compares himself to autumn leaves; in the second, to twilight; and in the third, to dying embers. From the union of these images emerges the dominant idea of impending death. There follows the completely justifiable couplet addressed to the young man and pointing out the conclusion to be drawn from the preceding lines:

This thou perceiv'st which makes thy love more strong
To love that well which thou must leave ere long.

Note that there is a pause after each quatrain, the longest coming appropriately after the third. This was the customary usage among the writers of sonnets in the English form.

SONNET 94: VARIED INTERPRETATIONS

The end of the poem is the beginning, according to the late T. S. Eliot; that is, in the democracy of criticism varying interpretations are deemed acceptable. This point of view may be illustrated by reference to selected critical comments on Sonnet 94. According to Wyndham (ed. *Sonnets*, 1898) Shakespeare first advances the argument of those who, with an outward beauty which is the source of temptation, are themselves cold and not easily tempted. They are the owners and masters of their destiny; but, in contrast, those whose beauty not only tempts but also leads them into temptation are the dispensers of it. As a symbol of the first, the Poet takes a flower which is sweet to the world around it, although it blossoms and dies to itself, self-contained and unrewarding. As a symbol of the second, the same flower is infected with a canker, in which case it is more offensive than a weed.

Mr. William Empson (*Some Versions of Pastoral*, 1935, p. 89 ff.) has his own explanation of the poem, which he insists is "a piece of grave irony." He tells us that, according to Shakespeare, superior individuals remain aloof and never submit to temptation. Nor in so doing are they being selfish, for they unconsciously do good, like the flowers. The Youth, the Poet continues, must be, indeed already is, quite like them. Yet even such superior individuals must remain alert not to fall from perfection if they are to avoid becoming the worst, just as "Lilies that fester, smell far worse than weeds."

A third interpretation is that of Mr. Edward Hubler (*op. cit.,* pp. 102-106), who approaches the poem in the light of Shakespeare's other works and who is quite aware of the fact that the poem "has been the object of more critical analyses than any other sonnet." Mr. Hubler points out that it makes use of Shakespeare's most familiar imagery and that the basic idea of the sonnet is to be found everywhere in the poet-dramatist's works. He emphasizes the irony of the first two quatrains: "It is preposterous on the face of things to proclaim as the inheritors of heaven's graces those who are 'as stone.' It can be other than ironical only to the cynic, for even the hardhearted man thinks of himself as generous and cherishes an abstract admiration for warmth." Mr. Hubler finds the octave to be "Swiftian in both method and force," the poet stating in specious terms that which he clearly considered to be false: "those men whose appearance does not square with reality, whose deeds do not fulfill their promise, who move others while remaining cold, are proclaimed the heirs to heaven's graces." Elsewhere in his works, Shakespeare insisted that "the sense of living without regard for others is intolerable," and he cites the examples of Rosencrantz and Guilderstern, Goneril and Regan, and others. At the end of the octave ("Others but stewards of their excellence") there is a full stop, and then the Poet introduces the familiar image of the summer's flower, which is beautiful despite the fact that it lives unto itself alone: an obvious analogy. Earlier and often in the sequence he had praised the flower's beauty, but saw it only as one of its attributes and not necessarily as the most important one. The beauty, he argued, is increased by the flower's odor, which represents that which is usefully good. In Sonnet 69, for example, he writes:

> But why thy odour matcheth not thy show,
>   The soil is this, that thou does common grow.
>
> (13-14)

And in Sonnet 54:

> O, how much more doth beauty beauteous seem
> By that sweet ornament which truth doth give.
> The rose looks fair, but fairer we it deem
> For that sweet odour which doth live in it. . . .
>
> (1-4)

In Sonnet 94, the flower, isolated, does not fulfill its function, despite its beauteous form. And "if it should meet with infection" (that is, if the expression of its function should be perverted), its odor (that is, its essence, its soul, its human utility as expressed in the deeds of the young man and the perfume of the flower) becomes worse than that of weeds—worse, that is, than that form which nothing was expected.

Mr. Walter Kaufman (*From Shakespeare to Existentialism,* 1960, pp. 5-8) vehemently rejects Mr. Hubler's interpretation of Sonnet 94, which he believes "celebrates Shakespeare's un-Christian ideal, which was also the ideal of Nietzsche. . . ." With reference to the first two lines of the poem—

> They that have power to hurt and will do none,
> That do not do the thing they most do show . . .

—Mr. Kaufman finds what he calls an exellent commentary in a passage from the German philosopher's chapter "On Those Who Are Sublime" in *Thus Spake Zarathustra:*

> One who was sublime I saw today, one who was solemn, an ascetic of the spirit; oh, how my soul laughed at his ugliness! . . . As yet he has not overcome his deed. . . . As yet his torrential passion has not become still in beauty. Verily, it is not in satiety that his desire shall grow silent, be submerged, but in beauty. Gracefulness is part of the graciousness of the great-souled. . . . There is nobody from whom I want beauty as much as from you who are powerful: let

your kindness be your final self-conquest. Of all evil I deem you capable: therefore I want the good from you. Verily, I have often laughed at the weaklings who thought themselves good because they had no claws.

"Shakespeare, too," the critic continues, "celebrates the man who has claws but does not use them." Kaufman sees nothing preposterous or ironic, as Hubler does, in the Poet's saying that the inheritors of heaven's graces are those who are as stone. "What seems preposterous to a Christian reader need not have struck a Roman or a Spartan as unseemly." He reminds his readers that Shakespeare was an actor and admonishes those "who would rather not believe that Shakespeare, the poet, moving others, was himself as stone. . . ." He sees the Poet, then, as one who endorsed the idea of the aloof superman, one who looked with contempt upon the common man and who viewed religion as mere superstition. Shakespeare himself would surely be among those quite startled at this bit of impressionistic criticism.

SONNET 116: AN EXERCISE IN DEFINITION

The essence of love and friendship for Shakespeare, it is apparent, is reciprocity or mutuality. In Sonnet 116, for example, the ideal relationship is referred to as "the marriage of true minds," a state which can be realized by the dedicated and faithful:

> Let me not to the marriage of true minds
> Admit impediments.
>
> (1-2)

These lines echo the marriage services in the Book of Common Prayer: "If any of you know cause or just impediment . . ." Thus we understand the Poet's attitude toward his subject. He then proceeds to define such love, first negatively—that is, explaining what it is not, always an effective rhetorical device:

> love is not love
> Which alters when it alteration finds,
> Or bends with the remover to remove.
>
> (2-4)

He continues this formal method of definition now by advancing an affirmative definition:

> ... it is an ever-fixèd mark,
> That looks on tempests and is never shaken;
> It is the star of every wandering bark,
> Whose worth's unknown, although his height be taken.
>
> (5-8)

The "ever-fixèd mark," to be sure, is the traditional sea mark and guide for mariners, the North Star, whose value is inestimable, although its altitude has been determined. The star, unlike physical beauty, we are told, is not subject to the ravages of Time. And so true love, which is not "Time's fool" (plaything, as here used). In his definition Shakespeare then introduces the great concepts of Space and Time, applying them to his idea of true love:

> Love alters not with his brief hours and weeks,
> But bears it out to the edge of doom.
>
> (11-12)

"Bears it out" means survives, and "edge of doom," Judgment Day. Finally, with absolute conviction, the Poet challenges others to find him wrong in his definition:

> If this be error and upon [against] me proved,
> I never writ, and no man ever loved.

This is his standard of friendship and love which he hopes that he and the Fair Young Man can achieve.

SONNET 129: THE STRINDBERGIAN MOOD

Perhaps no poem illustrates how far Shakespeare could depart from the Petrarchan tradition of love poetry than Sonnet 129, which has been called an almost Strindbergian poem on the power of lust. In a hortatory mood he writes:

>   ... lust
> Is perjur'd, murderous, blood, full of blame,
> Savage, extreme, rude, cruel, not to trust. ...
>
> (2-4)

Here especially he asks why the heart should be moved by what he knows to be worthless. But, obviously bound by passion, he cannot escape despite his better self, and he endeavors to convince himself that the Dark Lady is better than he knows her to be. As R. C. Trench wrote (*Household Book*, 1868, p. 392), "The bitter delusion of all sinful pleasures, the reaction of a swift remorse which inevitably dogs them, Shakespeare must have most deeply felt, as he has expressed himself upon it most profoundly." As a testimonial of profound and powerful emotions, this poem, in the words of J. A. Symonds (*Sir Philip Sidney*, 1886, p. 153), is "the most completely powerful sonnet in our literature." Bernard Shaw (*Nation,* London, 1910, VIII, 543) described it as "the most merciless passage in English literature."

The poem requires little annotation. *Expense* in the first line means "expenditure"; in the same line *spirit* has the double meaning of "vital power" and "semen." *Past* in lines 6 and 7 means "beyond." And *made* in line 9 means "when experienced." *Dream*, line 12, may well refer to a nightmare in view of the context in which it is used. Finally the *heaven* referred to in the last line is the "sensation" (or possibly "place") of bliss.

QUESTIONS

1. What evidence can you adduce to support the belief that the sonnets are autobiographical?

2. Which sonnets seem to you to be most conventional and imitative?

3. In which sonnets does Shakespeare express originality?

4. What are three ways in which he departs radically from the Petrarchan tradition?

5. Select two sonnets from each of the two major divisions. How do they differ in mood and the treatment of love?

6. What are the structural virtues of Sonnet 73 as compared, for example, with Sonnet 30?

7. In which sonnets does the Poet pun wittily — and sometimes shockingly?

8. What evidence is there that Shakespeare sought to avoid af-

fected and pretentious language? To what extent do you believe he succeeded?

9. What structural virtues do you find in the Shakespearean form of the sonnet as opposed to the Italian? What are the dangers which are not always avoidable?

10. In the sonnets, what views does Shakespeare express as regards (a) the nature of true love; (b) the miseries of misplaced love; (c) the obligations of stewardship?

11. What are five adjectives used to describe time in the first large division?

12. In what ways does Shakespeare indicate that time may be conquered? In which of the ways do the poems themselves prove to be right?

13. What do you take to be the respective ages of the man addressed and the poet? Why?

14. What evidence do you find that the young man is of high social rank?

15. Aside from love, what themes does the Poet develop in the sonnets?

16 What views of the acting profession does Shakespeare advance? Why?

17. What words does the Poet use to describe (a) the man addressed; (b) the Dark Lady?

18. What lapses in the character of the youth does Shakespeare note? What is his reaction thereto?

19. Sonnet 146 has been described as one of the two most powerful poems in the sequence. What do you find to be the source of its power?

20. What use does Shakespeare make of nature in the sonnets?

BIBLIOGRAPHY

Bray, Sir Denys de Saumarez. *The Original Order of Shakespeare's Sonnets.* London, 1925.

——————— *Shakespeare's Sonnet Sequence.* London, 1938.

Chambers, Sir E. K. *Shakespearean Gleanings.* London, 1944.

Cuttwell, Patrick. *The Shakespearean Moment,* New York, 1960.

Herrnstein, Barbara, ed. *Discussions of Shakespeare's Sonnets.* New York, 1964.

Hubler, Edward. *The Sense of Shakespeare's Sonnets.* Princeton, 1952.

———————, Northrop Frye, Leslie A. Fiedler, Stephen Spender, and R. P. Blackmuir. *The Riddle of Shakespeare's Sonnets.* New York, 1962.

Knights, L. C. *Some Shakespearean Themes.* London, 1960.

Krieger, Murray. *A Window to Criticism: Shakespeare's Sonnets and Modern Poetics.* Princeton, 1964.

Landry, Hilton. *Interpretations of Shakespeare's Sonnets.* Princeton, 1964.

Leishman, J. B. *Themes and Variations in Shakespeare's Sonnets.* London, 1961.

Lever, J. W. *The Elizabethan Love Sonnet.* London, 1956.

Prince, F. T. *The Sonnet from Wyatt to Shakespeare.* Stratford-on-Avon Studies, 2, 1960.

Quennell, Peter. *Shakespeare.* New York, 1963.

Robertson, J. M. *The Problems of Shakespeare's Sonnets.* London, 1926.

Rollins, Hyder E., ed. *A New Variorum Edition of Shakespeare: the Sonnets.* 2 vols. London, 1944.

Rouse, A. L. *Shakespeare's Sonnets.* New York, 1964.

Willen, Gerald and Victor B. Reed. *A Casebook on Shakespeare's Sonnets.* New York, 1964.

Wilson, J. Dover. *An Introduction to the Sonnets of Shakespeare.* New York, 1964.

NOTES

NOTES

NOTES

This is the TITLE INDEX, indexing the over 200 titles available by Series, by Library and by Volume Number for both the BASIC LIBRARY SERIES and the AUTHORS LIBRARY SERIES.

TITLE	SERIES	LIBRARY	Vol
Absalom, Absalom!	Basic	American Lit	4
	Authors	Faulkner	3
Adonais (in Keats & Shelley)	Basic	English Lit	1
Aeneid, The	Basic	Classics	1
Aeschylus' Oresteia (in Agamemnon)	Basic	Classics	1
Agamemnon	Basic	Classics	1
Alice in Wonderland	Basic	English Lit	3
All That Fall (in Waiting for Godot)	Basic	European Lit	1
All the King's Men	Basic	American Lit	6
All Quiet on the Western Front	Basic	European Lit	2
All's Well That Ends Well	Basic	Shakespeare	1
	Authors	Shakespeare	8
American, The	Basic	American Lit	2
	Authors	James	6
American Tragedy, An	Basic	American Lit	3
Animal Farm	Basic	English Lit	5
Anna Karenina	Basic	European Lit	3
Antigone (in Oedipus Trilogy)	Basic	Classics	1
Antony and Cleopatra	Basic	Shakespeare	2
	Authors	Shakespeare	9
Apology (in Plato's Euthyphro....)	Basic	Classics	1
Aristotle's Ethics	Basic	Classics	1
Arms and the Man (in Shaw's Pygmalion....)	Basic	English Lit	6
	Authors	Shaw	11
"Artificial Nigger, The" (in O'Connor's Short Stories)	Basic	American Lit	7
As I Lay Dying	Basic	American Lit	4
	Authors	Faulkner	3
Assistant, The	Basic	American Lit	6
As You Like It	Basic	Shakespeare	1
	Authors	Shakespeare	8
Autobiography of Benjamin Franklin	Basic	American Lit	1
Autobiography of Malcolm X, The	Basic	American Lit	6
Awakening, The	Basic	American Lit	2
Babbitt	Basic	American Lit	3
	Authors	Lewis	7
"Bear, The" (in Go Down, Moses)	Basic	American Lit	4
	Authors	Faulkner	3
Bear, The	Basic	American Lit	4
	Authors	Faulkner	3
Bell Jar, The	Basic	American Lit	6
Beowulf	Basic	Classics	3
Billy Budd	Basic	American Lit	1
Birds, The (in Lysistrata....)	Basic	Classics	1
Black Boy	Basic	American Lit	4

This is the AUTHOR INDEX, listing the over 200 titles available by author and indexing them by Series, by Library and by Volume Number for both the BASIC LIBRARY SERIES and the AUTHORS LIBRARY SERIES.

AUTHOR	TITLE(S)	SERIES	LIBRARY	Vol
Aeschylus	Agamemnon, The Choephori, & The Eumenides	Basic	Classics	1
Albee, Edward	Who's Afraid of Virginia Woolf?	Basic	American Lit	7
Anderson, Sherwood	Winesburg, Ohio	Basic	American Lit	3
Aristophanes	Lysistrata * The Birds * Clouds * The Frogs	Basic	Classics	1
Aristotle	Aristotle's Ethics	Basic	Classics	1
Austen, Jane	Emma	Basic	English Lit	1
	Pride and Prejudice	Basic	English Lit	2
Beckett, Samuel	Waiting for Godot	Basic	European Lit	1
Beowulf	Beowulf	Basic	Classics	3
Beyle, Henri	see Stendhal			
Bronte, Charlotte	Jane Eyre	Basic	English Lit	3
Bronte, Emily	Wuthering Heights	Basic	English Lit	4
Brown, Claude	Manchild in the Promised Land	Basic	American Lit	7
Buck, Pearl	The Good Earth	Basic	American Lit	4
Bunyan, John	The Pilgrim's Progress	Basic	English Lit	2
Camus, Albert	The Plague * The Stranger	Basic	European Lit	1
Carroll, Lewis	Alice in Wonderland	Basic	English Lit	3
Cather, Willa	My Antonia	Basic	American Lit	3
Cervantes, Miguel de	Don Quixote	Basic	Classics	3
Chaucer, Geoffrey	The Canterbury Tales	Basic	Classics	3
Chopin, Kate	The Awakening	Basic	American Lit	2
Clark, Walter	The Ox-Bow Incident	Basic	American Lit	7
Conrad, Joseph	Heart of Darkness & The Secret Sharer * Lord Jim	Basic	English Lit	5
Cooper, James F.	The Deerslayer * The Last of the Mohicans	Basic	American Lit	1
Crane, Stephen	The Red Badge of Courage	Basic	American Lit	2
Dante	Divine Comedy I: Inferno * Divine Comedy II: Purgatorio * Divine Comedy III: Paradiso	Basic	Classsics	3
Defoe, Daniel	Moll Flanders	Basic	English Lit	1
	Robinson Crusoe	Basic	English Lit	2
Dickens, Charles	Bleak House * David Copperfield * Great Expectations * Hard Times	Basic	English Lit	3
	Oliver Twist * A Tale of Two Cities	Basic	English Lit	4
	Bleak House * David Copperfield * Great Expectations * Hard Times * Oliver Twist * A Tale of Two Cities	Authors	Dickens	1

AUTHOR	TITLE(S)	SERIES	LIBRARY	Vol
Dickinson, Emily	Emily Dickinson: Selected Poems	Basic	American Lit	2
Dostoevsky, Feodor	The Brothers Karamazov * Crime and Punishment * Notes from the Underground	Basic	European Lit	3
	The Brothers Karamazov * Crime and Punishment * Notes from the Underground	Authors	Dostoevsky	2
Dreiser, Theodore	An American Tragedy * Sister Carrie	Basic	American Lit	3
Dumas, Alexandre	The Count of Monte Cristo * The Three Musketeers	Basic	European Lit	1
Eliot, George	Middlemarch * The Mill on the Floss * Silas Marner	Basic	English Lit	4
Eliot, T.S.	T.S. Eliot's Major Poets and Plays: "The Wasteland," "The Love Song of J. Alfred Prufrock," & Other Works	Basic	English Lit	6
Ellison, Ralph	The Invisible Man	Basic	American Lit	7
Emerson, Ralph Waldo	Emerson's Essays	Basic	American Lit	1
Euripides	Electra * Medea	Basic	Classics	1
Faulkner, William	Absalom, Absalom! * As I Lay Dying * The Bear * Go Down, Moses * Light in August	Basic	American Lit	4
	The Sound and the Fury * The Unvanquished	Basic	American Lit	5
	Absalom, Absalom! * As I Lay Dying * The Bear * Go Down, Moses * Light in August The Sound and the Fury * The Unvanquished	Authors	Faulkner	3
Fielding, Henry	Joseph Andrews	Basic	English Lit	1
	Tom Jones	Basic	English Lit	2
Fitzgerald, F. Scott	The Great Gatsby	Basic	American Lit	4
	Tender is the Night	Basic	American Lit	5
Flaubert, Gustave	Madame Bovary	Basic	European Lit	1
Forster, E.M.	A Passage to India	Basic	English Lit	6
Fowles, John	The French Lieutenant's Woman	Basic	English Lit	5
Frank, Anne	The Diary of Anne Frank	Basic	European Lit	2
Franklin, Benjamin	The Autobiography of Benjamin Franklin	Basic	American Lit	1
Gawain Poet	Sir Gawain and the Green Night	Basic	Classics	4
Goethe, Johann Wolfgang von	Faust - Parts I & II	Basic	European Lit	2
Golding, William	Lord of the Flies	Basic	English Lit	5
Greene, Graham	The Power and the Glory	Basic	English Lit	6
Griffin, John H.	Black Like Me	Basic	American Lit	6

AUTHOR	TITLE(S)	SERIES	LIBRARY	Vol
Haley, Alex	The Autobiography of Malcolm X	Basic	American Lit	6
see also Little, Malcolm				
Hardy, Thomas	Far from the Madding Crowd * Jude the Obscure * The Mayor of Casterbridge	Basic	English Lit	3
	The Return of the Native * Tess of the D'Urbervilles	Basic	English Lit	4
	Far from the Madding Crowd * Jude the Obscure * The Mayor of Casterbridge The Return of the Native * Tess of the D'Urbervilles	Authors	Hardy	4
Hawthorne, Nathaniel	The House of the Seven Gables* The Scarlet Letter	Basic	American Lit	1
Heller, Joseph	Catch-22	Basic	American Lit	6
Hemingway, Ernest	A Farewell to Arms * For Whom the Bell Tolls	Basic	American Lit	4
	The Old Man and the Sea	Basic	American Lit	7
	The Sun Also Rises	Basic	American Lit	5
	A Farewell to Arms * For Whom the Bell Tolls The Old Man and the Sea The Sun Also Rises	Authors	Hemingway	5
Herbert, Frank	Dune & Other Works	Basic	American Lit	6
Hesse, Herman	Demian * Steppenwolf & Siddhartha	Basic	European Lit	2
Hilton, James	Lost Horizon	Basic	English Lit	5
Homer	The Iliad * The Odyssey	Basic	Classics	1
Hugo, Victor	Les Miserables	Basic	European Lit	1
Huxley, Aldous	Brave New World & Brave New World Revisited	Basic	English Lit	5
Ibsen, Henrik	Ibsen's Plays I: A Doll's House & Hedda Gabler * Ibsen's Plays II: Ghosts, An Enemy of the People, & The Wild Duck	Basic	European Lit	4
James, Henry	The American * Daisy Miller & The Turn of the Screw * The Portrait of a Lady	Basic	American Lit	2
	The American * Daisy Miller & The Turn of the Screw * The Portrait of a Lady	Authors	James	6
Joyce, James	A Portrait of the Artist as a Young Man * Ulysses	Basic	English Lit	6
Kafka, Franz	Kafka's Short Stories * The Trial	Basic	European Lit	2
Keats & Shelley	Keats & Shelley	Basic	English Lit	1
Kesey, Ken	One Flew Over the Cuckoo's Nest	Basic	American Lit	7
Knowles, John	A Separate Peace	Basic	American Lit	7

AUTHOR	TITLE(S)	SERIES	LIBRARY	Vol
Shakespeare, William	Troilus and Cressida * Twelfth Night * The Winter's Tale	Basic	Shakespeare	1
	All's Well that Ends Well & The Merry Wives of Windsor * As You Like It * The Comedy of Errors, Love's Labour's Lost, & The Two Gentlemen of Verona * Measure for Measure * The Merchant of Venice * Midsummer Night's Dream * Much Ado About Nothing * The Taming of the Shrew * The Tempest * Troilus and Cressida * Twelfth Night * The Winter's Tale	Authors	Shakespeare	8
	Antony and Cleopatra * Hamlet * Julius Caesar * King Lear * Macbeth * Othello * Romeo and Juliet	Basic	Shakeapeare	2
	Antony and Cleopatra * Hamlet * Julius Caesar * King Lear * Macbeth * Othello * Romeo and Juliet	Authors	Shakespeare	9
	Henry IV Part 1 * Henry IV Part 2 * Henry V * Henry VI Parts 1,2,3 * Richard II * Richard III * Shakespeare's Sonnets	Basic	Shakespeare	3
	Henry IV Part 1 * Henry IV Part 2 * Henry V * Henry VI Parts 1,2,3 * Richard II * Richard III * Shakespeare's Sonnets	Authors	Shakespeare	10
Shaw, George Bernard	Man and Superman & Caesar and Cleopatra * Pygmalion & Arms and the Man	Basic	English Lit	6
	Man and Superman & Caesar and Cleopatra * Pygmalion & Arms and the Man	Authors	Shaw	11
Shelley, Mary	Frankenstein	Basic	English Lit	1
Sinclair, Upton	The Jungle	Basic	American Lit	3
Skinner, B.F.	Walden Two	Basic	American Lit	7
Solzhenitsyn, Aleksandr	One Day in the Life of Ivan Denisovich	Basic	European Lit	3
Sophocles	The Oedipus Trilogy	Basic	Classics	1
Spenser, Edmund	The Faerie Queen	Basic	Classics	4
Steinbeck, John	The Grapes of Wrath *	Basic	American Lit	4
	Of Mice and Men * The Pearl * The Red Pony	Basic	American Lit	5

AUTHOR	TITLE(S)	SERIES	LIBRARY	Vol
Steinbeck, John	The Grapes of Wrath * Of Mice and Men * The Pearl * The Red Pony	Authors	Steinbeck	12
Stendhal	The Red and the Black	Basic	European Lit	1
Sterne, Lawrence	Tristram Shandy	Basic	English Lit	2
Stevenson, Robert Louis	Dr. Jekyll and Mr. Hyde *	Basic	English Lit	3
	Treasure Island & Kidnapped	Basic	English Lit	4
Stoker, Bram	Dracula	Basic	English Lit	3
Stowe, Harriet Beecher	Uncle Tom's Cabin	Basic	American Lit	2
Swift, Jonathan	Gulliver's Travels	Basic	English Lit	1
Thackeray, William Makepeace	Vanity Fair	Basic	English Lit	4
Thoreau, Henry David	Walden	Basic	American Lit	1
Tolkien, J.R.R.	The Lord of the Rings & The Hobbit	Basic	English Lit	5
Tolstoy, Leo	Anna Karenina * War and Peace	Basic	European Lit	3
Turgenev, Ivan Sergeyevich	Fathers and Sons	Basic	European Lit	3
Twain, Mark	A Connecticut Yankee * Huckleberry Finn * The Prince and the Pauper * Tom Sawyer	Basic	American Lit	2
	A Connecticut Yankee * Huckleberry Finn * The Prince and the Pauper * Tom Sawyer	Authors	Twain	13
Virgil	The Aeneid	Basic	Classics	1
Voltaire, Francois	Candide	Basic	European Lit	2
Vonnegut, Kurt	Vonnegut's Major Works	Basic	American Lit	7
Walker, Alice	The Color Purple	Basic	American Lit	7
Warren, Robert Penn	All the King's Men	Basic	American Lit	6
West, Nathanael	Miss Lonelyhearts & The Day of the Locust	Basic	American Lit	5
Wharton, Edith	Ethan Frome	Basic	American Lit	3
Whitman, Walt	Leaves of Grass	Basic	American Lit	1
Wilder, Thornton	Our Town	Basic	American Lit	5
Williams, Tennessee	The Glass Menagerie & A Streetcar Named Desire	Basic	American Lit	6
Woolf, Virginia	Mrs. Dalloway	Basic	English Lit	5
Wordsworth, William	The Prelude	Basic	English Lit	2
Wright, Richard	Black Boy	Basic	American Lit	4
	Native Son	Basic	American Lit	5

INDEX OF SERIES

<u>BASIC LIBRARY (24-0)</u>

THE SHAKESPEARE LIBRARY: 3 Volumes, 26 Titles (25-9)
- V. 1 - The Comedies 12 titles (00-3)
- V. 2 - The Tragedies, 7 titles (01-1)
- V. 3 - The Histories; The Sonnets, 7 titles (02-X)

THE CLASSICS LIBRARY: 4 Volumes, 27 Titles (26-7)
- V. 1 - Greek & Roman Classics, 11 titles (03-8)
- V. 2 - Greek & Roman Classics, 2 titles (04-6)
- V. 3 - Early Christian/European Classics, 7 titles (05-4)
- V. 4 - Early Christian/European Classics, 7 titles (06-2)

ENGLISH LITERATURE LIBRARY: 6 Volumes, 55 Titles (29-1)
- V. 1 - 17th Century & Romantic Period Classics, 7 titles (07-0)
- V. 2 - 17th Century & Romantic Period Classics, 7 titles (08-9)
- V. 3 - Victorian Age, 11 titles (09-7)
- V. 4 - Victorian Age, 10 titles (10-0)
- V. 5 - 20th Century, 10 titles (11-9)
- V. 6 - 20th Century, 10 titles (12-7)

AMERICAN LITERATURE LIBRARY: 7 Volumes, 77 Titles (33-X)
- V. 1 - Early U.S. & Romantic Period, 11 titles (13-5)
- V. 2 - Civil War to 1900, 11 titles (14-3)
- V. 3 - Early 20th Century, 9 titles (15-1)
- V. 4 - The Jazz Age to W.W.II, 11 titles (16-X)
- V. 5 - The Jazz Age to W.W.II, 10 titles (17-8)
- V. 6 - Post-War American Literature, 13 titles (18-6)
- V. 7 - Post-War American Literature, 12 titles (19-4)

EUROPEAN LITERATURE LIBRARY: 4 Volumes, 29 Titles (36-4)
- V. 1 - French Literature, 12 titles (20-8)
- V. 2 - German Literature, 7 titles (21-6)
- V. 3 - Russian Literature, 7 titles (22-4)
- V. 4 - Scandinavian Literature, 3 titles (23-2)

<u>AUTHORS LIBRARY (65-8)</u>

- V. 1 - **Charles Dickens** Library, 6 titles (66-6)
- V. 2 - **Feodor Dostoevsky** Library, 3 titles (67-4)
- V. 3 - **William Faulkner** Library, 7 titles (68-2)
- V. 4 - **Thomas Hardy** Library, 5 titles (69-0)
- V. 5 - **Ernest Hemingway** Library, 4 titles (70-4)
- V. 6 - **Henry James** Library, 3 titles (71-2)
- V. 7 - **Sinclair Lewis** Library, 2 titles (72-0)
- V. 8 - **Shakespeare** Library, Part 1 - The Comedies, 12 titles (73-9)
- V. 9 - **Shakespeare** Library, Part 2 - The Tragedies, 7 titles (74-7)
- V. 10 - **Shakespeare** Library, Part 3 - The Histories; Sonnets, 7 titles (75-5)
- V. 11 - **George Bernard Shaw** Library, 2 titles (76-3)
- V. 12 - **John Steinbeck** Library, 4 titles (77-1)
- V. 13 - **Mark Twain** Library, 4 titles (78-X)

Moonbeam Publications ISBN Prefix: 0-931013-

HARDBOUND LITERARY LIBRARIES

INDEX OF LIBRARIES

This is the INDEX OF LIBRARIES, listing the volumes and the individual titles within the volumes for both the BASIC LIBRARY SERIES (24 Volumes, starting below) and the AUTHORS LIBRARY SERIES (13 Volumes, see Page 6).

BASIC LIBRARY SERIES (24 Volumes)

THE SHAKESPEARE LIBRARY: 3 Volumes, 26 Titles

Vol 1 - The Comedies (12 titles)
*All's Well that Ends Well & The Merry Wives of Windsor
* As You Like It * The Comedy of Errors, Love's Labour's Lost, & The Two Gentlemen of Verona * Measure for Measure * The Merchant of Venice * A Midsummer Night's Dream * Much Ado About Nothing * The Taming of the Shrew * The Tempest * Troilus and Cressida * Twelfth Night * The Winter's Tale*

Vol 2 - The Tragedies (7 titles)
*Antony and Cleopatra * Hamlet * Julius Caesar * King Lear * Macbeth * Othello * Romeo and Juliet*

Vol 3 - The Histories; The Sonnets (7 titles)
*Henry IV Part 1 * Henry IV Part 2 * Henry V * Henry VI Parts 1,2,3 * Richard II * Richard III * Shakespeare's Sonnets*

THE CLASSICS LIBRARY: 4 Volumes, 27 Titles

Vol 1 - Greek & Roman Classics Part 1 (11 titles)
*The Aeneid * Agamemnon * Aristotle's Ethics * Euripides' Electra & Medea * The Iliad * Lysistrata & Other Comedies * Mythology * The Odyssey * Oedipus Trilogy * Plato's Euthyphro, Apology, Crito & Phaedo * Plato's The Republic*

THE CLASSICS LIBRARY (cont'd)

Vol 2 - Greek & Roman Classics Part 2 (2 titles)
*Greek Classics * Roman Classics*

**Vol 3 - Early Christian/European Classics Part 1
(7 titles)**
*Beowulf * Canterbury Tales * Divine Comedy - I. Inferno
* Divine Comedy - II. Purgatorio * Divine Comedy - III.
Paradiso * Doctor Faustus * Don Quixote*

**Vol 4 - Early Christian/European Classics Part 2
(7 titles)**
*The Faerie Queene * Le Morte D'Arthur * New Testament * Old Testament * The Prince * Sir Gawain and the
Green Knight * Utopia*

ENGLISH LITERATURE LIBRARY: 6 Volumes, 55 Titles

**Vol 1 - 17th Century & Romantic Period Classics
Part 1 (7 titles)**
*Emma * Frankenstein * Gulliver's Travels * Ivanhoe *
Joseph Andrews * Keats & Shelley * Moll Flanders*

**Vol 2 - 17th Century & Romantic Period Classics
Part 2 (7 titles)**
*Paradise Lost * Pilgrim's Progress * The Prelude * Pride
and Prejudice * Robinson Crusoe * Tom Jones * Tristram
Shandy*

Vol 3 - Victorian Age Part 1 (11 titles)
*Alice in Wonderland * Bleak House * David Copperfield
* Dr. Jekyll and Mr. Hyde * Dracula * Far from the Madding Crowd * Great Expectations * Hard Times * Jane
Eyre * Jude the Obscure * The Mayor of Casterbridge*

ENGLISH LITERATURE LIBRARY (cont'd)

Vol 4 - Victorian Age Part 2 (10 titles)
*Middlemarch * The Mill on the Floss * Oliver Twist * The Return of the Native * Silas Marner * A Tale of Two Cities * Tess of the D'Urbervilles * Treasure Island & Kidnapped * Vanity Fair * Wuthering Heights*

Vol 5 - 20th Century Part 1 (10 titles)
*Animal Farm * Brave New World * Cry, The Beloved Country * The French Lieutenant's Woman * Heart of Darkness & The Secret Sharer * Lord Jim * Lord of the Flies * The Lord of the Rings * Lost Horizon * Mrs. Dalloway*

Vol 6 - 20th Century Part 2 (10 titles)
*Nineteen Eighty-Four * Of Human Bondage * A Passage to India * A Portrait of the Artist as a Young Man * The Power and the Glory * Shaw's Man and Superman & Caesar and Cleopatra * Shaw's Pygmalion & Arms and the Man * Sons and Lovers * T.S. Eliot's Major Poems and Plays * Ulysses*

AMERICAN LITERATURE LIBRARY: 7 Volumes, 77 Titles

Vol 1 - Early U.S. & Romantic Period (11 titles)
*Autobiography of Ben Franklin * Billy Budd & Typee * The Deerslayer * Emerson's Essays * The House of Seven Gables * The Last of the Mohicans * Leaves of Grass * Moby Dick * Poe's Short Stories * The Scarlet Letter * Walden*

AMERICAN LITERATURE LIBRARY (cont'd)

Vol 2 - Civil War to 1900 (11 titles)
*The American * The Awakening * A Connecticut Yankee in King Arthur's Court * Daisy Miller & The Turn of the Screw * Emily Dickinson: Selected Poems * Huckleberry Finn * The Portrait of a Lady * The Prince and the Pauper * Red Badge of Courage * Tom Sawyer * Uncle Tom's Cabin*

Vol 3 - Early 20th Century (9 titles)
*An American Tragedy * Babbitt * Call of the Wild & White Fang * Ethan Frome * The Jungle * Main Street * My Antonia * Sister Carrie * Winesburg, Ohio*

Vol 4 - The Jazz Age to W.W.II Part 1 (11 titles)
*Absalom, Absalom! * As I Lay Dying * The Bear * Black Boy * A Farewell to Arms * For Whom the Bell Tolls * Go Down, Moses * The Good Earth * The Grapes of Wrath * The Great Gatsby * Light in August*

Vol 5 - The Jazz Age to W.W.II Part 2 (10 titles)
*Miss Lonelyhearts & The Day of the Locust * Native Son * Of Mice and Men * Our Town * The Pearl * The Red Pony * The Sound and the Fury * The Sun Also Rises * Tender is the Night * Unvanquished*

Vol 6 - Post-War American Literature Part 1 (13 titles)
*100 Years of Solitude * All the King's Men * The Assistant * The Autobiography of Malcolm X * The Bell Jar * Black Like Me * Catch-22 * The Catcher in the Rye * The Color Purple * The Crucible * Death of a Salesman * Dune and Other Works * The Glass Menagerie & A Streetcar Named Desire*

AMERICAN LITERATURE LIBRARY (cont'd)

Vol 7 - Post-War American Literature Part 2 (12 titles)
*The Invisible Man * Manchild in the Promised Land * O'Connor's Short Stories * The Old Man and the Sea * One Flew Over the Cuckoo's Nest * The Ox-Bow Incident * A Separate Peace * Shane * To Kill a Mockingbird * Vonnegut's Major Works * Walden Two * Who's Afraid of Virginia Woolf?*

EUROPEAN LITERATURE LIBRARY: 4 Volumes, 29 Titles

Vol 1 - French Literature (12 titles)
*Candide * The Count of Monte Cristo * Cyrano de Bergerac * Les Miserables * Madame Bovary * No Exit & The Flies * The Plague * The Red and the Black * The Stranger * Tartuffe, Misanthrope & Bourgeois Gentlemen * The Three Musketeers * Waiting for Godot*

Vol 2 - German Literature (7 titles)
*All Quiet on the Western Front * Demian * The Diary of Anne Frank * Faust Pt. I & Pt. II * Kafka's Short Stories * Steppenwolf & Siddhartha * The Trial*

Vol 3 - Russian Literature (7 titles)
*Anna Karenina * The Brothers Karamozov * Crime and Punishment * Fathers and Sons * Notes from the Underground * One Day in the Life of Ivan Denisovich * War and Peace*

Vol 4 - Scandinavian Literature (3 titles)
*Giants in the Earth * Ibsen's Plays I: A Doll's House & Hedda Gabler * Ibsen's Plays II: Ghosts, An Enemy of the People & The Wild Duck*

AUTHORS LIBRARY

Vol 1 -Charles Dickens Library (6 titles)
*Bleak House * David Copperfield * Great Expectations ** *Hard Times * Oliver Twist * A Tale of Two Cities*

Vol 2 - Feodor Dostoevsky Library (3 titles)
*The Brothers Karamazov * Crime and Punishment ** *Notes from the Underground*

Vol 3 - William Faulkner Library (7 titles)
*Absalom, Absalom! * As I Lay Dying * The Bear * Go Down, Moses * Light in August * The Sound and the Fury * The Unvanquished*

Vol 4 - Thomas Hardy Library (5 titles)
*Far from the Madding Crowd * Jude the Obscure * The Major of Casterbridge * The Return of the Native * Tess of the D'Urbervilles*

Vol 5 - Ernest Hemingway Library (4 titles)
*A Farewell to Arms * For Whom the Bell Tolls * The Old Man and the Sea * The Sun Also Rises*

Vol 6 - Henry James Library (3 titles)
*The American * Daisy Miller & The Turn of the Screw ** *The Portrait of a Lady*

Vol 7 - Sinclair Lewis Library (2 titles)
*Babbitt * Main Street*

Vol 8 - Shakespeare Library, Part 1 - The Comedies (12 titles)
*All's Well that Ends Well & The Merry Wives of Windsor
* As You Like It * The Comedy of Errors, Love's Labour's
Lost & The Two Gentlemen of Verona * Measure for
Measure * The Merchant of Venice * A Midsummer
Night's Dream * Much Ado About Nothing * The Taming
of the Shrew * The Tempest * Troilus and Cressida *
Twelfth Night * The Winter's Tale*

Vol 9 - Shakespeare Library, Part 2 - The Tragedies (7 Titles)
*Antony and Cleopatra * Hamlet * Julius Caesar * King
Lear * Macbeth * Othello * Romeo and Juliet*

**Vol 10 - Shakespeare Library, Part 3 - The Histories; Sonnets
7 titles)**
*Henry IV Part 1 * Henry IV Part 2 * Henry V *Henry VI
Parts 1,2,3 * Richard II * Richard III * Shakespeare's The
Sonnets*

Vol 11 - George Bernard Shaw Library (2 titles)
*Pygmalion & Arms and the Man * Man and Superman &
Caesar and Cleopatra*

Vol 12 - John Steinbeck Library (4 titles)
*The Grapes of Wrath * Of Mice and Men * The Pearl *
The Red Pony*

Vol 13 - Mark Twain Library (4 titles)
*A Connecticut Yankee in King Arthur's Court * Huckle-
berry Finn * The Prince and the Pauper * Tom Sawyer*